# DEFIANCE
## Fighting Elitism and Racism
## at LSU in the '70s

Theodor Schirmer

*Printed in the United States of America*

For my children and my granddaughter Clara Rose Schirmer.

# Table of Contents

# Preface

In the fall of 1970, LSU was a bastion of Southern conservatism. Only the year before had the administration stopped requiring that all incoming male freshmen join the Reserve Officers' Training Corps (ROTC). To this day, LSU still uses the term "Ole War Skule" to describe itself.

A few years earlier, women couldn't wear pants or shorts on campus and were even required to wear dresses when attending off campus LSU functions.

Also, there were no Black players on the LSU football team. And that wasn't the only area of student life not open to Blacks. LSU was still steeped in Confederate traditions.

The stories and accounts written in this book come from my recollection of events and extensive research. Some names, locations and identifying characteristics have been changed to protect the privacy of those depicted. Quotations come from news articles or were recreated from memory. The opinions expressed in the book are my own.

# Fall and Spring Semesters, 1970–1971
## MY FIRST SEMESTER AT LSU

I decided to attend LSU in the fall of 1970. What was I thinking!

In all my years growing up, I don't remember ever considering going to college. In fact, I had to talk one of my teachers into changing my grade from an F to a D so I could graduate from high school. After two tours of duty in a Navy Inshore Undersea Warfare Group 1 unit in Viet Nam ("UWG 1" we called ourselves) and doing little to no reading or writing during that time, I was pretty damn close to being functionally—if not actually—illiterate. I had trouble filling out a simple job application. Oh yeah, I also did not realize I had ADHD. Hell, I could not even spell Attention Deficit Hyperactivity Disorder let alone know what it meant.

After being discharged from the Navy on April 15, 1970, I spent the summer in McHenry, Illinois, living with my brother and working for a minimum wage as a spotter and presser at Crystal Lake Cleaners. During that summer, I morphed from a conservative military man into a full-blown hippie. That transformation was helped along by attending two three-day rock festivals plus seeing the musical *Hair* in Chicago.

Now there I was, a long haired hippie driving in my 1959 Volkswagen van to Baton Rouge to enroll at LSU. I had attended an LSU football game while on leave from Viet Nam and wanted to experience more of that unbelievable excitement. In short, like many times in the past, and many more times to come in the future, I had not thought—I just acted.

I did not have a clue what was required in order to succeed in college. How was I even able to get my foot in the door of a university of higher learning and go where the vast majority of the children of the poor are not usually allowed to go due to a lack of a good public school education or money? I had escaped high school with a D grade point average. I never took the SAT or ACT. How could a person with all those strikes against him ever get into LSU?

Well, I want to thank the one person who made that possible, the politician who opened the door to a higher education for myself and all the other poor children raised in Louisiana, the children who wanted to better the life that they had been born into by getting a college education. Who was that person? Governor Huey P. Long, that's who! I thank you, Governor Long, for giving me the opportunity to attend college and thus opening the door for me to later attend law school. My life and my family's life would have been very different if not for the progressive changes your administration brought to Louisiana. But for you, thousands of poor Louisiana children, like me, would have been doomed, as generations before us were, to a life of poverty.

Governor Long passed a law that stated, since Louisiana taxpayers were pouring millions of tax dollars into LSU to improve it (and replace Tulane as the top university in the state), LSU had to admit any student who graduated from a Louisiana high school. There was no other requirement, like a good SAT or ACT score.

My stepdad had been a professional musician, so my family moved every year, or even more often, and I attended many schools as I grew up. But we settled in Baton Rouge in 1965, and I had managed to graduate (escape) from Istrouma High School in 1966 (the first person in my family to graduate high school) before going into the military. So, LSU had to accept me!

At registration in the fall of 1970, I soon had my first fight with the LSU administration on my hands. My mom had died while I was in Viet Nam, but my stepdad, Bill Schirmer, still lived in Baton Rouge and had agreed to let me stay with him with the understanding that I would not "start any trouble" at LSU. (I would soon find out that exercising my First Amendment rights was included in "start any trouble.") However, at registration, I was told by the first person I met, a student worker, that all incoming LSU freshmen (except married freshmen) had to live on campus in the student dorms. I said that I could not afford to pay the dormitory fee. I had just gotten out of the military and had only my

2

GI benefits to live on. Also, having spent four years in the Navy, there was no way I was going to live in a dormitory on campus even if I could afford it. That student told me that, if I did not live on campus, I could not enroll. I asked if I could talk to someone about getting a waiver. He said that the requirement could not be waived unless I was married. But I blew him off as just a cog in the machine and walked across campus to the Registrar's Office in the hope of speaking to someone with the authority to waive that requirement.

After being told by two other people at the Registrar's Office that it couldn't be changed for anyone, I decided to see the vice chancellor. He informed me of the reason behind the requirement. LSU had built new dormitories, anticipating that students would want to live on campus, but the dormitories were staying half empty. That was why the Board of Supervisors instituted the requirement that all freshmen had to live on campus. I explained that I was not to blame for the Board of Supervisors' obviously bad decision to build those dormitories, and I would do whatever I had to until I was allowed to enroll without living on campus. After going around and around for about 10 to15 minutes, the vice chancellor finally took out a paper with an LSU logo on it and wrote a one sentence waiver for me. LSU did not even have an official waiver form for allowing students not to live on campus.

When I later met with the Veterans Affairs counselor, I was told that in order to receive the total monthly VA Educational Benefit, which I needed for living expenses, I had to be enrolled full-time at LSU. That meant taking at least 12 hours of accredited classes. That fall I took a Philosophy class titled Man and Society, a Human Geography class (I was very interested in who I was and why), Elementary Spanish (I had taken a Spanish class in high school), and the required classes of English Composition and Freshman Orientation (Orientation was not a credit course, so I kind of blew it off).

With all due respect to LSU, it was not one of the most academically strenuous universities in the country at that time. Like the line in Randy Newman's song "Rednecks": "College men from LSU / Went in dumb, come out dumb, too." Even so, after a couple of weeks of attending classes, it became painfully obvious to me I was totally unqualified and unprepared for college.

All during my first semester at LSU, I was just trying to hold on. I finally accepted that I could not handle a full course load. Even if it meant less money to live on, I would have to drop a couple of classes in order to save my sanity. I decided to drop my Philosophy and Spanish classes.

Spanish was a five-credit course that met five days a week. It was a foreign language to me but, at that time, so was English. I had no resistance from the Philosophy professor when I presented him with the drop card to sign, but when I took the drop card to my Spanish teacher, Miss Watts, she talked me out of dropping her by telling me that she was sure I would get at least a passing grade. So, I kept Spanish, even though I had serious second thoughts about it since Miss Watts was using English grammatical terms to teach Spanish grammar. I had not learned any formal English in school. I did not even know what the object of a sentence was, or a verb, a pronoun, let alone a prepositional phrase, etc. I ended up getting an F in Spanish. I had to take Elementary Spanish three more times in order to finally get an A to offset the F.

My Human Geography class was taught by Professor Rob Haswell. He was a visiting professor from South Africa at the time of apartheid. Professor Haswell played rugby in South Africa as a scum-half. Every Friday he would show a film of an epic rugby game. About halfway through the semester, he invited any male student interested in starting a rugby side (team) at LSU to meet him at the Tiger Lair in the Student Union (Union) for beers (on him).

Since my family moved many times when I was growing up, I was often the new kid in school. In order to make friends and fit in, I learned to play all the different sports—football, basketball, baseball, and even track. That fall of 1970, I was once again the new kid at school. I knew no one at LSU. I was also as ill-prepared for college as I had been for the many public schools I attended as a child. I was happy to turn to rugby to help me get my mind off my plight and, hopefully, to make new friends.

Professor Haswell and Jay McKenna, a graduate student who had played rugby at another university, were the organizers. I attended a couple of the practices that semester, but the next semester I got too involved with student issues on campus. I did not get back to playing rugby until 1977. Then I played and became president of the LSU Rugby Football Club, plus I went on two rugby tours: one to Freeport, Bahamas, and the other to England and Wales.

With all of my struggles in the classroom, what kept me in school that fall semester was LSU football. Yes, if it was not for LSU football, I probably would have dropped out of college in 1970. But I had become hooked, and I needed my Student ID to get into the games.

Texas A&M was the first game I saw as an LSU student, and it was my real first experience of "Saturday Night at Tiger Stadium." While the game was played at night, the event was an all day and night happening. I got to campus early Saturday morning so I could get a good parking place on campus, ate breakfast, scramble eggs and grits, at the Union, then spent the rest of the day walking around campus enjoying the party atmosphere. Even in 1970, tailgating with the Tiger fans was a big part of game day at LSU. The scene on campus was of tents and canopies placed everywhere there was space to pitch them. Every type of South Louisiana food you could think of was being cooked somewhere on campus. I was still wearing my jungle greens jacket and boots around campus, so, even though my hair was starting to get long, I was seen to be a veteran and invited to share food and drink with several of the groups of people tailgating.

I figured that getting to the stadium an hour before kick-off was early enough to get a good seat. Man, was I wrong! I learned that night that there was a privileged class of students on the LSU campus. The best seats in the student section were being saved by pledges from the many different fraternities on campus. The pledges had orders to be the first at the stadium when the gates opened so they could save rows of

5

the best seats for their fraternity brothers and their sorority dates, who would stay at their frat houses getting smashed until game time.

When I got into the stadium, I did not realize that all those rows and rows of empty seats on the 50-yard line were being saved by pledges. Shortly after I sat down though, a young pledge, who could not have been more than 18 years old, came running up to me while yelling, "These seats are saved. These seats are saved." I asked him, "All of these seats?" as I gestured at row after row of empty seats. He had gotten close enough to me to see I was not your average LSU student. I was much older than him, and I was wearing my jungle greens and boots from Nam. He immediately seemed very uncomfortable as he weakly said, "Yes, sir." It was a little bit of a shock hearing this young kid address me that way. I looked around and saw young men scattered all around the students' section who were obviously attempting to save rows and rows of seats for their frat brothers. By then the young man was standing right by my side with a very pleading pitiful look on his face. I started feeling sorry for this kid. Normally I would have refused to move, but I realized that this kid would get a lot of shit from his frat brothers for failing to do his job, so instead I got up, shaking my head, and moved up the walkway to sit down on the concrete at the top of the seats.

As I sat there, I observed more and more students arriving who were confronting the pledges over all the rows of empty seats that they were saving. Some of those confrontations almost turned into fights. At that time, I did not know anything about fraternities and sororities. As a matter of fact, I believe I had never even heard of those organizations. But as I watched the pledges struggle to save seats, I found myself wondering why. Why were these guys putting themselves through this obviously stressful situation, not to mention the unfairness of denying all those seats to students who made the effort to get to the stadium early? This was my first introduction to how the children of the elite believe that the rules do not apply to them.

This excerpt from an article in the 1971 edition of *The DELTASIG Magazine*, a publication of the Delta Sigma Pi Louisiana State Baton

Rouge Beta Zeta Chapter, shows the attitude of the fraternities about this practice:

> After an excellent rush program, consisting of an informal smoker, a football rush party, and a professional program, 18 men were pledged, two of whom are in the MBA program. The pledge class seems quite capable and we are expecting great things from them. (Any pledge class that can reserve a quarter section in Tiger Stadium on Homecoming deserves honorable mention.)

And as my years at LSU went by, I learned that the LSU administration fully supported this elitism exhibited by the Greeks. Why did the LSU administration turn a blind eye to this type of elitist behavior and even more deadly behavior, like fraternity hazing? As I would learn later, it was because the Greeks did not rock the boat. They did not demonstrate against the Viet Nam War or any controversial issues of the day. And more importantly, they never seemed to complain about what the LSU administration was doing or not doing. As a matter of fact, more times than not they were on the administration's side, and against the rest of the student body on issues.

Furthermore, the Greeks were allowed to discriminate against minorities when selecting who could join their organizations even though the fraternity and sorority on campus houses were on state property and labeled student housing, which was supposed to be open to all students. This would later come to a head when LSU Black students formed Harambee (Swahili for "all pull together"). The Black students demanded a house like the fraternities and sororities had on campus. Even though at the time there was an empty fraternity house that Harambee wanted, there was no way in the 1970s that the LSU administration was going to allow a Black fraternity to be on campus. In 1972, the administration created a Harambee House off campus.

I went back to McHenry, Illinois, to spend Thanksgiving with my brother Terry and my girlfriend Susanna. I met Susanna in the summer

7

of 1970, when she was a senior in high school and we both worked at Crystal Lake Cleaners.

At that time, LSU was undefeated and ranked No. 6 in the country and about to play, for the first time in LSU football history, Notre Dame on November 21, 1970. Notre Dame was the No. 2 team in the country. That was the first time that Notre Dame played a team from the Southeastern Conference.

The game was to be played at Notre Dame Stadium. Since it was not that far away from Chicago, I decided to try to get tickets at LSU, but I found that the game had been sold out for weeks. Someone suggested that, if I were in Chicago the Friday before the game, I could try to get tickets at the LSU Board of Supervisors and Alumni party that was going to be held at the Palmer House Hilton.

That Friday, I took the train down to Chicago and went to the Palmer House. At that time, my hair was past my shoulders, plus I was wearing my favorite cold weather coat, a World War I winter coat, along with my drill instructor hat. In other words, I did not look anything like a typical LSU student. I walked into the lobby and spoke with the man at the desk. I told him I was from LSU and I was looking for the LSU party. He said the party was being held in the conference room.

As I stood at the door of the conference room for a moment, an older man walked up to me and asked, "Can I help you?" I told him, "I am an LSU student without any tickets for the game tomorrow. Does anyone have any tickets?" A shocked look came over his face as he said, "You're an LSU student?" I took out my LSU Student ID card and handed it to him. He said, "I'll be damn!" Then, while still holding my ID, he turned toward all the people standing in the room, saying, "Hey, we have an LSU student here who came up for the game and needs tickets." He turned back to me asking, "How many tickets?" I said, "Two." Then he turned back toward the other people, "He needs two tickets." He motioned for me to follow him as he went into the room.

As I followed, I realized everyone had stopped talking and was staring at me as if I were some kind of alien, which I guess to them I was. A couple of older men walked up to us. If I remember correctly, one of the men was on the Board of Supervisors and the other was the president of LSU, Martin Woodin. The two of them looked at me, asking, "You came up for the game and need two tickets?" I said, "That's right, I am a big LSU fan." That brought a smile to their faces. Soon the first man I had met came back with two tickets in his hand and gave them to me. I asked, "How much do I owe you?" He told me, "Nothing. Enjoy the game." I was taken aback, but I thanked him and left without even looking at what seats were designated on the tickets.

Susanna and I took the train to the game. It was over a five-hour train ride to South Bend. The game was to start in the early afternoon. The train left McHenry around 7 A.M. and got into South Bend at around noon. We arrived at the football stadium about 30 minutes before the game started.

Until then I did not know if our seats were very good or not. Man, was I in for a shock. They were great seats! They were three or four rows back from the LSU sidelines and on the 50-yard line. When we took our place, there was a Catholic priest sitting next to me. I kiddingly asked, "Aren't you on the wrong side of the field?" He looked at me with a smile on his face as he pulled back his jacket. There pinned to his vest was a button. Written on the button was "Go to Hell Notre Dame."

Unfortunately, LSU missed two field goal attempts early in the game, and Notre Dame made its only field goal attempt to beat us 3-0 with just a few minutes left in the game. But what a game!

LSU had been told by the Orange Bowl Committee that if they beat Tulane and Ole Miss in the final two games of the season, they would be invited to play in the Orange Bowl on New Year's Day. LSU survived a very good Tulane team and then kick the shit out of Ole Miss and Archie Manning, 61-17, as oranges rained down onto the field from the student section. I was one of the first students in line the next morning to buy two tickets to the Orange Bowl in Miami.

When I told that to Susanna, who was in her first year at the University of Northwestern nursing school, she wanted to meet me in Miami. She arranged for another nursing student and herself to get paid to drive an ambulance to the Miami port in order for it to be shipped to Israel. Susanna told me sometimes they would turn the ambulance's siren on as they sped down the highway.

I met up with Susanna at the Miami Port where she turned in the ambulance. Since the game was to be played on January 1st at the Orange Bowl in Miami, we had a couple of weeks to see Florida. We decided to spend those two weeks in Key West.

In the 1970s, the Keys were not as built up as they are now. Shortly after I had parked the van for the night on a street in Key West, a police car pulled up. He told me that there was no parking on the streets at night. I said OK and pulled away. I soon found a big empty lot and parked there for the night. Early the next morning, we were wakened by a cop banging on the side doors of the van. To my shock, it was the same cop. He told me that it was against the law to sleep in your vehicle in Florida. I tried my Viet Nam veteran line on him, but he was not impressed. He told me he would arrest us if he caught us sleeping in the van again. As he turned and started walking to his vehicle, I shouted out to him, "Merry Christmas!" He froze for a moment, then continued on to his car and drove off.

Well, I knew we had to figure out where we were going to be staying for the next two weeks. As fate would have it, we decided to eat at an A&W drive-in that morning. As we were waiting for our food, a blue Ford van with a bunch of hippie types in it, pulled into the space beside us. I struck up a conversation with them and asked if they knew of any place we could spend the night in my van. And they did! They told us about Ohio Key where there were no buildings. It was just an empty Key. They said some freaks were already camping out there.

It took a couple of trips down U.S. 1 to find the turnoff. It was not easy to turn around on U.S. 1. Finally, we drove down a dirt road leading to Ohio Key and found two or three vehicles parked there. One was a truck with a camper on it. There was a guy sitting on the back of the camper wearing Viet Nam clothing. He turned out to be a fellow veteran. I asked him about staying there, and he told me that it was ok. He said a very cool older couple owned that half of the Key and did not mind people staying there. We had found our home for the next two weeks.

A couple of days later, a half dozen Canadian teenagers, ages 15 to 16, showed up. They had been hitching around the U.S. after having already hitched all around Canada first. They also had found out about Ohio Key from the guys in the blue van.

I was very impressed with how mature the Canadians were. There soon became a friendly rivalry between Yankees and Canucks. It included a drinking contest that I would have won if I had not started throwing up and then passed out. Over the years, I would visit them in Canada, and they would visit me in Louisiana and California. John was in my wedding. I am still friends with John.

One day the blue van from the A&W drive-in came to Ohio Key. The guys had some dynamite marijuana and got us all stoned, then drove away. We never saw them again, but I think fondly about them to this very day.

After a while, there were about 25 or so young people staying on the Key. On Christmas morning, a Mercedes sedan came down the dirt road and an old couple got out of their car. They told us all to gather around. They both said Merry Christmas to us all and opened their trunk. In it were cooked turkeys with other Christmas food, plus beer, wine and cigarettes. It turned out that they were a couple of old hippies. They told us that they had bought half of the Key with money they made from smuggling marijuana into the country. They would put the marijuana in specially made pockets inside a big coat the wife would wear coming over the border. They never were stopped at the border, just waved through every time. They were a very nice couple.

New Year's Day, game day, finally came. Susanna and I drove to the Orange Bowl early to take part in the tailgating and drinking that LSU fans are famous for in the college football world. LSU was ranked 5th in the nation and Nebraska was ranked 3rd. Earlier that day No. 1 Texas and No. 2 Ohio State had lost their bowl games, so Nebraska would become National Champions if they beat us. Nebraska won the game 17-12 and won the National Championship.

11

Even though LSU football kept me in school, I still barely passed my first semester with a 1.09 grade point due to that F in Elementary Spanish, a D in English Composition, and a B in Human Geography. I may not have learned a lot in my courses, but I did learn to drop classes I was not passing, which I should have done with my Spanish class.

In the spring of 1971, the issue of student grooming standards, which had come up the previous semester in the College of Education, was once again front and center on campus. Not only did the College of Education require a student to look a certain way in order to enroll in that college, but also the LSU Marching Band would not let a past band member enroll because of the length of his hair. I believe a total of six colleges on campus had grooming standards.

Well, that really pissed me off, especially since LSU was a state school. That was the issue that prompted my first appearance at LSU's Free Speech Alley.

During my first semester in the fall of 1970, I did not attend Free Speech Alley, much less speak at it. I was only interested in LSU football and desperately trying to hang on academically. There is a good chance that, if the issue of grooming standards had not been happening at that time, I might have neither attended nor spoken at the Alley that semester. But I felt that the colleges and even the LSU Band director did not have the right to deny a student the right to look however he wanted to look while attending a state college.

Also, I had decided to take Speech Fundamentals that semester, and I thought speaking at the Alley would help me in that class. Those factors together gave me the courage to speak for the first time. I know it will come as a surprise to some that I ever worried about speaking in public, but, at that time, that could not have been further from the truth. Like most people, I was very hesitant, if not outright scared, to speak in front of a crowd. My palms would sweat and my breathing would increase as I waited my turn to speak. But once my blood is up about something, I do things that, after the fact, I wonder, what was I thinking?

A little about LSU's Free Speech Alley. The Alley was started in 1964, with no official rules, under the Oaks behind the LSU Union. By 1968, the official rules (if they could be called rules) were: "A sense of fair play should be kept in mind while the speaker is questioned." Further, "The use of the soapbox is limited to faculty and students of LSU." Later, while I was attending LSU, anyone could come on campus and speak at the Alley.

The term Alley came about when that event got moved from the Oaks to the alley between the Union book store and the theater. By the time I spoke at the Alley, it had been moved to the front of the Student Union, and students would sit on the steps to listen to the speakers. When there were a couple of hundred students at the Alley, keeping a path clear into the Union was a problem. During my time, and yes, David Duke's time, it was such a consistent problem that the SGA had to bring out movie theater ropes to keep a path open. The Union administration was constantly threatening to move the Alley because of that, citing fire department rules.

The Alley meetings usually began on the second or third week after classes started each semester. They were sponsored by the Student Government Association, the SGA. The SGA president would appoint a moderator, who would bring out the wooden "soap box" for the speakers to stand on. It was a foot-high platform, about four feet by four feet, which was painted yellow. In addition, the moderator would have a sign-up sheet for individuals who wanted to speak at the Alley.

Sometimes there were time limits on how long a speaker could speak, but most often the students listening to a speaker decided when they had heard enough. The more entertaining the speaker was, the longer that speaker could stay on the soap box, especially if there were not a lot of names on the sign-up sheet. But if there were a lot of people who wanted to speak, then the moderator would establish firm time limits. Sometimes that would encourage tag team speakers, who would speak on the same subject, one right after the other.

When I first enrolled at LSU the previous fall, I was older than the average student, a Viet Nam veteran (a war that was becoming unpopular even in the south by 1970) and, if that were not enough, a long haired hippie type attending a Deep South college. I did not fit in at LSU. In my classes, especially English class, I felt as if I were again that kid who sat in the corner in front of the class with a dunce hat on his head, or was placed under the teacher's desk and kicked every time I moved or spoke, or had to drag my desk out into the hallway to sit there the entire school day as the other kids went to and from their classes and recess—to name just a few of the humiliating incidence I experience as the poor new kid in school. Tiger football had become my sanctuary, but when the spring semester began, there was no LSU football, and I had not yet gotten into LSU basketball as I would in the fall of 1975. What was going to be my sanctuary without LSU football?

That turned out to be Free Speech Alley. At first, it was just a sanctuary from my struggles in the classroom. Sure, I could not understand things being taught in my classes, and I couldn't keep up with the required reading or the writing assignments—which led to my dropping classes or outright failing classes. But at the Alley it didn't matter that I could hardly read or write. I could talk!

I could communicate my feelings about things happening on campus with honest emotions and even passion. I was not ashamed of who I was outside of the classroom, nor of the poverty of my childhood. I talked freely about that part of my life, not in a poor me downer way, but with the humor I had learned to use to deflect the condition life had put me in. I would also speak in a more serious and firm tone when the subject required it. Liking people as I do, I soon got over any jitters about speaking in front of a crowd.

After the first couple of semesters, I began to see the Alley as, to paraphrase the Chicago Clubs saying, "the friendly confines of Free Speech Alley." I felt I fit in at the Alley. I found I could become the voice of the students who did not belong to a fraternity or sorority, whose families struggled to help them attend LSU; the students who had to work to earn money for school even while wishing they could put that time into their studies. The Alley became my validation of why I was attending LSU; it became my calling as a college student.

In later years at LSU, I would kid that I was majoring in Free Speech Alley with a minor in Union Coffee. The Union was where I and others, who had attended the Alley, would often gather to continue our discussions.

Students who first heard me speaking at the Alley were in for a shock. This was because I was fresh out of the Navy and cussed like a sailor when I spoke. Some of my favorite cuss words were fuck, mother fucker, son of a bitch and asshole. As a matter of fact, I did not attempt to stop cussing until, after a couple of times speaking at the Alley, a graduate student complimented me and told me that he agreed with what I was saying, but that I would be more effective if I did not cuss so much. After that I cut down how much I cussed, but I never stopped completely. It was just who I was at the time.

Years later, I tried to analyze why I became so popular at the Alley. I concluded that one of the main reasons students came to Alley to hear me was not that they agreed with whatever stand I was taking, but that they found me quite entertaining. Not only did I cuss like a sailor, but I would cuss out faculty and administrators in public, something many of them may have wanted to do but were afraid to. This was very new for LSU at the time.

The Alley audience was made up of young people born and raised, for the most part, in conservative families in Louisiana and other Deep South states. I still remember the shocked looks on students' faces when I would call a college dean or an administrator a son of a bitch or a fucking asshole. I was not doing this intentionally to shock them, I was just talking like any poor white trash sailor talks. As I spoke at the Alley, larger and larger crowds of students showed up to hear me.

Speaking at the Alley really did help me in my Speech Fundamentals class. I remember one speech I gave in class a few weeks after I had started speaking at the Alley. We were told to prepare a speech about something we had done in our life. I choose to speak on Rock Festivals.

I still had a pair of my Navy white bell-bottom pants and I had an artist friend of mine draw bright psychedelic colored images on them. Then I put another pair of pants on over them. As I started speaking about the many things, like drugs, which people do at Rock Festivals, I started unbuttoning my shirt. I then went into how drugs, combined with rhythmic hard-driving rock and roll music, would lead to people swaying back and forth to the music. By then I had undone all the buttons on my shirt, and I took it off, throwing it on the classroom floor. I then started explaining that this combination of drugs and rock and roll music would lead some people to take off their clothes.

While I was saying this, I started undoing my belt buckle and unfastening my pants. As I was yanking down the pants I had worn over my psychedelic pants, I saw the teacher, who was sitting in the back of the classroom, jump to his feet with a terrified look on his face. As I continued to speak, with a smile on my face, I pulled my outer pants all the way off and threw them on top of my shirt on the floor. As I looked at the professor, I saw a broad smile on his face. He knew I had learned one of the most important lessons in his class. A speaker has to get his audience's attention at the very beginning of his speech, then keep their attention.

I talked about some of my experiences at the Kickapoo and Stevens Point Rock Festivals, which I had attended the previous summer in Illinois. When the class was over and the other students had left, the professor told me he thought for sure I was going to strip down right there in his class.

I do not remember how many speeches I had to give in his class, but I made an A on all of them. However, I only made a C on the written tests, so I got a B in that class. I also made a B in my Human Geography class. Human Geography was all multi-choice, matching or filling in the blanks. I saw that was the kind of test I could pass, so I kept taking both geography and geology classes. That is why I graduated with a Bachelor of Science degree in General Studies.

In the middle of April, my Speech professor asked me if I would like to compete in the Speech Department's annual Persuasive Speaking

Contest that was coming up on April 26th. He told me that each section of undergraduate Speech was allowed to send two students to the contest. The winner would get a cash prize, and the second and third place winners would be awarded certificates of excellence. I would have to give a four-to-six-minute speech on any topic designed primarily to persuade. I did not care about the certificates of excellence, but the cash prize got my attention. I don't remember how much the cash prize was, but it was enough for me to agree to compete.

I decided my speech would be on gun control. This was one of the few times I went to the library to research. I put together a speech that covered our country's number of deaths caused by guns compared to that of Japan and England. One of my examples of gun violence in the United States was a story of the accidental shooting to death of a young daughter by her father when she burst into the master bedroom late one night. I also discussed how other countries dealt with gun ownership by its citizens. And I attacked the myth that gun ownership was important to defend the country in the age of intercontinental ballistic missiles.

When I went to the first round of the competition, I opened with the line, "At this time I could pull out a gun and kill any number of you." Then I went into the main body of my speech. Well, much to my surprise, I won the first and second rounds and found myself in the finals. I thought, "Hey, I could win this thing and get the prize money." But in the finals I was competing with seniors majoring in Speech. I knew winning this was not going to be easy. I had an idea. My friend Phil Brady had a Colt .38 revolver, so I asked him if I could borrow it for the finals. Phil let me borrow it, of course, without any ammunition. I also decided to wear my Viet Nam jungle jacket and stuck the revolver in my belt under the jacket.

Graduate students in the Speech Department were the judges in the first two rounds, but, for the finals, Speech professors were the judges. I think there were four or five other finalists in the room with me. When my name was called, I went up to the front of the room. As I paused to collect myself, I noticed that one of the three professors judging the contest was obviously still writing notes about the finalist before me. I

17

started by saying, "At this time I could pull out a gun and kill any number of you." I pulled the revolver out from under my jungle jacket and aimed it right at that professor. I can still see the wide-eyed shocked look on his face as he glanced up to see me pointing that revolver at him. I had all of the judges' attention at that point. Regretfully, seeing that professor freak out so much threw me off my speech, and I stumbled through some of my parts and did not win. But that professor came up to me later to tell me he gave me first place. I am not sure if he did because I listened to those senior Speech majors' speeches and they were really good and smooth. Later I thought that it was very risky to have used a real revolver. The LSU Police had just been armed that semester and, if one of them had looked into the classroom window and saw me pointing that revolver at those people, he might have shot me.

## THE GROOMING ISSUE

The grooming issue became prominent in 1970 when a junior music major, who had been selected the outstanding freshman Tiger bandsman two years earlier, was dismissed from the band by LSU band director William F. Swor. An article appeared in the LSU student paper *Reveille* (December 2, 1970) stating:

> Swor described the student's hair as "excessively long and poorly groomed" and said it would present a bad image of the band on television. He added that it detracted from the uniformity of the group if one person in particular was not "well groomed."

The article further pointed out, "Guess who cut his hair in September at Swor's request, but was still not allowed to register for the course?"

The administration upheld Mr. Swor's right to dismiss students on the basis of appearance. A *Reveille* article (December 2, 1970), titled "Student seeks appeal in long hair dismissal," referred to a letter, written by then Vice Chancellor Paul Murrill, that was sent to the SGA ombudsman's office, defending the individual professor's right to set dress requirements. It stated, "We are not convinced that Mr. Guess [the student] has been wronged. Each instructor has the authority to determine whether a student is properly attired in class."

These prejudicial standards were especially emphasized by the College of Education. It was commonly regarded as one of the more conservative colleges on the LSU campus, which is saying a lot considering that Baton Rouge, Louisiana, is located in the Deep South. As a *Reveille* (December 9, 1970) article pointed out:

> Under the section Admission to and Retention in the College of Education it states, "Teachers should rank high in mental alertness, physical appearance, personal attractiveness, power of expression, and professional enthusiasm." This adds up to what? It adds up to being kicked out of the College of Education if you have long hair, a beard, bad breath, a gimp left foot, a bad case of acne, or any mental, physical or other personal handicap detrimental to successful work with children.

Unlike the previous fall I found myself actually reading all of the *Reveille,* not just skipping to the sports page in order to read about the upcoming football game. One of the first articles I read about the College of Education's grooming policy was an interview with Dean Garrett in the *Reveille* (January 12, 1971). Garrett maintained that, since the grooming policy has been attacked, he had been contacted by superintendents of education across the state supporting his stand concerning the grooming regulations. Garrett stated:

> "...that most of the superintendents told me that they would not hire a teacher who appeared before them groomed or dressed in an unconventional manner....We realize that the times change but we cannot allow our teach-

ers to appear before impressionable children with exceptionally long hair or improperly dressed....Education students enrolled only in courses not requiring contact with children are given more consideration on questions of hair length and dress....Unconventional grooming by a few students tends to make all students less attractive to persons who come to the university to interview education majors for postgraduate teaching positions."

In the spring of 1971, I decided to jump into the College of Education grooming standards controversy. I came to realize that, unlike when I volunteered for an unjust war, I needed to volunteer my time and efforts to fight against the arbitrary and unjust policies of LSU. I teamed up with a fellow student, Frank Cornish, and together we prepared a letter (Frank did the writing) to the Editor of the *Reveille* (February 17, 1970) and two petitions: one opposed to the College of Education policy and one in support. We wrote two petitions because I felt it would allow students who supported the policy to express that support. Plus, I felt that, if the petition in support of the policy did not collect as many signatures as the petition against the policy, it would give more weight to that petition. With SGA support we set up a table in the Union to gather signatures.

On February 17, 1971, I made my first appearance at Free Speech Alley. As a front-page article in the *Reveille* (February 17, 1971) stated, when I was asked why I was taking on the grooming issue, I replied, "I was waiting all last week for someone to do something and it dawned on me that at LSU no one was going to do anything."

At Free Speech Alley, I encouraged students, both for and against the School of Education's policy, to sign the petitions, in other words, to express their opinions. At the signing table I had a sign made by another student saying in big letters, "Speak Your Mind."

On February 25, 1971, I presented the petitions to Dean Garrett at the College of Education. A front-page article in the *Reveille* (February 25, 1971) proclaimed, "Grooming petitions accepted by Garrett." There were 2,542 names opposing the grooming policy and only 177 names supporting the policy. As the article pointed out, there was a back and forth between myself and Dean Garrett that got nowhere. "After the meeting Schirmer said it is evident that the students against the actions of the College Education are not going to get anywhere with the petition. We need another step, and it is already planned. It will be a rally next week."

I tried to get permission to hold a rally on campus, but in order to use campus facilities, a request by a recognized student organization was required. I could not even get a room in the Union for a meeting. We had to meet in the Tiger Lair to plan our next move. We decided to organize a rally at Peabody Hall, where the College of Education was located, and then picket the school. We thought it was best to organize by word of mouth since that way we would not show our hand until the day of the rally/picket. We chose Wednesday, March 10, 1971, the same day as Free Speech Alley was scheduled, with the idea that those students would join the rally.

I learned a lesson about political actions. Unlike today, when social media platforms like Facebook and Twitter can organize a protest rally or flash mob without much notice, organizing that type of action is damn near impossible. I asked Dean Garrett if he would address the rally. He declined. When I got to Peabody Hall, there were only a few other people there plus a cop. So I went to the Alley to rally support for our effort at Peabody Hall.

I told the Alley audience, "The administration does not know you as well as I thought they did [because] there's a cop patrolling around Peabody 'cause they thought you'd be over there. Well, there're only two people there. You really showed them." There were more than two students at Peabody Hall but I knew saying "two" would be more effective. Then David Dirks, who was an SGA presidential candidate, came to my aid saying, "I don't know exactly how much good a picket does but if you're going to have a president at least have an energetic one." Being a good student politician, he knew an opportunity when he saw it. Dave and I led the Alley crowd over to Peabody Hall. As a front-page *Reveille*

21

(March 11, 1971) article, titled "Alley crowd joins pickets to protest education rules," reported:

> The picketers proceeded in an orderly line through the first
> and second floors of the building carrying signs reading,
> "Teach, don't preach," "Mind your mind not mine," "Ability
> or appearance?" "Robots awaken" and "Dean Garrett, re-
> sign or accept 1971 A.D."

As the picture on the front page showed, that last sign was carried by Gus Tabony, who was front and center in the picture. Gus would always make sure he was in any pictures taken of any political actions students organized or participated in. In addition, he always was the one at meetings who promoted actions that either bordered on illegal or were out right illegal. Years later we found out why. Gus was an undercover police officer for the Baton Rouge Police Dept. Gus was always trying to sell me dope, but fortunately I had my own sources.

Several of the students stopped in Dean Garrett's office to talk with him since he had said he would meet with students in his office. A *Reveille* (March 11, 1971) article stated that, "Garrett reaffirmed his support for the college's dress and grooming standards in a later interview with students. 'They [the standards] are realistic and not unreasonable. They represent what is expected of a teacher in a professional role,' Garrett said."

What was surprising to me was that there was no negative blow back from the students. All the student letters to the *Reveille* (March 17, 1971) were positive. In addition, as pointed out in an editorial (March 12, 1971), titled "Picketing for change," by Charlie East:

> The Picketing of Peabody Hall, home of the College of Edu-
> cation, Wednesday was successful in terms of what such a
> protest rally should accomplish. Not only did it confront
> Dean Garrett with the problem by bringing the opposition
> to his door step, but it captured the attention of both the
> university and the Baton Rouge community through news

coverage by the Daily Reveille and the State Times and Morning Advocate....Jon Ferguson, president of the College of Education Student Council, has noted that picketing was not the proper course of action to take. On the contrary, the picketing was entirely justified in view of the lack of response which Garrett has shown.

## THE PROGRESSIVE STUDENT ALLIANCE (PSA)

On March 15, 1971, a few days after the rally and picketing of the College of Education, we organized a meeting to discuss our next action. We decided that we could not depend on the administration, or the SGA, or any other recognized student organization to help in this matter. We had to organize ourselves. That was the birth of the Progressive Students Alliance (PSA).

In addition to the grooming issue, there was also the textbook issue. In the fall semester, the *Reveille* (September 8, 1970) printed a two-page editorial analysis of the history of the Union Bookstore and the other three off campus bookstores. It accused them of forming a "captive" market. These four bookstores had an almost exclusive right to provide 18,000 students with their needed textbooks. As the article stated: "Every semester hundreds of thousands of dollars' worth of textbooks change hands between students and these bookstores. Complaints are voiced by students who claim they are victimized by high prices and low rates of return on used books." The discontent increased to the point that one of the bookstores was boycotted by LSU students.

These two issues, the length of one's hair and the high cost of textbooks, hit me directly and prompted me to become a citizen activist. Some of the actions I am going to write about may seem petty, but each of the actions I was about to get involved with at LSU would teach me a lesson about organizing people.

A group of us met in the Union to discuss over coffee how to go about creating a student organization. The group included Charles Teddlie, Richard (Dickie) Eberhart, August (Gus) Tabony, Tom Ingallinera, Tal Pomeroy, Jeff Sharp, Doug Lambert, Steve Irving and myself. There may have been some women students, but I do not remember their names. Some of the other guys probably could remember every woman's name who was involved in the beginning because later they told me the reason they got involved in the first place was to meet women.

Getting PSA recognized as a student organization would allow us to reserve LSU facilities, grounds and equipment, get money from SGA, plus receive other perks. We decided that first we needed to get a room in the Union, then advertise in the *Reveille*, post flyers around campus and, at the next Alley, encourage students to come to an organizational meeting of PSA.

I reserved a room in the Union. We set the meeting for Friday at 7 P.M. on March 19, 1971. After extensively promoting the meeting, only about two dozen students came. We learned another important lesson: do not have meetings on a Friday night. But in another vein, the students who did come were really motivated (or just did not have anywhere else to go on a Friday night).

I was able to get the room reserved because I said it was an organizational meeting for a new student organization. But to continue to be able to get rooms for our meetings or the right to use other LSU facilities for our events, we were required to present to the administration a mission statement, a constitution, and bylaws, and to elect officers. In addition, we needed a faculty adviser. Fortunately, there were just enough motivated students at the meeting to form committees to write all the necessary documents.

Since I could not write (I did not tell the students there that I could not write), I volunteered to find a faculty member for our faculty adviser. I do not remember how I met Jim Borck, a young (only a few years older than me) English professor, but he agreed to be PSA's faculty adviser. He definitely looked the part. He had dark black curly hair that kind of looked like an afro and a mustache that ran down the sides of his mouth. He was our man! Jim always stuck by us no matter how much heat we were getting from the administration. And we would soon be getting some serious heat from them.

After PSA was organized, we elected officers. I was elected president. We considered whether or not to expand our organization's involvement beyond just the grooming and admissions policies of the College of Education. After discussing a number of issues that members wanted us to get involved with, we voted for protesting against the Viet Nam war by joining a march sponsored by a conservative Baton Rouge organization, Concerned Parents Association. They were protesting Lt. William Calley's conviction for killing Vietnamese old men, women and children. In addition, we decided to support the action of women students fighting Margaret Jameson, Dean of Women, for women students' rights.

The first thing I did was drop two of my classes that I was having trouble in. Once I was down to just two classes, Speech Fundamentals and Human Geography, I could throw myself into organizing PSA even though I had no idea how to do so. Later I would read *Rules for a Radicals: A Pragmatic Primer for Realistic Radicals* by Saul Alinsky, a 1971 book, on how to organize and run a movement for change.

## PROTEST AGAINST LT. CALLEY'S CONVICTION

At the PSA meeting, I had argued against teaming up with such a conservative group as the Concerned Parents Association. We could get branded by this action. (We found out later the Concerned Parents were not only very conservative, but also that they were linked with David Duke's White Youth Alliance.) Further, I thought all of the Army officers who ordered this action should have been tried, not just Lt. Calley.

Even though Calley was given a life sentence, in my opinion, he should have been shot for what he did at My Lai. Calley only served one day in prison at Fort Leavenworth because President Nixon ordered him transferred from prison to house arrest at Fort Benning pending his appeal hearing. After just three and half years of house arrest, he was released following an appeals court ruling.

But others thought the march was a chance to get some exposure for our new organization, plus they saw it as a chance to speak out against the war. I believe Gus Tabony was the big pusher of the idea to join in this action. Looking back, I am sure it helped him with his superiors at the Baton Rouge Police Department. Gus told me later, after he was uncovered as an informant, that when he was first recruited to be an informant, he was only making a few hundred dollars. But after PSA formed, he started getting paid over $800, plus, he said that the Police Department would give him marijuana that the police had seized from defendants in order to sell to support his cover.

At our meeting we discussed what we should do separately from the Concerned Parents. One of the crazier ideas was offered by a founding member of PSA. He was a chemistry major at LSU who used to make mescaline for our parties. He wanted to make some napalm and napalm a live turkey at the draft board to demonstrate what is happening to the Vietnamese after our planes drop napalm. Since I was a vegetarian and "of sound mind" I told him we were not going to kill a turkey by na-palming it to prove a point. Tom piped up, "We can just get a turkey at the grocery store. It doesn't have to be alive." We just looked at him while shaking our heads, saying "no"!

The final decision was that we would just participate in the march as a student organization, and members who wanted to could make signs to carry. I believe we also decided that none of us would speak to the media. We would let the Concerned Parents handle all the press inter-views. This is supported by the fact that in the *Reveille* (April 6, 1971) article covering this action, titled "Students, citizens unite against Calley verdict," only people connected to the Concerned Parents were named. PSA was mentioned as the student organization with them, but no members' names appeared in the article.

There were around fifty people who participated in the action. It was decided that we would meet at the State Capitol the day of the action.

PSA had the largest group that morning. Then the comedy of errors started.

As it turned out, the Concerned Parents did not have a clue how to organize an action. As we would discover, they had not done any advance planning. They had only written a letter to present to the draft board demanding that they resign so that no more Louisiana boys could be drafted and go to Viet Nam because of the conviction of Lt. Calley.

We were told by the Concerned Parents that we were to meet with Governor McKeithen, but, once at the Capitol, we were informed that we could not meet with him. On hearing that, the leader of Concerned Parents decided to march us down to the draft board. Since we were taking a subordinate role in this action, Mrs. Claude Groves, the only person quoted who was identified in the *Reveille* article, led the march to the Federal Building, where the draft board's offices were located. Lo and behold, the Federal Marshals would not let us in, so Mrs. Groves went in by herself. Mrs. Groves told us that the draft board members said they would address us there at the Federal Building, but they were a no-show. After a while, I figured that the draft board's members were never going to meet us.

I was starting to get a little frustrated with the Concerned Parents' incompetence. Mrs. Groves then said we should march down to the Baton Rouge Municipal Building to present the letter to Mayor-President W.W. Dumas and ask him to lower the flag to half-mast until the Viet Nam War was ended. So off we marched to the Municipal Building.

When we got there, a spokesperson came out to tell us that the mayor was out of town. It figured! A large number of Baton Rouge Police had gathered in front of the building. Another man in a suit spoke with us. I think it was Sargent Pitcher, Jr., Baton Rouge District Attorney. He said that he had served in the Korean War and would proudly serve today. I then shouted up at him, "I served two tours in Viet Nam and there is no way in hell I would ever serve again." The man just went silent, looked at me, then turned and walked into the Municipal Building. That was the end of that meeting.

Since our vehicles were at the State Capitol, we marched back to it. Once there, I finally decided to take the lead. I said, "Let's go up to Governor McKeithen's office and demand to speak to him." I believe the only people who went up were PSA members and other students from LSU.

When we got to the Governor's office, we all squeezed into the reception area. The Governor's secretary told us that the Governor was out of town. I asked her, "What about the Lt. Governor?" The secretary picked up the phone and made a call. I could tell she was very nervous with all these antiwar protesters in the room. After speaking with someone, she hung up the phone and told me that Lt. Governor Aycock would see us in his office. Now, we had been marching all over town, so I just said, "Have him come to us."

I turned to everyone saying, "Let's sit down and wait for the Lt. Governor," and sat down on the carpet. I was just tired, and I did not feel like going up to the Lt. Governor's office to probably be told he was not in or some other bullshit. As we all sat down on the floor of the Governor's office, the staff began freaking out. It was not my intention to have some kind of antiwar sit-in in the Governor's office, but it became very obvious that the Governor's staff thought that was exactly what we were doing. In a couple of minutes, Baton Rouge police officers, Capitol police and even State Highway Patrol officers started sliding into the reception area, taking positions along the walls. In about five to ten minutes, there must have been a couple of dozen law enforcement officers lining the walls around us. Then Lt. Governor Taddy Aycock managed to squeeze into the room. As I watched, he carefully walked around all the students sitting on the floor making his way to me. When he got to me, I stood to greet him. I thanked him for coming and handed him the letter, asking him to give it to the Governor while explaining why we were there in the first place. He promised he would give it to the Governor when he got back in town. Everyone got up, and we left the Governor's office under the watchful eyes of all the cops lining the walls.

After all the frustration of the day, some of the students actually felt like we had accomplished something by holding a successful sit-in at the Governor's office. I didn't do anything to burst their bubble by telling them I really had not sat down for the reason they thought.

As we were descending the State Capitol's steps, we were laughing and carrying on about the Governor's staff being so worried that they called all those cops into the Governor's office. I didn't remember any television stations covering our march earlier in the day, but I guess someone in the State Capitol Building must have called them about a perceived sit-in at the Governor's office because cameras were waiting at the bottom of the steps as we came out of the building. We stuck with the plan and no one from PSA spoke with the press. But somehow the media had gotten my name and broadcast my name when the tape was shown on the local evening news.

That is where one of my stepdad's fellow workers must have seen it because, the next day, he asked Bill at work, was that his son demonstrating at the State Capitol? When I got to the house that evening, Bill was eating at the kitchen table and, without looking up, he said, "When are you leaving?" He had told me I could stay in his house as long as I did not cause any trouble, and what I did was trouble to him. I knew his rules and the punishment for breaking them. I told him that I would move out and walked into my room. I moved out the next day.

I was homeless for a couple of weeks after Bill kicked me out of the house for demonstrating against the Viet Nam War and had to sleep in my van. To avoid detection by Campus Police, I would park my van in different locations around campus at night. Mostly though, I would park in the football stadium parking lot. Back then, male students lived in dorm rooms underneath the stadium seats and parked their vehicles in the stadium parking lot at night. Before class, I would shower at the Pentagon dormitories.

Each day, I would ask everyone I met if they knew of any houses for rent—that is a house I could afford on my small fixed income from the VA. After about a month, I was told about some cheap houses on Highland Road. Mr. Cheney, who owned a farm on Highland Road, bought houses around Baton Rouge that were going to be torn down and moved them to his property on Highland Road. I found two other students, Jeff Sharp and Bill Malone, who were also looking for a place to live. Bill was the brother of Dave Malone, co-founder of the New Orleans band The Radiators, and Tommy Malone was the founder of the band The Subdudes. Both bands were very popular in New Orleans and all around Louisiana.

The house, which had three bedrooms with screened-in front and back porches, was not in that bad of shape. The rent was $65 a month. Because Jeff and I had bigger bedrooms, our share was $25 each and Bill's, whose bedroom was smaller, was $15. I would live there until 1972, when I moved back to McHenry.

## SUPPORTING EQUAL RIGHTS FOR FEMALE STUDENTS

The PSA and I then became involved in protesting against Margaret Jameson, the Dean of Women. She enforced antiquated rules and regulations governing women students on and off campus. Even though there was a women's organization, the Association of Women Students (AWS), on campus, they took a more conciliatory approach to Dean Jameson's heavy-handed dealings with students. A *Reveille* (May 4, 1971) article titled "Protesters oppose committee's ruling," explained what we were protesting.

> The controversy stemmed from a December 14th walkout in which coeds gathered at the Episcopal Student Center in violation of dormitory curfews to protest the alleged discriminatory regulations imposed upon women students. The coeds had appealed their cases to the Associated Women Students Judicial Board, which decided in February to exonerate them of any punishment in conjunction with the walkout. The board ruled that the coeds had acted as an organized political body with assured provisions for their safety and were exercising their rights of free speech and

assembly....Dean Jameson overturned the board's decision in March on the grounds that the coeds knowingly violated a university regulation and should have been prepared to serve the resulting penalty."

Such a blatant disregard to the constitutionally protected rights of citizens, including college students, was a consistent attitude of the LSU administration, as I would discover over and over again.

That decision of Dean Jameson's led to an appeal by the coeds to the Committee on Student Conduct, which upheld the dean's decision. By that time, a number of the original women who participated in the walkout were PSA members. At a PSA meeting, they asked PSA to protest what was happening in the hope of getting this injustice reversed.

About 35 PSA members, the vast majority being women students, went to Dean Jameson's office to discuss the issue with her. I attended the meeting. Dean Jameson later stated that I laid down in her office before she told me to leave her office. I do not remember that, but I do remember that she told me to leave her office because the meeting involved only the women students who had participated in the walkout. I pointed out to her that a number of them were members of PSA and had asked me to come with them. She replied she was not going to start the meeting until I left her office. That left me with no choice but to leave, but as I was leaving, I turned to her and retorted, "I did not know Hitler had a sister." Her face turned a bright red and I could tell she was fighting mighty hard not to respond to my comment.

After I left her office, I waited in the reception area. In a very short time, the PSA women came out of her office upset. They said that Jameson basically blew off their claims that they were exercising their constitutional rights, and that they knew they had violated university regulations by participating in the walkout.

The coeds who gathered in the dean's office in Thomas Boyd Hall carried signs such as "Free the Prisoners in the Dorms" and "We have prisoners in Vietnam—we have them here." We then gathered at the bottom of the steps leading up to her office. There was a photo on the front page of the *Reveille* (May 4, 1971), and an article quoted me, as the leader of the rally and the head of the PSA, saying:

> "I urge all students with prior, present or future troubles with Dean Jameson to come out now. Don't sit and mull over your beer and just bitch about it....This is a thing involving the whole university, not just an isolated segment like with the College of Education," Schirmer said, referring to recent conflicts between students and administrators over alleged discriminatory standards in the colleges....Schirmer said that the peaceful protest would continue all this week. He urged all concerned students to meet on the front steps of the Union [first] so that the students can go as an organized group.

I was not the only one in PSA who felt that students' rights were nonexistent on the LSU campus. A *Reveille* (May 12, 1971) article, titled "Student alliance discusses plans for 'fall offensive,'" asserted that, regardless of the fact that the vast majority of students were of adult age, the LSU administrators acted like they were our parents, and that what they said goes. The article was written by Richard Eberhardt, a founding member of PSA. The article stated that PSA was planning a 'fall offensive' which included picketing on campus and other non-violent actions:

> Beginning with fall registration, PSA members will "start picketing and won't stop," Schirmer said....In the field of dorm hours, suggestions ranged from girls jumping out of windows for *Reveille* photographers to breaking pencil points off in door locks and putting epoxy in the locks to keep the doors from being locked at night...."We need all the hard-core members that we can get back in the fall," Schirmer said, likening PSA members to the Vietcong, which he called the hardest fighters in the Viet Nam war. He did mention that the analogy was poor, however.

Sure enough, I had to explain later what I meant. A *Reveille* (May 13, 1971) article titled "Alliance head explains rap session atmosphere" stated:

> "The call for a "fall offensive" next fall...may have given a misguided impression that the group, which is dedicated to working with the system and with administrators, may have turned to more violent methods.... Sometimes, due to frustrations, things are said which do not necessarily reflect the feelings of the group, as evidenced by what I say," Schirmer said..."I have high regard for the man [Chancellor Taylor] and can feel the same frustrations of the man caught in the middle with administrators on one side and progress on the other....I hope what readers construe from stories in the Daily Reveille will not kill freedom of expression at the PSA meetings."

Just to make sure the administration did not think I was trying to water down what PSA may be planning to do in the fall, the article ended with, "He added that no plans for the 'fall offensive' have been finalized but rather were only discussed [at the meeting]." I was not letting the administration off the hook.

## THE PEACE ACTION GROUP PROTEST

At the end of April, PSA participated in another antiwar protest organized by the Baton Rouge Peace Action Group. A front-page article in the *Reveille* (April 30, 1971), titled "Antiwar activism to be stepped up," reported that the protest was to go on over a three-day period. There was going to be an all-night vigil, rally and speeches focused on how important it was to participate in the march to the State Capitol. A number of professors were to speak, including Political Science professor Dr. Cecil Eubanks, English professor Dr. Herbert Rothschild, and Chemistry professor Dr. Joel Selbin. In that article I was quoted as saying that "members of the Progressive Student Alliance were interested in serving as marshals for the protest march." I pointed out that, "These people are experienced in pickets—they're northerners." This comment provoked "laughter from the audience."

The article stated that, "Peace Action spokesman Jim Penny said arrangements are being made to invite a number of Viet Nam veterans who oppose the Indochina war to speak at the Capitol. He further indicated that some of the veterans may turn in their combat decorations in symbolic protest."

At this time, I was not one of these Viet Nam veterans. I still found it hard to go all out against the war because of my friends who had been killed in Viet Nam. I felt at the time that this would be supporting the very people who had killed Danny and Terry. This march and what was said at the State Capitol would soon change my thinking.

In the article, Doug Lambert was reported saying, "'[I] urge marchers to carry U.S. flags if 'possible.' Displaying U.S. flags would underline the fact that the group was just as patriotic as anyone else who supported the Viet Nam war. 'It's my flag too,' he said."

There was a heated discussion about whether or not Viet Cong flags should be allowed at the march. The article reported that, "One intense onlooker said, 'I'm prepared to turn in my Bronze Star, but not if Viet Cong flags are carried' ....Dr. Joel Selbin spoke in support of the march but urges students not to display Viet Cong flags in the march saying, 'You've got an uphill battle all the way [in Louisiana], and you'll lose it before you start if you carry Viet Cong flags.'" It was decided that no Viet Cong or North Vietnamese flags would be allowed at the march.

The LSU vigil and march were to coincide with protests going on in Washington, D.C. The D.C. antiwar protest was organized by the National Peace Action Coalition and called the Viet Nam War Out Now march. It was said that it was the largest protest march ever at the Capitol. Over 200,000 citizens participated in the peaceful march on April 24, 1971.

The LSU activity was scheduled to start on May 4, 1971, with a Peace Vigil beginning at 9 P.M. and lasting all night, in the Memorial Oak Grove behind the Union. Everyone was told to bring materials to make

34

posters, banners and arm bands for the march the next day to the State Capitol. There was one big problem for LSU female student's attending the vigil: Dean Jameson.

The cochairman of the event, Rose Kamere, met with Dean Jameson to discuss allowing the female students living in the dormitories on campus to attend the all-night vigil. Surprisingly, Dean Jameson gave permission under certain circumstances. These conditions were explained in the *Reveille* (May 4, 1971) article titled "Coeds may sign out for antiwar vigil." "Girls wanting to sign out for the vigil must have parental permission by either letter or phone call." The article does not mention if this applied to older female students living in the dormitories. Jameson had originally stated that female students could not sign out for the vigil unless restroom facilities were provided. That was solved when the Episcopal Center on campus agreed to allow the female students participating in the vigil to use their restrooms at the Center. Organizers urged that "Blankets, sleeping bags, pillows and *cigarettes* (emphasis added) should be brought by participants to keep them more comfortable." That was definitely a different time.

Even though I went to the vigil along with about 25 or so other PSA members, unlike the others, I did not spend the whole night in the Memorial Oak Grove. After the last speaker, I went home to sleep and returned the next day for the rally and march.

That afternoon, we all attended a rally at Memorial Oak Grove before marching down to Nicholson Road. At the beginning of the march, PSA members, wearing armbands designating us as marshals of the march, marched along side of the main body of marchers in order to keep order and to keep others not involved in the march from physically harassing the marchers.

As we left the campus and started walking down Nicholson Road, I noticed a couple of men in suits and ties, with cameras, hiding behind a couple of oak trees on the LSU campus. They really stood out to me because it was unusually hot for May. The temperature was in the 80s with the usual high humidity for Baton Rouge. Yet these men were wearing suits and ties. Local law enforcement individuals in Louisiana would never wear a suit and tie in Baton Rouge in the heat of the day. These men had to have been from the Federal government. This sight immediately brought to mind the saying, "Only mad dogs and English men go out in the midday sun." Even though we marchers were out in the "midday sun," we were all wearing T-shirts, sandals, cut-offs, and shorts. Some may have been in long pants but not a suit and tie. As we marched down Nicholson toward the State Capitol building, the men would step out from behind the oak trees, take some pictures, and then step back behind the trees. I thought this was pretty funny. Did they think that hiding behind these oak trees would somehow make them invisible to us? And really, were we that much of a threat? Well, their superiors may have thought so considering what had happened in Washington D.C. two days earlier during the Mayday protest. I am pretty confident that those men were FBI agents. I also believe that, if I have an FBI file, it started that day.

Once at the State Capitol, we all gathered on the steps to listen to a number of individuals speak out against the war. One of them was Lloyd Lindsey, Jr., a former Marine Corps lieutenant. He was an LSU graduate and recipient of the Purple Heart for wounds incurred in combat. He stated that he had "witnessed civilian killings many times," explaining that every night numerous Vietnamese people are killed in "free-fire zones." He said it was an everyday occurrence for his men to receive orders to "harass civilians." "When you are ordered to fire 75-millimeter guns, that's killing, not harassing," Lindsey said. He also, "noted that Army Lt. Calley, convicted of the civilian massacre at My Lai was, "a dirty little murderer," but then added that he guessed he was, too, since he had also killed in Vietnam.

Both Professors Cecil Eubanks and Herbert Rothschild spoke at the rally. A *Reveille* (May 6, 1971) article stated that, "Four young Viet Nam veterans turned in combat medals and citations as a symbolic gesture of sympathy with the demonstration." As I stated earlier, I was not planning on turning in my medals at the demonstration, but one of the veterans, who had served in the Army Rangers in Viet Nam, had tried, all during the march to convince me to do so. I was still resisting that request when Lloyd Lindsey Jr., the Marine Lieutenant, stepped up to the microphone and, while tossing his medals into a box that was going to be sent to Washington, he said, "I will accept medals from my country when the medals are for peace, not war." The Army Ranger looked at me as he turned to toss his medals into the box, asking me, "Well, what are you going to do?" What Lloyd Lindsey had said broke through my resistance to turning in my medals. It made sense to me in that I should not be proud of medals given for a war that we should not be involved in and that was killing so many innocent people. When Lloyd came back over to me, I told him that I did not have my medals or ribbons with me. At which point he reached into his pocket and pulled out ribbons that matched the medals he had just thrown into the box and handed them to me, saying, "Use these as substitute for your medals." And as the *Reveille* article pointed out, "Also relinquishing medals were Ted Schirmer."

As I rode back to campus with my fellow PSA members, a feeling of righteousness swept over me. Shortly afterward, I would become a founding member of Viet Nam Veterans against the War at LSU.

## Summer, 1971
### THE CELEBRATION OF LIFE FESTIVAL

I had made a number of new friends due to my involvement in PSA and speaking at Free Speech Alley. Frank Hall was one of them. We talked about the rock festivals I had attended. At some point, he asked me if I wanted to get involved with a rock festival that summer in Louisiana called Celebration of Life. Even though he told me I would not get paid, I jumped at the chance. That meant I could not attend summer school and, therefore, I would not get my school money from the VA, the only money I was living on at the time. So, to get a chance to work on a rock festival, no matter in what role and for no pay, I had to get a job to support me for the summer.

I believe I met Dave Brown at LSU. Dave was the son of Jim Brown, who owned a local carpet store. I am not sure if Dave asked his dad if he needed help or if he just told him he did. Somehow, I ended up meeting Jim, and, after talking with him and his wife, who did the books, he offered me a job working in the warehouse with Dave.

Jim was a real decent, down to earth man. And Mrs. Brown reminded me of the type of strong women I had known my entire life—women like my mother. When things were slow, Jim and I would talk about life. Like me, he came from a hard life as a child. By then I had been growing my hair for over a year, and it was getting long. Jim, unlike almost any other employer in Baton Rouge in 1971, hired me in spite of my long hair. That doesn't mean he did not give me shit now and then about my hair, but it never was mean spirited. I always felt it came from his heart. He cared about how long hair could affect my life, especially in Louisiana. Another thing I liked about Jim was that he was not a racist. Jim had a Black carpet installation team. He treated them with the respect that they deserved. I remember the boss on the team taking me out on a couple of jobs in an attempt to teach me how to lay carpet. I learned how, but was not very fast or good at it.

I do not believe I was paid much, but I did not need much money. The work at times was hard: taking big ass rolls of carpet off a stack of carpets to measure and cut pieces for the installers to take to their jobs. Dave actually got a hernia from picking up rolls of carpet. But I never was afraid of hard work.

I did take a lot of shag carpet scraps home and glued them to my bedroom walls. In addition, I painted the ceiling of my bedroom flat black, then painted stars and planets on the ceiling. All I needed was a moon shaped globe for my overhead light. Then one night, some of us were eating in a spaghetti restaurant right off campus on Highland Road when, on the way to the bathroom, I noticed the ceiling light in the hall had a round white globe. Yep, I unscrewed the globe and left out the back door with it.

All this time I worked at Jim's, I was waiting to hear from Frank about what I was to do relating to the upcoming festival. He had instructed me to keep quiet about the festival because information about it was being kept under wraps. It seemed they were trying to sneak it by the authorities. I finally called Frank. He asked me if I knew where to get a lot of bales of hay. I told him I probably could get them from my landlord. Frank told me to buy a number to be used in the Arts and Craft tent at the festival, and I would be reimbursed. I forget how many bales of hay I purchased from Mr. Cheney, but I had them ready when the time came to take them to the site of the festival. (I was never reimbursed for the hay.)

Another role I had was to provide a way station for a number of the people coming into Louisiana to work on the festival. A dozen or so people showed up at my house the night before we were to head to the festival site. They were all about my age and appearance. After they got settled in, it seemed as if every one of them pulled out a lid of marijuana and rolled a joint. Now, a dozen or so long haired freaks with out of state license plates coming to my house did attract the attention of the Baton Rouge Police Department.

This was June in Louisiana, which means hot and humid, and the only air conditioner in my house was a window unit in my bedroom, so everyone laid their sleeping bags, pillows, etc. on the front porch floor. It must have been sometime after midnight when a knock came at my bedroom door, and one of my guests told me there were some pigs (cops) pulling into the driveway.

I jumped up out of bed, got dressed, and went out to the front poach. Sure enough, there were two Baton Rouge Police officers getting out of their patrol car and walking past my van toward the house. I navigated around the sleeping bodies on the floor and latched the hook on the screen door as I waited for the two cops. They climbed the steps, and one of them put his hand on the handle and tried to open the screen door while asking, "Can we come in?" I looked him in the eye and said, "No." That, and finding the screen door latched, seemed to startle them for a moment. One of them shined his flashlight on the floor where everyone was sleeping. The other one started telling me, "We had a call about a gray van being involved in a store robbery." "Oh, really?" I said, "Well, my van is blue." As both cops spun their heads toward my van, the cop with the flashlight shined his light on my van. For a moment they both stared at my blue van, then the cop who was doing the talking said, "Yeah, I see," and asked again, "Can we come inside?" Again, but more firmly, I said, "No!" They looked at each other, turned, walked back to their patrol car, and left.

The next morning, my overnight guests and I all waited to hear where the festival's site was located. One of the original sites proposed for the festival had been Mississippi, but the authorities there had not liked that idea, as was pointed out in the *Reveille* (June 17, 1971) article titled "The Proper Pop Festival" by David Dirks:

> There is a lot of hassle with the Mississippi authorities right now....Frank Hall, a junior in law school, who's working with Kaplan [the festival promoters], promises that all the final preparations can be done within five days of the starting date, June 21....Hall assured me [Dirks] that the site of the festival is already decided and final preparations are being completed now. A press conference today will release the details to the public.

Other vehicles started arriving at my house that morning, including one with Frank Hall in it. The first information we got about the site was that the festival was being held somewhere in Pointe Coupee Parish. I was told I could leave my van at my house because the trucks were coming back to Baton Rouge to pick up more equipment. So, I rode in a truck with Frank and the hay I had bought and other equipment for the festival. As we backed out of my driveway, we knew that the festival site was going to be in Pointe Coupee Parish. The question was, where in Pointe Coupee Parish?

The site had been decided on only ten days or so earlier when the authorities finally agreed that the festival could start. An excellent article covering the festival later appeared in the *Rolling Stones* (July 12, 1971) magazine. It was titled "Life Celebration: A Report from the Front: Drugs, death and rock & roll at the Louisiana music festival."

Because of the late start, the pressure was on to get to the site and begin working on getting the set up and running. Even without specific directions, it was decided to head off in the direction of Pointe Coupee Parish. Now, this was before cell phones, so it came down to our caravan of trucks and vans having to make frequent stops at gas stations and country stores so the leaders could call someone for directions to the site.

As we wandered around Pointe Coupee Parish back roads, it got later and darker by the hour. Even though I would subsequently make a number of runs to Baton Rouge and back, I would often get a little confused about directions: was I going in the right direction, was it the right road, was I coming or going? That I was under the influence of different drugs each time may have added to my confusion a little.

I remember we finally stopped at this little country store sometime after dark. The owner of the store, who did not realize that a rock festival was about to descend on his very small community, directed us to our final destination. In about a half mile, there was a dirt road leading up to the top of the Atchafalaya River levee.

But when we arrived at the levee, it was so dark no one could see far. All the vehicles stopped, and a discussion among the leaders of what to do commenced. It was decided that, since no one knew what the site looked like and the headlights from the vehicles were insufficient to light up the area, we would just park there until daylight. More vehicles were expected to arrive that night, so a rope was put up to keep them from going further onto the site before we could see the lay of the land.

A couple of us needed to drive back to Baton Rouge to get our vehicles and our personal supplies. A number of those vehicles were at my house. When we reached my house, all the other individuals got in their vehicles and drove back to the site.

I decided to stay and sleep in my air-conditioned bedroom in my own bed. The next morning, I decided to take my time getting back to the festival site. Hey, it was mid-June in Louisiana. That meant it was very hot and very humid. I did not have any assigned duties that I knew of and had no desire to stand around doing nothing in that heat and humidity. Plus, I needed to buy supplies like food and water for myself. I knew enough about festivals by then to realize that food and water can become pretty expensive. I did not have much money, and I would need what money I had to buy gas and dope—dope, literally, was a bare necessity for a rock festival.

As I drove down the country roads to the festival site, I noticed more and more hippie types wandering around like bees looking for honey. Even though there hadn't been a formal announcement yet about where the festival was going to be held, people were already wandering the Pointe Coupee roads looking for it.

As I passed the country store, I saw there were already vehicles there and parked along the dirt road leading to the festival. When I got back to the site, I headed for a trailer where the headquarters of the festival was. Frank was in the trailer and obviously very busy. I asked him what he needed me to do, but he was not sure at the time and told me to check with him later. I asked him where I should I park my van. He suggested I park behind the stage and reached into a small box and handed me a button. He told me the button would get me into any area on the festival grounds. I looked at the button. It was light blue with the word "Family" printed over a peacock, the symbol of the festival.

I was surprised at how much work on the stage area had either been finished or was underway. A tall wooden fence had already been completed around the stage site, with the stage itself already starting to take form. I drove my van up to the gate of the stage area and showed my "Family" button to the man standing at the gate. He looked at it, looked at me, then turned and opened the gate. As I drove to the back of the rapidly rising stage, I thought, "Man, I have a ringside view of the construction of a stage at a rock festival." I also knew I had a good chance to see rock and roll stars up close and maybe even meet some. As I looked down at my "Family" button I said to myself, "Damn! This is a goddamn good button to have!"

All around the stage area some very skilled young men were working on various sections and parts of the stage. Since I was not skilled at anything related to building a rock festival's stage, I decided to keep out of the way and go explore the festival grounds.

Typically, during Louisiana summers, rain storms formed in the late afternoon. At 2:30 or 3:00 P.M., you would see black clouds approaching from the south. That is what happened on Tuesday at the festival. People in Louisiana knew that, when they saw black clouds approaching, it was time to "batten down the hatches," but those workers from out of state did not know how quickly a violent storm could develop. Because they were behind schedule and hurrying to get the stage completed, men were still up on the towers when the storm hit. Sure enough, when the winds hit, the tower on the left side of the stage came crashing down. Why did it fall? No one had placed the pins at the base that would have anchored the tower to the stage. Two guys working on the tower were injured. One was reported to be fully conscious but on the ground with a pole sticking through him.

Strangely enough, in the summer of 1973, when I was working in McHenry, Illinois, I took a rare Saturday off so I could attend a party. There I overheard a guy talking about how he was once seriously injured while working at a rock festival in Louisiana. That got my attention. I turned, and asked, was that the Celebration of Life festival? Yep, he was the guy who was run through by the scaffolding. I explained that I was one of the people coordinating efforts to get him to a hospital in Baton Rouge. What a coincidence. There I was talking to the guy who most of us thought had died. Dan Peacock was his name and he had been a Ranger in Viet Nam. He and I became fast friends.

The festival was finally ready to open three days late on Wednesday, June 23rd, but then the local sheriff's deputies started blockading the entrance gate, hassling people leaving and keeping food and water from entering. Some of the people who had stayed at my house decided to leave. They were bummed out by all the law enforcement personnel outside the festival and the fact that the promoter had hired a New Orleans motorcycles gang, the Galloping Gooses, as security. Those bikers were beating, robbing, and threatening people all over the festival grounds.

Before the festival opened, I had spent some time talking with one of the guys who would leave early. John had worked on other festivals and had hoped to smoke dope with John Sebastian, formerly with The Lovin' Spoonful. It seems that Sebastian likes to get high with the stage crew before he went out to perform. One of the first performers to appear on the first day was John Sebastian. Sure enough, as I was standing with some of the stage crew getting high, Sebastian and his girlfriend walked up, dressed in what looked like the same tie dye clothes he had worn at Woodstock, and asked if they could join us. We had no objection, so he and his girlfriend joined our little circle of dope smokers. As the pipe was being passed around, my thoughts went to John, who had wanted so badly to smoke dope with John Sebastian, and I smiled. If he had only stayed, his dream would have come true.

As I looked out to the back of the stage area, I saw Chuck Berry, standing out in the hot Louisiana summer sun, waxing his black Cadillac. Sweat was pouring off him. I guess he knew the tight rope we all were walking, smoking dope in plain view. He knew damn well that, even though there were 200 Louisiana sheriff's deputies outside of the festival grounds, there were also numerous undercover narcotics officers working inside the festival area and maybe even backstage. He wasn't taking any chances. He was staying as far away from us as he could get. As a Black man, he knew what southern cops were like.

John Sebastian's performance was ok, but maybe because I knew he was stoned, I thought he looked stoned. Chuck Berry was the best performer on the first day by far. He must have played for two hours. When he played "Johnny B. Goode," he did his famous duck walk across the stage. The crowd went crazy.

Another performer, the singer Melanie, had started to sing her hit, "Brand New Key," when a bug flew into her open mouth. She gagged a little, shook her head, then said to the crowd, "Yuck! I just swallowed a bug." After spitting out what remained of the bug, she continued with her song.

I missed a lot of the other performers because of my trips to Baton Rouge to report on the festival for *The Word,* a new underground Baton Rouge newspaper. George Blair was editor-in-chief, and John McGinnis was managing editor. They had asked me to write an article for them about the Celebration of Life rock festival. I told them I could not write very well, but they said someone on the paper would help me. They just wanted a behind the scene story by someone working on the inside. I agreed and got my picture taken for my State of Louisiana press credentials. I had to drive to Baton Rouge to dictate what I had seen to a reporter who wrote it down. I think they put only my name on the article.

Due to the sheriff's blockage, food was running short at the festival. Stewart Enterprises of Houston had bought the concession rights at the festival for $35,000 (that would be a little over $217,000 today) and were operating many stands at the festival. At first the prices were normal festival prices, but by Friday, due to the blockage of incoming supplies by Louisiana law enforcement officers, the vendors had increased their food prices to three or four times in accordance with the old capitalistic adage of price and demand. Well, those vendors did not realize that people attending rock festivals did not believe in that capitalistic adage. They saw it only as taking advantage of others' misfortune to make a buck (which in my opinion is the real meaning of price and demand).

I had just met Jerry Rubin and Carlene Tanner (I found out later that was an alias) earlier that day. She was a Weatherman (Weatherwoman) wanted by the FBI for being involved in the bombing of a room in the Capitol in Washington D.C. that same year. I don't remember who introduced Rubin to me, but I was "starstruck" to meet him. So much so that it took me a while to realize that Jerry Rubin was an egotistical asshole. But that is a later story.

So, Rubin, Carlene and I were sitting in front of the stage rapping, when I noticed about a dozen people marching through the crowd chanting "free the food." One person was carrying a sign that had the same written message on it, "Free the Food." Since I had brought plenty of food with me, I had not gone to the concession area and was, therefore, unaware of the food situation at the festival. The crowd grew and soon there were over a hundred people chanting "free the food." The three of us got up and started following the crowd. When the front of the crowd got to the vendors, they just rushed the nearest food stand, knocking the person manning it down. I believe the stand was selling hot dogs. While those at the first stand were grabbing hot dogs, buns and anything within reach, a large part of the crowd rushed the other stands.

Vendors and their workers tried to fight off the crowd, but they were way out numbered. During the food riot, the power poles, which were only 12 feet or so high and 8 to 10 inches in diameter, started getting knocked down. At the same time, one of the vendors pulled out a revolver and fired a shot in the air. That froze everyone for a moment. But a couple of people in the crowd started yelling and cursing at the vendor with the gun. It seemed like blood was going to be spilled at any time. Then a power pole fell down right between the vendor with the gun and the crowd. It was hissing and sparking. Someone yells, "Look out, that's a live wire!" Talk about great timing. That was just what was needed to prevent the crowd from rushing the vendor with the gun, which probably would have gotten people shot. After all, it was Louisiana!

By then Rubin, Carlene and I had worked our way up front. A couple of us started trying to defuse the situation. Rubin just stood there as if he were waiting for the situation to go to the next level. I started talking to the vendor with the gun telling him I was a Nam veteran and to put the gun away. He had this panicky look on his face, realizing how close he had come to shooting someone. As I was talking with the vendor, others were getting the crowd to settle down. I know some people wrote that it was the police who settled things, but that was not what happened. The sheriff's men stayed outside of the festival grounds.

There was the suggestion that we form a committee with representatives from the vendors and representatives from the crowd. The vendors agreed to this, as did the people in the crowd. By then the crowd had grown to several hundred people, but they were peace loving hippies and thought talking was a better solution than violence. I guess because I addressed the vendor with the gun, I was asked to be one of the representatives. Then, thinking that Rubin had experience in these kinds of matters, I pointed to him. "Jerry Rubin should be in on this, too." I do not believe any of the vendors had ever heard of Jerry Rubin, but a lot of the people in the crowd sure had. It was almost like announcing that we had a ringer on our side. That really mellowed the crowd who believed Rubin would get them a fair deal. I felt the same way. Man, was I in for a shock.

The vendors had picked their representatives, which included the man with the gun. He had tucked the gun in his belt, but in plain view. I thought that was a little provocative, but I realized he was scared of all those long haired hippies demanding free food.

The negotiators all sat down on the ground in a circle, and all the other people formed a larger circle around our circle. As the discussions started, Rubin said one of the stupidest things of the whole meeting. He said the vendors should just feed the people the food they had left for free since, he declared, "You have made enough money off the people." He was obviously playing to the crowd. I turned to see if he was serious. He was! I looked at the vendors. They had stunned looks on their faces, their mouths gaping open. Then their mood turned to anger.

They all started talking about the money they had invested in their stands and the costs to operate them. The authorities' blockade of traffic into the festival was keeping them from bringing in more supplies and jeopardizing their chances of even recovering their investment. I quickly acknowledged that fact. Looking at Rubin, I said to them, "You have a right to at least get your money back with a little profit, but not to charge three to four times the price you were first charging." The authorities' choice to blockade the festival was not our fault, nor the vendors' fault; so everyone had to help each other out. They agreed to sell their remaining food at a profit of only 10%. All the vendors did not agree with this proposal, nor did everyone in the crowd like that idea, especially Rubin. Eventually, though, it was agreed to set up a free food kitchen to feed those with no money, and the vendors agreed to lower prices at the concessions for those with money.

The vendors only had another couple of days to try to get their investment back. I believe a lot of them thought that the festival was going to be for eight days as advertised, and that 60,000 people would be there. Neither one of those things materialized. After seeing Rubin's behavior in the meeting, you would think I would have realized then and there that he was an asshole. But no, I was still starstruck. It wasn't until later that I learned: never assume a celebrity is who he appears to be in the news or on television. He could be, but, more likely than not, he is a completely different person in private than the one in the public eye.

After the meeting broke up, a hippie came up to Rubin and gave him some mescaline in cocoa. The three of us went down to the Atchafalaya River to cool off and make a drink with mescaline cocoa.

All that time I was wearing my "Family" button on my shirt. While we drank our mescaline tea, Rubin asked me about the button. When I explained the button to them, they both started giving me a hard time. They said the button was a symbol of elitism and other shit. By then I was standing in the river up to my thighs. I could already feel the current of the Atchafalaya swirling around my legs. Well, still starstruck and tripping on mescaline, I declared, "I am no elitist!" Taking the button off, I tossed it over my shoulder into the river. Instantly I realized I had fucked up! My van was parked behind the stage. I could not get to it without that button. I quickly turned around while shouting, "FUCK!" The button had already sunk into the water. I began wading out into the river, and I had taken no more than two steps when I felt something smooth under my foot. I reached my hand down into the muddy river water, felt around on the bottom, and pulled out my "Family" button. Talk about good karma or just flat out luck. As I turned back around, I saw Rubin and Carlene just standing there laughing at me.

Even after that I still did not let myself see those two for who they were. Later that day, I brought up the idea of asking Rubin to speak at LSU to help PSA raise both political consciousness and funds for the organization. He said sure, then gave me his phone number and address and invited me to visit him in New York City.

Walking back to the stage area, we came up to some of the others who had been involved in the food riot earlier. They were building a communal kitchen. Other festivals had kitchens, like the Hog Farm at Woodstock that relied on people to donate food to feed people for free. The ex-rioters had gotten the wood left over from building the stage. The vendors had donated large pots and pans plus a cooking stove. All that was needed was more food to cook.

I volunteered to drive to Baton Rouge to get food since I could get back into the festival. I had a press pass. One of the conditions set by the promoters of the festival was that, once ticket holders were at the festival, if they left, they could not get back in without buying another ticket. In addition to my press pass, I still had my "Family" button.

Rubin showed no interest in participating in this free food project. He had just hooked up with a young woman and walked away from the group. Carlene Tanner told me she would come with me to Baton Rouge. She wanted to take a shower at my place. Another guy from the festival came with us. I do not remember his name, but I do remember he gave Carlene and me more mescaline.

Since I was driving, I realized that I should not be taking any mescaline, but, once again, I was pressured into doing something I knew was wrong by Carlene, or should I say by my fascination with her as a Weatherwoman who was on the FBI's 10 Most Wanted list—not to mention she was attractive. So, I took the mescaline. What a trip I went on. I had already traveled a couple of times back and forth to the festival from Baton Rouge. But this time, I kept getting confused about whether I was coming to the festival or driving to Baton Rouge.

I was struggling with this when a long ass caravan of sheriff's vehicles passed us heading to the festival. As I watched the cars pass, I noticed that they were from many different parishes around Louisiana: East and West Baton Rouge, Saint Landry, Saint Martin, Lafayette, Evangeline, and West Feliciana parishes. I thought, all these redneck sheriffs wanted to get in on the action of busting hippies' heads. Despite the fact the festival had been blockaded for over a week, only some of the vendors and very few people had left the festival. I am sure the authorities were planning some kind of action in the event they had to go into the festival to clear it out.

After what seemed like days, we finally got to my house. The other guy wanted to take a shower also, so I looked at Carlene and said, "To save hot water, we should take a shower together." She just winked at me and said, "Sure."

After we had all showered and gotten dressed, we drove up to Vince's Grocery store, just a little way from my house on Highland Road. It was the nearest grocery store, so I had visited it on many occasions. We were in luck: the owner was in the store. I told Vince what was happening at the festival, how young people were running out of food and many could not afford to buy what food there was at the vendors' stands. I told him about how others at the festival were building a communal kitchen, and that some of the vendors had donated kitchen supplies, even a stove, to the communal kitchen. What we needed was food.

He said he had seen that on the news, and that it was terrible how the young people were being treated by the authorities. He told us to follow him. He took us back to a storage area where there were restaurant size cans of beans, corn, tomatoes, and other foods, plus sacks of rice and dry beans. He also owned a restaurant. While telling us to take the cases he pointed out to us, he said he was going to call the manager of Hostess Bread and ask if he could help us out.

After we had loaded about a dozen cases of canned goods and about 30 pounds or so of rice, we thought that was good enough. We did not want to abuse his kindness. At that point, Vince came out and told me to go to the Hostess factory. It was late at night by then, but the manager himself was going to open up the factory and give us some bakery goods. That just blew our minds. We thanked him over and over again.

We then drove to the Hostess factory. Sure enough, a man was sitting in a car as we pulled into the parking lot. He introduced himself and told me to pull my van around in back to the loading dock. The loading dock doors slid up, and the manager waved us inside. He told us to fill my van up with as much bread as we could get into it. Wow. We did just that. We stacked bread from the floor all the way up to the ceiling. We also thanked him over and over again for his kindness.

Man, were we excited about getting back to the festival with all that food. It was pretty late when we approached the site. I noticed there were only a couple of sheriff's officers at the gate. As I slowed down, they did not signal for us to stop. I drove to where the communal kitchen was being built when we left.

When I stopped the van by the kitchen, all three of us jumped out, eager to show them how much food we had gotten. Were we shocked when we saw all kinds of boxes and bags full of every kind of food. I asked the people manning the kitchen, what had happened? It turned out that when it hit the news that the authorities in Pointe Coupee had been trying to starve out the people at the festival, it upset a number of people. One of them was Woody Dumas, Mayor-President of Baton Rouge. He flew over to the festival in a helicopter loaded with food. He went on television and lambasted the authorities behind that strategy.

Free kitchens then sprang up all over the festival grounds. I was told that Stephen Stills, who went to LSU in the '60s, manned one of the kitchens before he had to perform. After that, I parted with Carlene and Rubin but made plans to visit them in New York City.

## VISITING JERRY RUBIN IN NEW YORK CITY

Back at LSU, as mentioned in an article on the front page of the summer *Reveille* (July 8, 1971), titled "Alliance plans protest rally," I said at the meeting of PSA that I was "planning to go to New York to explore the possibility of bringing such speakers as Jerry Rubin and Abbie Hoffman to the campus." One of the members of PSA stated that, "Rubin has an ability to show people what is really lacking. He is good at 'radicalizing' people." A picture of me sitting on a table at the meeting showed the effects of spending days out in the sun at the festival. Even though it was a black and white picture, you can tell I have a very deep, deep tan.

My plan to go to New York had one big problem. Since I had been involved with the festival most of the summer, I had very little money. PSA members all chipped in until I had about a $100 or so. It was not enough to buy a bus ticket and live on, so I decided I would hitchhike up to New York. Now, I had only hitchhiked to New Orleans when I was in the Navy. At that time, I wore my Navy uniform, which made it very easy to get rides. But I remembered those young Canadians, whom I had met the previous Christmas, telling me how they had hitchhiked all over Canada and the United States. Hell, if those 15 and 16-year-olds could do it, I felt I could hitchhike 1,400 miles to New York City. I packed my Navy seabag with what I thought I would need for the trip and had Susanna drive me to the I-10 Interstate Highway to start my adventure.

I never took into consideration my new look. By then I had long hair and a beard. I wore bell bottom jeans and T-shirts. After Susanna had left me on the Interstate, I immediately started to think this may not have been a good idea. I was surprised when I caught a couple of rides pretty quickly. I made it into Mississippi before my thumb went cold.

I had been walking along the highway with my thumb out for about an hour with no luck. I was starting to worry when a '57 Bel Air with a Dixie license plate drove by. In the vehicle were two young white men. As they passed me, we made eye contact. I noticed they both had flattop haircuts. Then I saw that they were pulling over to the shoulder of the highway a little way past me. I could not help but think they might be a couple of rednecks deciding to kick some hippie's ass. After all, I was in Mississippi.

I saw the Chevy begin backing up at a high rate of speed. Their car came right up to me, forcing me to step back. Shit! I was preparing for the worst. Plans of how to defend myself were running through my head when the passenger said to me, "We aren't going far but far enough to get you high." Instant relief swept over me, and I replied, "Hell yes!"

The passenger leaned forward to let me get in. I threw my seabag in and climbed in back. True to their word, the passenger lit a joint and handed it back to me. He asked where I was heading. I told them I was going to New York to see Jerry Rubin. I could tell they had never heard of Jerry Rubin, but, despite their appearance, they were very hip for southern boys.

I had only time to take a few hits off the joint when the driver said they were taking the next exit. As I climbed out of the car with my sea-bag, the passenger held out the remainder of the joint, asking me if I wanted the rest. I thanked him but said, no, too risky. He smiled. They both wished me luck and drove off leaving me stoned on that Mississippi highway.

I was starting to feel the full effects of the joint. That was good dope, I thought. Then the paranoia hit me full force. Not only was hitchhiking on the Interstate illegal, but I was doing it in Mississippi as a stoned long haired freak. I thought maybe I should get off the Interstate. I could buy a map of Mississippi, then hitchhike the back roads until I got out of Mississippi. I quickly realized that was a fucking bad idea. A long haired- hippie hitchhiking the back roads of Mississippi. What could be wrong with that!

As I started to have a complete melt down right there on the side of the Interstate, an eighteen-wheeler pulled over in front of me. I quickly ran over to the rig and climbed into the cab feeling very relieved at not being on the highway. The driver was a white man who didn't look much older than me. He told me he usually never picked up a single man hitchhiking, only couples, but what the fuck. He asked me where I was headed. I told him New York. With a smile on his face, he said, "I am not going that far, but I will get you out of Mississippi." Wow, another cool white man in Mississippi. Someone was looking after me.

I am not sure how far I rode with him, but it was for a number of hours. It was the first time I had ridden in the cab of an eighteen-wheeler. A person has quite a view because of how high up one sits in the cab. It was July in Mississippi, and I had a clear view of the woods lining the Interstate. I had never realized how this part of Mississippi was rolling hills. It may have been because I was still a little stoned, but

Mississippi was really beautiful. I have never seen it again looking so beautiful.

The driver had been carrying a rig full of live pigs but had unloaded them in New Orleans. He reached behind him and pulled down a box of Babe Ruth candy bars. He told me he had been given these candy bars to feed to the pigs to help keep their weight up during the trip to New Orleans. He said to help myself to as many as I wanted. I stuffed a bunch of the candy bars in my pockets.

While we were still in Mississippi, as we approached a weighing station, he pulled over on the shoulder. He explained he would get into trouble if the company knew he was picking up hitchhikers, so I should meet him on the other side of the station. I tossed my seabag out, climbed down, and started walking down the highway while he pulled his rig into the weight station. I had walked only a few hundred yards when he stopped and let me in again. It was night when he finally pulled over to let me out. He pointed to the road down under the over pass we were on and told me, that's my road. He wished me luck. I thanked him for the ride and the candy bars.

In 1971, the Interstate system was far from completed. I found myself at one of those uncompleted sections. I believe it was Interstate 40. When I walked down to the highway, I found a two-lane road to my left that dead ended into the beginning of the newly built section of the Interstate on my right. There were no vehicles at all on the road. I figured I might as well sleep there until morning. Right under the over pass, there was a ledge about two feet wide with bird and rat shit on it. I cleaned off the ledge, took my sleeping bag out of my seabag, and bedded down for the night. I only vaguely remembered hearing one car go by that whole night.

The next morning, as I was rolling up my sleeping bag, I noticed that someone had written something on the concrete wall. It said, "Been here two days, no rides." Holy shit, I thought. Two days. Fuck! I was pretty depressed at that point. I walked down to the road and started walking. I was not going to just sit there for days waiting for a ride. I had not gotten very far when I heard a car coming, I quickly turned and stuck out my thumb. The car pulled over. What luck! Even the driver knew how lucky I was because he mentioned that he normally did not pick up hitchhikers but knew that road was not well-traveled. I would have been there for some time if he had not come along. He dropped me off at a busier part of the Interstate, and from there I was able to get a number of short rides until dark.

At that point I was a few hundred miles from Washington, D.C., so I decided, since I had never been to our Capitol, I would pass through D.C. on the way to New York. But as I stood there with my thumb out, I did not have much luck. It was getting very late at night, so I went into a restaurant by the highway to get a cup of coffee to go. When I came back out, there was another hitchhiker standing where I had been hitch-hiking just a few minutes ago. It's tough enough for a single male to get rides, but for two males it is nearly impossible.

He was an older man, maybe in his late 40s. His demeanor told me he was an experienced hitchhiker. He immediately said that we both cannot hitchhike in the same spot, and that I would have to go farther up the road. But that was a good spot since it was right across from a restaurant where people were stopping to eat at and get coffee. I told him I would go sit down off the road while I drank my coffee, giving him a chance to get a ride. If after I finished my coffee, he still had no luck, I would walk farther up the road. All the while I was talking to him, he kept his thumb out. To our total astonishment, a car with a woman driver pulled over right in front of us.

We walked up to the car as she leaned over and rolled down the passenger side window. She said she had been driving for two days and was totally exhausted. She needed to get to D.C. that night, but she needed help driving. She asked us if we had driver's licenses. When we both said yes, she told us to get in. He climbed in the back seat, and I sat in front.

We had only traveled a few miles when she said, "If you are going to rape me, get it over now. If not, which one of you wants to drive?" After getting over the shock of what she had just said to us, the man in the back said he would drive so she could get some sleep in the back seat.

They changed places, and we were off again. She fell asleep immediately. I made some small talk with the guy, but I was thinking I would have to drive next, so I needed to sleep.

I must have been really exhausted because, when I woke up, the women were driving again. I looked in the back seat. The other guy was gone. She told me that she had let him out a way back. She then said that we were arriving in D.C. and asked me where I would like to be let off. I told her I had never been to the Capitol, so anywhere would be fine. It was by then around 2 A.M. She let me out by the Lincoln Memorial, thanked me, and drove off. I didn't even get time to thank her. Since I hadn't driven any, I thought, did she just thank me for not raping her?

Here I was at our Capitol. A little excited thrill came over me. There was a sign that showed where all the memorials and museums were located. Since it was two o'clock in the morning, all the museums were closed, but I could at least see all the memorials before leaving for New York.

I decided to start with Lincoln's Memorial since I was much closer to it than the Capitol. After I was done at the Lincoln Memorial, I thought I would walk over to the Jefferson Memorial. I was really inspired by him (that was before I learned more about the man). Statements by him, such as "The tree of liberty must be refreshed from time to time with the blood of patriots and tyrants," fit my view at the time that our country needed a revolutionary change. Hopefully, not a bloody one, but considering what happened at the 1968 Democratic National Convention in Chicago, the violence in the south surrounding the Civil Rights Movement, the killing of the four students in 1970 at Kent State by the National Guard, plus other violent actions by the government, it seemed possible that a violent revolution was coming.

The Jefferson Memorial did not appear to be that far away, so I hoisted my seabag on my shoulder and off I went. Well, distances on maps appear shorter than they are in reality. I was over two miles away from the Lincoln Memorial. Since my seabag carried everything, I thought I might possibly need for as long as a week, it was quite heavy.

But even after a long trek, I thoroughly enjoyed the Jefferson Memorial. It was so early in the morning that there were no people around and little sound of traffic from the roads that ran near-by. I had a one on one with Jefferson as I read the writings on the wall of his Memorial.

It was then around four in the morning. I decided not to walk over to the Capitol building but just go to the Washington Monument and the White House, then hit the road for New York.

After walking around the Washington Monument, I headed for the White House. When I got there, to my surprise, there was a table outside the north portico manned by several people. I stopped to talk with them about what they were up to.

It turned out they were Quakers. That summer, a Quaker Action Group had transformed itself, in response to the Viet Nam War, into the Movement for a New Society. This newly formed group was operating a 24/7 protest against the war outside the White House. I told one of the young men that I was a Viet Nam veteran and that I strongly supported what they were doing. At some point, I said I was hitchhiking to New York, and he told me he knew of a girl at his school, Georgetown University, who was driving to New York that day. He offered to ask her if she would take me with her. He also offered to let me rest awhile at his apartment. I was pretty tired after walking five to six miles around D.C. carrying my heavy ass seabag, so I said, sure. We left immediately for his apartment.

After arriving, he brought out a tray of marijuana and rolled a joint. I told him I thought Quakers did not partake in those kinds of things. He said with a smile, "It's ok in moderation." He lit up the joint, and we got stoned.

He wanted to know about my experience in Viet Nam. I explained how my beliefs about the war, or any war, had changed since serving in Viet Nam. He then said, "I have a book for you." He gave me a book that did indeed help me with my evolution from a supporter of war to a strong opponent of wars. The name of the book was *The War Prayer* by Mark Twain. Being stoned, I did not think I would be capable of reading anything right then. My new friend said sure I could, it was very short. When I opened the book, I was pleased to see, not only were there very few words on the pages, but every other page came with an illustration to go with the words. *The War Prayer* became one of my favorite books. Like some other books, I felt it had a great message, and I later brought copies to give to my friends. My new Quaker friend told me the book was a gift from him to me.

When I woke up the next morning, I found out he had spoken with his classmate, and she had agreed to take me to New York. When I met her, I offered to pay for gas, but she told me it was not needed, she was going to go to New York anyway.

We got to New York on August 1, 1971, and she dropped me off near the address I had for Rubin. He lived in the Bowery at the time. When I got to his apartment, I knocked on the door. To my surprise, who opened the door but Carlene.

Carlene looked surprised when she saw me standing there, but she gave me a hug, then took my hand and led me inside the apartment. She called out, "Jerry, come see who is here." Rubin came out of what I learned later was his bedroom. With a grin on his face said, "You made it here." He walked over to me and gave me a hug.

Since neither one of them addressed me by my name, I figured that both of them could not recall it. As I looked around the apartment, I saw there were three other men in the room. I walked over to one of them, stuck out my hand and said, "Hi, I am Ted Schirmer from Louisiana." That man shook my hand, saying, "Stew Albert." I did not recognize the name. Later, I learned he was quite an activist himself. He had appeared in front of several grand juries that were investigating the bombing of the United States Capitol by the Weather Underground in March of 1971. That was the same event that put Carlene on the FBI's most wanted list. Looking back, I marvel how Carlene was hiding from the FBI in plain sight.

I then turned to the other man, who did not look familiar either. As he stuck out his hand he said, "Allen Ginsberg." I had heard of him. I found out later why he was there. He was very concerned about the suffering of victims during the Bangladesh civil war that was going on. He wrote his famous poem "September on Jessore Road" after returning from touring refugee camps. There he witnessed the plight of millions fleeing the violence. Bob Dylan put his poem into a song by the same name, and he would sing it at the Concert for Bangladesh. Before I could say anything, Rubin spoke up. "Yeah, Ted was at the festival I told you about."

I then turned to face a man who was standing by himself as someone said, "He's from Chile and doesn't speak much English." I said, "*Buenos dias.*" He gave me a queer look and said, "*Buenas tardes.*" I quickly said, "*Buenas tardes,*" with a smile on my face. My F in Spanish was showing.

I sat down on the couch and started talking with Albert and Ginsberg. They both were very interested in my experiences in Viet Nam. They also were interested in Louisiana, especially in what kind of activism was happening in that racist state. We had not been talking long when Rubin interrupted, saying, "We have to leave for Abbie's." I presumed that was Abbie Hoffman since I knew he and Jerry Rubin were friends. I still did not know about the Concert for Bangladesh that was to take place that night. In hindsight, they may have thought I did, and that was why I was there on August 1st.

Albert and Ginsberg got up to leave with Rubin. Albert gave Carlene $20 while telling her to take the Chilean down to the train station. He instructed her to help him buy a ticket to where his relatives lived in New York. Carlene told me to come with them. She said that, after she got him on a train, she was going down to the Garden [Madison Square Garden] where George Harrison was putting on a Concert for Bangladesh to raise money for the Legal Defense Fund. If we were lucky, we might cop a couple of tickets to the concert. That sounded good to me.

Why was there a Concert for Bangladesh? As they left India, the British had partitioned their former colony into (mostly) Muslim Pakistan and (mostly) Hindu India. A part of the Indian province of Bengal was designated East Pakistan. A civil war, called the Bangladesh Liberation War, broke out when the Bengalis attempted to create an independent state called Bangladesh. This civil war resulted in around 6 to

7 million displaced people fleeing into neighboring India. This happened shortly after the area was devastated on November 12, 1970, by the Bhola cyclone that killed an estimated 500,000 people. Then, in March of 1971, the Bengalis were hit by torrential rains and floods that led to a humanitarian disaster. In an attempt to put down the uprising, the Pakistani army went from village to village, home to home, raping and slaughtering Bengalis under a military action titled Operation Searchlight. At least 250,000 civilians were murdered by the Pakistani army and militia. The surviving Bengalis, who had fled to Calcutta, were facing starvation and an outbreak of cholera. The concert was an attempt to raise money for their relief.

In an interview a few months after the concert, George Harrison stated that his friend Ravi Shankar, a Bengali musician, was very upset and distraught about what was happening in his homeland. That was why he approached George Harrison for help in trying to alleviate the suffering of his people. Harrison was so moved by what was happening, he not only agreed to help put together a benefit concert, but he went into a Los Angeles studio to record a song he wrote for the benefit, "Bangla Desh." The song explained the reasons for a benefit, and the origin of the idea for a benefit concert.

Shankar was hoping to have some kind of benefit concert that would raise $25,000. The two concerts were attended by 40,000 people and raised $250,000. The concert, record and film raised millions of dollars.

The planning of the benefit concert started in earnest the last week of June, only around 6 weeks before the August 1st date for the concert. The organizer was George Harrison, a former Beatle, and the list of performers he hoped to get to play at the benefit concert was very impressive. It included the other former Beatles, Paul McCartney, Ringo Starr, and John Lennon, plus he invited Eric Clapton, Bob Dylan, Leon Russell, Jim Keltner, Voormann, Billy Preston and the band, Badfinger among others.

Paul McCartney shot down any idea that he would play at the benefit almost immediately because he still had bad feelings because of the legal hassles over the break-up of the Beatles. That fit my image of Paul

McCartney perfectly: refusing to perform at a very worthy benefit concert because his feelings had been hurt.

John Lennon agreed to perform, even with the condition that Harrison insisted on: that his wife and musical partner at the time, Yoko Ono, was not to perform. Then it was alleged that Lennon and Ono got into a massive argument over the fact that she was not invited to perform, and, as a result of this argument, Lennon left New York a couple of days before the concert date.

Ringo Starr, like a true friend, was completely different than the other two former Beatles. He let it be known in no certain terms that he was in. So much so that he stopped the filming of his movie *Blindman* in Spain in order to play at the benefit.

Bob Dylan was being Bob Dylan. On July 29, 1966, he had crashed his motorcycle in upstate New York and quit touring. Apart from a few public appearances, he withdrew from the public for many years. Therefore, when Harrison asked him to perform at the concert, he had serious doubts about performing in public for the first time in over five years, especially at an event at the Garden, in such a highly charged atmosphere with so many other famous musicians. He would not commit to play at the benefit. Dylan did not show up for any of the rehearsals until the final rehearsal the night before the concert.

All of these doubts as to who would perform at the concert just added to the excitement and electricity outside of the Garden that day and night. In all, 75 stars, including Bob Dylan, Ringo Starr, Eric Clapton and the others, billed themselves as George Harrison and Friends.

When Carlene, the Chilean and I got to the train station, Carlene bought him a ticket for $5 and pointed out the train he was to get on. As I watched the Chilean board the train, I turned to Carlene and asked her, "The $20 was for the Chilean. He did not have any money. Why didn't you give him the change?" As she turned to walk away, she said, "He didn't know how much the ticket cost." That was another incident that should have convinced me that these people did not deserve my admiration or respect. But I was still ego tripping on the fact that I was running with real revolutionaries. My eyes were not opened until later in Baton Rouge.

When we got to the Garden it was quite a scene. A couple of hundred people milled around the entrance to the Garden. There were people with all kinds of petitions advocating various political, religious and environmental issues. There were, of course, Hare Krishna members dancing around. It was clear that the concert had been sold out for a long time because there were a number of ticket scalpers hawking their tickets for exorbitant prices. I knew there was no way I could afford to buy a ticket from those scalpers. But I had my Louisiana press pass in my wallet, and I started wondering if I could use it to get into the concert.

Carlene and I went over to the Legal Defense Fund people. After talking with Carlene, they handed each of us a clipboard with a petition supporting the work of the Defense Fund and instructed us to ask people to sign the petition, then ask for a donation. So, we stood in front of the entrance to the Garden working the crowd. At some point, Carlene just disappeared on me. For all I know, she probably met up with Rubin, Ginsberg and Albert to go inside to the concert. Hey, to them I was nobody, just some hippie from Louisiana that they had met at a festival. Rubin probably never thought I would take him up on his invitation to come to New York. But I did not mind. I was getting off on the crowd.

The closer it came time for the first show to start, the larger the crowd got by the entrance. All the time, the well-to-do and rich were arriving in their limousines and taxis. Each time a limousine would pull up and let a number of people out, the ticket scalpers would swarm around them, holding one, two or more tickets in the air. I returned the petition and the donations I had gotten for the Fund and decided to see if I could use my Louisiana press pass to get into the concert. I went up to the ticket window and showed my press pass to the person manning the ticket booth. I told him I was there from Louisiana to cover the concert. I was informed that I would have had to request press credentials for the concert days ago. Oh well, the best laid plans of mice and men.

When I got back out front, hundreds of people were still milling around, as if waiting for tickets to the concert to fall out of the sky or some other miracle to happen, so they could get into the concert. Since I was not going to get into the concert, I thought I might as well enjoy what was happening outside of the Garden.

By then people were getting very antsy. It did not help rumors started spreading through the crowd that "Dylan may be coming to play." When the afternoon performance ended and people exited the concert, it was confirmed: Dylan had indeed performed at the first show. This information was like throwing gasoline on a fire. It was around 5 P.M. when the first performance ended. In the next three hours before the 8 P.M. performance, the news that Dylan was performing at the concert spread, not only through the crowd, but, by the number of new people descending on the Garden, the news must have spread through all of New York City. This was getting exciting.

The ticket scalpers, in response to this news, doubled and even tripled the already exorbitant prices of their tickets for the evening performance. Some of them were asking $200 for a ticket. In today's dollars that would be over $1,200. The upper echelon of New York society started appearing in larger numbers without tickets and were very willing to pay the outlandish prices that the scalpers were asking. Keep in mind, those transactions were taking place right on the sidewalk in front of the Garden, in plain view of the hundreds of young people who had been outside of the Garden all day trying to cop tickets. It really pissed them off.

By 8 P.M. the scalpers had sold all of their tickets, but still the taxis and limousines continued to come for about a half hour. But there were no tickets to be had. It was funny to watch the faces of those privileged individuals getting upset that their wealth would not get them into the concert. Not to be sexist, but the women were more upset than their husbands or dates that they were not going to get into the concert.

One would have thought that the crowd would have started to thin out. Well, a few people left, but not many. It seemed as though there was a hardcore of about two hundred or so individuals that appeared to

63

be up to something. I did not know exactly what. I positioned myself at one end of the glass doors leading into the Garden. Around 8:30 P.M., the glass front doors had been closed and locked.

I think some of these hardcore New Yorkers took this as a personal insult, especially after seeing so many rich folks getting into the concert. Some of them started beating on the glass doors shouting, "Let the people in!" Soon there were a number of what appeared to be New York police standing on the other side of the glass doors inside the Garden. About an hour after the glass doors were locked, a police barricade was used to break through the glass door at the end farthest from where I was standing. All of the security ran down to that door as dozens of people ran through the shattered glass door. Then, with military precision, another group smashed the glass door at the end where I was standing. Then even more people ran through.

*The Village Voice* (August 12, 1971) article "Who Clubbed the Clown?" stated, "…midway through the evening show, a crowd of 200 non-ticket-holders charged and broke through the doors of Madison Square Garden." There were so many people coming through both of those broken doors that the security guards appeared to be retreating. As I saw all of these people running into the Garden, I thought, "What the fuck?" and joined them.

Shortly after entering, I realized that the security guards had not retreated very far. In fact, it soon became obvious to me that they only retreated a little way to await reinforcements. I also noticed that security personnel were sweeping down the hallway that led to the concert. They were pushing and hitting people as they went. I quickly got out my press pass. When I saw a security guard rushing toward me with his club raised above his head, I quickly flashed my press pass in front of his face and yelled, "I'm a press reporter!" This brought a puzzled look on his face as if he were caught in a dilemma: should I hit this guy or not? Even though I had long hair and beard and was dressed in hippie attire, this was New York City, not Louisiana, so it was not out of the realm of possibilities that indeed I was a news reporter. He shouted at me, "Get out of here." I had turned to head for the doors when the son of bitch hit me hard in the back with his night stick. I spun around but he was already running over to where a couple of the security guards were beating a young woman who was on the floor with her arms over her head trying to protect her head from the blows that were raining down on her. I put my back against the wall and slid down it toward the exit, keeping my eyes peeled in case another security guard attacked me.

The scene in front of me was like something out of a newsreel. Security guards were beating people right and left. Some of the people were putting up a fight only to be knocked down and beaten by more of the SOBs. Later I found out that one of the people seriously injured was Wavy Gravy of the Hog Farm, made famous by the Woodstock movie. *The Village Voice* article by Ron Rosenbaum pointed out that Wavy had a ticket to the concert. He still got beaten when he was unable to obey an order to run because of a recent operation on his back. This did not save him as a security guard hit him right in the back with his club. He had to be taken to the hospital that evening.

By the time I worked my way out to the street, buses loaded with New York police in riot gear had arrived. They filed out of the buses and smartly marched single file around the Garden. I saw a captain standing by one of the buses observing his men. Still pissed off, not to mention still hurting from the where the club had hit by back, I went up to him, showed him my press pass and said, "One of your officers just clubbed me after I showed him my press pass." I emphasized again, "AFTER I SHOWED HIM MY PRESS PASS!" The captain could tell I was very upset and to his credit he calmly said, "That was not one of my officers." "What?" I said in astonishment. "I saw his uniform. It's the same as yours. He even had a badge on his shirt." He responded calmly, "I know. Security companies, including the Garden's security, wear identical uniforms to us, and their badges are very similar." He went further, "We get these types of complaints all the time, of people being beaten by our officers, when in fact it was a private security guard. We have been demanding that City Hall do something about this confusion. But no luck so far. The security companies argue that looking like they are New York police officers helps them control problematic people."

I went back over to the entrance and looked more closely at the uniforms and badges the security guards were wearing. The badges were definitely not the same as the police. I even believe that MSG Security was on the badges. But that was the only difference between the security guards' uniforms and the New York police uniforms.

I made my way back to Rubin's apartment, my back hurting the whole way. I was still sore the next morning when Rubin asked me to ride with him and Stew Albert to the airport. He needed me to drive his car back from the airport to his apartment and park it behind the building. They were flying to Chile that afternoon to see what was happening since the 1970 election of Salvador Allende to the presidency of Chile.

On the way to the JFK Airport, I again raised the idea of Rubin speaking at LSU to help PSA raise money. He agreed to come and told me all we had to do was pay for his plane ticket and cover any of his expenses, like food, etc. He told me to call him with the details when he returned from Chile.

I then managed somehow to navigate New York streets to get Rubin's car back to the apartment and parked it where he had told me to. Since I had very little cash left, I decided to spend only one more night at Rubin's apartment before heading back to Baton Rouge. I had not gotten much sleep the night before and just did not feel like hitchhiking back to Baton Rouge. I decided to call my brother Terry to ask him to loan me the money for bus fare back to Baton Rouge. Even though he acted as if I were asking him for a kidney, he wired the money to me.

PSA brought Rubin to speak at LSU on November 14, 1971. That was a Sunday, but Sunday was the only day we could get the Cotillion Ballroom. The right wing, i.e., most of Baton Rouge, protested Rubin coming to LSU to speak. All that did was give us a lot of free publicity and ensure we were going to sell a lot of tickets. Indeed, the ballroom had an overflowing crowd of over 800 people. PSA did not have a way to sell tickets in advance, so the tickets were only sold at the door the night of the event. The tickets were sold at 75 cents for students and $1.50 for non-students.

Rubin stayed at my house. Susanna and I gave him our bed to take a nap in before he spoke. After he woke, we all drove to LSU. At the Cotillion Ballroom, about five minutes before the event was to start, Rubin demanded we pay him $500 dollars or he was not going to speak. (That was the equivalent of over $3,000 today.) I was flabbergasted! I explained to Rubin that PSA was only making a little over $500. He insisted he wanted $500 or he was not going on. We tried to bargain with him, offering him half of the money we netted from the event. "No," he said. "$500 or I am not going to speak." The PSA officers discussed this among ourselves, but we really had no alternative. That overflowing crowd would have gone crazy if Rubin did not speak. Not to mention, it would be the end of our organization. We told him we would give him the money. Then the SOB wanted the money right then. I told him he could take our word on it, but, no, he wanted the money before he spoke. We had to delay the start so we could get the money from the PSA members who had manned the doors.

The real kicker was that I then had to go on the stage to introduce him to the audience. That was very hard. I cut my intro down to just a couple of sentences. That was the incident that finally ended my awe of Rubin.

Since then, I learned that one should reserve your opinion of a public figure until you have a chance to meet him. That does not mean one cannot like or dislike what the public figure is doing or saying, but just do not think that is who that person really is until you get to know him.

## Fall Semester, 1971
### A GIFT FROM MOROCCO

My girlfriend Susanna was attending the Nursing School in Chicago in the fall of 1971. She had told me during our summer together in Baton Rouge that she wanted to quit nursing school and stay with me in Baton

Rouge. I urged her to stay in nursing school. She only had two years left to become a registered nurse. She seemed to agree and left for school at the end of the summer. However, one fall day after school had started, I returned home from class and found her sitting on the steps of my house. She had quit nursing school.

One Sunday, we pulled over to a gas station to get gas. I do not remember what gas station it was, but it was closed. The station had a big daisy, in a green pot, spinning in the wind on top of the roof. It was made out of some light weight metal. I thought that it would look great on our house. I climbed up on the roof and took down the daisy. When we got back home, Susanna and I put it on the roof of our house on Highland Road.

Later, in the fall semester, I came home from school to find a package in the mailbox addressed to me from, of all places, Morocco. I thought, what the hell? I did not know what it was, but, because I had a high my profile, I decided not to open it right away. I figured that if I were being set-up by the authorities, they would show up in a few days. But after time passed and nothing happened, I thought it was safe to open the package.

It was wrapped in some type of colored aluminum foil. Inside was a note from my Canadian friend John and a brick of Morocco hash. In the note, John said he was stuck in Morocco and needed money to get back to Germany to catch a freighter back to Canada. I think he wrote he just needed $15 dollars. The first thing I thought was that hash must be dirt cheap in Morocco since John said he was broke. I sent him the $15 and apologized that that was all I could afford. I think he may have really wanted me to sell some of the hash to raise money for him. But I did not sell drugs.

There was no way I could smoke all that hash John had sent me, so I decided to use it to entertain all my friends and people I knew in the local movement. Over the next couple of weeks, Susanna and I had a number of parties at the house. As is the case at parties, a number of people you do not know showed up.

As a matter of fact, one of these people I did not know was so impressed with the hash, he asked to swap some powdered cocaine for some hash. Well, I had never done coke. It was the rich man's drug at the time. Also, trading hash for cocaine would not make me a drug dealer, so I said, sure. I was highly disappointed with cocaine. First cocaine cost way too much money. Plus, good speed and good marijuana taken together was much better. Matter of a fact, for a couple of years when I went to Mardi Gras, I would have speed, marijuana and a plastic gallon jug filled with tequila and orange juice. The marijuana would mellow me out, the speed would keep me moving, and the tequila would be the icing on the cake. *Laissez les bon temps rouler!*

Then, one day after I had been throwing hashish parties at the house, I was sitting in the Student Union at LSU drinking coffee when I heard a person at the table behind me talking about a house on Highland Road with great hash. I heard another voice ask where on Highland Road? The first voice started explaining that you could not miss it because the house had a big daisy flower on the roof. Shit! As I picked up my books, I looked over my shoulder at the guys sitting at the table. I did not recognize any of them. That was not good. Just to play it safe, I decided it was time to get rid of the hash. At the next party I gave everyone who wanted it a chunk of the hash until it was all gone. Once again, nothing was worth risking my freedom for.

In the fall of 1971, Ossie Brown was running for East Baton Rouge Parish District Attorney for the first time. He was running against the incumbent District Attorney Sargent Pitcher. I knew enough about Pitcher to disgust me. I guess you could say he was the typical racist politician in Louisiana at the time. He was a proud member of the racist organized White Citizens' Council. So one day, when I was asked if I wanted a bumper sticker speaking out against Pitcher, I said, "Sure, give me one." The bumper sticker had written on it, "Sargent Pitcher Bugs Me." I put it on my van.

That same night my friends and I were on the way to a party when Sweet George, the local drug dealer, asked if I could give him a ride home first. His car had broken down, and he lived pretty far down

Highland Road. I said, no problem. Just as we were driving off of LSU's campus, I saw a Baton Rouge police car behind me with its lights on. I called out to everyone in the back that I was being pulled over by a cop and to keep quiet. I did not know if any of them had dope on them, but it was a good bet that at least one of them had at least a joint. I pulled the curtains to the back of the van closed as I stopped on the side of the road.

I watched the two officers in my side mirror get out of their patrol car. They seem to be talking to each other, but I couldn't tell about what. One of the officers came up to my window and asked for my license and registration. I handed them to him. As he was going over them, without looking up at me, he said, "So, Pitcher bugs you, does he?" I realized then they had been talking about the sticker on my van. I was not going to be intimidated for my political view, so I said, "Yeah, he sure does."

The officer looked up at me with a smile on his face. He then handed my license and registration back to me. As he started back to his patrol car, he said over his shoulder, "You better get your brake lights fixed." After they pulled away, I could hear laughter coming from the back of the van.

When we got to Sweet George's home, he told us to wait a minute. He ran into his house. In a little bit, he came back out and handled me a rolled-up baggie. He told me it was mescaline cut in cocoa. I told him thanks and stuck the mescaline in my pocket.

Later at the party, I had gotten pretty damn stoned and decided to try some of the mescaline. I licked my finger, stuck it in the baggie, and then licked my finger. It tasted just like Nestle's cocoa. Without realizing it, because I was stoned and had the munchies, I kept dipping my finger into the bag of mescaline. I do not know how much I took, but fortunately one of my friends saw me doing this. He and another of his friends took me home with them.

I had one of the most intense trips I ever had. I could swear I actually stopped time. That was one long night. The two friends took turns staying up with me all night. At one time as I was sitting in my chair, I could not distinguish where the chair started and my body stopped. I was unable to feel any connection to my body. I took off my shoes and socks and walked outside barefooted. It was cold enough outside that I was able to "rebuild my body" starting with my feet and working my way up to my head. I had to do that a couple of times. What a night!

Later I had a bad LSD trip during Mardi Gras. After that I swore off man-made hallucinogens and only ate mushrooms or peyote. I quit those by 1978. I had heard people say that when you eat peyote, you see God; when you eat mushrooms, you talk to God. I have eaten both, and, while I had some mind-blowing trips, I never saw nor talked with God.

## PSA AND HARAMBEE CHALLENGE THE GREEKS

In the fall of 1971, PSA was unhappy about the lack of success in changing the grooming standards and was trying to decide what its next actions were going to be. In a *Reveille* (November 11, 1971) article, titled "Alliance described as 'nothing definite,'" I was quoted as saying, "For this university, PSA may be radical, but anywhere else it wouldn't be….A university should be a mellow place, and maybe by creating tension now we can make this place a better university."

In the *Reveille* (October 6, 1971), there had been a letter to the editor from Javier Loustaunau, a graduate student complaining about fraternities saving rows of seats at football games. The letter was titled, "How long?"

> This is a questioning letter to LSU students, asking how long they are going to tolerate the abuse of two to three students reserving (owning) 50 or more square feet of sitting area for the football games….There is nothing against people that want to sit together but I think that they should go together and not send their "emissaries" to hold half of the stadium until their "good buddies" arrive at the start of the game to take "their reserved seats." There are no reserved seats in the student section of the LSU stadium. Any person

with the proper ID card can and should sit in any vacant place....This abuse will persist as long as the rest of the students continue to tolerate it.

This letter, and my own experience with pledges' saving seats, prompted me to argue to PSA that we should demonstrate against what the Greeks on campus were doing. We could accomplish two things. First, show other students what can be done to stop this abuse and, secondly, sock it to one of the elitist fraternities on campus. Tom Ingalliners, treasurer of PSA, announced to the *Reveille*, "PSA plans to demonstrate civil disobedience at the Notre Dame game and on Thanksgiving....we may be arrested for it [but] we will be doing more than bitching, which gets old after a while."

PSA united with Harambee, the first Black student organization at LSU, for a demonstration at the LSU vs. Notre Dame football game. We agreed to occupy the Sigma Chi fraternity's seats. It was one of LSU's premier fraternities. In 2015, Sigma Chi was kicked off of LSU's campus for at least three years for hazing and substance abuse.

The protestors all agreed to meet at the football game hours before the gates opened so we could go into the stadium as a group in the hope that a large group would discourage any of the frats from starting a fight. We also needed a large number of students to participate so we could occupy as many rows as possible. I think around 50 PSA and Harambee members showed up. Some of them had never been to a LSU football game before since, unlike me, they were not at all interested in LSU football.

Sigma Chi's seating area was on the 50-yard line where there was an excellent view of the football field. I always wondered if the Interfraternity Council at LSU had assigned sections to each fraternity based on their status to prevent fighting among the different fraternities at the games.

As expected, there were around a half dozen pledges reserving rows of seats in that part of the stadium. As we climbed the stairs heading toward the Sigma Chi section, I noticed a worried look on the pledges' faces as they watched this large group of Blacks and freaks heading toward them.

We had decided not to bring dates to this demonstration just in case a fight broke out. Considering the terrible treatment that couples had received in the past from frats when they attempted to sit in their "reserved seats," the odds were that a fight was very likely. The pledges attempted to stop us from sitting in the section by shouting the typical line, "These seats are reserved!" We just shouted back, "There are no reserved seats in Tiger Stadium. It is first come, first served." In one way, it was kind of sad to watch the anguish and despair on these young students' faces who, as freshmen, had just gone through Sigma Chi's hazing to become a member. These poor pledges were milling around in despair not knowing what to do or what their newfound frat brothers were going to say.

We had enough PSA and Harambee members that we were able to occupy every row of Sigma Chi's section except one. About 10 to 15 minutes before the start of the game, the drunken Sigma Chi members started arriving with their dates. Those were some pissed off frats when they saw us seating in "their sections." Some of them even attempted to threaten us with violence if we did not give up the seats. As a group we all stood up basically saying, "Oh yeah? Bring it on!" That action quickly defused that threat. Some of the Sigma Chi members sat on the steps while others walked around with their dates looking for seats. They knew this was not a game an LSU football fan wanted to miss. In the game, we got our revenge for the previous year, beating Notre Dame 28 to 8 that night. The stadium was rocking all during the game and the celebration continued all night after the game.

## MORE PSA PROTESTS

The fact that a small group of students were talking about holding protest rallies and sit-ins would not sweat university administrators at any college campus today. But at the beginning of the '70s in the Deep South, it must have worried the shit out of LSU's administration. Also, the fact that PSA was being led by a long haired, foul speaking Viet Nam veteran must have given them some serious concerns.

In the start of the fall semester of 1971, it wasn't just the administration that took notice of PSA's comments. Jim Lestelle, the new *Reveille* editor for the fall semester, and SGA President Bentley Alexander took exception to all this talk from PSA about disrupting fall registration, sit-ins, etc. and, more specifically, to me.

An editorial titled "Long haired tactics" appeared in the *Reveille* (September 14, 1971) along with a political cartoon showing a long haired hippie jumping up and down with a clenched fist smashing something that had the caption, "Oh, we're scared!" The editorial stated:

> The Progressive Students Alliance's scare tactics lately have failed to make the persons to whom they are directed tremble. It's a good thing. The group's unwarranted and libelous attacks, especially by president Ted Schirmer, are a black mark on the entire long hair profession. One of their top-secret plots was leaked last week to a girl as she registered to vote at the Registrar's table manned by PSA members in the Union. One member said the group was going to take over the Student Assembly if the *Reveille* didn't get in their way. Asked about their plans, the member said they were the only ones who had filed for vacant Assembly positions and that, once in, they would fight to "swamp" the elected group. Well, he shouldn't have said that because now the *Reveille* is going to get in their way, or at least it will try.

The next day a letter titled "Clarifications" appeared in the *Reveille* (September 15, 1971) from Steve Irving, the newly elected president of PSA. In it, Steve pointed out:

> First, Ted Schirmer is no longer PSA president. He speaks for himself and not for the organization. Second, the rumor

concerning PSA's swamping of the SGA elections is a fact. I spread this rumor myself....PSA was founded to serve as a campus political party. This is what a party is supposed to do. It is hardly secret as this is stated in the PSA charter.

The *Reveille* (September 16, 1971) reported: "Free Speech Alley opens with rain, verbal battles." SGA President Bentley Alexander came to Free Speech Alley, and he and I carried on a debate over the fact that, after it became known that PSA members were running for positions in the SGA Assembly unopposed, he extended the time period for students to qualify for the upcoming elections. Bentley was a very smart guy with a great sense of humor. When a student asked Bentley where all the people came from after the deadline was extended, he replied, "God created them." We disagreed about a lot, but I sure enjoyed listening to him talk. He later had to resign as SGA president because of the pressures of law school. I could relate to that because I was so busy with all these activities that I flunked out of LSU after that semester.

In a front-page article in the *Reveille* (September 23, 1971), titled "Four PSA members win Assembly seats," it was pointed out that, "Only two PSA candidates were defeated in their effort to 'swamp' the Student Assembly elective posts. Frank Dixon, Doug Lambert and August Tabony [later to be exposed as an undercover cop for the Baton Rouge Police Department] and Bernard Duhon were elected."

I may have flunked out of school, but at least PSA had a solid foothold on the LSU campus as a strong student organization that fought for students.

# 1972–1974, On Scholastic Probation
## BACK IN MCHENRY

After being put on scholastic probation, I went back to McHenry, Illinois, to work. Susanna and I rented a little house, and I got a job as a night stocker at the McHenry Eagle grocery store. I made $6.25 an hour, and for 1972 the pay was excellent, but the days and the hours I had to work sucked. I had to work every night except Tuesday and Sunday. I went to work at 10 P.M. at night and got off at 7 A.M. in the morning. That left very little time for socializing with my friends. When I heard that my nights off at Eagle were going to be Tuesday and Sunday nights, I thought, there went my social life. But it turned out to be a blessing for going to concerts and shows in Chicago. Not only did a lot of concerts play in Chicago on a Tuesday night, it was also easy to get good seats on a Tuesday or Sunday.

I made the decision that I would see as many as I could of the big name rock and roll bands that came to Chicago. In addition, I would see every rock opera (rock music that told a story). That would include *Tommy*, the first rock opera, and *Jesus Christ Superstar*. Both of those rock operas had a great effect on the transformation of who I was and on what I believed in and how I looked at the religions of the world. Susanna and I even went to *Godspell*, thinking it was similar to *Jesus Christ Superstar*. It was not only not a rock opera, it wasn't anything like *Jesus Christ Superstar*. As a matter of fact, Susanna and I left right after the first act. We decided to go see *Hair* again.

Some of the concerts I got tickets for were Deep Purple, Moody Blues and Alice Cooper. I was a little hesitant to go see Alice Cooper at first. He was a little too bizarre, even for me, but his *Billion Dollar Babies* album was the No. 1 album in the U.S. and the song "Billion Dollar Babies" was a top ten single. I bought tickets for his Billion Dollar Babies tour on April 10, 1973, which was a Tuesday. I believe the tickets were six or seven dollars. It was billed as: "The most elaborate theatrical show ever conceived." The stage was indeed the most glitzy and excessive stage of any rock group I had seen up to that time. Our seats were in a good section at the Amphitheater in Chicago, just off the floor right near the stage. Susanna, being short, had trouble seeing over people if we were on the floor.

Alice Cooper opened with "Hello Hooray," then played "Billion Dollar Babies." Before he sang "No More Mr. Nice Guy" he went behind the stage and soon reappeared, walking up to the very front of the stage with a rolled-up poster in his hand. He stated waving the poster over the heads of the people right in front of the stage while saying, "You think I'm crazy do you! You think I'm crazy! Here is an autographed poster! Signed by all of us." He pointed the poster back toward the rest of the band. "Who wants it?" he asked.

I watched as the audience went into a frenzy. People, who were way in back on the floor, started rushing toward the front. Soon there were people standing 20 to 30 deep in front of the stage. Alice Cooper then threw the poster out into the crowd. I watched as the people ripped the poster to shreds. Cooper then turned and walked backstage again. This time, he emerges with an arm full of posters. When the crowd saw this, a roar went up as even more people rushed to the front. He started pacing back and forth in the front of the stage all the while again shouting, "You think I'm crazy do you! You think I'm crazy!" Then he threw the whole armful of posters out into the crowd. It kind of reminded me of those movies showing piranha fish feeding on a carcass in a river. People in the crowd were pushing and shoving each other while reaching for a poster. I do not believe any of those posters made it intact to anyone. I thought to myself, "He made his point." After that, Susanna and I would never buy tickets for the floor for any concert in a big city.

## OZARK MUSIC FESTIVAL

In the summer of 1974, the Ozark Music Festival was held over the weekend of July 19th thru the 21st at the Missouri State Fairgrounds in Sedalia, Missouri. Sedalia was just under 500 miles away from

McHenry, where my friend Ronny Etherton, Susanna and I were sharing a house together. The promoters told the town that only about 50,000 people would show up at the festival. It turned out that estimates of the actual crowd size varied from 150,000 to 300,000. I believe it was closer to 150,000 people. The promoters also told the town and state officials that the festival would be a bluegrass and rock festival with arts and crafts stands and baking contests— basically just another county fair.

Since I had made a decision that I would never miss a rock festival within 500 miles of wherever I was at the time, I was determined to go to the Sedalia festival. I felt that we could go there and still make it back for work, and, even if we did not make it back in time, we could just call in sick. So, it was agreed: Ozark Music Festival here we come!

We drove there in Ronny's 1950 Buick Dynaflow. It was a great car. One time Ronny drove it off the road and down a hill. Ronny wasn't hurt, and neither was the Buick. That car was built like a tank. It had an outside visor over the front windshield, plus the front windshield was divided in two parts. When I sat in the front passenger seat, I felt as if I were inside the head of a Chicago Cubs baseball player looking out. Yes, I was high at the time.

By Thursday, July 19th, the citizens of Sedalia did not know what had hit them. The gates to the fairgrounds were to open at noon on that Friday, but thousands of people from all over the country had already arrived in Sedalia on Thursday. On Friday morning, the traffic was so bad that people who lived in Sedalia could not get to work. By the time we got to Sedalia, the traffic was backed up for miles and miles from the town. We sat in line for what seemed like forever, but no one seemed to care that much. As a matter of fact, waiting in line took on a festival atmosphere itself with people booming out rock and roll music from their vehicles, smoking dope and generally having a good time.

Looking at the movies and pictures of the festival online, I just kept saying to myself, "It was hot! It was damn hot!" It was 99 degrees on Friday and 100 degrees both Saturday and Sunday. If it were not for the music and drugs, it would have been a living hell. Whatever drug you wanted could be found at the festival, mostly in the tunnel leading into the racetrack.

I think that was where I purchased a ball of opium. I had never tried opium before, and I was curious what it was like. I was hoping it would help me cope with the heat. I knew I wanted nothing to do with heroin. I had seen friends of mine become addicted to it, and I even had two friends die of overdosing.

Susanna and Ronny didn't want to smoke any, so I smoked the opium in our tent by myself. It was unbelievable. I felt total bliss, as if I were floating in the clouds. It not only wasn't hot to me anymore, I did not have a care in the world. It was wonderful. We had to leave for the stage area because the Nitty Gritty Dirt Band was going to play. Their record "Will the Circle Be Unbroken" was one of my and Susanna's favorite records. Before leaving the tent, I decided to take off all my clothes. Susanna and Ronny, let's say, were a little taken back by my decision to walk around naked. Matter of fact, they told me to walk in front of them. They did not want to be seen walking with me. Yes, I got burned in places I had never been burnt in before or since. Afterwards, I put opium in the same category as heroin, i.e. don't fuck with it! You may love it so much it will kill you!

Since the promoters had sold the festival to the state and town as a bluegrass and rock festival (small 'r'), they booked not only Bachman-Turner Overdrive, Aerosmith, Eagles, America, Ted Nugent and the Amboy Dukes, Lynyrd Skynyrd, Joe Walsh and Barnstorm, REO Speedwagon, Bruce Springsteen (but his bus broke down so he did not play), Boz Scaggs, and Blue Oyster Cult, to name only a few of the rock bands. They also booked the Nitty Gritty Dirt Band, Earl Scruggs Revue, The Ozark Mountain Daredevils, The Flying Burrito Brothers, The Charlie Daniels Band and the Southern-Hillman-Furay Band and other bluegrass/country bands.

The Earl Scruggs Revue played on Saturday. The audience, being a rock and roll audience and not a bluegrass audience, mostly sat on their hands. I could tell the band was feeling as though it had made a mistake in agreeing to play at the festival up to when they played the Beverly

Hillbillies theme song. The audience immediately jumped to their feet, clapping, cheering and singing along. You could tell that was what the band needed.

Lynyrd Skynyrd played on Saturday night. When the band came on stage to a thunderous applause, they dropped a huge Confederate flag behind them. Then they broke into "Sweet Home Alabama." This was the song that they wrote in response to Neil Young's "Southern Man." That must have pissed off some person right in front of the stage because he started throwing rocks at the band. The band stopped playing, and Ronnie Van Zant, glaring down into the crowd, said in a very pissed off tone, "Whatever mother fucker is throwing those rocks, I'll meet you backstage afterwards, but stop throwing the damn rocks." Not only did the rock throwing stop, but the audience went crazy.

We were right up front of the stage, maybe 20 deep, when the Nitty Gritty Dirt Band came on. We had gotten there early in the day to get up front. The band came on the stage after their equipment had been set up. This festival had two large performance areas on the stage so that one side could be setting up while a band played on the other side of the stage. That worked very well. There was very little stop time in between bands. Both stages had a tarp high above the stage for shade for the performing bands.

I guess because it was Sunday, the last day of the festival, the tarp was not completely deployed over the Nitty Gritty Dirt Band. It was 100 degrees that day, and the sun had been shining on the equipment that had been placed on the stage by the roadies. The band came out on the stage. I do not remember what the first song was, but at some point, John McEuen had to set down the instrument he was playing and pick up his brass banjo. It must have been hotter than hell, because as soon as he picked the banjo up, he did a perfect imitation of someone trying to hold on to a hot potato. He was juggling the banjo so much he almost dropped it. This was all happening behind the backs of other band members. McEuen quickly put the banjo down and picked up a guitar just in time to play his part. Because it was supposed to be a banjo playing, as soon as he played a few notes, the rest of the band members looked over at him. He just shrugged his shoulders and kept playing the guitar. They played "Mr. Bojangles," a favorite, but what I loved the most was that they closed with "Will the Circle Be Unbroken."

## GROWING POT

Having to move from the house where Susanna and I were staying, we found out that the house right next to her mother was for rent. We asked Ronny if he wanted to go in on it with us, and he did. The two-bedroom house had a barn and sat on about five acres. The farmer, who owned it, kept trying to get me to buy it and the land. I think he wanted around $15,000. My mind was set on going back to LSU, so I told him, "No." I had to tell him "no" a couple of times.

Back then, the marijuana a person would buy came with stems and seeds. Like Cheech and Chong sang in one of their skits about making a television ad for legal marijuana, "No stems, no seeds that you don't need. Acapulco Gold is bad ass weed." Since I was renting a place on West Wright Road, I figured, why not plant some of these seeds I kept getting in my marijuana.

I planted some seeds behind the barn where there had been a pig pen. The soil was almost jet black it was so rich. In addition, I planted a couple of seeds in the same dirt that I placed in an old coal bucket and put in the house. The seeds in both places quickly started growing. After all, marijuana is just a weed.

One day, after the plants had grown about three or four feet, I went back behind the barn to tend to them. As I came around the corner of the barn, I saw a large groundhog standing on its hind legs, leaning against a plant while he nonchalantly chewed on the marijuana plant's leaves.

I shouted, "Hey!" thinking that would scare the groundhog away. Not a chance. He just slowly turned his head, looked over at me, then turned back to the marijuana plant, bit off another leaf, and kept chewing. He was one big groundhog. I could clearly see his big ass teeth as he ripped off my leaves. I noticed that he had eaten all the leaves about a foot or so from the ground. I realized then that was one stoned groundhog. I started jumping up in the air while waving my arms and shouting, "Get out of here!" He again turned his head in my direction and stared at me for a moment, as if to say, "You still here?" I started yelling even louder and waving my arms even faster in the air. He finally kind of fell to his side, got up and staggered away. I watched him disappear into the tall grass (not the kind you smoke).

I examined the plants. They seemed fine except that one of them had a lot of its leaves stripped off. The stem was in good shape though. I knew I had to do something to protect my plants from this stoner groundhog. I bought some chicken wire and posts to build a barrier around my plants. After that, I would check the plants every day to make sure my druggie groundhog could not get to them. It turned out that I did not have to do that for too many more days.

I still had to buy marijuana while waiting for my plants to mature. I was over at my friendly drug dealer's house buying another quarter pound of dope when a lot of people started showing up with beer, whiskey and food. They were about to party, so I could not just buy my dope and run. I stayed until midnight partying with them.

By the time I was ready to leave I was so messed up that I backed the car off the side of his driveway right into the ditch running alongside the road. I did not just drive into the ditch, I straddled the ditch with my car. I could not get the car off the top of the ditch. My friend the drug dealer offered to drive me home and told me to come back tomorrow to have my car towed off the ditch. That sounded good to me. I left everything in the car, including the quarter pound of dope I had just bought from him. It was in a brown paper bag that I had set on the front seat of the car.

The next morning, I got a ride over to my friend's house to recover my car. When I got there, I saw that it was gone. I knocked on my friend's door and asked what happened? He said he was awakened by noises out in front of his house. When he looked through the window, he saw a police car and a tow truck pulling my car off of the ditch and towing it away. Shit! I told him that the quarter pound he had sold me the night before was on the front seat of my car.

Once again, my friend drove me home. I feared that since the car was towed by the police, they would probably take an inventory of the things on the inside of the car. That meant they would find the quarter pound of marijuana on the front seat. When I got home, I told Susanna what had happened and that I thought the police were probably getting a search warrant to search our house. I thought we had better get rid of all of our dope. Susanna was not big on throwing away all of our marijuana. She said we could take the plants and our stash over to her mother's house next door. The police are not going to search an old lady's house, especially since any warrant they get would be for our house, not Mary's. I thought, good idea.

I ran to the back of the barn, pulled up those marijuana plants, and wrapped them in a tarp to take them over to Mary's. Susanna carried the plant in the coal bucket over to her mother's. We went through the house to make sure there was no dope or even marijuana paraphernalia in the house. Then we waited for that knock at the door.

After a couple of hours of waiting, I decided to take the offensive. I called the police station to inquire about my car. They had no record of my car being towed. I hung up the phone. That just made me worry more. Are they still in the planning stages of busting me? Fuck it. I decided to push the issue. I called the police station back, telling them that a person saw one of their police cars with a tow truck towing my car away. He then gave me the name of the towing company that they used. I called them and, sure enough, they had my car. I asked them who authorized them to tow my car. The man told me the police had called them about a car that needed to be towed. I complained that it was taken out of my friend's yard. He explained, "No. The car was straddling the ditch which is city property." He then told me what it would cost for me to get my car. I said I was coming right over with the money. I then thought that the police were just waiting until I claimed the car, with the dope inside, to bust me.

I thought this over, but realized that I had to play this thing out no matter what happened. I needed my car. I had no choice but to go get it. Susanna drove me over to the towing company. As I got out of the van, I told her to leave in case this was a trap. I'd meet her back at the house, I hoped.

As I walked into the towing company's yard, there was my car parked across from the tow company's office. I went inside, expecting that, at any time, cops would start popping out from behind every door with guns drawn. Instead, the man said how much I owed him. I handed the man the money, and he handed me a receipt. I kept glancing around as I turned to walk back outside. As I stepped out of the door, I pause for a moment, still expecting cops to start yelling, "FREEZE!" Nothing.

I walked over to my car's driver side with my keys in my hand. As I was putting the keys in the door, I looked inside the car. There, on the front seat, right where I had left it the night before, was the paper bag with the dope in it. I started the engine. Still no cops. I put the car in gear. Still no cops. I started driving out of the tow company's yard. Still no cops. Looking around, I did not see any cops anywhere. It became clear that no one had entered my car. I guess to them, the paper bag was just a paper bag with something in it.

I was still a little paranoid. We decided to play it safe for the next few days, so we kept our dope over at Mary's for a while longer. The cops never came. What did happen was that Susanna had set the plant in the coal bucket on her mother's front steps. This plant was about two feet tall and very bushy because I had been topping it. Two days after Susanna put the bucket there, a county road crew came by the house working on the road. The next day, we saw that the coal bucket with our marijuana was gone. We figured some of the young men working on the crew recognized the marijuana plant and took it. Bummer!

We tried smoking the leaves from the plants that were behind the barn that I had pulled out of the ground. Well, to quote another skit by Cheech and Chong, "Man, this shit wouldn't get a fly high." We had to throw out the rest of the plants. Later, I felt it was probably for the best

84

since it was a serious felony in Illinois at the time to cultivate marijuana. The good ole Yin and Yang. In every bad there is a good, and in every good there is a bad.

## THE MOTOROLA SKIT

I left Eagle and went to work at Motorola in Schaumburg, Illinois, as a stock chaser. My duties were to keep three assembly lines stocked with the parts that the people working the lines needed to assemble military radios. Motorola's plant in Schaumburg at the time made mostly radios and other electronics for military and police forces around the world. Mostly women worked on my three assembly lines. There were some younger women, but mostly women in their 40s and 50s or even older.

Motorola was a non-union shop in Northern Illinois, the land of unions. In an attempt to prevent the employees from unionizing and demanding more pay, and also to reduce their high turnover rate, Motorola gave their employees stock options and had elaborate festivals for the four seasons. I started working there a few months before the Spring Festival. The festival's events included dance contests, a skit contest, and other events over the lunch period, which was extended so everyone could participate and watch.

Two women I had met at work wanted to perform a pantomime for the skit contest and asked me if I would join them. Well, I knew a thing or two about pantomime, since I had watched my stepdad Bill and the Korny Kats, the band he was in when I was young, perform Spike Jones' "Hawaiian War Chant" and other Spike Jones songs.

My friends had decided to do a skit with the Andrew Sister's song, "Boogie Woogie Bugle Boy," a song that appeared in the 1941 Abbott and Costello movie *Buck Privates*. They thought that they could win the skit contest because so many women working at Motorola were over 50 years of age and knew the Andrew Sisters' work. I agreed to go over to their place to kick around some ideas and practice. I definitely had some ideas on how to perform the skit. I just had to convince the two women that my ideas would go over with the audience.

They had three Women's Army Corps (WAC) uniforms they had gotten at an Army/Navy Surplus store. I suggested that I should wear the skirt and put two big balloons in my blouse. In addition, I would wear an Army military cap, an Army jacket and my Viet Nam jungle boots. By then my hair was way past my shoulders and I had a beard. The women wore army slacks and one had an Army jacket, the other an Army shirt. Both had soft Army hats.

We spent a good amount of time choreographing the song. The hardest part was convincing them to use some of the hand signs I wanted to make while miming the words. They had no problem with pointing our index finger up in the air at the line "He was the top man at his craft." However, they did not want to do the next hand sign I suggested for the lyrics "but when his number came up." I urged that we should lean forward toward the audience, extend our arms, and flip the bird. The two of them were aghast that I would make such a suggestion. They thought the older women, and maybe even the bosses, would freak out seeing us flipping the bird at the audience. I argued that because of the Viet Nam war, they knew men were getting screwed by the draft. They would grasp the message we were trying to send. It took a while, but I finally got them to agree to it.

When Friday came to perform at the festival, I was given time off to get dressed and meet up with the two women. Motorola had put out flyers all week advertising the contests, including the entertainment that was going to be performed at the festival. A buzz had started to build up around the plant among the older women about the "Andrews Sisters" act. My cohorts were right about the older women really loving an Andrews Sisters skit. The women at work did not know who was in it, only that the people in it were going to perform the "Boogie Woogie Bugle Boy."

A section of the floor had been marked off to act as a stage. There was an act before us. I think it was a takeoff of a sock hop. As we waited out of sight. I could see more and more gray-haired ladies gathering out in front. By the time we were up, it looked like a couple hundred older women were standing around the stage, or sitting at tables in the area.

My two cohorts were getting nervous. I, on the other hand, was getting excited about performing. We received our cue and walked out front. When the audience saw me in my WAC's skirt and blouse, with very big breasts, jungle boots and long hair with a beard, laughter went through the audience. I think it helped to relax my fellow performers when they realized that the audience was going to be watching me, not them.

Then the song started. Being Patty, I was in the middle with each of the women as LaVerne and Maxene, on either side of me. We started with the motions that the Andrews Sisters executed while miming the words. Then when we got to "but when his number came up" both of them were in perfect sync with me. We all leaned forward, extended our right arms, and flipped the bird at the audience!

The front line of the audience was standing only about 10 feet from us. It was funny as hell to see the faces of those old ladies. They were at first swinging and singing along with us. Then when we leaned forward and flipped them the bird, they were just frozen in place with looks of shock on their faces, like they did not believe what they just saw. Literally, some of the women's jaws dropped.

We were already in the act of throwing our thumbs past our heads as the lines "and he was gone with the draft" played. It was as though the audience needed to hear that part of the song to make the connection. Then a huge roar of laughter went up from those gray-haired women. They were laughing so hysterically it completely drowned out the song. I do not believe most of them even heard the rest of our routine.

When we finished, it seemed as if the applause that erupted was louder than the previous laughter. As I scanned the audience, I saw people applauding and laughing at the same time. The applause and laughter seemed to go on forever. We kept bowing. We must have bowed a half dozen times. I threw my arms out, bowed my head and went down on one knee. I never knew how hard it was going down on one knee in a skit. By then people were coming from all over the plant to see what the commotion was all about. To say the obvious, we won the contest.

I was not sure how the prizes worked, but I got two tickets to see Cheech and Chong live. I flipped out. I had already bought all of their records. The seats were great and so were they. They did not disappoint.

## A VISIT TO CANADA

That summer, Susanna and I went to visit John in Montreal Canada. We traveled up there with Brad and Deb. Brad was the younger brother of my friend Randy and also worked for Eagle. He had just bought a new car, so we went in it. John lived on the shores of a beautiful lake outside of Montreal. We only visited for a couple of days since Brad and I had to get back for work.

While in Canada, I decided to stock up on Export rolling papers. I liked how easy it was to roll a joint with those papers, plus the joint held together while burning. I bought a case of the papers to take back to the States.

Since we were still carrying some of the marijuana that we had not smoked in Canada, plus the case of Export rolling papers, we decided to arrive at the border early in the morning, thinking that was a better time to cross into the US. We had no problems driving into Canada, but we did worry about crossing the border back into the States carrying dope.

When we got to the Canadian and U.S. border at the Ambassador Bridge Port of Entry at Detroit, Michigan, it was around two in the morning. We thought that it would be better if Susanna and Deb carried the marijuana, thinking the border agents wouldn't search women. We hid the rolling papers in a tissue box. Damn, it is hard to believe I was that stupid.

That plan was doomed from the very beginning. First, crossing that early, we were the only traffic on the bridge. Therefore, the border agents had nothing else to do but hassle us. We should have crossed during rush hour traffic. Looking back, if I were a border agent, I would have found two couples, one guy looking like a hippie, crossing the border at two in the morning mighty suspicious.

The border agents asked us to pull the car over in front of their office. Then we all were asked to come inside to answer some questions while they searched our car.

We were at the counter talking to an agent when another agent walked in carrying the case of Export rolling papers. Then, a minute or so later, a Jack Webb-looking agent came in holding what looked like a joint in his hand saying, "Look what I found." My brain started racing. How in the hell did we leave a joint in the car? I thought maybe one of the others had forgotten it. Later, after we talked, we realized that the joint the agent was holding was not our dope. The agent was using it to justify a search of our persons.

Right after that, Brad and I were told to go into separate rooms for a strip search. I was keeping my cool for once, but then the Jack Webb looking agent pointed to the upside-down American flag I had sewed on my pants, saying, "What a disrespectful way to treat the American flag." Well, it was on!

I told him, "I was a Viet Nam veteran and did two tours in Nam. I will wear this flag anyway I want to." As predictable as the sun rises in the East, he said, "I served in Nam, too," as he was going through the clothes I had taken off. As usual, the next words out of my mouth were, "In what outfit?" He then stated some Marine Corps outfit. That response from him stopped my normal line of, "That chicken shit outfit." Instead, I looked him in the eyes as I said, "It figures, a dumb ass Marine." For a moment, I swear he was going to attack me right then and there. But he got control of himself and just threw my clothes back at me. He told me to get dressed and left the room.

Of course, it turned out that there were women border agents whose job it was to search women. They had only one woman on duty at the time so, when I got back out to the waiting room, Deb was still there waiting to be searched. I sat down right next to her. Since all the agents were busy up by the counter, she leaned a little toward me and slipped the marijuana she had into my pocket. I then yelled up to the agents at the counter that I had to go to the bathroom. One of the agents looked at me suspiciously, but the Jack Webb agent said that I had been searched, so it was ok for me to use the bathroom. Once there, I flushed the marijuana down the toilet.

When I got back out to the room, Deb was gone, but Brad and Susanna were sitting there. Susanna had a very worried look on her face. As I sat down next to her, she whispered to me that they had found marijuana on her. I could not think how we were going to get out of this one. We were really fucked. In all of the states in the U.S. in 1974, simple possession of marijuana was, not just a crime, but in some states it was a felony. In almost all of them, if not all of them, a person would spend some time in jail.

After Deb joined us, we were all called up to the counter. To our great relief, attempting to bring that small amount of marijuana into the U.S. was not a crime, but there was a fine of $500 for illegally attempting to bring contraband into the United States. That was good news. Now the bad news. We did not have $500. In today's dollars that was close to $2,700. They wrote us a ticket, then impounded Brad's car until we paid the fine. What was even more of a problem was that they told us we couldn't stay at the office. We would have to leave. Man, it was 3:30 A.M. in the morning, and very dark.

As we were trying to figure out how we were going to stay alive in that part of Detroit, I found a pay phone and called my brother Terry. Luckily Terry got up really early in the morning to catch a train to Chicago where he worked as a plumber. I told him what happened and that we needed $500. He asked me where we were in Detroit so he could wire the money to the nearest Western Union. Where we were, people had shot out the streetlights, so I could not read the street signs. I finally told him by the Ambassador Bridge. He said he would wire the money to a Western Union station near us as soon as they opened. He said some other things about never again and how stupid I was, but I was used to that from my brother, so I don't remember the exact words.

We waited, huddled in a dark doorway of some abandoned building right under the Ambassador Bridge, until daylight. During that time, I wished I had not flushed the marijuana down the toilet. We sure could have used a joint then. To quote the Fabulous Furry Freak Brothers,

"Dope will get you through times of no money better than money will get you through times of no dope."

A couple of hours later, we had the money. We got the car out of the Border Patrol impound lot and hit the road. About 15 to 20 miles from the border, there was a very loud explosion from under the hood of Brad's car. He quickly pulled over. We popped the hood and looked at the engine. One side had just blown. Brad just threw up his hands and fell backwards down an incline on the side of the road. I rushed over to him and helped him to his feet.

While sitting there, a highway patrol car stopped. After seeing what had happened, the officer called a tow truck. When the tow truck driver took a look at the engine, he immediately asked if the car had been impounded at customs. When we said yes, he explained that Brad's was the third car that month like that. He suspected Border Agents were putting mothballs, or something like that, in the gas tanks of people they did not like. My guess was that damn Marine had done it. I didn't say anything to Brad or Deb, but I was known to do things like that to people who pissed me off when I was in the military. But only when I was in the military. I had changed, and so should that damn Marine. Since the car was new, I believe Brad's insurance company paid for a new engine.

# Fall and Spring Semesters, 1974–1975
## BACK AT LSU

As the summer of 1974 ended, after four years together, Susanna and I had our first break up. I ended up borrowing my brother's truck to move my stuff down to Baton Rouge. I contacted a friend of mine, Tom Smith, and I learned that Tom, his girlfriend Betty, and another friend were renting a house by the State Capitol in Spanish town. They had an empty small loft- type room with a kitchen on the top floor and offered to share their rental with me. I took it.

As I went through fall registration, I was very excited about being back at LSU. No, it wasn't just the anticipation of going to another LSU football game, although that was a big part of it. It was a realization that I did not like working in jobs that were not challenging or enjoyable.

That excitement carried over to until I went to buy my textbooks for that semester and learned how damn much my books were costing me. I had managed to save only a couple of hundred dollars, figuring it was enough to last until I got my first VA check. I knew I would need money to rent a place to live since Bill was not going to allow me to live at his house. But I had not calculated the cost of textbooks. Buying the textbooks I had to have for my classes ate up most of the money I had saved. The high cost of textbooks would soon become a driving issue for me, as it was for thousands of LSU students.

I was determined to do better at school than I had previously. Therefore, I decided not to get involved in campus politics this time around. PSA had good leaders and seemed to be doing well as a student organization, but I wanted to keep my nose in my textbooks.

At that time, I thought that the reason I had trouble reading and writing was because of having moved so many times when I was young. Since I was never in the same school for more than a year, I never had the opportunity to learn grammar or to read well. I thought all I had to do to be able to succeed in school was to consistently put more time into my studies. I would not find out until much later that I had learning disabilities.

I had not even heard of ADHD until my first child was diagnosed as suffering from it in 1990–91. That was when a doctor friend of mine said, "Ted, maybe that is why you did so poorly in school." He arranged for me to be tested. Sure enough, I was not only dealing with ADHD but also mild dyslexia. ADHD kept me from being consistent in my studies, and mild dyslexia made it very hard to for me to learn to read and write better.

It was very hard for me to succeed in an academic environment. I would get very frustrated when I had to struggle just to read a handful of pages each night. As the weeks went by, I found myself falling further and further behind in my classes.

I was taking a full load of 12 hours: Physical Geology, a Philosophy class titled Man and Society, Analytic Philosophy, and Child Psychology. All of these courses required, what was for me, a lot of reading. In addition, I had to buy a dictionary because I did not know the meaning of many of the words. I was constantly having to stop to look up a word. I am not just talking about technical language but words that anyone going to college should already know. Looking back, I realize that I probably had the equivalent of a middle school student's vocabulary and knowledge of grammar. If that! All this was not really clear to me at that time. I thought that just flat-out hard work would get me through.

I worked hard in my classes, but I seriously considered dropping a couple. When I went to check on dropping classes, I was told that LSU had a $5 drop fee, the equivalent of nearly $27 today. Since money was so short for me then, it stopped me from dropping any classes. But it pissed me off that, once again, because of my lack of money, I was being stopped from doing something I wanted to do while people with money could do it.

To truly understand the impact that poverty has on children, one must have experienced at least some of the hardships of the poor. With my background, I could relate to those individuals who had suffered through the Great Depression. Those conditions had caused the rise of many movements and politicians, like Louisiana's Huey Long, who fought against the privileged class and the state and federal politicians who supported them. I decided to speak about it at the Alley.

A *Reveille* (October 24, 1974) article, titled "Disappointed ticket buyers, others complain at Alley," mentioned that, "Ted Sherman [sic] voiced his sentiments on the $5 fee for dropping courses." I was quoted as saying, "A lot of people can just barely make it, but the rich don't suffer. They just write daddy and mommy and ask for more money. The poor are suffering again." That was a sore point with me.

The *Reveille* identified me as "Ted Sherman" for a little while. When I was called Sherman, I would respond, "No, I'm not the guy with the lighter. I'm Schirmer." I was referring to Sherman's march to the sea when his army burned a fifty-mile-wide swath through Georgia during the Civil War. In addition to the *Reveille* getting my name wrong, they published a picture showing the back of me speaking to the audience at the Alley with a caption reading, "This speaker obviously has found a sympathetic audience." That was how unknown I was at LSU in 1974, even though I had been so involved in 1971–72. Ah, fame is so fleeting.

## THE NONPROFIT BOOK RENTAL PROGRAM

I still was trying not to get too involved so I could focus on my schoolwork. But after speaking at the Alley, several students came up to me to discuss how they felt they were being ripped off by the Student Union bookstore. I agreed that something had to be done to make textbooks more affordable. That discussion led to us getting a room at Prescott Hall for a meeting of likeminded students. Unlike the Union, where only a recognized student organization could reserve a room, any full-time student could reserve a room in an academic building on campus.

Afterward, I spoke for the first time at the Alley about the idea of a Book Rental. As a *Reveille* (November 7, 1974) article, titled "Gripes on frats, politics, book prices mark Alley," stated:

> Ted Sherman [sic] introduced an idea of setting up a Book Rental because "students are being ripped off by the school bookstore....Southeastern University has used a book-rental system since the origin of the university....We would like to start things off by handling 4,000 to 5,000 students next semester....If we could get it set up everyone would want to participate."

Where we got those numbers from I haven't a clue. Really! I don't think I was stoned when I said that, I only sounded like it.

> Sherman said eventually the rental would have books for all courses. "If it is successful, we would receive about $400,000 per semester, and the administration will not have any control of it."

Even then, I was arguing for student independence from the administration. They weren't our parents. I felt we could solve our own problems if we would only unite. That would be the underlying foundation to my whole activist career in college and law school: student independence from the administration. How else can young people, with the ability and means to attend college, become good citizens in our democratic republic if they don't believe they can solve the problems facing our republic?

At the Thursday, November 7th meeting, about a dozen students showed up. I went over the idea of a Book Rental with them. In the *Reveille* (November 8, 1974) article, titled "Book rental plan explained; support for project asked," I pointed out what the issues and goals were for setting up a Book Rental at LSU.

> Warning students that trying to set up a Book Rental is like dynamite, Ted Schirmer explained his plan for a rental and asked for student support in a meeting Thursday night. [The *Reveille* finally got my name right.] "We are talking about taking a lot of money away from people who have been making it a long time," Schirmer said. "Books are big business here." He said the only way to get administration approval is to set up the rental as a nonprofit organization. Schirmer said the Student Government Association is solidly behind the plan. "Everybody I have talked to sounds excited about the idea," he said. "One problem we have now is to get the idea out to the people."....Schirmer said he is

encouraging fraternities and other campus organizations to back the plan.

There was only one fraternity or sorority that showed any interest whatsoever in the idea of a Book Rental. That was Phi Sigma Epsilon, the financial fraternity. That was even before the other fraternities developed a deep hatred of me. Those students didn't need help in buying their textbooks. Most of their members came from families that could afford to buy the books for their children. In addition, they did not seem to care about any of the problems of the other students at LSU, as exemplified by their belief that it was their right to reserve seats at LSU football games.

The *Reveille* article continued:

> Schirmer said books would be rented at a rate of $5 per course or no more than $20 per person. "Students who donated books would be allowed to rent books first," he said, "and then the rental would be open to the general public....Schirmer said the only way the plan can fail is through present apathy.

We needed the Student Government Association to be a strong supporter. I went to an SGA Assembly meeting for the first time, but I was not a member of the Assembly, so I could not speak. Richard Eberhardt, a PSA founding member, moved to form an ad hoc committee to investigate the need for a Book Rental. I thought the need for a Book Rental was already understood.

Soon after that, we created a student organization called the Student Nonprofit Book Rental Service. That was necessary in order to get official recognition, and, more importantly, money, from SGA. Even so, we were still having trouble getting many students to join us.

At the SGA Assembly on November 22nd, there was a discussion about funding the Book Rental. A front-page article in the *Reveille* (November, 23, 1974), titled "SGA Assembly approves funds for escorts, book plan," reported:

An appropriation of $1,500 was passed for the Nonprofit Book Rental Service beginning in January. The amount includes stickers, publicity, supplies and buying students' books at a competitive price with the local bookstores....Phi Sigma Epsilon, the financial fraternity and the only fraternity that helped, offered to handle the business aspects of the program. The Men's Dormitory Association, Circle K and the Progressive Students' Alliance are providing services for the rental.

We finally had not only operational money, but, even more importantly, other organizations, like the Associated Women Students (AWS), were supporting the Nonprofit Book Rental. I knew there was still a lot of work to do but, it seemed we were getting the support necessary to move on to the next phase.

The fall semester was coming to an end. We had to get organized and be ready to buy and, hopefully, receive donated textbooks. We spent some of the money we got from SGA on a two-page ad in the *Reveille*. The ad stated in large letters,

SUPPORT YOUR STUDENT NONPROFIT BOOK RENTAL – DONATED BOOKS NECESSARY FOR OUR SUCCESS AND SURVIVAL. Next semester there would be a minimum cost per student of $3.00 a course and a maximum cost per student of $12.00 (full load). For Book Drop-Off Centers contact the SGA Office...or just look for tables in front of bookstores during dead week.

At the end of the semester, we put tables right outside the Union bookstore. I joined some other members of the Book Rental to man the table. I remember students, who were heading into the Union bookstore to sell back their books, looked really uncomfortable walking past our table. Some of them would say they were sorry, but they needed the money. I would always tell them not to worry, we are getting books from other students. I was trying to make them feel better, because I certainly knew what it meant to need every dime. Some of the students came back out all pissed off and handed us their books, complaining about how little the bookstore was paying for them. They would rather give their books to the Book Rental than sell them back to the Union Bookstore for a quarter of what they had paid for them at the start of the semester.

We collected over 1,100 books. It blew all of our minds. We ordered stickers made saying "LSU Book Rental" to put on the outside of the books. That was not only to mark the books as the Book Rental's but as an advertisement. The next semester when students saw the stickers, they would realize that the books they just bought they could have rented for only $3 a book.

I thought it had been a good semester. In spite of spending a lot of time working on the Book Rental, I managed to pass all of my courses with one B and three C's and finished with 12 credits. On top of that, the Book Rental seems to be taking off. The downside was that the Tigers did so poorly that semester they didn't go to a bowl that year. But if the team had won more games, I may not have gotten involved in the Book Rental.

## MAGIC MUSHROOM CAPITOL OF LOUISIANA

On first arriving back in Baton Rouge, I started living in a house in Spanish Town with Tom and his girlfriend Betty. When we broke up in McHenry, Susanna had driven to Boulder, Colorado, to stay with our friend Sandra, a Cajun, who had lived in the house next to ours on Highland Road in 1970. Sandra was born and raised in Louisiana. When she came back from Colorado, Susanna came with her, and we made up.

The apartment I had been living in was a converted attic. It was too small and hot for Susanna, me and my German Shepherd Baron to stay in. I started looking for another place immediately. I was trying to find a place out in the country but close to LSU. I had checked Highland

Road, but had no luck. I decided to look down River Road. The road, as its name suggests, runs along the Mississippi River.

As I was driving down River Road, about six miles from Skip Bertman Drive, I saw a large, abandoned house setback 20 feet or so from the road. It turned out to be an old overseer's house. I wanted to check it out, but I had to climb over a locked gate that had massive blackberry bushes growing on either side. (Later, when the blackberries were ripe, they turned out to be the sweetest blackberries I had ever eaten.) I managed to get over the gate and walk up to the front of the house.

The house sat up off the ground about three feet on brick piers, which was common for houses that close to the Mississippi River. The river was right on the other side of the levee, just off River Road. A porch ran the length of the front of the house without any steps to get up on it from the front yard. That was one of the first things I had to build for the house.

The house had a steep tin roof. Later, I would build a very long ladder so we could climb up on the roof at night for the breeze. Also, the roof was high enough that mosquitoes did not fly that high, so we could enjoy the summer nights looking up at the stars while watching the river traffic go up and down Ol' Man River.

In order to get down from the roof, a person had to scoot down the tin on his/her butt to get to the ladder in order to climb down. One night, my good friend Marion Campbell decided to slide down the roof fast. His plan was to stop himself by slamming his feet into the big brick chimney at the very back of the house. He only did that once because, when he hit the chimney with both feet going at that speed, the chimney started rocking a little, then just fell away from the house, crashing to the ground. That chimney had probably been there for over a hundred years, but no more!

I was to discover that the house had been stripped of all of its pipes and had no indoor plumbing. In the back of the house was an outhouse, which turned out to be our only toilet. Next to the outhouse was a chicken coop with a fair size chicken run, which I would put to good use in due time.

On the left side of the big house, about twenty yards away, was a typical Louisiana shotgun house. These houses were so named because a person could fire a shotgun straight through the front door and out the back door. It looked as if it had been abandoned even longer than the big house.

A large pecan tree was about 15 feet away from the house and another large pecan tree was located between the big house and the shotgun house. Pecan trees make good shade trees in Louisiana. As I looked around the property behind the house, I saw there were pecan trees everywhere. Taking in the size of the trees and the way they were spaced, I figured the trees must have all been planted at the same time, many years ago.

Later, I would learn that there were Jackson, Oconee, Caddo, Sumner, Elliott, Candy and Melrose pecan trees. Damn near every type of pecan is grown in Louisiana. The trees stretched as far back into the pasture as the eye could see. I learned later that two different varieties of pecan trees should be planted for cross-pollination, and that was exactly what whoever planted all these pecan trees had done. During pecan season, Susanna and I would harvest pecans in 25-pound sacks. We would collect up to 300 hundred pounds of pecans each year and take them up to McHenry, Illinois, to sell. They would sell like hot cakes. We would sell out in a few days. People who bought them would come back asking for more. Yankees sure did love Louisiana pecans, even if they couldn't pronounce the word right. They would say, "How much for the pe-cans." I would have to stifle a laugh. Those Yankees mispronounced another Louisiana food staple: crawfish. They said crayfish. Did I really use to live among these people? Only kidding, I loved the North as much as the South.

The house had the 12-foot ceilings typical of houses built back in the days of no air conditioning. They let the heat rise to try to keep the house cool. There was a single light bulb hanging down from each ceiling on a vintage cloth covered electrical cord.

The layout of the inside of the house was two rooms in front, two rooms behind those rooms, and another room in the back that served as the kitchen. All the rooms were the same size with the kitchen a little larger than the other rooms. All the rooms had fireplaces, the largest in the kitchen. There was only one piece of furniture in the house: a very large pantry. It was made from the same wood covering the interior walls of the house, that old slat board that was used all over Louisiana and probably all over the South. When we moved from that house, Susanna wanted to keep that pantry, so we drove it up to her mother's house in McHenry.

After exploring the house and property, I then had to find out who owned it. I found an old rusty sign out in the pasture with Charlie Brown's Livestock Auction House painted on it. I thought that was a beginning. So, the next day I drove to the auction house out on Airline Highway. It turned out that Mr. Brown leased the land the house was on for his cattle. When I told him I was interested in renting the house, he said it was not livable, that the house had no running water. I told him the story of living under similar conditions on Hogg Ridge Road, Kentucky, when I was a kid. He still seemed very hesitate to rent me the house, so I pulled out my ace of spades. I started telling him about my time in Viet Nam. That I had lived in tougher conditions there than I ever would be subject to living in that house. That did it. He agreed to rent the house to me for $25 a month since I would have to put a lot of work into it. We shook hands to seal the deal with no written agreement. That would come back later to bite me in the ass.

Some of our friends, including Sandra, came over to the house to help us clear the old house and paint three of the rooms. I got some large throw rugs that covered most of the floors in the two front rooms. We were given some furniture and brought other pieces at the Salvation Army. It would be our home for over two years.

Our bedroom was the left front room, and the right front room was our living room. The only other room we used was the kitchen. There was a sink attached to the wall, but no water pipes under the house. To get water we saved the one-gallon milk containers we bought and soon had over 25 of them. I would take them to LSU, fill them, and bring water home. We used the outhouse for our toilet but had to take showers at LSU or at friends' houses. I, myself, had lived that way before in my life. Susanna had not, but she seemed to adapt to it so well that we both loved living in that old house.

There were lots of cattle on the property. In southern Louisiana, grazing cattle meant that there was a good chance that you would find Psilocybin mushrooms (magic mushrooms) in the fields. When the cows eat grass that has magic mushrooms in the fields, they consume millions of microscopic mushroom spores. The spores then travel through the cow's multiple stomachs but are not affected by any stomach acids because the cow is one of the few animals that does not have stomach acid. Then, after germinating in the cow's stomach, they come out in the cow's dung. After a little rain, of which Louisiana has an abundance, the magic mushrooms appeared. Susanna and I decided not to depend on the random act of the cows eating grass that may or may not have spores on it. In the first couple of months, whenever we picked magic mushrooms, we would set them on a sheet of aluminum overnight. That would let the spores drop on the aluminum foil. Then we took the aluminum foil out to the cows' salt licks in the pasture and rubbed the spores on the salt blocks. After a few weeks of this, I could sit on the roof and look out over a sea of magic mushrooms. When people would ask me where I lived, I would fondly say, I live at the mushroom Capitol of Louisiana.

We had several magic mushroom parties at the house. One of the more memorable ones was before the Rolling Stones concert in 1975. There were future Baton Rouge judges, lawyers, and doctors at the party, plus assorted hippies like me. We prepared mushroom spaghetti, mushroom sandwich, or just mushrooms washed down with mushroom tea. I would ask friends, before letting them partake in the mushrooms, whether they had ever eaten mushrooms or peyote or had they taken any hallucinogens. If people had never tripped before, I would try to explain that mushrooms were not for everybody, that mushrooms affected everyone a little differently. One thing I understood about hallucinogens was, if you had demons in your head that you were consciously or unconsciously suppressing, there was a damn good chance that those demons would come out after eating mushrooms.

If my friends still wanted to eat mushrooms that night, I would add one more word of advice. I told them that if they started to have a bad trip on the mushroom to remember that the mushrooms will just work their way out of your body in time. I would stress that they have nothing to fear eating mushrooms, unlike manmade hallucinogens. I explained that when I used to take LSD, not knowing who made the LSD or what was in it, increased the paranoia I would experience from a bad trip. That was why I quit taking any manmade hallucinogens. I stuck with only hallucinogens from the earth.

When it was time to leave for the Rolling Stones concert, everyone was feeling good except for two individuals. One was having a bad trip. Childhood demons were tormenting him. He had attached himself around Susanna's legs, obviously terrified by something in his head. We comforted him until he came down. He later became a judge in Texas.

The other individual was visiting from Illinois. He and another friend of mine, Terry, who would later become a District Judge, were riding with us in my van to the concert. When I slowed down to cross the railroad tracks by Alex Box Stadium, Terry's friend jumped out of the van and started heading north on the railroad tracks saying, "I am going home." Terry jumped out to try to talk his friend back into the van, but no dice. Terry waved us away as he continued to follow his friend up the railroad tracks.

## A TRIP TO MEXICO

During the Christmas break of 1975, Susanna, Peter, Susanna's older brother, and I decided to go to Mexico for two weeks. Peter came in from Nevada, where he was living the life of a mountain man, to go with us. I had an account at All Hands Credit Union in New Orleans from when I was stationed on the USS *Hyman*. I took a $1,500 student loan from the credit union to have funds to travel on.

103

The plan was to drive to Brownsville, Texas, then take a bus from Matamoros, Mexico to Palenque, Mexico. Palenque is a Maya city-state that flourished in the 7th century. I had studied about the Mayans in my anthropology class and was very interested in them. The Maya script was like Egyptian hieroglyphics. I was so fascinated by hieroglyphics in the third grade that I wrote my name in them until my teacher forbid it.

My Philosophy teacher, Bill Smith, had told me that he once lived in Oaxaca and had traveled to the Mayan city of Palenque. He added that there were Psilocybin mushrooms outside of Palenque. That the Maya people called the mushrooms "God's flesh" and used them in their religious ceremonies. That's all it took to inspire me to plan a trip to Palenque.

We drove non-stop to Brownsville, Texas. It was only then that I realized we had gotten stoned before leaving the house and I had not put my seabag, with all my clothes, toilet articles, etc., in the car. Big mistake. We went to a Salvation Army store to buy clothes. I also brought a wig to put my long hair under to cross the border.

Another thing we did not plan out was where we were going to leave the car for those two weeks in Mexico. All the parking lots in Brownsville were expensive. A lot of people parked their vehicles in the parking lots so they could walk into Mexico or take a bus. We had money but did not want to spend so much of it on parking. Since Peter and I were both Viet Nam combat veterans, I came up with the idea of trying to see if we could leave the car on a military base in the area.

We drove out to the nearest Army base. I spoke with a very friendly Army sergeant, who had also served in Nam. He let me park my car on the base. We put our weed in the glove compartment and locked the car, then took the city bus back to the Greyhound bus station in Brownsville and brought our tickets to Mexico City.

I went into the bus station's bathroom and put the wig on. We had no problems leaving the U.S., but, when we got to the Mexico side, everyone had to get off the bus with their luggage and go through Mexican customs. I was the last person in my line. I was nervous about my long hair, so I was not paying attention to what was happening to the people in front of me as they were being questioned and their luggage searched. When I got to the Mexican Border Agent, he asked my destination and how much money I had with me, all the time running his hands through the suitcase I had bought at the Salvation Army. He kept running his hands through my suitcase until someone on the bus yelled, "Give him a dollar!" I reached into my pocket, got out a dollar, and handed it to him. He took the dollar, shut my suitcase, and pushed it at me.

I had been told about how you had to give all Mexico government workers bribes, but I had forgotten that gem. It was a way of life in Mexico. I also was told that if you find yourself being arrested by Federal police, to immediately offer a large bribe to that officer. Because, if you wait, you will have to bribe more and more officers who either arrive on the scene or are at the police station.

Back on the bus, we started off to Mexico City, which was over 1,000 miles away. We were no more than a hundred miles out of the city of Matamoros when the bus was stopped at an Army roadblock. Soldiers came on the bus and walked down the aisle eyeing everyone. Outside of the bus, other soldiers were looking in the bus's luggage compartment. That happened two more times before we reached Mexico City. I found out that the soldiers were looking for weapons. The Mexican Dirty War, where a hundred plus students were killed by the Mexican Army, was still hot. It had only been four years since the Corpus Christi Massacre in Mexico City by Mexican soldiers, who had been trained in the United States. The massacre was featured in the 2018 movie *Roma*.

Mexico City was crazy. It was dirty and crowded like New York City, but even dirtier. Another big difference was, unlike New Yorkers, it seemed every Mexican was constantly spitting, not just on the sidewalks, but in the bus station and everywhere. You had to be careful where you walked and even where you sat. We could not wait to get out of the city. We also were in a hurry to get to Palenque.

We caught a bus to Palenque shortly after getting into Mexico City. Palenque is in the Mexico state of Chiapas, the southernmost state of Mexico. Palenque had just been declared a city in 1972. The home of the future Zapatista Army of National Liberation, better known as the Zapatistas, and Subcomandante Marcos (even though he is not an indigenous Maya). We fully realized that we were in for another long bus ride, over 14 hours, but our plan was to travel at night and sleep on buses to save money by not having to rent a room. I had slept on buses several times in my life, but Susanna and her brother had not. After looking over the different buses parked in the lot, we decided that a 2nd class Mexican bus would be all right. It was no Greyhound bus, but it was not bad.

We got to Palenque the next morning. In 1974, Palenque was still a little Mexico village. They were just building a *zocalo* in the center of the village. There weren't any modern hotels or motels, only the typical Mexican motel. We were too tired and hungry to do anything but eat a sandwich and crash. The rooms were very bare: a bed, a small table with a light hanging from the ceiling. Even though it was December, the temperature at night was still in the 70s. We could not open the windows because of the mosquitos, but I was so tired I fell asleep immediately, and we slept into the evening.

When we got up, we went looking for a cheap restaurant. The ones in the center of town, we felt, were too expensive. We found a restaurant on a side street that was empty, but the prices were good. We ended up eating there all the time we stayed in Palenque. During the next couple of days, we got to know the owner. He spoke a little English, so between our little Spanish and his English we could carry on a conversation.

I had been told to only drink bottled soda or beer but not the water, or there was a good chance I would get Montezuma's Revenge. That is what non-Mexicans called the bad case of diarrhea tourists got from drinking the water in Mexico. Susanna's brother, Peter, on the other hand, started drinking the water. When I mentioned what I had heard could happen to gringos drinking the water, Peter only said, "You gotten be tough." That recklessness almost killed him by the time we got to Oaxaca, Mexico, a week later. After eating, we went back to the motel and crashed again. After that we decided that riding so many hours in a row on buses was just too exhausting.

The next day we decided to go looking for magic mushrooms. I had learned to say the Spanish word for mushrooms, *hongos*. What I did not realize at the time was that a person could get in a hell of a lot of trouble for picking mushrooms in Mexico. I would only find that out later. As we walked around town, I would ask Mexicans we ran into, "*Donde esta hongos?*" The first couple of Mexicans just shook their heads and walked away. I thought they must not like Americans. I could understand that, knowing as I did, what America had done, and was doing, in Latin America. Finely, a man, with a smile on his face, pointed to a dirt road leading out of town. He then turned and walked away from us. I only understood a little Spanish, but we understood the gesture. Off down the dirt road we went, not knowing how far we had to go to find those mushrooms.

As we walked down the road, we would pass Mexican houses with people swinging in hammocks on the front porch. I would ask, "*Donde esta hongos?*" They would laugh and smile while pointing down the road saying, "*Hongos, hongos!*" I learned later that these local residences once were farmers, but, when they plowed their fields, they would uncover Mayan artifacts. They would then sell these artifacts and buy cattle (I am sure some of them just looted the Mayan ruins as was evident by the tombs that had been broken into at the Palenque site). Now, they were no longer farmers but cattle ranchers.

We had walked several miles when we spotted a herd of cattle in a pasture. We thought where there were cows, there would be mushrooms. We climbed over the fence and headed out into the field. After walking a short distance, we came upon what we had traveled nearly 1,900 miles and over 24 hours on buses to find: "God's flesh," the same mushrooms the Mayans themselves had eaten.

We walked through the pasture filling our pockets with mushrooms. Then I decided to fall to my knees and eat a mushroom down to the cow dung. I thought that may have been the way Mayan's had eaten them. Susanna and Peter ate a couple of mushrooms each. We walked into a nearby wooded area by a stream, then split up to experience the coming trip undisturbed.

I sat in the woods by the steam that ran toward the cow pasture. I found myself contemplating on why I was attending LSU. What was I trying to achieve in life? Just as I started to think about Nam, I found myself engrossed in the stream, the beautiful colors of the water, the sound that the stream was making as it flowed over the rocks, the wind gently blowing over me. I started looking around me. The colors of the grass, sky, trees, everything seemed more vivid than I had ever seen before. I had never experienced that visual sensation on LSD, mescaline, peyote, or even the mushrooms in Louisiana.

I must have been in that state of mind for hours until I realized that Susanna was sitting next to me. I smiled at her. Susanna and I had taken the same philosophy class with Professor Smith, who had told me about Palenque. I barely made a C in his class while Susanna made her usual A. She had written her paper on Friedrich Nietzsche for that class and had gotten an A+ with glowing comments written all over the page by the professor. As she looked into my eyes, she said, "I finally understand Nietzsche!" Only later did I see how ironic it was that she had gotten one of the highest grades in philosophy class, but only after eating Palenque mushrooms did she really understand Nietzsche. At the time though, I only nodded my head in an understanding way.

It was getting late, so we went looking for Peter. We were interested in what kind of experience he had had. Peter had returned to Viet Nam. He had been a gunner on Navy Seawolves, the Navy's Huey helicopters. He had two helicopters shot down and was awarded the Silver Star for saving the life of one of the crew members. I could understand why he may have traveled back to Nam.

As we were walking back toward town, a Policia Federal jeep passed us heading toward Palenque. We could see there were a couple of young white people in the back with very worried looks on their faces. Only after that did it dawn on us, we could have gotten into serious trouble for picking and eating mushrooms. I figured that some of the Mexicans I had asked where the mushrooms were had called the Federales. What saved us was going into the woods, which kept us from being seen from the road. After that, we kept a low profile when we ate the remaining mushrooms we had in our pockets.

We again had dinner at the hole-in-the-wall restaurant. This time, after the owner brought us our food, he just pulled up a chair to talk with us. He was a very pleasant man. I could tell he was very pleased that we had chosen to return to his restaurant. I don't remember any nightlife in Palenque. Matter of fact, I do not remember any streetlights or nightclubs.

We decided we would visit the Mayan ruins the next morning. To save money, we did not take the bus to the ruins, rather we walked there. It turned out it was a pretty good walk. Then Peter or I, I can't remember which one of us, thought, since they charged money at the entrance, why don't we just climb up the mountain and cut through the jungle to the ruins; that way we would save even more money. I think the owner of the restaurant put that idea in our heads. He knew poor gringos when he saw them.

So up the mountain we went. Again, we had no idea of how far the ruins were up that mountain. We ended up stumbling upon a Mexican (maybe Mayan) family homestead in the middle of that jungle. As we stepped out of the jungle, we were greeted by naked, barefoot children just staring at us in shock. I am sure they had never seen gringos popping out of the jungle in the middle of the day before. As we made our way past chickens and pigs running free, a man and woman stepped out of the doorway (there appeared to be no door), looking even more shocked than their children. We just smiled and waved as we continued up the mountain.

By then all our clothes were soaking wet from sweating. At one point, the way was so steep we were on our hands and knees climbing up the mountain. We finally burst through the jungle into the ruins site, startling the shit out of a group of tourists. I am confident in saying that we all thought that climbing up the mountain to save money was a stupid idea. I mean, I think the entrance fee was only one U.S. dollar. We definitely were not going back down the mountain that way.

At that time, there were only a few ruins exposed at the site and the jungle was right up to the edge of even those buildings. We climbed up the Temple of the Inscriptions, where the tomb of Pacal the Great had been located in 1952. We could not go down into the tomb. The tomb held a sarcophagus or tomb lid that showed King Pacal, in elaborate head-dress, leaning back in a seated position. I had read the book *Chariots of the Gods* by Erich Von Daniken, which speculated that the king was actually an extra-terrestrial being, and that the carving depicted him in his spaceship. That theory has since been totally debunked, but back then it was food for thought.

We also visited the Temple of the Skull and the Palace of Palenque. By then we were tired and sweaty. It was at this point that we were told by some young people, I think Canadians, who had come out of the jungle, that there was a waterfall and swimming hole down the hill. That was just what we needed: a cool swim in the same water hole that the Mayans had swum in. That spot had appeared in the film *Predator*. It was where Arnie (Arnold Schwarzenegger), who was being hunted by the Predator, dives off a waterfall. I could see why they picked that spot. It was beautiful.

After resting we headed back up the hill to the ruins. As we got out to the parking lot to look for a ride back to town, out of the jungle walked three real live Mayan Indians: a male and two females. The Mexicans got so excited it was as if rock stars had just walked out of the jungle. I found out that to the Mexicans they were stars, just by being who they were: Mayan Indians.

The male was maybe five feet two inches tall. He had long black hair with a bow across his back and what looked like some kind of quiver with arrows in it. He wore no clothing on the top half of his body, only a loincloth. He had no footwear. Various items hung from his waist. I got the impression he had things to trade.

The two women were different in height and age. The older woman looked about 4 feet 10 inches tall, while the younger woman was a couple of inches shorter. They both were bare-breasted and had only loincloths around their waists. They too were barefooted. One of the Mexican men there told us that the two women were the male Indian's wives. He said it with a tone of admiration in his voice. I could not tell if it was because both women were very attractive (which they were) or because the male Mayan Indian had two wives. In ancient times, Mayan couples were usually monogamous, except for the wealthy nobles who practiced polygamy.

We took a bus back to town and went to the motel to get cleaned up. Since we were leaving tomorrow morning and were totally exhausted, we wanted to eat and then go to bed. We went back to "our" restaurant.

Once again, there was nobody else in the restaurant, so, after the owner brought us our food, he again sat down with us to talk. We had only just begun to eat, when none other than those same three Mayan Indians walked into the restaurant. He must have finished his trading.

The owner jumped out of his chair and ran over to them. He led them to a table on the other side of the restaurant from us. I don't think he put the Indians on the other side of the restaurant because we were Americans, but because he wanted them to have privacy. As he passed our table to get them water, he looked at us saying, "Great honor, great honor." Each time he would pass our table to go to and from their table to the kitchen, he repeated, "Great honor, great honor." He seemed to be bursting from the seams with pride that the Indians had chosen his restaurant to eat at while in town. I thought it might have been because his restaurant was on a side street away from the more populated center of town. Considering how excited the Mexicans had appeared to be when they saw the Indians, they probably wanted a quiet place to eat.

As we finished eating our meal, we watched the owner, and then his wife, fawning all over the Mayan Indians. The Indians seemed to take it in stride. They must have become used to that kind of attention and commotion whenever they came to town. I felt as if I were interrupting something very sacred and important when I asked the owner for our bill. He smiled at me as he handed me the bill saying again, as he looked over at his wife talking to the two Mayan women, "Great honor." He then hustled back over to the Mayans' table. We put our money on the table, with a large tip, and left the restaurant. I looked back to wave goodbye but neither the owner, nor his wife, took their attention off of the three Mayan Indians.

We had decided to spend Christmas at the beach in Salina Cruz, another area that I had been told I should visit. It was located on the coast of the Pacific Ocean. The next morning, we bought our tickets to Salina Cruz on a third-class bus. Before getting on the bus, Peter thought it would be a good idea if we ate the rest of the magic mushrooms. Was that a bad idea!

The most direct route to Salina Cruz from Palenque is by way of Rt. 199. Palenque was around 200 feet above sea level. From there we were going to travel to a mountain pass which was at 7,200 feet, the highest point on Rt. 199.

When we got on the bus, there were people with chickens, pigs, and even a goat on the bus. The bus was packed because, I am sure, it was the cheapest way through the mountains to Salina Cruz by way of San Cristobal de Las Casas. The bus started climbing into the mountains and in an hour or so we got to the first little mountain village. By then I was tripping my ass off on the mushrooms. I am telling you, tripping on a third-class Mexican bus, packed with people and their livestock, going through the mountains in one of the poorest areas of Mexico, was not a good experience.

The minute the bus stopped at the first village, several local vendors, hawking food, drinks, and an occasional souvenir, came onto the bus. These were mostly children, I think because more of them than could fit on the bus. Outside of the bus, adult vendors were going from window to window, trying to sell their goods. To my tripping self, their faces seemed completely distorted. I am sure it was because of the mushrooms and the wear and tear of life on these people living in these mountains. It was freaking me out so much, I had to close my eyes.

To my relief, we finally got back on the road. I had noticed around all the bends and especially the cutbacks there were lots of flowers and shrines with religious items like glass candles and crosses on the edge of the road. I found out that these items marked where a bus had gone over the edge, killing many people. That information did not help my tripping one bit.

It was getting dark when we started hitting more cutbacks on the road. I noticed that the driver, when approaching one of these many cutbacks, would turn his lights off. What that fuck was he thinking? Up in those mountains, it was pitch black at night. A Mexican on the bus who spoke some English, noticed my look of, should I say, deep concern about this maneuver. He explained to me that it prevented blinding the drivers of oncoming buses driving on the outside of the road and kept them from going over the edge. A bus driving on the inside, like the one I was on, could only hit the mountain. That helped a little.

It was around a 10-hour trip to Salina Cruz. We got there at night and found a cheap motel where we could spend the night. It was Christmas Eve. The next day we walked around the town. Since we were going to be riding more buses in Mexico, we decided we needed to get some Valium so we could sleep better on the bus. We had found out that a person did not need a prescription to get Valium in Mexico. That was good, but none of us knew how to pronounce Valium in Spanish. Someone wrote the word down on a piece of paper for us. Peter then went into a pharmacy, handed them the paper and, sure enough, they sold him a bottle of Valium.

Later, that day we went a little way out of town to a nearby beach where there was a Mexican campground. They rented out *hamacas* (hammocks) right on the beach for a tenth of what the cheap motel charged us. The hammocks were very wide and were tied to two poles in the sand. There were about a dozen hammocks on the beach and more under a pavilion. We got three hammocks beside each other. I had never slept in a hammock before or on a beautiful Pacific beach.

That night, Christmas, we went into town to watch the Christmas celebrations. I experienced another first. I saw a Black baby Jesus and Madonna. Of course, unlike what Americans think, Jesus was closer to Black than white. I did not know that at the time, so I was taken aback when I saw the people parading with that Black Jesus and Madonna. They marched into a very old looking Catholic Church, so we followed

113

the crowd. They placed the Black baby Jesus in a cradle in a manger with animals. That night, back at the camp site, I decided to take one of the Valium pills. I slept like a baby that Christmas night.

The next day we wanted to get on the road to Oaxaca but decided to spend one more day on the beach and leave for Oaxaca that afternoon. Oaxaca was only around five hours away. After all those 11 to 14-hour bus rides, we figured that a five hour ride would be a piece of cake, so we did not get out of Salina Cruz until late. What we did not know was that we had to change buses in Tehuantepec. We got to Tehuantepec around 7 P.M. and had to wait for the bus to Oaxaca. Thinking that I could get some sleep on the bus, I took a couple of Valium pills. Well, I took too many because I started falling asleep on the street while waiting for the bus.

When the bus finally arrived, the Mexicans rushed the door of the bus like a Rugby scrum. Peter managed to get on the bus with the Mexicans, but Susanna was having to deal with me. She managed to get me to my feet and onto the bus, but we, along with a young Mexican man, were the last three who were able to squeeze on. Susanna had to sit on the hot engine cover, while I had to stand right in front of the bus's door.

Even though it was December 26, it was still hot, and the bus did not have air conditioning. The bus driver left the door open so air could flow into the bus. After traveling only a few miles, I must have fallen asleep again because the next thing I remember I was being pulled back into the moving bus by the young Mexican man. I had started falling out of the open door of the bus. Susanna warned me to stay awake. No matter how hard I tried, I kept falling asleep only to be woken as the Mexican was pulling me back into the bus. The bus driver never even slowed down as I was falling out of the bus. Finally, only after the young Mexican insisted that this American was going to kill himself falling out of the bus, did the driver finally close the door. That really upset the other passages on the bus. My guardian angel, the young Mexican, came to my defense, but I could tell that some of the Mexicans didn't give a shit if an American fell to his death.

We got into Oaxaca late. Fortunately, Professor Smith had given me the name of a good hotel in the center of the market, the Rex Hotel. When we got there, it was after midnight. There was no one at the desk, but there was a buzzer to ring. While waiting for someone to answer the buzzer, I looked around the lobby. There were glass cases lining the walls. In the cases were some of the most beautiful butterflies I had ever seen. I learned that the owner of the hotel collected butterflies from all over Latin America.

A man finally appeared at the desk. He was the owner of the hotel and spoke English. I mentioned Professor Smith's name, saying that he had highly recommended that hotel to us. He said he remembered the professor and asked how he was doing? He then said he did have a couple of rooms for us.

The next morning, Susanna and I decided to walk around the market to look for a place to eat breakfast. We stopped by Peter's room and knocked on the door. We told him through the door what we were going to do and asked if he wanted to come with us. He said "no" through the door, so Susanna and I went by ourselves.

The Oaxaca market was famous for, not only its size and the many items in the market, but also for the fact that the indigenous peoples would come down from the hills to trade and sell their goods there. I ended up buying a hammock in the market. Regretfully, it was not as good as the hammock I slept in at Salina Cruz. It was not as wide as those, but I still used it for several years. I also fell in love with some hand-painted wall plates of Mayans, which I still have today.

After a couple of hours, Susanna and I walked back to the hotel. As soon as we entered the lobby, the owner came running up to us, saying that our friend was very sick. He stated that our friend's mattress and sheets were soaking wet, and that Peter looked very pale and was sweating profusely. He had given him the address of a doctor and said Peter had left over an hour ago. We headed off to the doctor to find him.

We both were very worried; Susanna was almost in tears. We had gone about four or five blocks when we saw Peter heading toward us. He said that he woke up sweating and with diarrhea. The doctor had immediately asked if Peter had been drinking the water. It was Montezuma's Revenge. The doctor shot Peter up with a lot of penicillin. I told Peter I hope he wasn't going to drink the water any more. Peter insisted that he was going to continue to drink the water. He felt, since he had gotten sick, his body could handle the water now. I was very skeptical of that logic. But Peter kept drinking the water, and I never saw him sick again.

We had planned to go to the ruins in Monte Alban, but was told by the owner of the hotel strangers were not welcome in the area. He said a lot of the local farmers were growing marijuana near where Monte Alban was located. The farmers were very suspicious of strangers. We felt that we didn't need the hassle, so we decided to just hang around the market and rest before heading to Mexico City.

We were having lunch at a restaurant in the zocalo (the main square in Oaxaca) when I heard two guys at the adjacent table talking. They were Americans, so I introduce myself, Susanna and Peter. They joined us at our table. Eventually, the conversation came around to how we heard about Palenque, magic mushrooms, Salina Cruz and Oaxaca. I told them about my professor. They both broke out laughing. They knew Professor Smith very well. They didn't elaborate. The following semester, I went to the professor's office to tell him about the two guys. He definitely knew them. He said, "They are the reason I am not living in Oaxaca right now." Since Professor Smith was gay, I figured it probably was a lover thing gone wrong.

We left Oaxaca after three days and headed back to Mexico City. We wanted to see some of the city even though we were not impressed when we saw it the first time. I wanted to see two things in Mexico City. One was the *Zocalo* (main square) of Mexico City because the picture of the *Zocalo* was in my Elementary Spanish textbook. I had taken Elementary Spanish three times already and was planning to take it another time to try to make an A to off-set the F I had gotten my first semester. Maybe seeing the *Zocalo* in Mexico City might help me get over the hump.

While I was setting on a bench at the *Zocalo*, waiting for Susanna and Peter, a Policia Federal officer approached me. At the time, I had my hair down and was wearing torn blue jeans with patches and a T-shirt. When I saw him heading toward me, I got up to leave. He walked right in front of me, causing me to stop in my tracks. He looked me up and down while saying, "You look like you do not have money, but I know you do." Fuck, I was about to experience a Policia Federal shake-down.

I took a step around him, turning as I did so I could keep facing him with my hands spread out while saying, "No, I don't have any money." He had a big grin on his face as he took a step toward me, saying, "You have money, you just dress like you don't." I kept backing away, shaking my head negatively, saying, "No money, I have no money." I knew if he got near enough, he might grab me and maybe plant marijuana or something on me. I kept shaking my head as I spun around and started walking away from him fast toward a crowd of tourist with a guide. I acted as if I belonged to the group. Only then did I dare to look back. The Policia Federal officer was walking in the other direction. I thought, that was too close for comfort.

The second thing I wanted to see was the National Museum of Anthropology. Anthropology was my favorite subject in college. The Museum is one of the largest museums in the world. It held significant archaeological and anthropological artifacts from Mexico's pre-Columbian heritage. We took the subway to the Museum. I thought the spitting on the street was bad, but the Mexicans were spitting just as much in the subway and on the train. We had already bought our bus tickets home, so we did not have that much time to spend at the Museum. Even worse, we missed the first subway train so, by the time we got to the Museum, we had to hurry through. It was huge. We skipped several areas and still had to hurry through the rest of the museum. I remember very little about the Museum of Anthropology. I thought someday I would return, but I have never been back to Mexico City again.

We got back to Brownsville, Texas, with no more adventures. I told Susanna and Peter to wait at the bus station and I would go out to the base to get the car. The car was right where I had parked it. When I got back to the bus station, there were two other people with Susanna and Peter: a young American guy and a young Mexican woman. I found out we were giving them a lift. The man was going to San Antonio, and the young Mexican woman was going to Houston. They were going to help with the gas. I don't know how I found this out, but the Mexican woman had no papers. She said she had family in Houston.

We were just outside of Brownsville when Susanna took the marijuana out of the glove compartment and rolled a joint. I don't know if the Mexican woman took a hit or not. Since the windows were rolled up because it was cold outside, the inside of the car was soon thick in marijuana smoke.

I was just driving over a little rise when, down the road a bit, was the biggest damn stop sign I had ever seen. Near the sign was a Border Patrol trailer. I quickly told everyone to roll down their windows. Since I was driving and stoned, I did not start rolling my window down. Susanna was gathering the marijuana and rolling papers and stuffing them in her panties. Finally, she rolled her window down, but still there was a lot of smoke in the car. I was almost at the stop sign and could see a Border Patrol Agent walking toward us. I was panicking. We were fucked with all that marijuana smoke in the car. I quickly rolled my window down. At that time a gust of wind blew through the car, blowing all the smoke out of the car just in the nick of time.

I came to a stop by the sign. The Border Patrol Agent walked up to my car window, stuck his head in the car and looked at everyone while asking, "Is everyone an American citizen?" As I said, "Yeah, we are all American citizens," my eyes landed on the Mexican woman in the backseat. Shit! I thought. But the Border Patrol Agent had stood up, apparently not noticing her. He asked me if we had any fruits or vegetables in the car. I said, "No." He asked to look in the trunk. I told him, "Sure."

I got out of the car, popped the trunk, and leaned against the car trying to act cool, as though I wasn't worried about anything. There, in plain view, was the Mexican woman's sack of oranges. The agent gave me a perplexed look. He shook his head slightly as he turned away from the truck saying, "Ok, go on." For a moment I was frozen in place because I was expecting a totally different comment from him. Then I shut the trunk and quickly drove off. It was just another close call in my life in a long line of close calls.

## PROBLEMS FOR THE BOOK RENTAL

In the spring semester of 1975, I signed up for an even bigger class load. I signed up for 16 hours: General Geology Historical, the Physical Geology Lab that was recommended with the General Geology class, American History (that was when I first met Professor Bob Becker), American Government, Psychology of Adjustment, Voice and Articulation. With this last class I was hoping to learn how to pronounce words correctly. Due to my increasing involvement with the Book Rental, I would eventually drop all the classes except for American History and Psychology. I made a C in both classes.

As I realized later, James Reddoch (the former dean who had become vice chancellor for student affairs) must not have thought that we would be as successful as we had been in acquiring books at the end of the fall semester (hundreds of students had donated books to the Book Rental). We were prepared at spring registration to rent those books, but we needed a location accessible to students. The Student Union refused to allow us to set up a table in the Union during registration. The Union administrator told us that we needed permission from Vice Chancellor Reddoch before he would permit that.

John Crochet and I went over to Reddoch's office to see what he was up to. His secretary told us to go in, that he was expecting us. Really? The Student Union administrator must have called him. As we entered his office, Reddoch was typing something on his typewriter. He gestured for us to have a seat in two chairs in front of his desk. As we sat down, I started complaining that the Union told us that Book Rental could not set up our tables to rent out our books. While still typing, Reddoch said that was because we had failed to meet the administration's regulations for a student organization operating a Nonprofit

Book Rental. I asked, "What regulations?" "These," he said as he pulled the paper he had been typing out of his typewriter. He picked up a pen and signed the page. John and I looked at each other.

Reddoch then called his secretary into his office and handed her the piece of paper, telling her to make a copy for Mr. Schirmer. I still did not know what he was up to. We all sat there not speaking. Then the secretary came back in and handed Reddoch copies of the paper. Reddoch gave one to me, saying, "These are the regulations that PSA will have to meet in order to operate a Nonprofit Book Rental on campus." I glanced down at the list of requirements. At the end there was a statement that we would have a 30-day grace period to meet those requirements. I was fighting hard not to lose my temper and say something stupid.

As we got up to leave, Reddoch, with a smirk on his face said, "You know the trouble with students? They don't do their homework." I really had to bite my tongue then. Reddoch had just created the damn regulations. How the hell could we have known what was required? I was coming to realize that the vice chancellor for student affairs indeed had a great deal of power over students and their organizations. That would not be the last time I would clash with Reddoch over what a student organization could or could not do.

I later realized that Reddoch, as vice chancellor for student affairs, probably had already pulled my LSU record. Therefore, he knew that, in January of 1971, I had been placed on scholastic probation and, in 1972, resigned from LSU. In addition, he would have known that I didn't make the necessary grades in my first semester after returning to LSU to get off scholastic probation. Furthermore, he knew that I was attempting to take 16 hours that semester, and I was exposing myself to flunking out of LSU again if I stayed too involved in the Book Rental. He was operating under the assumption that I was a normal student attending college, and that making good grades was the most important thing to me.

Of course, I was not the normal college student. I am not your average anything. Realizing that put a whole new light on his statement that

120

"the trouble with students is that they don't do their homework." He was sending me a message that he was fully aware of my academic position, and, if I expected to stay at LSU, I had better "do my homework" and quit spending time working on the Book Rental.

A *Reveille* (January 23, 1975) article, titled "Reddoch Okays Book Rental plan," reported that Reddoch stated:

> The University has no objection to the Book Rental being operated by students for students on campus, but it has an obligation to students to see it operated in a proper and businesslike way....The vice chancellor said that at a meeting with Schirmer in mid-October, he "verbally" outlined the conditions for using University facilities for a fund-raising or nonprofit program....According to Reddoch, Schirmer said that he understood the requirements but did not return with the necessary documents to show how the Book Rental was to be operated.

What bullshit. The vice chancellor for student affairs generated those requirements when John and I had gone to his office to ask why the Union was not letting us set up the Book Rental table.

Reddoch added that "failure to meet the requirements will prevent the program from operating in summer school or next fall." The sonofabitch was doing everything he could to kill the Book Rental. As I pointed out before, selling books was big business for the Union Bookstore.

I knew from my many previous battles with people in positions of power over me that the fight was on. That was going to require as much of my free time as I could give if we were going to have any chance of getting a Book Rental set up at LSU. I remembered how hard I had had to work the previous semester in order just to pass all of my courses while doing the limited work I had done on the Book Rental then. I would have to drop classes if I were going to have the time to work on the requirements that Reddoch had outlined, not to mention the other roadblocks I figured would be coming down the pike.

A later *Reveille* (January 28, 1975) article reported, "PSA also discussed what it called a 'lack of responsiveness on the part of the campus newspaper' to allow a rebuttal to an interview with Vice-Chancellor for Student Affairs James Reddoch printed earlier this week." I had wanted to correct what Reddoch had said in the interview, but we were not allowed a rebuttal of the article.

I may not have been a Journalism major, but I had read enough newspaper articles to know that, when something is said by a person being interviewed about another individual, the reporter contacts that individual for a comment.

During most of that semester, the editors and staff of the *Reveille* were opposed to what I was trying to accomplish on behalf of the students. They were as conservative as the vice chancellor and the professors of the College of Journalism who appointed them to the *Reveille* staff.

Since the *Reveille* editor refused my request to rebut Reddoch's interview, I attended the first Free Speech Alley of the spring semester. A *Reveille* (January 30, 1975) article, titled "Mass transit, Book Rental discussed at free speech," stated that:

> Ted Schirmer, a member of the Progressive Student Alliance and organizer of the student Book Rental program...stated he asked the Reveille editor for a chance to comment on Reddoch's version. Schirmer said the editor denied him this. Schirmer concluded his two major points were: 1. Get rid of Reddoch and 2. Give the *Reveille* to the students.

The *Reveille* received student money out of every full-time student's tuition. Therefore, I felt the paper should become a true student newspaper with the editor and staff elected by the students. That was done on other college campuses. The *Reveille* staff was too easily controlled or intimated by the administration and Journalism faculty. Hell, not only were their grades controlled by those professors, but their future jobs in journalism could be jeopardized.

I talked with a professor in LSU College of Business about getting the Book Rental on its feet. The professor stated the number one thing was to get a source of seed money, ideally, over a span of time, but at least for the first year of operation. We came up with the idea of asking students if they would be willing to tax themselves to set up a Book Rental on campus.

The proposal, which PSA wanted to put before the student electorate, read: "All full or part-time students shall be assessed a $1 fee per semester, for one year only, to be applied to the LSU Nonprofit Book Rental, Inc., for the purpose of permanently establishing a low-cost Book Rental program for the students of LSU." The way the proposal was written, correct grammar, no spelling errors, coherent, it was easy to tell I was working with actual college students, students who were educationally qualified to be college students, not pretenders, like myself.

The *Reveille* (March 12, 1975) published an editorial by Mary Ellen Halterman Smith asking, "Another Fee?" In the editorial Ms. Smith stated:

> The Progressive Students Alliance is trying to get 10 per cent of the student body to sign a petition. If they get the required number of signatures, the Student Government Association must place a referendum asking students to approve or disapprove assessing $1 a semester for the nonprofit Book Rental. The idea of a nonprofit Book Rental run for and by the students is certainly progressive. It even can be said to be a "real service" to the students. But putting another mandatory fee on students who may choose not to use the Book Rental is unfair. According to the proponents of the fee assessment, "more than 10,000 students in the fall of 1976" will be able to use the rental. Well, this is 1975 and there are more than 10,000 students who will have to pay the fee if the referendum passes (if the PSA gets the required signatures).

I my view, this is the typical conservative argument of thinking only of yourself, not what is best for all the people. It seems that conservatives believe that if something doesn't benefit them personally and, even worse, may cost them money, then it should be resisted to the point of destroying a damn good idea, no matter if the idea would help many people less fortunate than them.

In order for the Book Rental to meet the requirements set down by the vice chancellor to use LSU facilities, we decided to work through the PSA. That was reported in the *Reveille* (1975) article titled "PSA votes Book Rental into constitution."

> The Progressive Student Alliance voted Wednesday to amend its constitution to include establishment of a Book Rental program, thus satisfying one requirement for formal recognition of the program by the University...the amendment was passed at the request of a faculty committee on student organizations. Since the Nonprofit Book Rental is a business and not an organization, the committee said it needed sponsorship by a campus organization, in this case PSA, in order to be formally recognized and eligible to use University facilities.

After the first week of the start of the 1975 spring semester, the Book Rental shut down after renting books to hundreds of LSU students. We stored the remaining books. We all felt the first semester of renting books was a success, considering that all the books we had received had been donated the previous semester. There had been several students who wanted to sell their textbooks to us instead of the bookstores, but we were unable to buy textbooks. Our inability to buy textbooks was due to the freezing of the funds that SGA had voted to give to the Book Rental for operating and to buy textbooks. The funds had been frozen due to questions that had been raised by the Young Americans for Freedom (YAF) and members of the Assembly who opposed the Book

Rental and opposed PSA spending of $4.50 for flyers. That was an example of the typical harassment that the Book Rental was receiving from the more conservative students at LSU.

At the SGA meeting of March 19th, the Assembly voted to unfreeze the funds of the Nonprofit Book Rental after the audit by the financial vice president of SGA, Dan Parker, was submitted to the Assembly. The report proved that the Book Rental hadn't misspent the funds allocated to it by the SGA.

An article in the *Reveille*, buried on page 16, titled "2,355 sign petition for Book Rental," reported that, "About 2,355 students signed a petition asking that a referendum be held to assess students $1 per semester for the Book Rental program....PSA said it would ask the SGA to make a resolution to have a special election for the Book Rental program."

Then a section in the *Reveille* (March 21, 1975), called "On the Spot," posed this question to ten students: "Would you favor adding $1 to your fees each semester for one year to support a Nonprofit Book Rental?" I am guessing that the editors were expecting a resounding "no" response. Instead, out of the ten students asked, seven said "yes," two said "no" and one student said he did not have enough information to make a judgment on it. I imagine those answers must have really upset Ms. Smith and the other *Reveille* staff who opposed the Book Rental. But I am sure they still believed that the referendum would never be put in front of the student body considering how conservative the Student Government Association leaders were.

But an article on the front page of the *Reveille* (April 3, 1975, titled "Vote on Book Rental fee set for Wed. by Assembly," reported, "Student Assembly members voted 28–12 Wednesday to put the referendum to the students after an hour of debate with Ted Schirmer, originator of the Book Rental idea."

Unfortunately, SGA President Gary Elkins, who was a conservative fraternity member, decided to step in before the SGA election and stop the referendum. A *Reveille* article the following day reported: "Elkins kills Book Rental referendum. Calls it 'extremely impractical.'"

As a result of the spring SGA election, another fraternity member, Paul Benoist, was elected the new SGA president.

Disappointed at the veto and angry at the constant attacks, I decided to resign from leadership of Book Rental. An article in the *Reveille* covering the Alley that day, titled "Schirmer quits Book Rental, PSA at Free Speech Alley," stated:

> Progressive Student Alliance member Ted Schirmer said at Free Speech Alley Wednesday he would no longer be involved with or speak about the Book Rental program. He said he quit the program because he was "being called a liar, a cheat, a thief; threats were made to bring me before the University Court and to have me expelled."
> Schirmer also attacked a statement made Monday by Student Government Association President Paul Benoist. Benoist was quoted as saying, "I don't see how a person with any iota of intelligence—even Mr. Schirmer's mother— could think it (the Book Rental program) would work." Schirmer, visibly overcome with emotion, said if anyone had made such a remark about his mother shortly after he had returned from Vietnam, "I would have cut his throat." Schirmer said his mother died while he was serving in Vietnam.

After that statement, no one said anything that personal about me or my family again. I am not sure if it was because they thought that Benoist went too far with his statement or a fear that I might actually cut their throats if they said something like that about my mother.

After I resigned from PSA and the Book Rental, another PSA member became the spokesperson for PSA and the Book Rental. That evening at the SGA Student Assembly meeting, they took up Elkin's veto. A number of other members of PSA were present. I was at home, feeling torn that I was leaving my child in someone else's hands to defend. It was not a very comfortable night for me, not knowing how the meeting was going.

In a *Reveille* (April 17, 1975) article, titled "SGA votes to uphold Book Rental veto 39–4," it was reported:

> The proposed referendum to fund the Book Rental Program will not be put before the student body. The Student Government Association voted 39–4 Wednesday to favor a past presidential veto of the referendum. The assembly had previously voted to hold the referendum and former SGA President Gary Elkins vetoed it.
>
> Assembly debate on the Book Rental program was primarily negative. Criticism centered on the charter, the feasibility of the program and the credibility of its backers.

What was it to criticize about "the credibility of its backers"? I thought that line was added as a dig at the students working on the Book Rental, especially me.

The next few days I didn't go to my classes nor go on campus. I needed to reevaluate what I was doing at LSU. Why was I taking this heat? The Book Rental was not going away, there were too many hardworking students manning the program for that to happen. That weekend, several PSA members came to my house to urge me to reconsider my decision to quit the PSA and the Book Rental. They convinced me that this fight was worth fighting for and that I was needed if the Book Rental had any chance of succeeding. They also pointed out all the time and effort that so many people had already put into the Book Rental and said that it would be wrong to walk away from it. I told them that I too was having second thoughts about my decision. I fully realized that I was responsible for people getting involved with this project in the first place. And I agreed with them that a lot of people had sacrificed their time and worked really hard to make the Book Rental a reality. Whether the Book Rental succeeded or not, I owed it to those people who believed in my vision not to quit on them. Because that is what I would be doing, quitting on them. I decided to get back into the fight.

At the last Free Speech Alley of the semester on April 24th, I returned to the Alley. Word must have spread throughout campus that I was going to speak. It was very crowded. It seemed as though all the PSA and Book Rental student workers came, and they all brought friends. It was the largest Alley that semester. The *Reveille* (April 25, 1975) noted my return with an article, titled "Schirmer back in saddle—SGA called 'leech' on student body."

> Ted Schirmer, who last week said he would no longer speak about the Book Rental program, criticized the Student Assembly Wednesday for upholding former SGA President Gary Elkins' veto of a referendum on the program. Schirmer, speaking to a large crowd at Free Speech Alley, said SGA wants to take the Book Rental program out of the hands of the Progressive Student Alliance. He said SGA will not allow any program unless it is something it can take credit for. "SGA is nothing but a leech to the student body," he said.

I must admit that I was a little uncomfortable as I walked over to the Student Assembly meeting that night. I wasn't sure how things were going to go down. Some of the individuals who were fighting to stop the creation of a Book Rental sat on the Assembly and were possibly going to make statements against me personally. How would I handle that? I was learning I would have to let those things roll off me like water off a duck if I was going to get back into this fight.

That was my first lesson in what happens if a person gets involved in a public issue or, for that matter, runs for office. You are going to get attacked personally. That was when I started to shed the old me: that poor kid who learned that if someone said anything about you or your family, you fought them, either verbally or physically. I had to civilize myself if I was going to fight the good fight. Otherwise, I would be hurting the causes I was fighting for more than helping them.

I actually received a very warm reception from several SGA Representatives and the legislative vice president, Jerry Giddens. That was the first time I talked to Jerry. To paraphrase a line from one of my favorite movies, *Casablanca*, "Jerry, I think this is the beginning of a beautiful friendship."

I explained to the Assembly that the PSA were in support of establishing a commission to study the feasibility and practicality of a Book Rental. Then I went on to argue for the Nonprofit Book Rental to keep the money the SGA had given it. I could tell that I was winning them over to our side. The *Reveille* (April 26, 1975) reported:

> A commission was set up by the Assembly to study the program and carry it out if found to be "feasible and practical." The commission will consist of members from the College of Business, SGA representatives, two faculty members, three other students and two students from the present Nonprofit Book Rental Program.
>
> Ted Schirmer was at the meeting to speak for the Book Rental. He said the issue was important and he had reconsidered his resignation of last week. Schirmer said he was pleased with the creation of the commission and would be willing to fund the commission from the Book Rental's budget.

## Summer Semester, 1975
### MY SUMMER OF FUN CLASSES

Normally, I would have looked for a job for the summer to save money so Susanna and I could travel. Since I had decided to jump back into the fight to establish a Book Rental at LSU, I felt I had to be on campus the summer of 1975 to work on it. As anyone who has taken summer classes at LSU knows, summer classes are hour-long for five days a week. That was because professors had to jam a regular semester's work into less time. Since I was not going to get a job that summer, I had to take a full load, which was six hours in the summer, in order to qualify for the full monthly check from the GI Bill that I depended on.

I decided if I was going to have to be on campus for the summer, I was going to enjoy some of the time. I enrolled in two traditional classes, General Geology Historical, since I had taken the class in the spring semester for a few weeks but withdrawn because of my work on the Book Rental, I figured I had a jump on the material. The other was Introduction to Law Enforcement because I was learning the importance of knowing your enemy given that I was a drug smoking political activist who had discovered he had been spied on by the Baton Rouge Police Department, i.e. Gus Tabony. I also was told that the course did not require a lot of work. Then I signed up for classes I knew that I would enjoy: Basic Golf, Basic Bowling and Basic Senior Lifeguard in the Huey P. Long swimming pool.

Once again, I had to withdraw from the General Geology Historical class. I wanted to learn about the history of Geology, but the amount of reading was stopping me. I was unable to overcome my learning disabilities (that I did not at the time even know I had).

The LSU Golf coach taught my golf class. I am sure he was a little surprised to see a long haired hippie in his class, but, after he saw how I could handle the short game and putting, he changed his opinion. He realized that I was taking golf because I wanted to learn how to play better, specifically, how to tee off using fairway woods.

When I played golf on the LSU golf course, I really enjoyed watching the tee shots with a wood go so much farther than the two iron I had been using. That was short lived because, after I injured my shoulder playing rugby softball, I was unable to swing a wood again as I had been taught in golf class. I received a B in that class for missing classes. I was once again busy working on the Book Rental. In addition, I did not do well on the class written exam.

My Senior Lifesaving class was also taught by a coach, LSU swim team coach Ted Stickles. He had been a record-breaking swimmer at Indiana University before being hired by LSU. Being a Yankee, he was not as surprised to see a long haired hippie in his class, especially after the jock in me rose up. In our class was a member of the LSU's swim team. Early on, the class was required to swim the same distance as we would be required to swim at the end of the class. Well, this athlete not only "smoked" the rest of the class, but, when he got out of the pool, he had a smirk on his face. I thought he was trying to show up the rest of the class or maybe just the long haired hippie in the class. Anyways, I decided to set my goal at beating him when we swam the same distance at the end of the semester. I would stay after class and swim 20 plus laps every day before leaving the pool. A young female classmate, I forget her name, would sit on the side of the pool, encouraging me to keep pushing hard through the water.

Then, a week before the swim test, I was called away to handle Book Rental business. I missed several classes, not to mention practices swimming fast. When the day came for our long distance swim, I did not beat the athlete, but I did push him. I came in with the second-best time right behind his. I got a B in that class for the usual reason, missing classes, which, because this was a Lifeguard class, was more serious than a normal class. Coach Sickles would point that out to me after I did poorly on the final written exam. Have you ever seen how thick that damn Red Cross Lifeguard Manual is? I had a difficult time reading that much material on any subject. I did get my Senior Lifeguard certificate though. I had passed all the rescue requirements.

I can't remember who the teacher was who taught my bowling class. All I do remember about him is that he looked like the typical male bowler in any bowling alley in the country. Let's say, he looked like he'd had way too many beers in his life. I had taught myself to bowl using the arrows on the lanes, but wanted to learn how to deliver the ball with a hook. Well, that didn't happen, but I still got a B in the class. Yes, for the same reasons, I missed classes and did not do well on the written exams. (Seems to be a pattern here.)

My Introduction to Law Enforcement was taught by a man who had turned his life around. He was a convicted felon but attended school both in prison and outside it to get his advance degrees in law enforcement so he could teach. Later, as a Public Defender, I learned that the word "felon" doesn't just cover those individuals who commit heinous crimes like murder, aggravated assault or battery, rape, etc., but it also includes drug charges, tax evasion, check fraud, forgery, etc. In other words, all felonies are not the same, so all citizens with a felony record don't automatically need to be feared.

We were given an assignment: to read the book *Serpico*, written by Peter Maas. We were not required to read the actual book but were told to buy the cliff notes version of the book. That was fine with me. After we had finished reading the book, the professor opened the class up to discussion. He asked the class, "How many of you feel what Serpico did, informing on his corrupt colleagues, was the right thing to do?" My hand shot up. I was sitting in the front row because I had gotten to that day's class late. As I turned my head to see who else had raised their hands, I saw that there wasn't another hand in the air. Then the professor asked, "How many here felt that Serpico did the wrong thing by informing on his fellow police officers?" The rest of the class all raised their hands, every last one of them.

Who were these students? They were either active Louisiana law enforcement personnel or people who wanted to be in law enforcement. A friend of mine, attorney Mary Howell, would later sue the New Orleans Police Department for police misconduct so severe that, at times, she feared for her client's safety and her own. I figured, at that time, the New York police had nothing on the New Orleans police department.

The debate was on! Me against the class. The professor kept a neutral position, but I could tell he thought that Serpico's actions were the right thing to do. A few of the comments from my classmates were: "If Serpico felt that way, he should have left the police department instead of turning on his colleagues." "He should have taken the money and given the money away if he didn't want it."

I found it shocking that these comments were coming from present and future law enforcement officers. I tried to counter these statements by my classmates. My argument was that, in order for citizens to trust their police, they must believe those police are not corrupt. As the discussion continued, I pointed out that I believed that corrupt police hurt the social fabric of society even more than the criminals. That went over like a lead balloon. To say the least, no minds were changed in that debate.

That class and another law enforcement class I would take later at LSU introduced me to several Baton Rouge officers, both present and future, with whom I became friends. I definitely believe it helped that I had served in Viet Nam for two tours in a Navy IUWG unit

The grades I made that summer made it possible for me to finally be removed from scholastic probation.

## THE BILL OF STUDENT RIGHTS

As the *Reveille* (July 29, 1975) reported:

> The Summer Executive Council approved a committee of 13 students that will revise the Bill of Student Rights. Herman Garner, ombudsman, will chair the committee and assistant ombudsman Randy Davidson will be assistant chairman. Other committee members are, Jackie Burnett, Lorraine Shelton, Lloyd Dore, Ed Butts, Dian Galatas, Betsy Bennitt, Ted Schirmer, Charlotte Portero, Badrig Maroujkian, Amit Sen and Mike Chittom.

Several of those students belonged to either YAF or College Republicans. I was the only PSA member on the committee. I had been asked personally by Herman to join the committee. Despite my other commitments, I thought this project very important and agreed to serve.

The Bill of Student Rights committee was broken into four sub-committees, Freedom of Expression; Right to Privacy; Campus Organization; and Disciplinary Sanctions. This last sub-committee was to study the disciplinary actions taken against students. As Herman pointed out, "We feel punishments are out of line with the offenses." I would find out just how "out of line with the offenses" the administration's disciplinary actions were when I ended up in front of the administration's Disciplinary Committee.

I worked on this bill with representative student leaders from all of the organizations at LSU. I was shocked at how far behind other universities LSU was concerning student equalities, rights, and freedoms. I saw the new Bill of Student Rights as going a long way toward addressing the long history of discriminatory practices by a certain segment of LSU's student body against minorities, and protecting students' right of freedom of expression, the right to protest, and the freedom of association or disassociation with campus organizations. We were attempting to drag LSU into the present, to ensure that LSU's students were treated the same as college students were treated in the rest of the United States. At a time when eighteen-year-olds were being drafted and had the right to vote, at LSU they were being treated like children.

This committee eventually drafted a Bill of Student Rights that was submitted to a vote by the student body in the 1976 spring elections.

## A COMMISSION TO STUDY
## THE PROPOSED BOOK RENTAL

Due to the great response of the student body, the Book Rental received hundreds of books donated to it at the end of the 1975 spring semester. Adding those books we already had nearly tripled our stock of textbooks to rent for the fall semester. PSA had voted not to run the Book Rental that summer.

The newly donated books had to be recorded into our inventory list, and Book Rental stickers had to be placed across their covers to have them ready to rent in the fall. Since so many of the students, who had been working on the Book Rental during the prior semester, had gone home or were working, the few of us left attending school that summer had our work cut out for us.

That summer in the State Legislature, a bill was introduced at the request of Mike Chittom, a Young Americans for Freedom student, which would prohibit both mandatory membership in the SGA and the collection of mandatory membership fees as part of tuition and registration fees. This issue would take up most of SGA president Paul Benoist's time that summer.

The *Summer Reveille* section "On the Spot" asked the question: "There is a bill in the state legislature that would eliminate mandatory fees for the SGA. Do you think the bill should pass?" Out of the eleven students whose responses were printed, ten students said "yes" they thought the bill should pass. Only one student said "no." In my opinion, it was a clear sign that a lot of students felt the SGA did not deserve to receive mandatory student fees every semester while doing little to nothing for the student body to earn those fees.

A front-page article in the *Reveille* (July 29, 1976), titled "Book rental program to begin again in fall," mentioned that:

> The Book Rental program will begin operating again at the start of the fall semester, said an original organizer of the program Monday. Student Ted Schirmer said the Book Rental will operate the same as previously, renting books for $3 per course, not to exceed $12 for any one student. He said the program did not operate this summer because the Student Government Association was to set up a commission to study the plan. Schirmer said he gave the remaining $1,100 of the $1,500 previously allocated for the program back to SGA to fund the commission.

The commission was never set up that summer, but a spokesman in the SGA office said it was hoped the study would eventually begin. A front-page article in the *Summer Reveille* (July 31, 1975), titled "No Book Rental study attributed to apathy," stated:

> The Book Rental commission appointments were not made this summer due to a general lack of student interest, particularly on the part of the originators of the program, said Student Government Association President Paul Benoist

> Wednesday....The commission charter calls for two stu-
> dents from the original program. Benoist said except for
> Ted Schirmer, the originators of the program did not ex-
> press interest in being on the commission, nor did Schirmer
> or they recommend anyone for the commission to Benoist.

That was more BS. Lack of interest wasn't what was holding up the creation of the commission. If you ask me, Benoist had no desire to set up the commission. In fact, Benoist had only "decided tentatively on five of the student appointments" and "they have not yet been notified." So that left four openings on the commission, not one, and Benoist didn't think it was his job to try to recruit members. What the hell did he think his job as SGA president was anyway, to sit and wait while collecting his SGA paycheck?

The summer semester turned out to be as frustrating as the spring semester, especially with the *Reveille* pulling out all the stops in the staff's efforts to kill the Book Rental referendum. It was lucky that I had the Huey P. Long swimming pool in which I could work out my frustrations.

# Fall Semester, 1975

## NEW SUPPORT FOR THE BOOK RENTAL PROGRAM

In the fall of 1975, I enrolled in five courses, General Anthropology, Basic Tennis (hey, what can I say? I enjoyed my HPRE classes that summer), the Philosophy class Religions of the World (I was still trying to find a spiritual system to believe in), Fundamental Issues in Politics, and, once again, Elementary Spanish. (One thing about me, I rarely give up on something I think is important and getting an A in Spanish to offset that F was very important to me.)

Because of all the demands on my time from the many issues and organizations I would get involved with that semester, I had to drop my Philosophy class. That class had a lot of reading plus, the dagger in my heart, papers to write. But I still managed to stay as a full-time student. At the end of the semester, I was able to pass all the remainder of my classes. I got a C in General Anthropology (I really enjoyed Anthropology), an A in Tennis, despite not being very good at serving, a B in Fundamental Issues in Politics, then (drum beat please) an A in Elementary Spanish. I would tell people that by then I could teach the first 12 chapters in Elementary Spanish.

Those grades raised my grade point average to 2.308. I know, for most students, a little over a C average wasn't something to brag about, but, for me, that was great. I had never been more than a C student in my entire life. If I could have done cartwheels I would have. Just finally getting that A in Spanish was worth a cartwheel or two.

With the start of the fall semester, there was a new *Reveille* staff and a new approach to the way reporters and other staff covered the Book Rental. At first it was just the coverage itself. As a *Reveille* (August 29, 1975) article, titled "Large selection available from Book Rental today," that appeared in one of the first fall editions, stated:

> The nonprofit-Book Rental will operate from 8 A.M. to 4 P.M. Friday in the Barataria Room on the third floor of the Union....Ted Schirmer, organizer of the Book Rental, said there was a very large selection of history books available along with many texts for other courses....Schirmer said the Book Rental is now accepting book donation and is looking for volunteers to work with the program. Last semester about 300 people used the Book Rental, said Schirmer, and at least the same number is expected this fall. He said the Book Rental has proven that it is needed. He hopes a referendum will pass this semester which will fund the Book Rental so services can be expanded.

That article was as good as an ad. What really drove home the reality that the changing of the guard at the *Reveille* would have a positive impact on the relationship with the Book Rental was an editorial by Mike Konvicka, the editor of the *Reveille* for that semester. Titled "Book Rental," the editorial, which appeared in the *Reveille* (September 3, 1975), said:

> In case you haven't been able to find it, the Book Rental is located on the top floor of the Union in the Barataria Room. The Book Rental will charge $3 per course or a total of $12 for all your books. Of course, you might not get a book in mint condition, and eventually, you'll have to give it back, but don't you think that for the amount of time you use it and the amount of money you're paying for it, that it just might be worth it?

That editorial was 180 degrees from the way Ms. Smith, the former *Reveille* editor, had spoken of the Book Rental. A new day had dawned for the relationship between the Book Rental and the *Reveille*.

Finally, after my consistent prodding and visiting the SGA offices, Benoist gave the Student Assembly names for the Book Rental commission members. At the meeting of the commission, we quickly got down to the nuts and bolts of the Book Rental. In a *Reveille* (October 24, 1975) article, titled "Budget, methods of buying discussed by Book Rental," it was reported:

> Commission member presented a rough budget based on an enrollment of 25,000 full-time students. The commission has proposed the rental program be funded by a one dollar voluntary student fee assessment during its first year.

Because of the delays in appointing the commission members, we were unable to get a report in front of the Student Assembly before the end of the fall semester, thus preventing the referendum from being placed in front of the student body for a vote in the fall 1975 election.

We would have to wait until the spring 1976 election to try to get the Student Assembly to place the referendum on the ballot.

## I AM ELECTED TO THE STUDENT ASSEMBLY

A *Reveille* (September 10, 1975) article, titled "Filing open for positions on Assembly," announced: "Filing is now open for 25 SGA representatives to be elected Sept. 26." I didn't even read this article. I had no interest in becoming an SGA representative. I had never even voted in an SGA election. I considered the SGA a Mickey Mouse organization. Little did I suspect others had different plans for me.

A later *Reveille* (September 19, 1975) article stated that, "Seventy-eight candidates are campaigning for the 28 vacancies on the Student Assembly." Well, not all 78. Unknown to me, John Grace had put my name in. The article listed the names of the candidates alphabetically and, down among those names starting with an S, was Ted Schirmer. I did not see this article. I was in the dark that my name had been entered in the SGA elections.

The night of the election, I was leaving the Student Union when I ran into John Grace and Bill Newchurch coming up the steps of the Union. When they saw me, Grace said, "Congratulations, Ted. You have been elected to the SGA Assembly."

"What?" I asked. "I didn't run for the Assembly."

But John Grace explained that they had put my name in to run for a position as an Off-Campus Representative. That stopped me in my tracks. He and Bill Newchurch had just come from the ballot counting and assured me that I had won. The next funny thing I heard was that the two of them were in a run-off for the remaining Off-Campus position. Grace would drop out of the run-off to allow Newchurch to have the seat on the Assembly since he was to graduate that December.

A *Reveille* (September 26, 1975) article, titled "SGA Student Assembly elected," listed the names of the students who had won their elections. Sure enough, there was my name as one of the winners of an Off-

Campus Representative position. I was not drafted into the military; I volunteered. But I was drafted into the SGA.

Elected to the Assembly, huh? After thinking about it that night, I decided that, by being on the inside of the SGA, I might have a better chance of getting the Book Rental approved.

An article on the front page of the *Reveille* (November 6, 1975), titled "Assembly circus performs again: SGA approves lobby liaison," stated that, "The Assembly also appropriated $663 for an SGA Leadership Lab to take place in a state park in Mississippi in the early spring. The Assembly sponsored the lab in lieu of a banquet. Last year their $1,000 banquet was met with heavy criticism."

I voted against the appropriation of money for a Leadership Lab, but later I was talked into going by Jerry Giddens and John Grace. University administrators who also participated included Kerry Pourciau, SGA president from 1972–73; Dr. Myron Mohr, director of the Crisis Intervention Center; Chancellor Paul Murrill; Union Director, Don Phillips, who showed the film *Twelve Angry Men*; and of course, Randy Gurie.

That was the first time I attended that type of an event. I made several friends there, plus I learned a fair amount about student government and the people in it.

I had already learned a great deal just from attending a few Student Assembly meetings the previous semester. I made it a point (no pun intended) to learn *Robert's Rules of Order*. I had seen how some of the Assembly members were able to kill measures brought before the Assembly, like pulling the Book Rental referendum off the ballot, by using parliamentary procedures. I had never belonged to any organization that followed *Robert's Rules of Order*, but I quickly learned to appreciate their importance, both in keeping order and in getting things done by individuals with different interests and points of view.

A number of us brought marijuana with us to the Leadership lab. Driving in a school bus up to the Mississippi state park, where the retreat was to be held, a number of us got stoned. This included the bus driver. Jerry, the only one with a chauffeur's license, was driving the bus. After stopping at a rest stop, we all piled back onto the school bus and hit the road. Soon, however, we were smelling something burning. We kept yelling for Jerry to stop, that something was burning. He blew it off until smoke filled the bus, and he had to stop. Jerry discovered that he had been driving the bus for over 20 miles with the emergency brake on.

## SPORTS EDITOR OF THE *GUMBO*

When Richard Hogan, the newly selected editor for the upcoming *Gumbo,* the LSU yearbook, approached me at the fall 1975 registration about being the sports editor, I thought he was kidding. To make me, the long haired hippie political activist that I was, the sports editor in a sports crazed college like LSU was mind blowing. But on second thought, being sports editor meant that I would get a press pass to attend all sporting events at LSU and away. Truly the football gods were smiling on me.

To be clear, the LSU student body was mostly football crazed. The students were not that much into LSU's track, baseball, and basketball teams. Those teams wouldn't start their winning ways until a few years later. And even though most LSU fans wouldn't openly admit it, if a Tiger team wasn't winning, they quickly lost interest in it. With the 1975 Tiger football team ending the season with its worst record in twenty years, I might have not gone to all the games either, except for the fact I was required to as sports editor of the *Gumbo.*

Notwithstanding the fact that LSU's 1975 football team's season was going to end badly, at the time when Richard offered me the job, I couldn't believe my luck. I was sure coach Cholly Mac would turn the team around.

I was excited that I would be sitting in the press box. I didn't even have a clue where the press box was located in Tiger Stadium, but I did realize immediately that being a sports reporter meant that I wouldn't have to arrive hours ahead of time in order to get a good seat. There would be one waiting for me. During that 1975 fall semester, due to the many things I was getting involved with, time became a valuable commodity for me, so not having to get to the game two or three hours before the gates even opened was great.

Like most fans, I had no idea how plays were called. I only saw the team from a fan's viewpoint. Being a sports reporter was going to change that. As a reporter, I would be able to go to the press conferences after the game and ask questions of the coaches. In addition, I could go into the players' locker room and ask questions. I would get a look, a small look, but none the less a look, at who was responsible for calling the plays on game day.

When Richard asked me if I wanted to be the *Gumbo's* sport editor, I wanted to be completely honest with him, so I told him in the clearest language I could, "I can't write!" He seemed not to be bothered with that, saying, "We'll have someone help you when it's time to do the writing." Here I was, about to write for another publication, as I had done for *The Word* when I covered the Celebration of Life festival, while having probably no more than a 7th grade education in English, if that. It was another example of how I appeared more educated than I was. But I sure in the hell wasn't going to look a gift horse in the mouth. I mean, refuse a chance to sit in the press box at LSU football games, are you kidding me!

When the time came for me to turn in my written material, I teamed up with Barry Lefleur, who would be my collaborator on the *Reveille* "The Mad Hatter" editorials. We wrote so extensively on each football game that we filled up pages and pages of material. But the only words Richard used in the *Gumbo* were, "The 1975 Football season was LSU's worst in 20 years." The *Gumbo* that year had only four pages on the football team. The four additional pages that normally would have been set aside for the football season were included in an earlier part of the *Gumbo* as blank pages with a sentence at the bottom of the first blank page stating, "The next four pages are dedicated to the apathetic majority of LSU." I always felt those four blank pages spoke volumes about the majority of students at LSU.

I attended every football and basketball game that was played on campus. Both of those sports had losing seasons that year. There was a big difference in how the coaches handled questions from me after a game, especially the questions I had for them after their teams lost.

LSU football coach Charles McClendon (Cholly Mac) ruled the roost among other coaches on the LSU campus. This was not just among the coaches on his football staff but among the other sports coaches as well. Football was king, not only on LSU's campus but throughout the state of Louisiana. LSU football coaches were major celebrities in the state—well, that is if the football team was winning. And Cholly Mac's teams had started on a downward spiral to mediocrity in 1974 with a 5–5–1 record. Then this was followed by the 1975 record of 5–6, the first losing football season since 1957.

Ole Miss was LSU's biggest rival in the SEC in the '50s and '60s. That rivalry would only start to cool off after the Archie Manning era at Ole Miss ended in 1971, but it was still plenty hot during my time at LSU. Even though both the LSU and Ole Miss football teams had losing records when they played in 1975, because of their past history, the game was being covered by a number of sports reporters. The game was played at the Mississippi Veterans Memorial Stadium in Jackson, Mississippi, and I was told that the stadium's press box was overflowing with reporters. When I showed up with my long hair and hippie attire and a LSU Sports Pass, I was immediately hustled over to the LSU's coaches' box. The man kept telling me there was no room in the press box, even though I didn't get a chance to confirm if that was true. I was told that I would have to sit with the LSU coaching staff. As I stood there looking at the coaches looking at me with stunned expressions on their faces, I didn't realize that I was about to hear and see how LSU plays were really called during an LSU football game.

The game didn't disappoint. It was a typical LSU/Ole Miss football game, a tough defensive game by both teams. LSU had the ball and was leading 13 to 10 going into the final minutes of the game. All we had to do was get one first down, then run out the game clock. LSU, at that time, had two great running backs: Terry Robiskie and Charles Alexander. On the first play, LSU handed the ball off to one of these running backs, I believe it was Robiskie. Ole Miss blitzed all of their linebackers, stopping Robiskie in his tracks for no gain. On second down, everyone in our box could tell that Ole Miss was going to have an all-out blitz again. Hell, they weren't even trying to hide the fact. Coach Amedee, the offensive coordinator, yelled, "Screen pass, Screen pass.!" Nope, it was another run play, and it was stopped for little to no gain. By the third down, Coach Amedee was beside himself, yelling, "They're blitzing again, throw any kind of short pass to counter the blitz." Nope, not Cholly Mac. He was as stubborn as he was conservative in his play calling. He tried to run the ball again. We were stopped again with little to no gain. We punted and Ole Miss marched down the field and scored the winning touchdown in the final minute of the game. I had suspected that Cholly Mac was the real play caller for the offense, not the offensive coordinator, Coach Amedee. At the Ole Miss game, I had witnessed it. In my opinion, we lost the Ole Miss game, and many others, because of conservative play calling by Charlie McClendon.

At the press conference, after raising my hand several times, Coach McClendon finally called on me. I stated that I had been in the coaches' box during the game and, during that last series of downs for LSU, I heard Coach Amedee call over and over again for a screen pass or any short pass because Ole Miss was blitzing on every down. "Why didn't you call for a short pass to counter the Ole Miss blitz?" I could tell that my question got the attention of every sportswriter present. There was what is referred to as "a pregnant pause." Then, to the surprise of all of us, McClendon got up and walked out of the press conference. A number of the sports reporters were really pissed off, especially the ones who didn't get a chance to ask a question.

Since the other reporters in the room earned their livelihood by asking McClendon questions, I decided I would not ask any more questions at future press conferences. But I did make sure that McClendon could see me sitting there. All through the press conferences, I didn't take my eyes off him, but I never raised my hand. I thought, by the way he was sitting, he was prepared to get up and leave the moment I raised my hand.

LSU's basketball coach, Dale Brown, was a completely different coach and man than Charles McClendon. As the *Gumbo* sports editor, I sat courtside during all the basketball games. Just as in football, all the sports writers would get the first half stats sheet. I used to love that because I could check on the number of fouls each player had and who was scoring the most points for both teams. Since my seat was courtside, I could usually watch Coach Brown as he coached his team during the game.

After the games, Coach Brown would talk with his team, then meet with the sports reporters. He would pull up a chair and sit among us like he was among friends. When I would ask a question, it felt as if I were having a one-on-one with Coach Brown. In contrast to the way Coach McClendon reacted when he saw a long haired hippie looking person sitting in the press conference, Coach Brown didn't seem fazed at all. This attitude carried over to when I would ask him a question. Unlike Coach McClendon, who acted as if it were drudgery to have to take questions when LSU lost a football game, Coach Brown, while not happy with the loss, would immediately put you at ease with his friendliness and demeanor. Even when the question was about a decision he made or didn't make during a game, he would be open and honest in his answers. His sincerity and care for his players showed through at every press conference I attended that season.

When the track season first started, I missed the first meets due to my involvement in student politics and covering LSU basketball games. Then I got a message that Coach May, the LSU track coach, wanted to see me. My first thought was that he was going to inquire why I had not been covering the track meets. Instead, he wanted to discuss Charles Alexander, LSU's phenomenal freshman football running back.

Coach May told me that he had called Coach McClendon, who was in Alabama on a duck hunting and recruiting trip, to ask for his permission to talk with Charlie Alexander about running track for him.

Coach May said that Coach McClendon told him he didn't care. Apparently, Alexander had signed an athletic scholarship for both football and track right out of high school. Coach May spoke with Alexander, and he was very excited about running in a track meet. I believe Alexander came in third, which wasn't bad since he had not been training for the race. When McClendon returned to Baton Rouge and heard that Alexander had run in the track meet, he called Coach May and started screaming at him, ordering him to never talk to one of his football players ever again. That one meet was the only meet Charlie Alexander ever ran for LSU.

I became too involved in campus politics to cover the LSU spring sports teams, so I resigned as sports editor. When the *1976 Gumbo* was published, I wasn't given the title of sports editor.

### WRITING "MAD HATTER" EDITORIALS

After the 1976 spring semester had started, I was asked by the news editors of the *Reveille* if I would be interested in writing a weekly editorial for the paper. I was told I could write about anything that I thought might be of interest to the rest of the student body. I got the impression that they were very interested in giving me a larger forum to speak out in more detail on student issues than I had at the Alley. I told them I would get back to them. I asked my friend Barry Lefleur if he would be interested in helping me write a weekly editorial. He agreed, so I told one of the editors, either Marti Quinn or Mike Farley, that I would be happy to write a weekly editorial for the paper.

I tried to think of a catchy title for the opinion piece. I decided that, since I was known for the WWI campaign hat that I wore everywhere, I would take that as my handle "The Mad Hatter." That was long before former football coach Les Miles got that nickname at LSU.

My first editorial was titled "The mad hatter—Reflections on leadership" and concerned the LSU-SGA Leadership Conference held at Percy Quinn State Park near McComb, Mississippi on January 16th and 17th. The lab was organized by Randy Gurie, Assistant Dean of Men.

146

That leadership conference was the impetus that led me to run for SGA president. That it was Randy Gurie who had organized the conferences was ironic because he became one of my major adversaries in the administration when I became SGA president.

Since I had made the decision to enter the SGA presidential race later that semester, I took the opportunity to write a small autobiography of myself in that first editorial. I told how the fall of 1970 had been my first semester at LSU. Like many thousands of freshmen, I didn't know what to expect. Earlier that year I had been discharged from the Navy and, as anyone who has been in the military knows, there is, aside from prison, no other environment so rigid and inflexible. I explained that after living within such a system for such a long time (four years), I came not only to cherish the freedoms I enjoyed as a United States citizen, but also to question how and why we have such freedoms.

I became involved in a fight to change the grooming standards in the College of Education. I pointed out that, after fighting this same conservatism in the Navy for four years, I was upset to witness it in a public institution attended by United States citizens, who took no oath relinquishing their rights when they applied for entrance to the university. This prompted my initial involvement with students' rights at LSU, and my involvement in student activities had grown with each semester.

Then I went on to explain how I had come to attend the LSU-SGA Leadership Conference. The program performed a very important service—it allowed students, who had in common their activities of involvement, to spend a day and an evening together learning about each other. In many cases, we were actually introducing ourselves to each other for the first time. I felt I came to know and respect several of my fellow students. Indeed, I became friends with a half dozen of them. All of this led to better communication between my fellow students and myself in the future.

I congratulated Randy Gurie on all the hard work he put into making the conference a success. Then I expressed my hope that the students who attended the conference realized the benefits of getting to know each other, but, most importantly, I hoped that the gap between the student body and the administration, the gap between what students needed or wanted and what the administration was willing to allow, had narrowed. I spelled out that we, as students, must realize that the administration was comprised of people who were being paid to operate a large university by maintaining a smoothly running system. That was no simple task, and it occupied the major part of each administrator's day. It was, therefore, the student leaders' responsibility to investigate and make known the students' demands for a more perfect system. The burden of pointing out the bureaucracy's faults lay with the student body as we bore the brunt of its imperfections.

My first editorial received very positive comments from both students and administrators. I felt I had made a positive first move in my attempt to explain who I was and how I felt: that, at certain times, student leaders had to stand up to the administration because they had inherently different objectives.

On January 27th, my second editorial, titled "The cost of freedom," appeared in the *Reveille*. This editorial was inspired by the outrage that both students and faculty were expressing over the State Legislature's decision to give $5 million for an expansion of Tiger Stadium (with a total projected cost being over $11 million) while LSU's academic needs were being neglected. As the 1976 *Gumbo* pointed out:

> In the last five years, this campus has experienced a 33% increase in enrollment, a gain of approximately 8,000 students since 1970. The campus now finds itself with sorely inadequate classroom space....The university now requires the departments to schedule 45% of their classes outside of prime time (8:30 A.M. to 2:30 P.M.). Spreading the classes throughout the day presents difficulties to those students who work or would like to work part-time. On the academic

side, many students are not able to schedule classes vital to their curriculum because there are physically not enough rooms for them. Three curricula—the Music School, the Architecture, and the Landscape Architecture departments— are now limiting their enrollment due to lack of space.

Considering the fact that LSU sat on the site of a previous plantation, I decided to use the two classes of slaves on a southern plantation, the field slave and the house slave, as an analogy for students and faculty. In the editorial, I admitted that, "Considering the extreme harshness of our past system of slavery, some may cringe at the following analogy, but it is a useful one." I was attempting to address the need for students and faculty to unite and warn that, until they do, very little can be accomplished on the issue of improving the academic side of the campus. What a roar their voices could be if only the field hands would stand with the house servants.

All of this effort was too little and too late to stop the funding of the stadium expansion over the academic needs of the campus.

My next editorial was titled "On jocks…and jerks." I was sure it was going to surprise many people on campus due to the fact that I, a long haired hippie activist who looked more like he belonged on the campus of Berkeley than LSU, was coming to the defense of LSU jocks. What were the student athletes' transgressions that would require someone like me to come to their defense? They were simply exercising their constitutional right to petition grievances to the powers that be, in this case, Coach McClendon, and getting a great deal of blow back from other students for it.

The *Reveille* (January 23, 1975) published an article, titled "Broussard Hall food protested by jocks," that reported on a group of football players who presented a petition to Coach McClendon calling for an increase in "the quality of preparation" of meals at Broussard Hall. The petition stated that the athletes needed to give their full attention to "studying and their athletic practice periods without the impediments of digestive upsets."

As the article reported, "McClendon said after the meeting that they were complaining about "a little too much grease in the chili." This was in reference to complaints about a Monday meal. McClendon added that everyone's taste buds are different and that he liked a "little extra grease in his chili." McClendon further stated, "that he saw no use in the petition" and "would be glad if the petition brought a serious problem to his attention."

That was the McClendon I had gotten to know when I was attending press conferences last semester. He dismissed those he disagreed with or didn't respect.

On campus, non-athlete students started having fun with what became known as the "Greasy Chili" protest. The other students saw LSU student athletes as a spoiled, privileged class of students who had no room to complain about their conditions. The *Reveille* soon received numerous letters ridiculing the jocks. On top of those letters, an editorial in the *Reveille,* written by the Editor Jere Longman, titled "Hold the Pickles," stated that the petition "was baseless and unfounded."

Mr. Longman than fanned the flames by stating that "athletes are the most pampered of all special interest groups on campus. In addition to receiving free tuition and room and board, athletes get scheduling and registering priorities as well as no-cost tutorial service. Few, if any, other students are so lucky." Then Mr. Longman pointed out that one of last year's football programs had a story about what was served to the athletes. Indeed, the jocks were served food that was, he wrote, "enough to make your mouth run like a river." I had no doubt that LSU's athletes ate better than other students on a meal plan. But he didn't stop there for he wrote, "If the athletes really wanted to complain, why didn't they protest against mandatory residence in Broussard Hall or against curfew restrictions? But as far as meals go, the only thing they can legitimately protest is too much good food."

Then came the concluding statement that was a stake in the hearts of all LSU football players who had to suffer through a losing season: "About the only things that appear to be greasy are their hands on Saturday nights." Ouch!

I had a close-up look at how last semester's football season went down and who, in my opinion, was to blame for it: McClendon. I wanted to come to the defense of LSU athletes, especially the football players. I felt the real issue had less to do with whether or not the food was good or bad. It was the right of student athletes to speak out on an issue affecting them and not be ridiculed and attacked by their fellow students for speaking out.

In that vein, I submitted the editorial titled "On jocks . . . and jerks" that appeared in the *Reveille* (February 3, 1976). It read:

> Why would a student want to attack a group of enslaved students for petitioning? Enslaved? Yes, the jocks are enslaved: no freedom of speech, no freedom of curriculum. In fact, they have many more restrictions than other undergraduate students....The athletes petitioned (a right sanctioned by real democratic individuals) to have quality food. Does anyone deserve less? An athlete requires a good and regulated diet. He should also have the right of every student: to petition, to free speech, and to participate in all fields (other sports also, Charlie Mac) of the university. Yes, Charlie Mac's personal policy is to pressure football players into ignoring all other varsity sports. This and lousy food are a lot to take, much less suffer in the silence imposed by the Charlie Mac gag rule. Instead of standing behind these fellow students all the way, the jocks are strapped, and we students hate them and oppose them. Attacking the slaves who have the guts to buck the system is no way to change the system.

I served in Viet Nam with men who were 17 and 18-years-old, the same age as most freshmen in college, who were willing to die for the belief, among others, that the First Amendment gave our citizens the freedom of speech.

You will hear or read a coach or athletic director saying how it's not all about winning, and that their job is to prepare young people for the rest of their lives as good citizens. Well, what are universities teaching these freshmen student athletes when they allow coaches to deny them the right of free speech? If the coaches are concerned about how the freshman student athlete will handle speaking to a reporter, especially one who is looking for a sensational story, then provide a course on how to do an interview with a reporter. Sure, this will require some extra effort outside of that coach's specific sport, but, I ask you, would that not be a better lesson to teach a young, talented athlete who may be dealing with reporters his or her whole sports career, than taking their First Amendment right away from them the moment they step on a state university's campus?

## REFERENDUM ON THE BOOK RENTAL PROGRAM

In January of 1976, I made another push to get the Book Rental referendum on the ballot. At the Progressive Student Alliance meeting on January 15th, I outlined once again, how the Book Rental would be operated. A *Reveille* (January 16, 1976) article, titled "Referendum sought by PSA to finance Book Rental plan," reported that Asst. Professor Hilary Zaunbrecher of the Accounting Department, had found that both the plan and the budget for the program, if the referendum passed, were sound and workable. I explained that once the Book Rental was on "solid ground" the management of the Rental would be turned over to qualified salaried personnel. In the event that the student body voted down the referendum, it would show that not enough students wanted the Book Rental and that would deeply affect the future of the program.

As of January, the Book Rental had 2,300 books that had been donated by participating students, but this was nowhere near enough books to serve even the freshman class attending LSU. The Book Rental needed the seed money that the $1 fee for a full academic year would provide in order to operate at a high level.

At the first meeting of the SGA Assembly on January 22, 1976, Ross Little, chairman of the Rules Committee, told the Assembly that his committee would present a favorable report on the Nonprofit Book

Rental. He further reported that the committee would probably recommend a student body referendum to add $1 to student fees for one year to help the Book Rental get started.

Supportive letters to the *Reveille* plus the positive report from the SGA Nonprofit Book Rental Committee and Rules Committee seemed to quiet the voices of dissent from fellow students. After a long fight, it appeared that all the hard work by the members of PSA, and later the SGA, to get a Book Rental on LSU's campus was finally about to come to fruition. The Book Rental referendum was going to be a part of the spring semester's SGA election on March 18th.

Even though we had won the fight, the administration was not throwing in the towel. In what appeared to be an attempt to affect the student vote on the upcoming referendum, Chancellor Paul Murrill gave an interview in a *Reveille* (February 26, 1976) article titled "Murrill says SGA should be realistic." Murrill felt that the SGA didn't:

> ...have the "resources or manpower to operate" an effective Book Rental program." He stated that SGA should focus on getting the university's book operations to operate in such a way to prevent practices that caused students to be ripped off. Furthermore, he thought SGA should "encourage more competition in the book stores off campus....[SGA] must realize where they stand and select a role within their capabilities" to be successful.

I was confident that the students would vote for the $1 addition to their fees. But even if they didn't approve the referendum, at least the students were being given the opportunity to vote for or against a Book Rental.

# Spring Semester, 1976

## ORGANIZING THE CAMPUS POLITICAL UNION (CPU)

While serving as a member of the Assembly, I started thinking of running for SGA president. I felt I could get more done for the student body than the past and present SGA presidents. Unlike other students seeking the position of SGA president, I had no plans for a political future in Louisiana after LSU. Hell, one look at my appearance alone would make that obvious I would think. Therefore, not being motivated to pad my political resume for future campaigns for political office in the state, I could be a much more effective fighter for the student body.

Still, by watching other SGA presidents struggle, I fully realized that I couldn't get much done as president without support from the Assembly. Having been a member of the Assembly for a year and having attended the Leadership Conference in Mississippi, I had made a number of new friends, who were way more politically savvy than I was. I started discussing my thoughts on running for SGA president and the idea of establishing a political party on campus similar to the Democratic and Republican parties. The goal would be similar to that of the Progressive Students Alliance when it attempted to "swamp" the Assembly with PSA members in the fall elections of 1971. At that time, PSA was more of a student activist organization than a student political party. I believed that, to bring about real change in student government, there had to be more progressive students in the Assembly and the executive branch. But to win more seats in the Assembly and the executive branch, more progressive students at LSU had to unite.

My years as a student activist at LSU had taught me that there were thousands of likeminded students on LSU's campus. All that was needed was to organize them into an effective block vote as the Greeks had done with their members on campus. This realization led me to team up with my new politically active friends, like Jerry Giddens,

154

among others, to organize a political party to counter the Greeks and hopefully get us all elected into student government offices.

The *Reveille* (January 30, 1976) article, titled "Schirmer advocates reformation for SGA," covered my beginning efforts to win control of SGA. The article reported that, at a meeting in the Union Board Room, "Ted Schirmer set up guidelines for a political party to be organized on campus to get more competent and effective leaders in SGA."

I characterized "the present system of SGA elections as a popularity contest in which fraternities band together to elect one of their friends." I pointed out that the university workers, after a long fought battle, finally got the right to unionize, making the "students...the only group still unorganized on campus." I told the students at the meeting that "I believe organization is the only way to get a voice on campus."

I stressed that the organization would be open to all students. I believed that "keeping membership open would prevent extremism in the group." This was despite the fact that there were those who thought I was an extremist. I brought up the fact that "Students feel that SGA is a 'Mickey Mouse operation' and SGA members are uninspired by students who they feel are apathetic." Jerry and I "urged those in attendance to apply for the 13 openings in the Assembly." "Once we have set a precedent for positive action, we can grow and provide more services for the students."

At the following Free Speech Alley, students were upset, rightly so, about the State Legislature canceling funding for several academic building projects while funding the Stadium expansion. I too was very upset by what happened. The *Reveille* (January 29, 1976) reported me saying that "the state was giving the LSU athletic department the whole loaf of bread and taking back the crumbs promised to education at the same time." I stated that the $12.7 million dollars allocated for educational buildings had been dropped "while a bond sale to finance the controversial stadium had been recommended. It's obvious this university just wants to produce jocks."

I then encouraged students to organize some form of union to give students a voice in the determination of spending priorities in the state.

I urged students to attend a meeting in the Union to organize such an association. Regretfully, these last statements about the meeting didn't make the paper. Only about a dozen students attended the first meeting. Most of those were students who have been involved in the Book Rental, members of the Progressive Student Alliance (PSA), and a good number of SGA Assembly members.

At this meeting on February 11th, Matt Barker, University College representative, suggested the name, Campus Political Union, for the group, saying the name would suit the purpose of the organization and would not be exclusive of any group.

It didn't take long after the forming of CPU that the first attacks on me showed up. In the *Reveille* (February 13, 1976), an editorial by David Dodson, titled "Reporter's commentary—"Schirmer's politics," appeared. In it he stated that in a democratic society, like America's, "it is always recommended to be suspect of altruistic 'big ideals' and 'lofty' intentions and motives." Then he pointed out how I had been fighting against the administration as "a self-styled 'voice in the wilderness'" and "generally making a nuisance of himself." He ended with a warning to the freshman and sophomores on campus, that if I "remain active in campus politics, you're going to have to live with it. And, in Ted's words, 'The people deserve whatever government they have.'" I was getting a good look at what to expect if I did run for SGA president.

At the next CPU meeting, as reported in the *Reveille* (February 25, 1976) article, titled "Schirmer nominated for SGA president," I was nominated as the CPU candidate for SGA president. There were complaints that I had created CPU all for the sole purpose of getting me elected SGA president. One such letter not only claimed that but accused the *Reveille*, by failing to print an article covering one of CPU's meetings, of not printing any negative stories about me. The author of that letter suggested that was happening because I wrote a column for the *Reveille*. In response, the *Reveille* (February 25, 1976) explained why the story of the meeting in question was late in being published. Then it went on to say:

However, the implication that we deliberately censored the story because it contained material adverse to Schirmer is completely unfounded. Had we any intentions of suppressing anti-Schirmer material, we would have printed the story with your remarks deleted. Our job is to report the news of the LSU community. Schirmer makes more news than any other here, excepting perhaps SGA President Paul Benoist. And as long as he continues to do so, his name will appear in this paper. However, since filing has begun for the SGA elections and Schirmer will no doubt become the CPU's candidate, his column will no longer be carried in the *Daily Reveille*.

The campaign was on, with CPU endorsing me for SGA president, Steve Pastorek for legislative vice president, Joe Cleveland for Arts and Sciences representative, Mary Teague for College of Education representative and Gaylord James for University College president. A number of Assembly members were also CPU members.

Luckily, I didn't know about the administration's rule that, to run for SGA president, a student had to have been a full-time student for the last three semesters. Fortunately, in the spring semester of 1975, I had gotten WC's in the two classes when I dropped from 12 hours (full-time) to 6 hours (part-time). A withdraw with a grade goes on a student's college transcript plus the student gets no refund. In some ways, it appears that the student is still considered a full-time student. That threw a monkey wrench in the effort of certain LSU administrators and students trying to disqualify me as a candidate for SGA president.

## MY CAMPAIGN FOR SGA PRESIDENT

Back when I was a truck driver for Barq's Root Beer right after I graduated from Istrouma High School in 1966, I had more in common with the majority of citizens in Louisiana than I did as an LSU student in 1976. When, on July 9, 1966, I volunteered to join the Navy and later volunteered for Viet Nam and served in Inshore Undersea Warfare Group 1, I am sure the vast majority of Louisiana citizens supported that action and continued to do so in 1976. However, I was no longer the same person I had been. I had made a 180 degree turn from who I was due, in large part, to my experience in Viet Nam and also as a result of the changes accruing in the United States during that time.

In order to reinvent oneself, one of the main steps a person needs to take is to associate with individuals who think differently than oneself. I had already started drifting toward the counterculture while still in the Navy. Afterward, while I was trying to live with the fact that I had taken part in the war in Viet Nam, I discovered that I wasn't alone in my search for answers. When I landed in Illinois after my discharge from the Navy, I soon hooked up with fellow Viet Nam veterans who were going through a similar metamorphosis. That helped to convince me I was not alone in searching to understand why we did what we did in Viet Nam. The killing, on May 4, 1970, of the students at Kent State who were demonstrating against the invasion of Cambodia by Nixon and Kissinger, was another brick in the wall sealing off that gung-ho individual I had been in 1966 and allowing the better part of me to blossom, helping me to evolve into the long haired hippie that became a big part of my identity for over a decade. It only took getting released from active duty for those changes to begin to blossom in me.

Remarkably, here I was in full bloom of the new me: hair halfway down my back, patched bell bottom pants decorated with the American flag and peace signs, my WWI Smokey the Bear hat, an openly proud democratic socialist hippie freak. I came out as a democratic socialist while speaking at Free Speech Alley in the '70s.

The *Reveille* (March 17, 1976) published a poll of 100 students who were asked their preference for SGA president in the upcoming SGA election. While 46 students stated they had no preferences yet, a whooping "36 students said they would not bother to vote at all." Of the 18 students who indicated a preference, Ted Schirmer was the favorite with eight." One student stated, "I'll vote for anybody except Ted Schirmer, because he's too much of a hippie freak." That pretty much covered what a lot of Greek and conservative students thought of me. Even the students who supported me stated, "I like him because of his offbeat stance" and experience. Of course, the reason why Greek candidates for SGA president were so hard to beat by non-Greeks was highlighted by one of the students polled. He explained he was going to vote for David Groner "just because he's in a fraternity."

At the first campaign meeting of my savvier political friends, a couple of weeks before filing for the SGA elections was opened, there was a discussion on how to run the campaign. It was agreed that I should speak at all of the fraternity and sorority houses. I was not excited by that idea. I had observed how the Greeks received preferential seating at football games and that the administration allowed their houses to be built on campus. It was my belief that holding a segment of the student body above the other students was elitism. When I expressed this point of view, Kathy Posey stressed the importance of visiting all the fraternity and sorority houses and volunteered to accompany me. I agreed to do this, but I made it clear I was not going to change my beliefs just to win votes. I didn't think I would be getting many votes from the Greeks anyway considering my talks at the Alley about them.

One of the first topics settled was the campaign's slogan that would be put on all the campaign materials. Ron Posey suggested the slogan "Schirmer for Students" since, he said, it summed up, in just three words what my years as a student activist were all about. I liked it.

Later, I went over to Steve Schultz, an artist friend of mine, to ask him to help me draw up a campaign flyer. At that time, one of my favorite bands was the Nitty Gritty Dirt Band. One of my favorite songs of theirs, and also the title of their album, was "Will the Circle be Unbroken." I wanted to use that in my campaign. Steve drew a circle in the middle of the flyer with the campaign's slogan, "SCHIRMER for Students" in the middle. On the outer edge of the circle, Steve drew individual pictures, each depicting a student movement I was or had been involved in. These were the elimination of grooming standards (1971), protests against women's dorm rules (1971–72), Union pay phone elimination (1971), Genesis house (1971), voter registration of students on campus (1972), Nonprofit Book Rental (1974–), re-evaluation of the F grade (1975), and the committee to revise the Bill of Student Rights (1975–). Then there was a last piece that did not quite fit into the circle, asking, "Will the Circle Be Unbroken?" In one corner at the bottom of the flyer was the logo of an old fashion key with the letters CPU, and in the other corner was written in bold letters VOTE!

I loved the way the flyer came out. I felt it really expressed the many things I had been involved with during my time at LSU. But when I showed it to my politically savvier friends, they explained to me that what I really needed was a "push card." I had never heard of this term. I learned that a "push card" is a piece of campaign literature used to introduce a candidate to a voter. It had to be small enough to "push" into the hand of a voter; thus, the term "push card." A push card would have the campaign logo, a picture of the candidate, and information about the candidate and the issues he supported. I said I would try to get one made.

I didn't want to burden Steve again about drawing up a push card since it had taken us all night to put together the flyer. After all, he was a student and, unlike me, he was at LSU first and foremost to get an education.

Fortunately, Richard Hogan, the editor-in-chief of LSU's yearbook, the *Gumbo*, and a couple of other *Gumbo* staff members, came to my rescue. They had the education and experience to compose, design and layout material to be published. It still took us hours in the *Gumbo's* office to decide on the best layout for the push card. I believe it was Richard who came up with the idea of two cards that could be printed on one piece of letter size paper and, when the individual card was folded, "Schirmer for Students" would stick out of a shirt pocket no matter how the person placed the card in their pocket. We used the picture, taken by a *Gumbo* photographer at Free Speech Alley, of me standing on the "soap box." The card was printed on the front and back with each side having three outlined boxes. On one side they were titled, EXPERIENCE, ISSUES and ISSUES, and covered all the issues I had been involved with at LSU. It took two committees to cover what we

160

felt were the issues important to the student body in the spring of 1976. On the other side was the picture of me at Free Speech Alley, a committee dedicated to the Campus Political Union, and a final committee with endorsements of my candidacy. Richard Hogan, Jerry Giddens, and Dana Wicks all provided a statement of endorsement. The last endorsement was from the Arab Club, written in Arabic. I had been a strong supporter of LSU's foreign students on campus, especially the Iranians who were demonstrating against the Shah of Iran. Iran was an American puppet at the time. How times have changed.

When asked the question of what color the campaign should use for its flyers and push cards, everyone suggested either red or blue from the flag. I, on the other hand, wanted to use my favorite color: green. So, green it was. In hindsight, I should have just gone with one of the more traditional colors. The green didn't stand out as well as red or blue would have on the campaign material.

When making all of our decisions, we had to keep in mind that there was a campaign spending limit of $150. Therefore, we had to get as big a bang out of the campaign money as possible. I was not comfortable asking for donations of money to my campaign, especially since all of my friends were students with very little money. With the exception of a few dollars' friends gave me without my asking for it, I put up the money, around $125. Yes, I also didn't have much money, but I was living in a house whose rent was just $25 a month and, being a vegetarian, I didn't spend much money on food. In addition, Susanna and I had made money from the pecans we had sold up in McHenry that winter.

Speaking of Susanna, she had to return to McHenry weeks earlier due to her father being terminally ill in the VA hospital in Illinois. Even though she was not close to her father, she wanted to help her mother, Mary, through this time. This allowed me to spend all my free time campaigning. Susanna didn't return to Baton Rouge until a couple of weeks after the election.

Even before my campaign for SGA president started, I realized that roadblocks were being put up to stop me from being elected. Jere Longman wrote an editorial in the *Reveille* (March 18, 1976) about the Election Board, which had been appointed by SGA president Benoist, a fraternity member. His editorial said that the Election Board "set election day during the midterm exams. As a result, candidates have less than two weeks to present their platforms around campus. Exams are sure to suppress voter turnout." The vote of the general student body would be suppressed but not the Greeks. The Greeks were very effective in getting out the Greek vote for a fellow Greek.

In the poll taken by the *Reveille*, students who stated they weren't going to vote in the SGA elections were asked, why not? "I simply don't care" was their most common reason, with one non-voting student emphatically stating, "I wouldn't waste my ---- time on it." The report said that 36 students polled stated they weren't even going to vote, while 46 students polled were still undecided and would probably not vote either. It concluded, "This year they will more than likely stay away in droves."

Then the editorial stated that, "Strong opposition is expected from David Groner." Groner was a Theta Xi, so his "strength should come from the Greeks who usually turn out in fairly large numbers because they are so easily mobilized." I fully realized that David was my main opponent, although I felt that football player Bill Edwards would also be a strong candidate. I admired his fight for better food for the jocks. David Groner also stated that he "expects to carry the Law School." Thanks to my friend Beno, that proved to be incorrect.

The editorial pointed out what I had come to believe over the years I had been at LSU, "that SGA has been nothing more than an administrative rubber stamp." I was determined to change that perception of Student Government, and also "the near total student apathy toward SGA." It was noted that only 35 people attended an SGA presidential candidates forum, with most of those people either representatives of the media or campaign staff members of the candidates.

During the campaign, I spoke out against students who had run for SGA president because of their future political ambitions. I maintained that such SGA presidents had allowed themselves to be manipulated by administrators and legislators to enhance their chances of later being elected to state office.

I also expressed my belief that the administration opposed an effective SGA president who would fight for what was in the best interest of the student body regardless of how that fight would affect him personally. The administration feared that the absolute power it held over the student body and student affairs would be endangered.

I continued to fight for the rights of athletes, especially football players, by pointing out again and again how Coach McClendon's refusal to let one of the football players, who was a star runner in his home state of Texas, participate in any future meets after running at just one LSU track meet. I surmised that track coach, Joe May lost his job for letting the student run. I would end this discussion with, "It is our duty to liberate the jocks!"

During the campaign I attended CPU meetings, but I kept a low profile. I wanted to let others take charge of CPU. And they did. CPU grew from just a few students at the early meetings to over 50 students. Fifty may not sound like many, but few organizations could claim to have that many members who were willing to take time away from their studies not only to attend the meetings but, more importantly, to work on CPU's candidates' campaigns and on student issues like the Book Rental.

After class, I would campaign in the male dormitories into the night. The only problem was that many times I would be invited into the students' rooms to get stoned. That would bring the campaigning to a quick end (but I did make a number of lifelong friends, like Mike Richmond). One night I got stoned and didn't leave until the next morning. This was a pleasant surprise and a perk of being the hippie, dope smoking presidential candidate that I was.

The SGA elections were held on Thursday, March 18th, the same day as Free Speech Alley. By then one of the candidates, George

McCullough, had dropped out of the race and endorsed my candidacy. Of course, the main topic at the Alley that day was the SGA elections. The crowd was one of the largest of the whole semester. It appeared that students were very interested in the SGA elections.

As usual, the Alley was set to start at 3 P.M. that afternoon. The night before, at a campaign meeting, everyone was assigned a location on campus. The volunteers were to hand out what was left of our campaign materials and urge students to vote for CPU candidates. I was assigned the Pentagon Dining Hall, now "The 5 Dining Hall," because it was one of the largest student dining halls on campus. We were all to arrive at our assigned stations before the first classes started except for those of us assigned to the dining halls around the campus who were to get there before the dining halls opened at 7 A.M. Lines of students would form 15 minutes or so before the doors opened, giving us time to talk to the students in line. I dutifully arrived at 6:30 A.M. (good military training) to hand out the remaining push cards I had left, which weren't many, and, more importantly, to talk to the students about my candidacy and the importance of electing our whole ticket of CPU candidates.

After the dining hall closed for breakfast, I went to campaign in front of the Middleton Library. That was where the *Gumbo* photographer took a picture that appeared in the yearbook of all four of the candidates for SGA president.

Since the large number of students with a meal plan for the Pentagon Dining Hall usually missed breakfast, I returned to the Pentagon Dining Hall for lunch to continue campaigning.

Around 12:30 P.M., a female student working on the David Groner campaign, came up to me obviously very upset. She started yelling at me while waving a flyer in my face, saying that this was the most disgraceful thing she had ever seen, and that I wasn't going to get away with it. I told her I didn't have a clue what she was talking about. That just made her madder. She got in my face so close she was spitting the words at me as she yelled, "You know damn well what I am talking about! All I can say is you aren't going to get away with it!" She stomped away without showing me what was written on the flyer.

She had caused such a scene that a number of students had gathered around us. I looked at them asking, "Do any of you know what she was talking about?" None of them knew what she was yelling about either.

A little later, one of our campaign workers showed me what appeared to be the same flyer the female student had in her hand. It was, I later learned, called a "blowout sheet." Blowout sheets are designed to motivate workers for a candidate into believing that the opposing candidate put it out to smear their candidate. These blowout sheets were usually put out on election day, making it hard for the candidate it was aimed at to have time to counter it. Of the many slights in the flyer, the one I think that may have made the female student so mad was a drawing of a young woman, with large breasts jiggling to and fro, saying "David, am I grown yet?" This was in reference to another blowout sheet that, among other things, showed three pictures of the same young female student whose breast were increasingly getting larger with each picture, with the caption, "Groner, Groner, Groner for SGA president." Again, this blowout sheet was intended to rile up Groner's campaign workers.

With this in mind, I headed off to the Alley to have a word with Groner about those "blowout sheets." Sure enough, Groner was at the Alley standing by John Porterfield. I attempted to discuss the "blowout sheets" with Groner, but he blew me off. That only pissed me off more. When it was my turn to speak, I immediately started in on Groner. As the *Reveille* (March 19, 1976) reported, "Schirmer raised eyebrows when he told the crowd, 'If you don't vote for me (for SGA president), please vote for anybody else besides David Groner'... 'some really filthy shit' had been spread by workers for one of the candidates. Schirmer said he knew 'the bullshit and slanderous crap' had not been spread by workers for either Bill Edwards or Mike Hilliard." Groner left the Alley after I had spoken without taking the box to speak himself.

At the end of Free Speech Alley, I was asked if I wanted to go with the group of campaign workers who were going to observe and monitor the opening of the voting machines and tally the votes. Observing the opening of the voting machines and making sure the vote tally was correct was the responsibilities of each candidate's campaign. I said, "Sure, that should be fun." And it was.

The voting machines were located in key areas around campus: out in front of all of the colleges, the law school and the library. SGA president Benoist and Election Board chairman, accompanied by SGA workers, went from one college to another to open the machines and tally the votes with the candidates' campaign workers observing and separately tallying the votes.

As the *Reveille* (March 19, 1976) reported, I led most of the boxes in most of the colleges. When the counting was done, I had received 1,914 votes, or 39.6 percent, to David Groner's 1,390, or 28.4 percent; a lead of 524 votes out of a total of 4,978 votes cast in the five man race.

Next would come the runoff election between me and the Greek candidate, David Groner. It would be a fight for the 1,674 votes that students had given to the three eliminated candidates.

## RUNOFF ELECTION FOR SGA PRESIDENT

David Groner's biggest vote count came from the Junior Division, but he won by only 584 to 529. This was a surprise to me because I figured that all the fraternities and sorority pledges had voted for him, and that the freshmen were new at LSU and did not know about my past work.

The CPU candidate for legislative vice president, Steve Pastorek, didn't do so well. As the *Reveille* (March 19, 1976) reported, "Dana Robert smashed fellow member Steve Pastorek for SGA legislative vice president by more than 2 to 1. Robert had 3,026 votes to Pastorek's 1,457 in perhaps the biggest electoral surprise of a surprising election." However, the rest of the CPU ticket did well. Ned Wright was elected SGA financial vice president without opposition. Wright had come to a CPU meeting before the filing date for elections and assured us that he would work with us. Therefore, CPU didn't put up a candidate for that position. That would turn out to have been a terrible mistake.

As I see it, Benoist and the Election Board had set the primary election on a Thursday and the runoff on a Tuesday because fewer students were on campus. Nobody wanted the Tuesday and Thursday hour-and-a-half long classes instead of the hour-long classes on Monday, Wednesday and Friday. A reduced number of students on campus gave a Greek candidate, like Groner, an edge over a non-Greek candidate like me.

On the way over to the library on runoff election day, I ran into David Ingallinera, the brother of Tom Ingallinera, who was one of the founding members of PSA back in 1971. David showed me a baggie full of rolled joints. As he hurried by me, he yelled over his shoulder that he was giving his friends one each to get them to go vote. I knew without a doubt that all of the long haired, dope smoking students were for me. The trick was to get them to vote. Easily 99% of them had never voted in an SGA election and probably would never do it again. It seemed that David had figured out a sure fire way to get them motived to go vote. As I watched him hurry away, I thought to myself, I hope they vote before smoking the joint or else they would probably never make it to the polls.

Later in the afternoon I went to the Union to campaign in the Union cafeteria. As I table hopped around the cafeteria talking with students, it became clear that most of them had already voted. Not only had they voted, most of them said they had voted for me and the referendum on the Book Rental and the Bill of Student Rights, which were on the ballot. I decided I would stop campaigning and get a cup of coffee.

Later, I met up with John Crochet, Joe Wills, and David Lofton, among others, to be present as the Election Board opened the voting machines and counted the vote. As the *Reveille* (March 19, 1976) pointed out, a fairly substantial number of students turned out to vote in the primary election. More than 5,000 students voted in the primary, about 29 per cent of full-time students eligible to vote. In this runoff election, it didn't appear to me that the number would be as high, which would be bad for me since overcoming the advantage that the Greeks had in these elections depended on a large number of students who normally wouldn't vote, voting.

This time, going around with the Election Board was even more exciting than the first time. I didn't really know what to expect the first time. In the primary election, I thought I would either win or be in a runoff, but I wasn't that confident that I would win the runoff.

We joined up with Benoist and the Election Board members. Groner and his people were already there, along with other candidates who were in runoffs. Altogether, there must have been around 40–50 students. Everyone there seemed to be extremely hyped up.

Our group seemed to hold our collective breaths, fearing bad news, while Groner and his supporters seemed to anticipate positive results. As we went from one voting location to another, there would be cheers and groans each time a voting machine was opened and the votes read out. The numbers for Groner and for me kept getting closer. This was completely different from the first election where I led by a large margin from beginning to end. It became clear that Groner was picking up more votes in the runoff than I was. In fact, I was barely matching the same vote total at each polling station that I had in the primary election.

By the time we got to the last polling place in front of the library, where the largest number of students voted, I was ahead by only 30 or so votes. There were several voting machines at the library polling station. As each machine was opened, I slowly gained more votes until the last machine was opened, sealing the election in my favor.

There are two pictures on the front page of the *Reveille* (March 19, 1976) taken as the last voting machine was opened. The first one shows me with an intent look on my face, and the other picture shows me with a big ass grin from ear to ear. This expression encompassed the realization that this was the funniest, most amazing thing that had ever happened to me. This poor white trash kid had beaten the elitist Greeks. I had become the first, and probably only, long haired, dope smoking hippie to be elected SGA president at LSU and likely anywhere in the Deep South at that time. To paraphrase the song "Spill the Wine" sung by Eric Burdon, this "long haired leaping gnome" has been elected student body president at Louisiana State University.

It was very close. My runoff vote total increased by only 528 votes to 2,442, while Groner's vote total had increased by nearly 1,000 votes to 2,218. I ended up winning by only 224 votes. Only twenty percent of full-time students voted in this election.

Even more importantly than my winning the presidency was the fact that the Book Rental referendum and the Bill of Student Rights both passed. The referendum on the $1 fee for the Book Rental was approved by a 2,432–1,812 margin. In an interview with a *Reveille* (March 24, 1976) reporter I stated I was ready to get to work and getting the Book Rental off the ground was my first priority.

An editorial in the *Reveille* (March 24, 1976) covering the election results, titled "SGA STILL POOR," stated that now the student body had Ted Schirmer, and if I failed to produce any results, students couldn't demand a reform candidate next year. "For if Ted is not a reform candidate, I'd like to see just who is." Then the editorial stated that I may just be the first SGA president who can get things done because I was independent. "That is because Ted is the first SGA president who wouldn't take all the old crap seriously." The editorial ended with the statement, "And year after year, after Schirmer is long gone, the 'history' of SGA will remain like the gray tide of a very polluted ocean." I wasn't sure if this editorial was complementary or not.

After hearing the last vote totals and realizing we had won, everyone wanted to head off to my friend Phil Brady's bar, Magoo's, to celebrate. I told them I would meet them there. I needed time to let what had just happened to me sink in. One of my friends, Marion Campbell, handed me a joint, telling me he would see me at Magoo's.

Being a Tuesday, there weren't many students still on the campus. It was around 7 P.M., and the sun was starting to set on the other side of the Mississippi River. The sky was already starting to light up with the colors that foretold one of Baton Rouge's beautiful sunsets was coming. With this in mind, I decided to walk across the Parade Ground to the old Law School building located just off Highland Road. I thought getting stoned and observing what promised to be a beautiful sunset would be an excellent way to cap off this amazing day in my life.

It was turning out to be one of those evenings in late spring that makes living through the hot and muggy summers in Baton Rouge worth it. It was March 24th, soon to be April. April is one of the best two months in Louisiana weather wise. The temperature was in the low 70s; there was little humidity (for Louisiana) and no wind. In other words, a very pleasant evening.

I crossed Highland Road and climbed to the top of the Law School steps. I had decided to sit down on the end of one of the podiums that bordered the steps. I walked to the end of the podium on the left side and sat down with my legs hanging over the side. I had a great view of the Memorial Tower on the other side of the Parade Grounds. The tower's Westminster Chimes were just marking the half hour as I pulled the joint out of my pocket and lit it up. As I smoked, the sunset sky behind Memorial Tower broke out in shades of yellow, pink, orange, and red.

My mind started to replay events. I had never thought something like this could happen to someone like me. Now that it had, I had to get my head around how I was going to do a good job as SGA president and pass my classes. On top of it, I remembered that it was the Baton Rouge campus' turn to be represented by its SGA president on the LSU Board of Supervisors. I thought, "What have I gotten myself into now?"

As I inhaled my second drag on the joint, the marijuana started tamping down my anxiety and replacing it with feelings of excitement over the upcoming challenge I was about to face. With a smile on my face, I started laughing out loud. Shaking my head, I thought to myself, "Shit!" I got up and started walking over to Magoo's, continuing to laugh at myself for jumping into something I hadn't really thought through. I just knew that, with the exception of the Greeks, the way the administration treated the student body had to change, and I believed that as SGA president I could help bring about that change. I would later understand this was just another ADHD moment in my life.

A long night of celebrating took its toll on me. I had no desire to try to drive home since I had drunk quite a bit. I ended up going home with Charlie, a new friend I made at Magoo's. I didn't have indoor plumbing at my house, so the next morning I took advantage of Charlie's shower before leaving for school. Since it was Wednesday, I had a full day of classes. Placing the election during midterm exams didn't help me academically.

While most students didn't give a high priority to working in student government, I didn't have the same priorities as most students. While many were getting an education in order to get degrees in professions that were geared toward helping others—like social work, medicine, and law—I was more focused on helping others in the present. For me, that was more rewarding than getting the top grade in some class I was taking.

Ever since returning from Viet Nam, I had been trying to learn to live with what I had been willing to do and what I had done in Viet Nam. I had come to realize that Hollywood war propaganda movies, like *Sands of Iwo Jima, Wake Island, The Battle of Midway* and similar movies, had programmed me and many others of my generation to march off to fight and die in an unjust war. For a poor white trash kid like me who had been ridiculed and shamed his entire childhood, dying, like John Wayne's character Marine Sgt. John Stryker in the *Sands of Iwo Jima*, was the most desirable and honorable way to end one's life. Talk about a sick puppy!

By the time I was SGA president in 1976, I had been mediating, smoking marijuana, and consuming mind expanding drugs on a regular basis. Also, I had chosen classes every semester that might help me answer the many questions I had. I felt I was getting a handle on making better decisions in my life. I had slowly learned not to hate myself for past actions, but to glean every lesson I could from them, then to lay those past acts down and move on. A person should only carry a bad event in one's life only as long as it takes to learn the lessons that can be found embedded in it after an honest and intense autopsy of the event. After applying this approach to the many terribly wrong decisions I made in my life, I was able to be at peace with myself.

That realization, along with what I had learned from my readings and discussions with individuals in the education field, only further reinforced my approach to attending LSU. And that was to fight the administration, and other students if necessary, for a better educational experience for all students. Soon, this became my top priority for attending LSU, not getting an education in order to get a job after college, not even attending Tiger Stadium on a Saturday night. I wasn't a good student in the classroom, but I felt I was a "good citizen" student outside of the classroom, a character that the university appeared to have no interest in developing.

In fact, it was the exact opposite. The administration actively suppressed any expression of "good citizenship" whenever it appeared on campus. It fought against social change by prohibiting students from attending the College of Education based on antiquated grooming standards, resisting Black students demands for more racial inclusion in the social life of the university, or telling female students they risked expulsion by protesting the discriminatory rules locking female students in their dormitories at night but not the male students. The LSU administration seemed to feel threatened by the most reasonable requests from the student body. I hoped my tenure as SGA president would make a difference in the lives of the LSU student body.

However, my tenure as SGA president would be very short lived if I didn't bring my grades up. In order to stay SGA president, I would have to maintain a full course load and a 2.0 grade point average. The Monday before the SGA banquet for the swearing in of new officers, I received my mid-term exam grades. I learned I was failing Economic Principal Problems and the American Revolution 1763–1789. I was really in a pickle. My administration was about to be over before it really got started. After all the work others had done to get me elected as SGA president, believing I would be the fighter for students' rights that they needed, I was facing losing the very office they got me elected to because of my grades.

I stayed after class to talk with the professors. My history exam with my friend Bob Becker had been an essay exam. Bob had drawn red lines through so many words and written so many red letter comments on my paper that I could hardly see what I had attempted to write. On the very top of the front page of my test paper, Bob had scrawled in huge red letters, "YOU CAN'T WRITE!" After the rest of the class had left, we went to his office. On the way, he kept expressing his astonishment that I could not write. He had the same look I had seen on teachers' faces my entire life, but none of them had also been friends of mine like Bob. I had taken Bob's freshman American History class in the spring of 1975 and had made a C in that class, so I thought my writing had been sufficient. When I brought that up, Bob said his graduate assistants had graded those tests. With a bewildered look on his face, he asked how I ever graduated high school. I explain that I had barely escaped.

I told him that I needed to drop his class and another class that I was failing, but I was going to have to figure out a way to do it in such a way that I could still stay SGA president. He told me he would give me a W-D when I withdraw from the class.

When I spoke to my Economics professor about withdrawing from his class, he also expressed disbelief that I had failed his class. He also stated he would also give me a W-D when I withdrew. Then all I had to do was figure out a way to keep the presidency after I withdrew from those two classes.

I called a meeting of my closest friends and advisers to tell them the bad news about the jeopardy our plans were in due to my failing two of my courses. I was hoping that these people, being more experienced in how the rules governing students at LSU were written, would know if there were any loopholes in them.

After much discussion, it was suggested I call a special session of the Assembly on April 1st, when I would officially be the SGA president, in order to ask for a vote by the Assembly on whether or not to allow the

SGA president to be a part-time student. We didn't have much faith that such a motion would pass, and, even if it did, that the administration would honor it.

Jerry Giddens offered an idea. When a student withdrew from a class so late in the semester that he got a W grade, that student didn't get any refund in fees nor have to surrender his full-time student ID. That allowed him to still qualify for all the benefits of a full-time student, like attending sporting events for free, using the Student Infirmary, etc. Jerry pointed out that Article I section 2 of the SGA Constitution states: "Every full-time student, as defined by the regulations of the university, shall be a member of the Student Government Association and shall have a voice and vote therein." Jerry concluded that, since the university considered a student to still be full-time if he dropped classes late in the semester with a W grade, even if the student didn't have 12 hours of classes anymore, I would still be considered a full-time student even if I dropped those two classes.

That was also how the GI educational bill worked in the '70s. As long as I enrolled as a full-time student and started the semester full-time, I would get my full VA check even after withdrawing from classes. I had been figuring my way around rules my whole life, and I thought this looked more promising than trying to get a motion through the Assembly. Jerry stated he would check this out with the Registrar. When Jerry spoke with the Registrar, he not only confirmed it, but, at Jerry's request, provided an official letter officially stating that policy.

The final date to drop classes was fast approaching, so I had to make a decision: Should I hope that the Assembly, called into special session, would pass an act authorizing an SGA president to go part-time and would the administration honor such an act by the Assembly? I had serious doubts about that approach. So, I decided to drop my two classes based on what the Registrar had told Jerry and the letter documenting that statement.

I waited until the afternoon of the last day for dropping classes to drop the two classes. I didn't want Vice Chancellor Reddoch to get wind of it. I knew if he became aware of what I was up to, he would stop me in my tracks. I fully realized that I was trying to put one over on the bullshit rule requiring SGA presidents to maintain a full class load while SGA president. I knew that I once again had "one foot over the line." If Reddoch stepped in, I was going to fight. I would expose how it only benefited the administration to force an SGA president to be a full-time student. Maintaining a full course load would dilute the president's effectiveness and thus make him/her less of a pain for the administration. In my opinion, there was no other reason for stopping an SGA president from choosing to go part-time in order to give more time to his/her duties.

I was interviewed about dropping two of my classes for a *Reveille* (April 2, 1976) article, titled "Schirmer averts hassle after dropping to part-time." I admitted that I was failing two classes and that "I could stop all work and do nothing but study, like Benoist." Most past SGA presidents just disappeared in their books, not even coming to the office, because athletes and student government officers had to maintain a 2.0 grade point. "But," I said, "I want to keep working for the students." The article pointed out that past SGA presidents have had similar problems. Bentley Alexander, SGA president in 1971, was put on scholastic probation in law school and had to resign his office in January 1972. The article alluded that the same fate befell Art Ensminger, who was in his third year of law school when he committed suicide.

The Ponchatoula Strawberry Festival offered the SGA crates of strawberries in order to promote the festival, but I thought I should check to be sure it was okay to accept the gift. As I walked over to Reddoch's office, I was wondering if he had heard about my dropping down to part-time. After waiting ten minutes or so, I was told that I could go in. As I walked in, my question was answered by the look on his face. A sort of painful grin said that I had got one over on him, and he didn't like it.

I was there to talk about being allowed to pass out free strawberries at the Alley, but Reddoch had other things on his mind. He started in on how I had misinterpreted what the Registrar had said. That policy he quoted was purely a financial policy. The requirement that all SGA officers be full-time was not affected by it. That policy had been established by the Chancellor's Committee. I just sat there listening to him talk down to me.

I knew he had probably already discussed my dropping to part-time with the chancellor, and they had obviously decided there wasn't anything they could do about it that wouldn't escalate the matter. They had been dealing with me for years, and they understood clearly that I would fight them tooth and nail if they tried to remove me from office. Reddoch stated he was not going to let it happen again because he had rewritten the policy to make it clear that SGA officers had to be full-time students to hold their office. I was the first SGA president in the history of LSU to be part-time. But not the last. Today there is no such requirement for the SGA presidents to be full-time. I was ahead of my time. ☺

## FIRST ACTIONS AS PRESIDENT

I knew the first Free Speech Alley after the election would be unlike any other I had spoken at before, and I was looking forward to it so I could thank all the people who had worked on my campaign. In addition, I was going to outline my plans for the upcoming year and the future of SGA under my administration. There was no doubt in my mind that our approach to governing was going to be totally different from how the Greek SGA presidents approached it.

As I was walking toward the Union steps, I could see that the Alley was being attended by one of the larger crowds of students that semester. The *Reveille* (March 25, 1976) article covering the Alley wrote that I made "an acceptance speech." As I rose when it was my turn to speak, another one of LSU's long haired student freaks at the Alley began playing "Hail to the Chief" on his guitar. I recognized him as one of the students who would sit with us in a circle of other long hairs on the Parade Grounds, playing his guitar while we smoked dope and sang. I thought this was pretty funny and started laughing. I mounted the soapbox with a big ass smile on my face. Every time I spoke at the Alley that entire year, he would be there and break out into "Hail to the Chief." Even at times when the shit was hitting the fan, it always relaxed me and brought a smile to my face.

I thanked everyone who had worked on my campaign and appealed to David Groner's supporters and the Greeks to come together with my supporters and not let the LSU administration divide us. I stated that winning the battles ahead of us in the coming year would require the whole student body to be united. I then discussed the Bill of Student Rights. I said that even though it had been approved by the student body in the recent election, "The fight isn't over to get the Bill accepted." It still had to go to the Faculty Senate, and a big problem for them would likely be the power that the Bill would grant to the students to review their teachers. There was also the issue of unauthorized searches of student rooms by dormitory counselors. This was taken out of the Bill of Student Rights by Vice Chancellor Reddoch before being put in front of the student body for a vote. I wasn't going to let this issue die. I was prepared to have SGA's ombudsman fight this issue in court, if possible. I urged all students who experienced this violation to contact me immediately, stating, "The more complaints we have, the better our case is going to be" when SGA filed a lawsuit.

The next day, at a Meet the Officers program at Coffee 2015 in the Union, with Legislative Vice President Dana Robert, Treasurer Ned Wright, and myself, I made my first attempt at communicating with my major opposition in the election, the Greeks. As reported by the *Reveille* (March 26, 1976), I stated that the Greek system had a lot of good things about it but if they "insist on infringing upon other students' rights (i.e., having their pledges reserve rows and rows of seats at the football games), it would be the duty of the SGA to resolve the conflict." In an attempt to lighten up this statement I explained, "Think of the poor freshman all excited about seeing his first LSU football game. He gets to the stadium real early and, much to his disappointment, finds all the seats reserved and that he has to sit in God's lap to watch the game." I further stated that, "Only the handicapped should have special seating."

177

I also discussed how wasteful it was for so much clothing and other items to be thrown away at the end of the semester when the students left since a few blocks off the campus were people who had very little and could use those items. I grew up wearing clothing that didn't fit me or were hand-me-downs. I knew how cruel teenagers could be to their fellow students who didn't have decent clothes.

In the last weeks of that spring semester, SGA advertised that the poor living in the neighborhoods surrounding LSU needed clothing and other items, and that SGA would have boxes at the entrances of all of the dormitories for donations from the students moving out of at the end of the semester. That semester's clothing drive was successful. We collected a large amount of donated clothing and furniture. We contacted local organizations and churches so these items could be distributed fairly.

I had heard complaints by students that the SGA office didn't have regular hours and it was closed more than it was open. Students couldn't get help from their own Student Government with problems they were experiencing. I promised that SGA offices would have regular hours, from 8 A.M. to 4 P.M.

An SGA banquet, organized by the outgoing president Paul Benoist, had been set for the following Monday night in the Union banquet hall. The banquet served as an inauguration ceremony for new officers plus a farewell event honoring the outgoing SGA president and executive officers. Awards were to be given to SGA Assembly members, one of whom was me. Before being sworn in, I was presented with the Art Ensminger Award for outstanding SGA Assembly Member.

Susanna still was in McHenry, assisting her mother in handling the death of her father, Jim. After the initial excitement of winning the election wore off, I felt down that I didn't have Susanna there. She and I had shared many exciting and fun experiences. It felt strange not to have her there to share this present one. I have always enjoyed my adventures more when I have someone to share them with, especially someone I loved as much as I loved Susanna.

I had hoped that Susanna would be back from Illinois in time for the inauguration banquet, but she felt her mother still needed her at home. Since I had never been to an event like the banquet before, I didn't know what to expect. After thinking about it, I really wasn't concerned about my attire. I was going to wear the same clothes I wore every day at school. I figured I could just flow with whatever was about to happen at this event, just as I had been flowing with every new situation I found myself in during my whole life.

Before leaving the house, I rolled a joint and stashed it in my shirt pocket. Hey, what can I say? I was a long haired freak.

When I got to campus, I walked behind the Union to the Oak Grove. There was nobody around, so I decided to smoke the joint under one of those magnificent oaks. They had been planted in 1926 and dedicated to the 30 LSU men who lost their lives in WWI. When I was alone among those oaks, especially at night, my heart would be filled with emotion for my fallen friends in Viet Nam and the cost of war. Bittersweet memories of Danny would fill my head. I would find myself talking to Danny about what was happening in my life. I knew Danny would have gotten quite a laugh out of my being elected SGA president at LSU, of all places. What better way to put things in proper perspective than to remember those who gave their all for this country?

Being sworn in as SGA president couldn't hold a candle to what I had already survived in my life. Thinking of that brought a smile to my face as I finished the joint, popped the roach in my mouth, swallowed it, and headed back to the Union. What was this new chapter in my life going to bring? I started laughing to myself, thinking, surprises are the things that make life worth living.

Walking inside, I noticed that there were more empty tables than tables with people at them. SGA was charging students to come to the event. I think it was around $15. That was a lot of money for a college student, especially for my supporters. I had let it be known that I didn't expect our people to waste $15 on attending the banquet. They had more important things to spend their money on, like dope.

I was sure that when Benoist made arrangements for the banquet, he, like a lot of others on campus, thought a Greek would win the election. Maybe when a Greek wins, his house requires attendance at the swearing-in ceremony of their brother. Well, the Greek candidates hadn't won, and my supporters were not as flush with money as the Greeks. The fact that I had won the election, I believe, kept the attendance down.

I asked someone, was SGA going to be charged for the empty tables? I was informed that, indeed, SGA was going to be charged for all the meals ordered regardless of how few people came. That blew my mind. What was Benoist thinking ordering so many place settings?

Whatever went into the planning, SGA would be paying for meals that weren't going to be eaten. There was no way I was going to tolerate that happening. One of my platforms was to cut wasteful spending by the SGA and here, on what was going to be my first night as SGA president, was the worst kind of wasteful spending.

I told the MC I would be back. I left the head table and went downstairs to the Union cafeteria. I started going up to students, who were waiting in the cafeteria line to buy food, asking if they would like a free meal courtesy of SGA. On a college campus it was not hard to find students who would accept a free meal. The *Reveille* (March 30, 1976) reported, "Earlier when it seemed the speeches would be delivered to a room full of empty seats, Schirmer stepped out into the Union to invite students to the banquet."

As I walked back up to the banquet hall with a dozen or more students in tow, I told them that, if they wanted, they could leave after eating. I just didn't want SGA money wasted on food that wasn't going to be eaten. Sure enough, most of the students who came back to the hall with me left after eating.

Benoist spoke first and became pretty emotional while recounting the events during his year as SGA president. He stated that the people at the university were second to the university itself and should take a back seat to what is important to the university. One of the individuals he sang praise for was Randy Gurie, Assistant Dean of Men. Since the others had started eating while I was rounding up students, I was still eating when Benoist made that statement. I almost choked on my food when I heard that. Randy Gurie and I had already butted heads and would do so even more in the coming year. Looking back on it after my experience as president, I think Benoist was tearing up because he was so relieved to get off the presidential hot seat.

After I was sworn in as SGA president, I gave what the *Reveille* (March 30, 1976) reporter wrote as a "fiery inaugural address." All I did was stress again that I was going to fight tooth and nail for the students. I wasn't going to take any crap from the administration, or any students opposed to our plans to help the student body. I again stressed the importance of unity among the student body, while knowing damn well there were students who would oppose everything we would try to do for the students. But if unity was not going to happen, it wasn't going to be because I didn't try to unify the students.

In closing, I said that some people claimed that "I was a leader from the '60s era. LSU is still in the '60s where students' rights are concerned." The South, as a whole, was 10 years behind the rest of the country and LSU was no exception, as shown by its archaic rules and disrespect for students.

After the banquet, I went with some of the others to Magoo's for a drink, then home. I had to clean the house because Susanna was coming home the next day. In addition, I wanted to get up early to get to the SGA office early to start my new job as president.

The following days I was busy interviewing and hiring staff and making appointments to the many vacancies in Student Government that the SGA president was responsible for filling. A top priority of mine was to stop any wasteful spending of SGA money.

Mike Richman immediately pointed out one area where SGA was wasting money. Mike, at the time, was working at LSU's telephone switchboard as an operator. When he learned there were separate telephone lines for every phone in the SGA office, Mike said that we could save hundreds of dollars by installing multi-line telephones, which would require paying for only one line, saving SGA big bucks over the year. I told Mike to make it so.

Office staff salaries was another area where SGA was spending money it didn't need to. SGA was paying the salaries out of SGA's budget. Since SGA was an official organization at LSU, Mike stated we should be able to get student workers assigned to the office. Those students workers received their salaries through the federal work-study program that provided part-time jobs for undergraduate and graduate students with financial need, allowing them to earn money to help pay education expenses. Sure enough, we ended up acquiring all of the office staff that way. These were just two of the changes we brought to SGA that saved thousands of dollars a year for the Student Government.

Susanna had returned from McHenry, and we decided to christen my office that evening. After everyone had left the SGA office, Susanna and I closed and locked the outer door and then went into my office, locking the door behind us. We had brought a large towel and a couple blankets from the house. We tightly stuffed the towel under the office door, then spread the blankets out on the floor. We got stoned, undressed, and made love until it was time for the student Union to close.

We got dressed and left the Union, feeling we had properly christened the office for the upcoming year. Afterward, whenever we won an especially hard fight, we would rechristen the office. I felt these christenings helped lift any bad karma lingering in the office. Well, that was our excuse for it anyway. Susanna and I hardly needed an excuse to get high and make love, no matter where we were at the time.

### PUBLICITY AND NOTORIETY

One surprising aspect of winning the presidential election was the amount of press coverage my election received from the Baton Rouge's news media. I hadn't had enough time to let winning the election sink in before I found myself being interviewed by George Cotton, a Baton Rouge staff writer for the *Morning Advocate*. In addition to the *Morning*

*Advocate*, I was interviewed by the Baton Rouge alternative paper *Gris Gris*, newly started by John Maginnis and others.

The two articles couldn't have been more different. The title of the *Advocate's* article was simply "Schirmer Wins LSU Student Post." The article stated my name, my age, 28, and that I had been elected SGA president in a very close election, which I won by a little over 200 votes. That was it.

This was in stark comparison to the *Gris Gris* (March 30, 1976) article, which was titled "The Man from S.W.A.T." I had explained that I had a dozen or so students willing to volunteer time to work for SGA. Sort of a student brain trust was what I called them: S.W.A.T. (Students Without Any Tactics). I actually was making fun of the television program on ABC titled S.W.A.T. about a Special Weapons and Tactics team in California when I made that comment. The television program was short lived, like our S.W.A.T. team. My friends all intended to work to improve students' rights, but found it took too much time away from their studies. I did make up key rings for them with the letters SWAT printed on them.

The article stated that, to look at me, the new LSU student government president, you wouldn't figure that I went to Istrouma High School, served four years in the Navy, and was "sneaking up on law school." The *Gris Gris* expressed amazement that the conservative students at LSU would elect "the ardent student activist over two fraternity men and a football player." The article reported that I told them we almost blew the election because the night before the primary was St. Patrick's Day, and "we all went out and got wasted and didn't campaign." I told the reporter that since I didn't have any future political ambitions, I was going to use the power that SGA had to improve the student life at LSU. I wasn't afraid to rock the boat. I had been rocking boats my whole life, and I planned to rock LSU's boat as hard as I had to on behalf of the student body regardless of the consequences to me personally. I informed the reporter that I had many plans and ideas, but no matter what we got done or what happens with my plans, I could assure everyone one thing for sure: the next year wasn't going to be dull or boring.

At the time, I was oblivious of the level of notoriety I was about to experience simply because of my election as SGA president at LSU. I think a lot of Baton Rouge citizens, not to mention the local media, were shocked to hear about my election. Long hair was still a novelty in Louisiana, and the state Capitol was no different. Now there was one of them damn hippies elected as president of the student body at LSU. What was this world coming to?

I don't know how to explain why it was that, while I was comfortable speaking in public, leading demonstrations and organizations, I didn't enjoy the notoriety that inevitably went with that activism. Sure, I had experienced some notoriety due to my student activism and antiwar protesting over the past couple of years at LSU, but nothing like what I was about to experience. Nothing had prepared me for what was to come. Notoriety was never my goal when I got involved in activities at LSU. Matter of fact, I didn't think about it at all. I just jumped into fights I thought were worth fighting regardless of how it would affect me personally.

Despite my outward behavior, I could be very comfortable staying out of the limelight. Considering the fact that I had ADHD, it may very well have been I didn't like overstimulation. I needed time alone or with my companions, away from whatever cause I was fighting for at the time. I found it quieting to be out of the spotlight. Matter of fact, I would later tell people who said they wanted notoriety, that they didn't know what they were wishing for. Public notoriety will invade one's private life to such a degree that literally your life no longer belongs to you but to the public.

Some people feel free to approach you wherever you are. There was more than once that, while urinating in the bathroom, men would come up to me and start a conversation. Of course, being a former Navy man, I would continue peeing while carrying on a conversation with a complete stranger. Then, when I was done peeing, I would turn around while putting my penis back into my pants. It seemed that only then did it dawn on them that they were talking with me while I was pissing. The expression on their faces as they quickly looked away was priceless. I realized these men were just excited that *the* Ted Schirmer was in the bathroom and not thinking about what I was doing.

Later, at the height of my notoriety, it became even more uncomfortable for me to go to parties, concerts, outdoor festivals, any place where there was a crowd because of the attention I would draw from total strangers. It got to the point that I couldn't enjoy going out with Susanna or friends. Hell, whenever I was introduced to a person whom I didn't know, I would stick out my hand saying, "Ted Schirmer, nice to meet you." You know, just the normal way of greeting new people. Inevitably, the person would exclaim, "The Ted Schirmer!" That made me very uncomfortable, so much so, that I would respond humorously, "You can just call me 'The'." I would always try to downplay any attempt to set me apart from other people. I felt that any importance I might have wasn't all that much in the scheme of things. SGA president! Really!

Maybe it was my experience in the war that gave me a bigger picture of life, but I soon only went to parties of close friends who "knew me when" in order to avoid meeting any new people due to these kinds of responses. I was still studying Buddhism in order to come to grips with why I had volunteered for Viet Nam. One of the strongest proclamations I got out of Buddhism, if not the most important one for me, was that one's ego needed to be tamed. One should struggle to develop an "egoless ego." Existence is suffering, suffering is caused by selfish craving and attachment, and suffering can be destroyed. Yes, I know this is a simple explanation of the Four Noble Truths, but I am a simple person. I am fully aware that I have the understanding of a child, if that, of Buddhism, but it helped me to understand who I was and why I did what I did. I was attempting to fight for changes that I believed would benefit all LSU students while at the same time putting up barriers to words and actions by others that could feed my ego. I always tried to downplay my role in things and to make fun of myself whenever I spoke in public.

What Susanna and I decided to do, because Susanna really loved parties, was just to have parties at our house. Regretfully, in an effort to invite all the people I wanted, or felt I had to, the parties got too big and rowdy at times. Fortunately, living out in the country on River Road, there was no one to call the cops on us. That is not to say the cops didn't show up. Twice, the deputy sheriffs drove all the way out to our house to fuck with us. They soon learned I was not the typical person that they could roust.

The first time the deputy sheriffs came, they made it onto the front porch before I knew they were there. Good karma was with me, for we were still setting up for the party and there was no dope out. When I saw them, I went out to the front porch, closing the door behind me. I asked them what they wanted. They said something about stolen property being reported at this location and could they look around. I said, "No, and I am busy right now, so could you leave?" That really pissed them off. One of them actually took a step toward me. Then Stuart Thompson, a friend of mine and a Baton Rouge attorney, who was helping us setup for the party, stepped out on to the porch. He knew one of the deputy sheriffs and was able to diffuse the situation. I wasn't sure how I would have dealt with the one getting aggressive with me but, knowing how I was back then, probably stupidly! I would have probably not only found myself in jail, but not in very good physical condition. Baton Rouge deputy sheriffs were very similar to New Orleans cops in 1976. They felt they had the right to beat the shit out of anyone who gave them lip, then to come up with a legal reason why they beat the shit out of the person later.

Stuart motioned for me to go inside, which I had sense enough to do. I watched Stuart through the window talking with the two deputy sheriffs. The one who had taken a step toward me made it clear he wasn't done with me, but the other one seemed to agree with whatever Stuart was telling him and led his partner back to their patrol car. When Stuart came back inside, he told me I had to be more careful. There were several Baton Rouge deputy sheriffs who would love to bust my head open and throw my ass in jail.

At the next party we threw, I informed everyone at the party what had happened before and asked those who were out on the front porch to keep an eye out and quickly let me know if they saw a sheriff's car driving up. Sure enough, the party was in full swing when a sheriff's car was spotted driving by the house. This time, there were all kinds of drugs out in the open, not to mention lots of people stoned or tripping on mushrooms. My place was the mushroom Capital of Louisiana after all.

When I made it out to the front porch, the squad car had turned around and was stopping in the road right in front of the house. I hurried down the porch stairs and out the front gate, closing the gate behind me. I stood there, watching the officers as they got out of their squad car. I didn't have to tell the people on the front porch to go inside the house. The sight of the squad car did that for me. Some of them were gripping the more stoned or tripping people by the arm and leading them inside the house. At the same time, others, either not tripping out of their minds or too stoned to talk, came out on the porch and up to the gate. I guess they were there to back me up. I was just hoping no one would do anything stupid—you know, like I had done at times.

By the time the officers had gotten out of their squad car and up to the gate, I knew there had been a complete "changing of the guard" on the front porch. In other words, some individuals had swept all evidence of drugs off the porch and inside the house. There were no laws being broken "in plain view." If the officers could see any illegal activity "in plain view" on the porch, they would have had the right to come onto my property without a warrant.

Knowing this, I was very calm as I asked them, "What's up?" I saw that they were two different officers than the last time. But like a broken record, the first words out of their mouths were about stolen property being at this location. I told them there was no stolen property here. Then they had the balls to say, "Can we look around?" Before either of them could take a step, I said, "No!" One of them said they could get a warrant to search the house. I told them, "Then go get the warrant, but you aren't coming on to my property without one." They stood there glaring at me for a minute, then, looking at each other, they finally turned and went back to their patrol car. As they drove away, I realized that, knowing Baton Rouge judges, they might just be able to get a warrant, so I told everyone they should head home. I also suggested that they go the long way back on River Road just in case the sheriffs were waiting down the road.

I believe it was this second incident that led the officers to go to the person I was renting the house from, Mr. Charlie Brown. They probably found out who owned the property and hassled him. That, in turn, led to Mr. Brown evicting us from the house.

What happened was that, one afternoon, two Baton Rouge deputy sheriffs came to my front door. They told me I would have to move because I had been evicted from the house. What? I told them I had not received any notice of eviction; that I had a right to notice. They told me that, if I did not move, I would be forcibly removed from the premises. In addition, I would be charged with all the cost of the move. I informed them that I had a right to my day in court before any eviction could take place. I was only guessing about that, but that made them leave.

I called my attorney friend, Stuart Thompson, to ask what I should do if they came back. He educated me on the eviction laws. He told me I was right, that I had to be served with an eviction notice. Then, if I refused to vacate the property, the landlord could file an eviction lawsuit. I explained that we had never missed a rent payment. That Mr. Brown had told me we could stay at the house for as long as we wanted. Stuart told me that it didn't seem like the landlord had good cause to evict us and offered to represent me in court if it came to that.

Nothing happened for a few days, then one day, two different Baton Rouge Parish deputy sheriffs arrived at my door to serve me an eviction notice. They told me I had five days to vacate the property, or I would be forcibly moved. Man, the same old line. The officers who serve those eviction notices must be trained to say that line every time. I told them the same thing: I could not be forced to move until I had my day in court. I thought we were safe since we had not missed a rent payment, and we also had kept copies of all the money orders we used to pay our rent.

At court, Stuart, true to his word, represented us for free. I was going to be educated the hard way about oral contracts in Louisiana. Mr. Brown's attorney called him to the stand and asked if he knew who I was. Mr. Brown said he had never seen me before. His attorney asked him if he had spoken with me. Mr. Brown said never. His attorney asked him a few more questions and ended asking if he had rented the house on River Road to me. Mr. Brown answered, "No!"

I sat there dumbfounded. All this time Stuart was calming me down, patting my arm. Stuart's turn came. He went over a little of what Mr. Brown had just testified, then showed Mr. Brown all our copies of the money orders with his name on them that we had used to pay the rent. Stuart asked if he received these money orders. Mr. Brown said, "No." The judge asked to look at the money orders. On each of them was Mr. Browns name, the date, and a notation reading "rent payment." Stuart put me on the stand. I went over where I had met Mr. Brown, our agreement, and that I had never missed a rent payment. In addition, I described all the work Susanna and I had put into the place. Stuart rested.

The Judge then went over the law governing oral contracts: that the contract can be dissolved if either party, under oath, denies the existence of the oral contract. Therefore, I was ordered to vacate the premise. The Judge added, the law normally gave 10 days to vacate, but he was giving us 30 days. Furthermore, he ordered that we could take anything that was ours from the house.

As I left the courtroom, I had to pee. I went to the bathroom. In the bathroom was the judge standing at the urinal. He was just finishing, as I walked over to an adjacent urinal. As the judge was washing his hands, he said, "Schirmer, you should know better than this. Get everything in writing."

Susanna and I then had to find a new home. I was told by friends who lived on Elbow Bayou that there were empty shotgun houses on

189

the property. I spoke with the owner, explaining what had just happened to me up the road, and that I did not want it to happen again. He said he was not like Brown, I could stay there as long as I wanted. I asked if he didn't mind writing that down. He did so.

There were two shotgun houses side by side, both in about the same shape as the overseer's house had been when we first rented it. Once again, the house had no running water. It did have a toilet, but no plumbing. The Black family up in front of our house ran their sewage into a ditch. I decided to run a large flex pipe from the toilet to an open area where I dug a hole. It was only a few feet deep. That's all I could go to because water would fill the hole.

I still had to tote in water, but we did get the stove to work with butane. We stayed at that house until 1979 when I graduated from LSU, but I had to pay more rent—$35 a month instead of $25.

## POLITICAL INFIGHTING WITH LAW STUDENTS

The SGA ombudsman is a student government official who investigates students' complaints against maladministration. This position is appointed by the SGA president. On April 1st, Randy Wells and Jeff Hollingsworth, who were ombudsmen in the prior administration, came to me to ask what my plans were for the ombudsman's office. I told them that I thought they were doing a fine job and agreed to keep them working in that office. I also, told them that I was planning to expand the ombudsman office by adding another ombudsman, Beno Duhan, in anticipation of upcoming fights with the administration and faculty over the Bill of Student Rights, especially the section about stopping dorm counselors from making unauthorized searches of student rooms

Later that day, I gave Beno a key to the ombudsman's office, which was located next door to the SGA offices. I don't believe Wells knew that Beno and I had been working together since the Progressive Students Alliance (PSA) days in 1971–72. I knew Beno, and he knew me. We both knew what to expect from each other. I didn't personally know

Wells or Hollingsworth, just that it seemed they had been during a good job for the past three months.

The following week, Wells came into my office all pissed off, demanding to know what Beno was during with a key to "his office." I explained again, I needed Beno in the ombudsman's office because I was planning to expand the office and, as my liaison to the ombudsman's office, Beno would be very valuable in that endeavor. Wells told me that he was opposed to giving Beno all the powers of an ombudsman. As I was in a hurry to get to a meeting of the Bicentennial Time Capsule Committee, I told Wells he could either work things out with Beno or resign from the ombudsman's office. As I was walking out the door, Wells stated that "working with Duhon would be unacceptable." I turned saying, "I want Beno in that office," and rushed off to the meeting.

The following Monday, April 12, Wells and Hollingsworth came to my office. Wells started off by demanding that I remove Beno from the ombudsman's office, that he was the ombudsman and wanted Beno out of his office. As I stated to the *Reveille* (April 20, 1976), "I thought I was being intimidated by the ombudsman. He was trying to deteriorate the power of the SGA president. Randy [Wells] wanted to be head man—no one else. He ordered me to take back the key from Beno. As far as I know, the ombudsman works for the SGA president. He doesn't' give him orders."

With Wells insisting that I remove Beno from the ombudsman's office, and in the same breath saying he wasn't resigning, I felt I had no choice. Even though I wanted him and Hollingsworth in the ombudsman's office due to the good job they had done in the previous administration, I felt even more strongly that I needed Beno in the ombudsman's office. Therefore, I told him, "Ok, Randy, then I am firing you."

Beno later said, in an interview with the *Reveille* (April 20, 1976), that Wells and Hollingsworth were "supporters of David Groner who are opposed to everything Ted does. That the opponents of my appointment are a group of people in the Assembly who are after Ted. They just want to nail him. They want to emasculate him."

I then discovered a problem that I am sure most student governments have: theft of supplies. I started getting information that a lot of pens, pencils, paper, and even rolls of stamps were disappearing from the office. We started locking up all of our supplies with only the office manager and executive officers given keys to the cabinet. Supplies still went missing, but it did narrow down the possibility of who was taking them. The prime suspect turned out to be Ned Wright, SGA's financial vice president!

I first met Ned Wright when he came to a CPU meeting to discuss our plans for recruiting candidates to run for offices in SGA. After becoming a member of CPU, he convinced us that he agreed with CPU's platform and wanted to be our candidate for financial vice president. After CPU voted for him to run as CPU's candidate, he stated he didn't want to be put on any CPU campaign materials so as not to alienate his Greek brothers and fellow law students. That would hurt him in the election. And we bought it! His name didn't appear on any of our campaign materials.

I found out later from Ned Wright himself that he had spoken to the Panhellenic Council and Interfraternity Council, telling them that they didn't need to run anyone for financial vice president because he would be running and would be a check on me and CPU. In addition, he had talked with other politically minded Law School students, and there were a lot of them, and persuaded them not to run for financial vice president. That is how he ran unopposed. I got the feeling that Wright was extremely proud of how he had managed this.

During the campaign, even though Wright had no opposition, he would show up at political events. I would watch him "glad handing" people as he walked among the crowd. I noticed that he would greet everyone with the same handshake and wink. I asked him at one of these events why he was campaigning, considering he was running unopposed. He told me that he was laying the foundation for a future career in Louisiana politics because he had plans after Law School to run for office. Basically, he was networking. He told me his political hero was Governor Edwin Edwards, and that he modeled himself after Edwards. Ned would stand in front of a mirror for hours practicing his handshake with the added wink. I was to find out, after the elections, that he modeled himself after Edwards in more ways than just a handshake and wink. He seemed to also copy Edwards' morals in relation to public service.

That Ned was a thief became apparent when I saw him leaving the SGA offices with a handful of pens and legal pads. When I confronted him about taking SGA office supplies, he didn't even stop but said over his shoulder as he left the office, "I needed some pens and writing pads." I assumed Wright had a legitimate reason for leaving with those supplies.

The following week, I confronted him again as he was leaving the office with more pens and legal pads. He tried to blow me off saying, "It's only some pens and legal pads" and kept walking. I found out that, even though SGA had no use for legal pads, law students sure did, and Wright had been purchasing a lot of them. But I couldn't believe that I had to tell a future lawyer that taking these items for personal use, or for his friends at the Law School, was stealing. I asked the office staff if they had observed Wright using SGA supplies for personal use. I found out that Wright had been printing out invitations for his, so called, victory party on SGA letterhead paper and making copies of the invitations on SGA's Xerox machine.

I told some of my friends in law school what was happening and asked if they knew of any suspicious activities of Ned's. I was in for another shock. They told me that they had seen Ned giving away rolls of stamps to his friends at law school. I realized that Wright was giving away SGA supplies to further his effort to build a network of lawyers for future political plans.

In order to prove that Wright was pilfering SGA supplies, I needed to see the SGA books. I told Wright the following day that I wanted to see the paperwork on how much SGA was spending on office supplies. He refused to give me any purchasing invoices. I was flabbergasted! I told him, as SGA president, I had a right to know what he was spending

SGA funds on. He insisted that he didn't have to show me the books, that he only had to show the books to the Assembly, and he left the office. I yelled at Wright that I was going to go to the Assembly that night to make him show me the books. I found out later, that he wasn't keeping any records of his spending.

That afternoon at the Alley, I noticed the presence of Ned Wright, John Porterfield and other Law students who were members of the Assembly. I hadn't planned to discuss what was happening between Wright and me, but with Wright and his friends present I decided to confront him publicly about his misuse of SGA supplies. As the *Reveille* (April 22, 1976) reported in an article titled "Free speech highlighted by verbal rift," "Political infighting used Free Speech Alley as its forum Wednesday as Ted Schirmer and Financial Vice President Ned Wright exchanged accusations, criticisms and denials."

After stepping up on the box, I started expressing my thoughts about Wright as financial vice president. I stated that Wright was "a politico whose ambition for a career after he leaves Law School overrides his duty to serve students." I went on to say that Wright, quite frankly, was committing white collar crimes as financial vice president.

Wright never denied what I accused him of, but he countered by claiming that "Schirmer is paranoid about people who disagree with him." I thought, what the hell did he mean by that? Did he disagree with me that taking supplies was theft? Then Wright went into my firing of Randy Wells, a fellow Law student, as ombudsman earlier last week. Wright further stated that, "The whole thing was just an example of Ted's playing power politics. Randy disagreed with him, and Ted took it personally. I don't like his getting personal."

Little did I suspect, but that was just the beginning. The next two weeks I found myself having to battle the blowback from firing Wells coupled with confronting Ned Wright over taking SGA office supplies. Damn, this was just the first two weeks of my taking office. I thought, what the hell was in store for me in the coming months? Fortunately, I had a lot of experience fighting for things I believed in during my life. I sure in the hell wasn't going to stop now. I believed I was voted into office to take on those issues and individuals.

## A TRAP SET BY THE LAW STUDENTS

When Free Speech Alley was over, I was walking back to my office when I was approached by a fellow student. He told me that he had transferred to LSU from Louisiana Tech, and he remembered Ned Wright from when Ned was a sophomore at Louisiana Tech and a Tech SGA senator. He had used telephones in the Louisiana Tech SGA office to make personal long distance calls, charging them to SGA. Wright was charged with misuse of SGA phones and later found guilty. This information was what I thought I needed to get the Assembly to order Ned to open up SGA's financial books. I hurried up to my office and placed a call to the Louisiana Tech SGA office to confirm this information. I was in luck. The person I talked to said that there had been an issue with Ned using Tech SGA's phones for personal long distance calls, but that person didn't know all of the details. I thanked him. I thought I had the information I needed if my word wasn't enough to get the Assembly to order Ned to show me the books.

On the night of April 21$^{st}$, a group of us met at the SGA office to walk over to the Assembly together. Assembly meetings were held at night in the old Law School building. Marion Campbell and John Crochet walked over with me. I was confident that the Assembly would order Ned to let me see his purchasing orders. After all, I was the chief executive officer of SGA. If there were any questions about my need to see how Ned was spending SGA funds, I would tell the Assembly what I had found out about Ned's time at Louisiana Tech. I would only use that information if I felt I had to.

As we walked into the Assembly meeting, I immediately noticed Ned Wright standing with John Porterfield. Additionally, I saw that the *Reveille* reporter covering the meeting that night was Jerry Fiegler. He and I had had had some words in the past. This concerned me some, but I had been fighting the conservative editors and reporters of the *Reveille* ever since becoming a student activist on campus.

On the Assembly agenda for that night were two of my cabinet appointments: Beno's for ombudsman and Naaman Eicher as my executive assistant. Naaman would later become a foe of mine on campus. In 1990, he and his father were sentenced to 46 months in federal prison, plus they agreed to pay $12 million in fines for mail fraud relating to their defunct Champion Insurance Company.

The plan was that, after my appointments were voted on by the Assembly, a CPU member of the Assembly was going to move to order Ned to open up his books to me. Since I was not a member of the Assembly, I stood to the side, and watched as, to my astonishment, the CPU member was out maneuvered by John Porterfield. When he rose to be recognized by the chair, Dana Robert, legislative vice president, who was the Chair of the Assembly, instead recognized John Porterfield. The next thing I knew, two bills had been introduced by John Porterfield and seconded. One bill had to do with taking away my power to appoint my ombudsman and giving it to an SGA Committee. Their other bill was to give Ned Wright, the financial vice president, the power to sign purchase orders, without the necessity of my signature, and to hire his own staff.

Since I wasn't a member of the Assembly, I couldn't be recognized by the Chair to speak. I had to have a supporter who was an Assembly member rise and be recognized by the Chair, then give me their time. But even then, there usually was a five minute time limit.

I had difficulty with a five minute window. Due to the fact I had never learned in public school how to organize on paper a coherent argument, I didn't speak that way. Again, unknown to me at the time, I had ADHD, which, without medication, made it impossible for me to organize my thoughts in a coherent way on my feet. Due to this, and how fast I spoke to try to get everything I wanted to say into the five minutes I was allocated, I could tell by the faces of the members of the Assembly that I was losing them. I also realized that Ned and his fellow law students must have lobbied them earlier because the vast majority of members weren't paying any attention to me.

The first bill, the one taking the power of appointing the ombudsman away from me and giving it to a SGA committee, passed 29–8. Eight was the number of CPU members on the Assembly. Even though we lost big time, I wasn't that concerned with losing that fight since I would veto the bill, and if my veto was overridden by the Assembly, I would appeal to the University Court. I was confident that I would win in court since it was clearly written in the SGA constitution that it was the prerogative of the SGA president to appoint the members of his administration, of which the ombudsman was one.

I was more concerned about the second bill. That bill would give Wright the power to sign purchasing orders and hire his own staff. Knowing what I did about what Wright was doing in the office, coupled with what I had learned about Wright's activities at Louisiana Tech, I felt I had to stop that bill.

During the debate on the bill, I walked over to a CPU member in the Assembly to consult with him about what I had found out about Wright at Louisiana Tech. As I did so, I saw Wright following me up the aisle and sitting down at a nearby desk. I shot Wright a "are you in for a surprise" look as I turned back to the Assembly member and started going over what I had found out about Wright. I suddenly heard Ned angrily say, "You better not say anything about that!" I told him if he didn't have his people withdraw the bill being debated on the floor, I would be forced to inform the Assembly of what I found out. Shaking with rage and jabbing his finger in my face, he started threatening to kick my ass if I said anything. Once again, it just amazed me how those law students thought they could get me to not do something by threatening me. That just showed Wright didn't know me at all.

By then, everyone in the Assembly was glancing over at us. Most of them observed what happen next. Wright was shaking his finger within an inch of my mouth while he was threatening me, so I leaned forward and forcibly bit down on it. He gave out a howl of pain and slung his other hand at my face, but I just knocked it away. He then started to try to get up from the desk. What a fool! There was no way I was letting him get up from that desk. I had the strategic advantage in this physical confrontation, and I wasn't planning to lose it. So, he just kept swinging at me with his left hand while I easily deflected it away from me.

While this was going on, I felt Marion Campbell's back pressing against mine. Marion literally had my back. Marion had become one of my closest friends. Growing up in New Orleans, and being Lebanese, he and his brothers had constantly been picked on in school, so they had started taking martial arts classes. They each mastered a different style of martial arts. The brothers told me that, after a couple of fights, they had established they were to be left alone. In short, Marion was a good person to have protecting my back.

I continued to swat away Wright's feeble attempts to hit me while sitting behind the desk. That was just good "military training" kicking in! Once you have the advantage in a fight, keep it until the fight is over, one way or another. Of course, I had learned a version of that as a child, but the hand-to-hand combat training I had learned in the military just reinforced that approach. I didn't see Ned as a future physical threat to me, so just letting him know I wasn't scared of him was enough. No need to hurt him any more than my bite did.

Like most fights, this confrontation only lasted a few minutes before the CPU member I had been talking to got between Wright and me and brought our little scuffle to an end. Wright would walk around for days with an ostentatiously bandaged finger. I think he was wearing it as a badge of courage.

As the debate over the bill continued, I and the CPU Assembly members kept trying to get the information about what Wright had done at our office and at Louisiana Tech in front of the Assembly. The clever use of parliamentarian rules kept blocking our efforts.

To the consternation of Assembly Chair Dana Robert, I was reduced to outbursts from the sideline to counter what Wright and Porterfield were stating about the need for passage of the bill. Dana was constantly trying to make me be quiet. Despite the information that I and other CPU members were trying to tell the Assembly, the bill passed 26–9, giving Wright the authority to purchase SGA office supplies with only his signature.

Now that the Assembly had given Wright the authority to hire his own staff, he immediately hired a secretary, paying her a $180 a month. With the financial vice president being paid $150 per month and his secretary $180 a month, SGA was paying $330 (nearly $1,500 per month in today's dollars) for the job Ned Wright was elected to perform.

An editorial in the *Reveille* (April 23, 1976) written by Jerry Flegler, the reporter who covered the Assembly meeting, and titled "Bell tolls for Ted" stated that I had taken "an eight count from the Assembly" after walking into a "carefully laid trap Wednesday night and didn't know what hit him." He went on to explain that from the beginning of my taking office, I had been "faced with a growing sentiment, possibly a conspiracy, to keep his reign in check and make sure his power over the Assembly and elsewhere is much less" than I expected. In reality, I really didn't know what kind of power an SGA president had from my little experience on the Assembly and from watching other SGA presidents in the past. Those presidents did little, or nothing, for the student body and never seemed to stand up to the administration.

The editorial pointed out that Ned Wright had surfaced as my "chief enemy in the SGA office and government." With no mention of the corruption by Wright that I had exposed, the editorial went on to describe how other conservatives on campus have "rallied around Wright" to prevent me from going too far. He claimed that those students had prevented me from getting much done other than "perform some social functions." WTF, it had only been three weeks since I took office. What the hell did he expect to be done in three weeks?

Flegler further wrote how I was unable to stop the Assembly from passing the two bills, and then implied those defeats were what led to a "slap fight between [me] and Wright." If he had checked with me before writing his editorial that same night, I would have corrected him. I know he must have heard Ned Wright's howl of pain after I bit him and later saw Wright's bandaged finger. Just another example of student journalism at its best. I didn't realize that I would experience much worst in the coming year. The editorial than stated that I had "retired from the room soon after in a mood of frustration…because the cards had been stacked against him."

To his credit, he pointed out "how easily the rules of the Assembly were manipulated to, first, allow the bills to reach the floor and, second, to disregard the unconstitutionality of the action." It was nothing more than law students at work. The Assembly totally disregarded the parliamentarian, David Lofton, who pointed out the unconstitutionality of the Assembly's action in passing both bills. Flegler ended his editorial with a line I agreed with a hundred percent: "The lines have been drawn."

After that night, due to the fact that the law students clearly established that they had control of the Assembly, I realized I would have to fight the Assembly, at least while the Assembly was composed of its present members. Since the semester was ending soon and a number of Assembly members would be graduating or dropping out of the Assembly due to grades or lack of interest, I thought I might have more luck getting things done in the summer and fall semesters.

## THE BICENTENNIAL CELEBRATION

While all this was going on, the administration and faculty were in the final stages of preparation for the Bicentennial Celebrations to be held on campus on April 30th in the Bicentennial year of 1976. A number of such events would lead up to July 4, 1976, the 200th anniversary of the adoption of the Declaration of Independence.

The state of Louisiana, including Governor Edwin Edwards, wanted in on the Bicentennial, so they started pushing for LSU to be named a Bicentennial University. A *Reveille* (February 7, 1975) article, titled "Edwards wants university named bicentennial school," reported:

> In a letter to Chancellor Paul W. Murrill, Edwards said,
> "Through the university becoming a Bicentennial Institu-

tion, an opportunity will be made available to highlight Louisiana's unique heritage and contribution to the greatness of America." Another heritage program would be the celebration of the 50th anniversary of the university's present location. Some tentative plans for this included a reenactment of the 1926 dedication service.

Chancellor Murrill said, "The involvement of the university in the bicentennial offers an opportunity for the university to pause and take stock of its influence."

LSU won the recognition as a Bicentennial University that they had sought, and the administration had been working hard on this event for a year. The problem I saw with all of this planning was that the only event involving the student body was the time capsule that the previous SGA president, Paul Benoist, had started. It was left to me to get together the SGA's items that were going to be put in the time capsule.

I wrote a letter, as SGA president, addressed to the 2076 students of LSU, describing how conservative LSU students were, but they still elected someone like me. I also wrote some things about rock festivals and the politics of the day. I concluded with a statement about how great the marijuana grown in Louisiana was and placed a handful of marijuana seeds in the envelope, writing that these seeds came from marijuana named Atchafalaya Red and Amite Blue, some of the best dope grown in south Louisiana. I put some magic mushrooms from my place on River Road in the envelope also, but they caused the envelope to bulge so much that I feared that it might burst open, so I removed them. Shit, I didn't want to get busted for trying to put dope in a time capsule. I put my letter to the future in with the other boxes of LSU items that had been purchased at the LSU Union bookstore by the pervious SGA administration and locked them in my closet.

So, the time capsule was the only SGA involvement planned for the Bicentennial Celebrations. That was it! I told my staff I thought that SGA should try to get the student body more involved in the Bicentennial. My first thought was to put on a free concert on the Parade

Grounds during the festivities on April 30th. My friend, Marion Campbell, got very excited by that idea and quickly volunteered to organize and run the event. That was going to be a tall order because he would have only about three weeks to pull it off. Since Marion was a full-time student, I was concerned it would interfere greatly with his classwork and upcoming finals. I asked how his classes were going. He told me he was doing fine in his classes, and he would have plenty of time after the 30th to prepare for finals. I said ok and appointed him to put on the concert.

Marion would later take the experience he got from organizing that concert to organize other SGA free concerts at the Greek theater on weekends and later the Registration Blues Festival in the fall. Regretfully, even though I constantly expressed my concern to Marion about his grades, he later dropped out of school. Allowing Marion to work on so many projects during my year as SGA president became one of the many things I regret in my life. Rest in peace, my dear friend.

The question came up, what time should we set for the concert to ensure that most students would be able to attend the concert? David Lofton pointed out that SGA had already issued Proclamation #3, which described the reason for and the importance of students attending the Convocation. It called "the student body of this university into session immediately south of the LSU Library beginning at 11 A.M. on Friday, the 30th day of April, 1976, and, it is further RESOLVED that all students are hereby requested and strongly urged to attend both the interment of the aforementioned container of artifacts and the aforementioned university-wide Convocation."

I had signed that proclamation on April 8th, and it was going to be interred in the time capsule with the other items from SGA. Since that proclamation, covering the Convocation ceremonies, had been very well received by the administration, why not issue another proclamation covering mid-morning of the 30th, including canceling classes in order to allow students to attend the free concert, which would be one of the Convocation events that day? The SGA constitution gave me the authority to call the student body into session. I liked it!

On April 22nd, the new proclamation was ready. I signed it, and we started delivering copies to colleges all over the campus. An article titled "Proclamation said to be nonexistent" appeared in the *Reveille* (April 27, 1976). As the article pointed out, my proclamation said the Bicentennial celebration would start at 7:30 A.M. and go until 8 P.M. with music by Light Years, Leon Bergeron, Bus Riley, the River City Revue and the Allen Brothers. An academic affairs spokesman stated that my "proclamation is a non-proclamation" and it "should not be taken seriously at all" because I didn't have the "power to dismiss classes."

When the reporter asked me about this, I told him I "was operating legally within the rules of the SGA in exercising [my] right to call the student body into session." I invited the faculty, administrators and staff to come and enjoy April 30th with us, the students.

All day Thursday, I watched as Marion and his crew built a stage on the Parade Grounds in front of the Bell Tower. I couldn't help but wonder if the stage would be ready by Friday. Marion had already lined up bands to play for free at the event in addition to acquiring all the equipment needed to put on a concert this size.

The morning of April 30th, I felt I had just the outfit to wear. After leaving the Navy, I had kept my navy bell bottom work dungarees. Even though I had been out of the Navy for seven years, the sewing skills of Mary (Susanna's mother) had kept them held together with patches. I had also had Mary sew red, white and blue fringe on the bottom of the dungarees. I felt those pants were perfect for celebrating the United States Bicentennial. In addition, I wore my Viet Nam jungle fatigue jacket with my World War I campaign hat, also known as my Smokey the Bear hat.

At the ground breaking ceremonies for the SGA time capsule, when Chancellor Murrill saw what I was wearing, he gave me one of those looks. I am sure that look was also related to my proclamation. Seeing him looking at me like that, I just smiled and swung my arms out to gesture in each direction. Surrounding the upcoming groundbreaking ceremonies were students standing five to six feet deep. He glanced around, then smiled back at me as the ceremony started.

After I had finished with all my duties of appearing and speaking at events around the campus, I went to the Parade Ground to relax, get high and enjoy the music with my fellow students. I sat down with some friends of mine to listen to Greg Wright's band Light Years. At some point, Marion came over to me and said that I needed to speak to the audience. I was pretty damn stoned at that point and told Marion that I was too stoned to go up on the stage. He argued that I should say a few words about us putting on the concert and asking everyone to help in cleaning up the Parade Grounds at the end of the concert. Even being stoned I realized that I had to also acknowledge the many people who had put so much work into pulling this concert off. I wanted to publicly thank Marion, Curtis Appleby and others for their hard work and long hours they had put in.

So I got up and walked carefully through the crowd to the stage. Now, if I had known I was going to speak at the concert, I wouldn't have gotten stoned, or at least not as stoned as I was at that moment. I climbed the steps of the stage and walked over to the microphone as one of the bands was setting up. All I can remember is that I started off pretty well, in that I named the students who did so much to pull this off and urged the crowd of a couple of thousand to give them a hand. I went on gushing about them until I was brought back to planet earth with yells of get off the stage. I quickly wrapped up with a call for everyone to help pick up trash after the concert was over, then hurried back to my friends. With a shit eating grin, I said, "Well, that went over well!" We all laughed and laid back to enjoy the rest of the concert.

I knew how important it was for us not to leave a mess on the Parade Ground. That would be all the administration needed to stop us from having other such events. We all stayed after the concert ended to help pick up the garbage. Regretfully, only about a dozen students stayed to help. Most of the students who did stay were people who had been working on the event all night and day. The amount of garbage wasn't as great as at the Celebration of Life festival, but it was a lot for just twelve people to pick up. It took us into the wee hours to finish. As I drove home, completely exhausted, I felt, in spite of everything, that the concert had been a great success. Then I said to myself, "Jesus, this was just the first month!"

## STUDENT REPRESENTATIVE ON
## LSU'S BOARD OF SUPERVISORS

In the '70s, the Board of Supervisors served as the management board for the Louisiana State University System. The Board consisted of sixteen voting members, who served overlapping terms. As of 1975, the Board also had the first student member of the Board who could speak on issues but had no vote. The student representative was the chairman of the LSU system's Student Government Association of Presidents. As the name implies, the organization is made of all the presidents of the LSU system's Student Government Associations. The Board position was to rotate among the different universities in the LSU system and, I knew it was LSU Baton Rouge campus' turn for the 1976–77 academic year.

On the morning of May 11th, I received word that the Student Government Association of Presidents was meeting that afternoon after lunch. The letter was signed by Billy G. Lyons, last year's SGA president at the LSU Shreveport campus, the out-going chairman of the Association of Presidents, and thus the student representative last year on the Board of Supervisors. I thought there would be some kind of ceremony involving Billy G. Lyons' leaving as chairman and my becoming the new chairman and student representative on the Board.

I asked John Crochet to meet me for lunch in the Tiger Lair so we could discuss how to handle the upcoming meeting after I became the new chairman. I always invited John to accompany me to any meetings I had to attend that might deal with parliamentary rules and procedures. I had learned that John, who gave himself the title of aide-de-camp to the president, was a wiz at matters dealing with such matters. Hell, he and David Lofton literally wrote the book on the SGA's parliamentary rules and procedures, which followed along the lines of *Robert's Rules of Order.*

When John met me for lunch, he, as usual, showed up with a binder. He had found time to map out some of the areas he felt should be covered at my first meeting as chairman. I went over his points while eating, then we walked over to the Board's conference room in Thomas Boyd Hall.

We arrived a few minutes before the meeting was to start. Opening the door, we walked into an empty room. The other SGA presidents hadn't arrived yet. We had the room to ourselves. John said that, since I was now the chairman, I should sit at the head of the long conference table. I sat down, took off my Smokey the Bear hat, and placed it on the table beside me.

We ended up sitting there for 10 to 15 minutes before the door opened. The first person through the door was Billy Lyons, followed by all of the other newly elected SGA presidents of LSU at Alexandria; LSU at Eunice; University of New Orleans LSU Medical Center (New Orleans) and LSU Medical Center (Shreveport). I got up to shake their hands and introduced John and myself to Lyons. As I was during this, he said he was sorry that I wasn't able to have lunch with all of them. As I looked at John, I said I didn't know anything about a luncheon meeting. He quickly added that it wasn't a meeting, just a chance for everyone to meet.

Before I could ask about their lunch, one of the other SGA presidents took my hand, turning me away while introducing himself. While I was busy greeting the other presidents, I noticed Lyons looking down at my hat at that end of the table, then walking down to the other end of the table to take a seat.

After everyone was seated, Lyons called the meeting to order. What was supposed to happen was a roll call and the reading of the minutes of the previous meeting of the LSU Student Government Association of Presidents. Instead, Lyons opened the meeting with a statement that he would entertaining a motion to select the new student member to the Board of Supervisors. Then a discussion broke out. Several from the northern part of Louisiana said that we weren't bound by last year's agreement about the selection order and argued that we had a right to choose among ourselves which one of us would sit on the Board.

Since we were under *Robert's Rules*, I stifled an outburst as I shot up my hand to be recognized to speak, but one of the SGA presidents from upstate said, "I so move." While I was still attempting to be recognized to speak, Lyons quickly asked if there was a second, at which point another SGA president from upstate seconded the motion. That was too much for me, and I shouted out, "What the fuck's happening? It's the Baton Rouge campus's turn to have their SGA president sit on the Board of Supervisors as previously agreed upon by all of the SGA presidents representing their schools."

From my standpoint, it quickly became obvious what their meeting at lunch had been about. That had been no simple meet and greet, rather an opportunity for Lyons to persuade the other presidents to ditch last year's agreement. The more I talked, the more upset I became, realizing that was why I hadn't been invited to the luncheon.

After a few more choice words by me, the question was called, and Lyons asked if there was any more discussion before taking a vote on to reopen the selection process for which campus' SGA president would be sitting on the Board. Only the New Orleans president spoke out against re-opening the selection process. He argued that an agreement made by the former SGA presidents should be honored by the current SGA presidents. No one else spoke either for or against the motion.

Lyons called for a show of hands in favor and who was against. The New Orleans president and I were the only "no" votes. Lyons, not being a student body president any longer, didn't vote. But I am guessing he didn't need to. He knew what the vote was going to be before they even arrived for the meeting.

Later, I pulled the minutes of the Board of Supervisors meeting that day, and there was an entry of Lyons telling the other members that "as the outgoing student member on the Board, he has called a meeting today of the several Student Government Association Presidents in the Louisiana State University System in order that the selection by them be made of his replacement for the upcoming year." I am guessing that after my election as the Baton Rouge SGA president, the first student member of the Board of Supervisors had been asked to convince the other new student body presidents in the LSU System to shit can the agreement negotiated last year.

They decided to tear a sheet of paper into six bits, wrote a number "1" on one piece, and left the others blank, then folded all six pieces multiple times for a blind drawing. The discussion turned to what to use to put the papers in for the drawing. I offered my hat, which was accepted. After our heated debate about screwing the Baton Rouge campus over, I was offered the first draw. I told them I preferred to go third, since three was my favorite number. They agreed to allow me to go third.

The six bits of folded paper were put into my hat, and Lyons held the hat above the head of the first-person drawing. I watched as he drew his paper and did not unfold it. He just set it down in front of him. The second person did the same. I don't remember anyone stating that this was required so, as the hat was held over my head, I reached up and pulled out one of the folded bits of paper. As Lyons was holding my hat over the next president's head for him to draw, I unfolded my paper. The number "1" was written on it. With a big smile of satisfaction on my face, I threw the paper into the middle of the table. I looked at them all as I got up out of my chair, saying, "Don't call me, I'll call you about the next meeting."

A week later I had to go to Governor Edwin Edwards' office in the State Capitol to be officially appointed to the LSU Board of Supervisors. I saw a group of reporters and TV cameras as I arrived and wondered what was up. Before I could speak to the Governor's secretary, a man hurried up to me. He quickly identified himself as Camille Gravel, executive counsel to the Governor, and stuck out his hand. As I took it, he guided me into what appeared to be a janitor's broom closet. I looked around at the brooms, mops, buckets and other cleaning objects, thinking, "What the fuck is this old dude up to?" Once inside the broom closet, he closed the door and asked me, would I mind if he gave me my appointment to the Board of Supervisors instead of the Governor?

I realized then why all those reporters and TV cameras were there. They were waiting for me to arrive. They must have heard that LSU's long haired hippie SGA president was to be appointed by Governor Edwards to the Board of Supervisors as the new student member. The Governor must have sent Gravel to intercept me before I could get to his office. There was no way that Edwin Edwards was going to allow any damn hippie to steal the limelight from him. Also, I am sure, the other two new members of the Board, Attorney Jerry McKernan from Baton Rouge and W. T. Hanna Jr., the owner of a car dealership in Shreveport, didn't want to have to answer questions about joining the Board with someone like me.

I laughed, telling Camille Gravel, "Sure, I don't mind at all," while taking the cardboard tube out of his hand. The tube contained a very elaborate and fancy certificate of appointment to the Board of Supervisors. Camille looked relieved and thanked me as he opened the broom closets door and gently guided me in the direction of the elevator. As a result, I made a friend of Camille Gravel. He was also a Board member and would help me a lot in the future.

Since I had never been a member of any organization like the Board of Supervisors, I really didn't think twice about just wearing my regular school clothes for my first Board meeting. Looking back, I was completely out of touch with what was expected of a member of the Board of Supervisors. Sure, I had seen pictures of the Board in the *Gumbo* that showed the men on the Board wearing suits and ties and Ruth Miller wearing a dress. It never dawned on me that they wore those types of clothes at every meeting. I thought that the members had dressed in suits and ties (and a dress) to have their pictures taken for the yearbook. That just showed how out of touch I was with that whole world of suits and ties. It is hard to imagine how unfamiliar I was at that time with the world outside of my life of poverty and in the military.

I know it must be hard for individuals who come from an entirely different socioeconomic status with their perceptions of social norms to believe that someone like me would not know how to dress as a member an organization as powerful as the Board of Supervisors. Looking back, I think I was like one of the Clampett family in *The Beverly Hill-billies*, except I was from Hogg Ridge Road, Kentucky, instead of the Ozark Mountains.

Unfortunately, on the day of my first Board of Supervisors meeting, due to my busy schedule as both a student and the SGA president, I lost track of time. When I remembered, I was already late for the meeting, so I hustled over to the Board meeting being held in Thomas Boyd Hall. I was wearing my Viet Nam jungle jacket, a T-shirt, my bell bottom pants, adorned with patches, sandals, and my WWI campaign hat. This was my normal attire on those many hot and humid Louisiana days. In addition, due to the heat and humidity, I was also wearing my hair in a ponytail.

When I got to the Board's outer office, only the receptionist was at her desk. The other staff members were already in the meeting. As I walked through the door, I saw a stunned look on the receptionist's face. Being a long haired freak in Louisiana, it was not uncommon for me to get those looks. I did not realize until later that it was because of how I was dressed to attend my first Board meeting. Hell, after getting to know the Board's long time head secretary, Kitty Strain, I realized that, if she had been at her desk, she would probably have tried to stop me from entering the meeting in order to protect the image of the Board.

Instead, when I asked the receptionist where the Board meeting was taking place, without saying a word, she just pointed at the door that led to the room. "Thanks," I said as I headed toward the door.

Having run across campus, I stopped for a minute outside the door to catch my breath. As I stood there, I wondered if any of the individuals I was about to meet for the first time had been behind the attempt to keep me off of the Board. I decided to watch their faces. That might tell me.

Realizing how late I was for the meeting, I attempted not to disturb it by slowly opening the door. I had never been to a Board of Supervisors meeting and didn't realize that I was using the door that non-Board members used. Therefore, when I stepped into the meeting room, I was in the section where administrators like Chancellor Murrill and Vice Chancellor Reddoch sat along with citizens attending the meeting. Board members had a separate entrance.

I saw all of these men dressed in suits and ties, and Ruth Miller in a dress, sitting in a semicircle of leather chairs facing toward me and the other people in the audience. Amazingly, I didn't feel uncomfortable about my attire. Since my childhood, I had learned to accept the fact that I was different from most people because I came from a poor family and not because I was a "freak."

However, this situation threw me off enough that I forgot all about trying to study the looks on Board members' faces. Instead, I saw some members, like Camille Gravel, Jerry McKernan and Gordon Dore looking amused while others looked disgusted and even angry.

After the swearing in of new Board members, Jerry Mc Kernan, W. T. Hanna, the Governor's gambling buddy, and myself, I just kept my mouth shut. (Yes, I know those who know me may find this hard to believe.) I was trying to figure out what the role of a non-voting student member of the Board entailed.

None of the members said anything to me about how I was dressed during the whole meeting or afterward. But Kitty Stain, the Board's longtime secretary, expressed her displeasure when I came over to the Board's office to pick up the next week's agenda. She pleaded with me to not go to the Board meetings in patched bell bottom jeans and T-shirts and urged me to wear a suit to the meetings. I could tell a couple of things from her request. One, she didn't have a clue that a person, like me, coming from the economically deprived life I came from, wouldn't even own a suit. Second, she wasn't taking into account that, except for rare Board meetings held on a Saturday, all the other meetings were during the week. I was a student at LSU trying to attend classes during the day. I wore the same clothes to Board meetings that I wore to school. Along with many other individuals, both in the administration and student body, I believe she felt that I dressed the way I did as some kind of act. The clothing I wore my first few years out of the military consisted of my old military clothes. And the many patches on

211

my clothes had as much to do with patching holes as they did with making a cultural statement.

I liked and respected Kitty and could tell that she was very upset over what I wore to Board meetings. I told her I would try to borrow a suit if it meant that much to her.

That weekend, my friend and attorney, Stewart Thompson, was over at our house for dinner. I mentioned what I had observed about how the other Board members were dressed. I said that I would be damn if I was going to buy a suit, but I was concerned if the way I dressed would affect my ability to represent students throughout the LSU systems. Stewart, who was around my same size, told me he would loan me a suit and tie to wear to the meetings. After a discussion, I agreed that it would be best for me to "clean up my act" in order to get the Book Rental and other matters approved by the Board.

Stewart loaned me a brown, three-pieces, corduroy suit that I kept in my office and wore to every meeting for the remainder of my time on the Board. The first time I wore it, I realized why Stewart didn't wear the suit: it was hot as hell in the Louisiana heat and humidity.

## Summer Semester, 1976
### RESOLVING THE NED WRIGHT PROBLEM

Even though as SGA president I was not required by SGA bylaws to be a full-time student during the summer semester, I did have to take at least six hours in order to collect my VA education benefits check. I signed up for two classes, Economics of Consumption (I still wanted to learn more about capitalism) and Political Parties in the United States. Late in the summer I had to drop my economics class with a W-D, but I managed to make a B in my Political Parties class.

Beside academics, my other major concerns, that summer of 1976, was the bill the Assembly had passed giving Wright the authority to purchase SGA supplies with just his signature. Because it was passed at the last Assembly meeting of the spring semester, and the Assembly did not meet again until the fall semester, I was not able to veto the bill. I feared that Wright would abuse this new authority even more than he had already abused his job as financial vice president. I was soon to find out I wasn't wrong to worry about him.

Shortly after the summer session started, I was contacted by Vice Chancellor Coco, LSU's comptroller. He said that he would like to see me. When I got to his office, he handed me a stack of papers asking if I was aware of this spending of SGA funds by my financial vice president. I thought to myself, I wish he was "my" financial vice president because I would fire his ass.

As I sat down, I noticed that he had handed me a batch of invoices and purchase orders. I didn't recognize any of these orders. Ned Wright's signature was the only name on the purchasing orders. It appeared that lots of money had been spent on office supplies in just the first month of my administration. The supplies included legal pads, pens and lots of rolls of stamps. There was no way SGA required that many stamps in less than a month. I was shocked at how blatantly Ned was purchasing SGA supplies without my knowledge or signature.

I told Mr. Coco that I had no clue how much money the financial vice president was spending or on what. I explained that I had asked Wright to show me the SGA's books, but that he had refused to provide me with any records of his spending. Vice Chancellor Coco told me that it wasn't good accounting methods to have only the financial vice president's signature on SGA's invoices and purchase orders. He explained to me that, as SGA president, I was the person who would be held responsible if funds were misused or stolen. He suggested having at least two signatures on all invoices and purchasing orders, one of them being mine, since I was the one ultimately responsible for where the monies of SGA went.

I explained what Wright and his supporters had done in the Assembly the previous spring semester. I told him my concerns about all of this and inquired how I could change it. He said, as SGA president, I only had to sign a form with his office to require all SGA purchase orders and checks have my signature on them. I filled out the form right there in his office and signed it. As I was signing the paperwork, making me the only one authorized to spend SGA funds, I realized that this was in direct defiance of the Assembly bill that had passed overwhelmingly last spring. It would likely embolden my enemies in the Assembly to file impeachment articles against me. Since I firmly believed I was doing the correct thing, I thought, fuck 'em, I would cross that bridge when I get to it.

As I left the vice chancellor's office, he told me if I had any more questions, his door would always be open to me. Vice Chancellor Coco and I would maintain a good working relationship for the remainder of my time as SGA president.

It turned out that any worries about my enemies acting against me for circumventing the Assembly's bill were put to rest a few days later when the *Summer Reveille* printed a number of articles about what Wright had done when he was in student government at Louisiana Tech.

The *Reveille* (June 10, 1976) printed three articles about Wright. The first article, titled "SGA financial vice president, Ned Wright, guilty of phone misuse at La. Tech," confirmed what I had tried to get the Assembly members to listen to last fall. The *Reveille* had contacted Mike Ruddick, the 1973 Louisiana Tech SGA vice president and chief justice of SGA's judiciary when Wright was a senator at Louisiana Tech. He confirmed that Wright had indeed been found to have used SGA phones for personal long distance phone calls and charged them to the SGA. After two judicial hearings, Wright was ordered to make restitution. The 1973 Louisiana Tech SGA treasurer, Don McGehee, stated he had found the illegal use of the SGA phones when he noticed inconsistencies when he broke down the phone bill for one month. The Louisiana Tech judiciary committee, made up of two faculty members and three students, had investigated the charges against Wright. Even after Wright had been asked personally by Mike Ruddick if he had made the phone calls, he stated he didn't remember making the calls. The former treasurer had to contact the phone company to trace the calls. At that time, he found out that the calls went to Ned Wright's parents' home. After confronting Wright on why he didn't admit that he had made the calls, he said he had forgotten to notify SGA he had made the calls and was embarrassed to admit it. What crap. Wright probably didn't think they would go as far as tracing the calls to him. He further alleged that it was a political hit job by other students because he was going to run for SGA president in the upcoming elections at La Tech. He indeed did run for SGA president and came in last.

Later, Ned Wright created a stir by publicly resigning from CPU along with Joe Wills, the chairman of CPU, and Naaman Eicher, SGA executive assistant to me.

Ned Wright's resignation from CPU I could understand. Wright told the *Reveille* (July 27, 1976) that he didn't "believe CPU is representative of students at LSU." Wright wanted to deflate CPU's influence among the student body and, at the same time, strike out against me.

The resignation of Joe Wills as chairman of CPU, on the other hand, really baffled me. Joe Wills stated in the same *Reveille* article that he was:

> ...resigning from the organization because it is "ceasing to provide any kind of functional service to the university. The two areas where CPU could help, giving free concerts and providing public services, can better be served by other campus organizations....Technically Ted has no control over CPU since he doesn't hold any office in it, but in actuality he has a great deal of control over it."

My involvement with CPU was my attempt to build a strong counterweight to the Greeks on campus. I never attempted to dominate CPU, rather to build an organization consisting of strong student leaders and workers in order to bring about change for the student body at LSU.

Naaman Eicher, executive assistant to the president of SGA, made his resignation from CPU public at the same time as Wright and Wills did but, as he told the *Reveille*, he wanted to:

> ...make it clear [that] his resignation had nothing to do with his opinion of Schirmer or Schirmer's involvement in CPU. His affiliation with other campus organizations and his "dis-illusionment with the present course and progress of CPU" were the sole reasons for his decision...."Under no circumstances is this to be construed as a personal rift between Ted and myself."

Naaman and I later worked together on such projects as the Registration Blues Concert at the beginning of the fall semester. But by the time of the SGA fall elections, things would change. All three of them, and some other former CPU members, would form a political party and run candidates against CPU for SGA positions.

Wills would later admit to me that, when he resigned from CPU and made the statements he did about me then and in the months leading up to the spring SGA elections, they weren't meant personally. He explained that by the summer, he simply was interested in running for SGA offices. He said he thought that by coming out against me, attacking me, he would generate a certain percentage of support from those students who were opposed to me. It was simply a Machiavellian maneuver to help him win office. He stated he still liked me; it was just politics. Really!! This reminded me of the line out of the *Godfather* when Michael Corleone is plotting to kill a corrupt police officer and drug dealer, "It's not personal...it's strictly business."

Ned Wright would be killed in 1988 while driving his 1982 Mercedes-Benz SL convertible in Monroe, Louisiana.

## REVISION OF THE BILL OF STUDENT RIGHTS

In the 1976 spring elections, when I was elected SGA president, the proposed Bill of Student Rights had been overwhelmingly approved by the students. But it still had to pass a review by the Faculty Senate before it went to Chancellor Paul Murrill for final approval. This led to the administration creating a committee of administrators, faculty and students to review and revise the bill before it was submitted to the Faculty Senate.

I became concerned about what the University Revision Committee would do with the bill and decided to step in. As a *Reveille* (June 24, 1976) article reported, "On the request of Ted Schirmer, who helped write the bill, officials are asking Murrill to allow the bill to go before the students again after revisions are made." I got a commitment from Chancellor Murrill that, if any changes were made to the Bill of Student Rights, then the SGA could put it again in front of the student body for a vote.

When the University Revision Committee met in the summer of 1976, everything went smoothly until the discussion turned to a section, which I strongly supported: Article 4, Section 5. It gave "students freedom of expression in public and in private as long as their means of expression do not disrupt essential operations of the university." Since I had been involved in organizing the first demonstration inside any college at LSU, in 1970 at the College of Education, I had worked hard on the language in this section. Defending this wording, I explained how classes weren't interrupted at all during our demonstration in the College of Education, even though our demonstration was during class hours. We had made it a point not to interfere with students trying to attend their classes. In order to establish how important these rights were to successfully bring about changes on the LSU campus, I explained how, due in large part to PSA's demonstration at the college, not only did the College of Education drop their grooming standards, but so did the other six colleges on campus. When students peacefully demonstrated their grievances to the administration, positive results were possible.

After a heated argument between me and the administrators on the committee, most of the committee members agreed "that the vice chancellor for student affairs had the ultimate power to decide at what point 'essential operations' were being impeded." Shit, I fully realized that it wouldn't matter what this section said about the rights of students to freedom of expression and dissent, if Reddoch had the authority to decide if "essential operations were being impeded." There was no doubt in my military mind that Reddoch's having the final say would make those rights meaningless. Even though students had voted for the Bill of Student Rights, I knew that was a long way from the bill going into effect. That was just another fight against the Greeks and the administration that I was going to have to continue in the upcoming year.

I was unable to attend the next meeting of the committee due to the fact that I, and a handful of other students, were busy trying to mail out 30,000 newsletters informing all LSU students of the threat by the administration to eliminate funding for the LSU Student Infirmary and urging them to contact their representatives at the State Capitol to support funding of LSU.

At least my ombudsman, Beno Duhon, attended. I had faith he would successfully defend the bill that the students had voted for. The bill was way too important to leave to student special interest organizations, like the Greeks, and the administration.

As reported in the *Reveille* (July 15, 1976), Vice Chancellor Reddoch was at that committee meeting. He must have also decided that this was too important a matter to leave to someone from his office. In addition to Reddoch, student leaders from four student organizations also attended: the Interfraternity Council (IFC), the Panhellenic Council, the Residence Halls Association (RHA), and the Association of Women Students (AWS).

Vice Chancellor Reddoch and two of the student leaders, representing the Interfraternity Council (IFC) and the Panhellenic Council, again attacked the last line of Article 5, Section 3 of the Bill Student Rights that read, "Campus organizations receiving funds, credits, property or things of value from the state cannot arbitrarily deny membership to any student who wishes to join." Their clever attack focused in on the word "arbitrarily," totally disregarding the sentence preceding which stated that all student organization "shall be open to qualified students without respect to sex, race, creed or national origin." The problem for the university and their favorite flunky student group, the Greeks, was this would affect the Greeks directly and indirectly.

The Greek houses sat on state property, so this alone should have prevented them from discriminating against students who wanted to join them. In addition, the university subsidized them by charging very little rent for the land the houses sat on, and, when the houses were built on campus, the university backed the bank loans. No bank was going to loan money to build a fraternity or sorority house on property owned by another party without that landowner's backing. Then the administration justified all this financial support by listing the Greek houses on campus under student housing. That was while allowing the Greeks to discriminate against Louisiana citizens who are students at LSU and Louisiana taxpayers. All of this support by the administration had paid dividends for them by the passive way all of the past Greek SGA presidents and Student Assembly members had dealt with the LSU administration when it came to bringing about positive changes for the student body that, for one reason or another, the administration opposed.

The *Reveille* further reported that, of the members of the committee present—which told me that the committee was poorly attended—for this meeting, "about half suggested the word be 'arbitrarily' replaced with 'prejudicially,' while the remaining participants called for the elimination of the sentence" all together.

That's when Reddoch decided to "advise" the committee that what they were doing stepped outside of the federal guidelines of Title IX. That Title IX specifically exempted fraternities and sororities from the guidelines. What a red herring! We knew that Title IX exempted fraternities and sororities from discriminating due to sex. They were also granted tax-exempt status. By so doing, they sanctioned discriminatory behavior by these organizations, which, as a Republic, we profess to be against.

Fraternities and sororities have a long history of racism and a lack of diversity. Hell, the national chapters had official race-based membership policies up to the 1960s. Dropping those race-based membership requirements did nothing to stop the racism in the Greek system. The traditions of racism and elitism are carried over each year in the chapters on campuses. The very foundation of each chapter is that, as the leaders in the chapter take office each year, they work hard to keep the traditions of that chapter alive. Unfortunately, in some chapters, that included their long history of racism. Even in the present day, some Greeks around the nation dress in "blackface" and hold parties and decorate Homecoming floats with racist themes.

The south, and the slavery that went with it, were the very foundation of at least two fraternities on LSU's campus. Sigma Alpha Epsilon (SAE) and Kappa Alpha Order (KA).

Sigma Alpha Epsilon (SAE), founded in 1856, was the first southern fraternity. SAE was initially restricted to only southern states, i.e. slave holding. There would be no damn Yankee chapters with their talk of ending slavery. But after nearly 27 years, the first chapter appeared in the north, and now SAE has the largest membership of any fraternity in the country. It was very common to see the Confederate Battle Flag displayed at chapter houses all around the nation. There were even worst exhibitions of racism by SAE chapters on college campuses, including LSU's. For example, in the 1976 LSU *Gumbo*, a picture taken in front of the SAE chapter house located on LSU campus, shows an SAE member in the front row holding a rope, with a noose around a man kneeling in front of him. This could easily be interpreted to represent the lynching of Blacks. Nearly 75% of lynchings occurred in the South. The chapter photo further exhibited its racism by showing a member hanging from the balcony by one hand, wearing a black gorilla mask and black gloves and holding a bottle in his free hand. SAE proudly let the university and the state know of its blatant racism.

When I was attending LSU, fraternity members of Kappa Alpha, which was formed in 1865 with Robert E. Lee being their "Spiritual Founder," often wore Confederate uniforms and exhibited the Confederate Battle Flag in front of their house on Dalrymple Drive, one of the main roads at LSU. It was mandatory that a picture of Robert E. Lee be prominently displayed in all chapters. The LSU chapter of KA had a huge mural of Robert E. Lee and Stonewall Jackson on their horses—not General William Tecumseh Sherman, who was the first president of LSU in 1859. In 2001, the National Chapter amended the Kappa Alpha laws to ban the Confederate Battle Flag. They didn't ban the Old South Ball or the Dixie Ball or the wearing of Confederate uniforms at that time. Finally, in 2010, the National Chapter banned them. This was more as cover for the fraternity than meant to actually stop these practices.

Greeks and administrators accused me of being anti-Greek, even though as SGA president I felt I had a responsibility to represent all students. As I stated before, I reached out to the Greeks right after the elections by visiting all of the fraternities and sororities that let me speak at their houses, which wasn't many. I will admit that there were times when I wore that accusation of being anti-Greek as a badge of honor.

## LOBBYING THE STATE LEGISLATURE

It was part of my job as the student government president to lobby the state legislature when bills that concerned students were under consideration. To do this, I attended committee hearings at the Louisiana State Capitol.

The State Capitol is one of the most beautiful Art Deco buildings built during the Great Depression. Built in 1932, thanks to Governor Huey Long, its craftsmanship and décor, inside and outside, are unmatched anywhere in the United States. Governor Long wanted the new State Capitol to be the tallest State Capitol in the United States. He achieved that. At 450 feet, Louisiana's Capitol was then, and is now, the tallest Capitol building in any state in the nation.

The entrance to the State Capitol is a sweeping stairway consisting of 49 steps leading up to the bronze doors of the main entrance. Each step, made of granite from Minnesota, is engraved with the name of a state in the order in which it joined the union. The first thirteen steps have the names of the original 13 states. Then there is a landing before the remaining thirty-six steps continue to the top 49th step, which has two states engraved on it, Alaska and Hawaii.

As I climbed those 49 steps for the first time as LSU's student body president, I realized that I had to change from a solo rebel fighting against injustices that I personally experienced into a representative of all LSU students, yes, even the Greeks. I had never lobbied before, and I was excited to see what it would be like to lobby as an elected official on behalf of all the students at LSU.

I had altered my appearance a little. I did realize that the clothes that I normally wore would not go over well at the State Capitol. With my new salary as SGA president, I was able to buy some new blue jeans (no patches needed) and a long sleeve shirt. That was my total accommodation. I wasn't cutting my hair. By that time, my hair was halfway down my back, and I had a full beard. I also wore colorful love beads in plain sight, tied tightly around my neck. Perched on top of my head was my WWI era Smokey the Bear campaign hat.

I am sure legislators had never seen a lobbyist like me before at the State Capitol. That was the period when seersucker suits, worn with white belts and shoes to match, were the fashion favored by the legislators at the State Capitol. To say that I got their attention when I arrived to lobby them would be an understatement.

I fully realized that the vast majority of those legislators would frown on me, if not downright hate me, for looking as I did. I had to break through this prejudiced opinion of long hairs like me. I wasn't going to surrender my self-identity in order to fit their prejudices, but I came up with a plan to at least give me a fighting chance to speak to them about the bills I was planning to advocate. It had everything to do with my newfound ally: Camille Gravel, the executive counsel to the Governor and my fellow Board of Supervisors member.

I felt that Camille had probably been embarrassed to give me my appointment to the most powerful board of higher education in Louisiana in a broom closet, though I had thought it was hilarious. By not making a big fuss about being snubbed and demanding that the Governor present me with the certificate in person, I made, not just a friend, but a powerful ally.

My plan to impress the Louisiana legislators was, whenever I saw Camille around the State Capitol, either in the halls outside of the House and Senate committee hearing rooms or outside of the House and Senate chambers, speaking with several legislators, I would walk toward him and say in a friendly, loud voice, "'Morning, Camille." As expected, he always smiled and said, "Morning Ted". Now, the expression of the legislators standing around Camille were priceless: a combination of shock and bewilderment. Some, of course, looked disgusted. Regardless, the result of my plan was to let them know that Camille and I where on friendly terms.

Once I went to the State Capitol with several members of the LSU Veterans Association, of which I was the sergeant of arms, to lobby in support of a Viet Nam veterans bill that was coming up before the Education Committee. Camille noticed us and said, "Good morning, Ted." While shaking my hand, he introduced me to the legislators as the student government president at LSU and a new member of the Board of Supervisors. He asked if I were going to speak at the committee hearing on the Viet Nam veteran's bill. I told him I was but didn't know how to go about it. He excused himself to the legislators he had been talking to, then took me by the arm and led me to some men standing in front of the Education Committee's meeting room.

Camille said to me, "This is the sponsor of the bill. Talk to him about speaking." He then introduced me to the legislator, wished me luck, then returned to the other men he had been talking to. I could tell the legislator had some doubts about my speaking in support of his bill. He asked if I had served in Viet Nam. I told him that I served two tours in Nam. That lit up his face. I figured he was thinking that here was a Viet Nam veteran, the LSU student body president, a member of LSU's Board of Supervisors, and just as importantly, maybe more importantly, an associate of Camille Gravel.

We all followed the state representative into the committee room. There was a clipboard for the names of individuals who wanted to speak on the bill. The president of the Veterans Association and I signed up to speak. The representative told us that, when called on, we would sit at the table in front of the committee with other individuals from the various veterans' organizations supporting the bill. He informed us that it wasn't looking good though. A preliminary head count of the committee showed eight against and only five for the bill. He told us to have a seat to wait for him to call us up to speak.

There were representatives of the VFW and the American Legion seated in the front row, waiting to speak. These two organizations were the largest veterans' organizations in the United States. They were made up of mostly aging World War II and Korean veterans with a spattering of Viet Nam veterans. The membership in the '70s believed in sayings like: "America—Love it or Leave it!" and "My country, right or wrong."

By 1976, the Pentagon Papers had been put into book form, and many Viet Nam veterans, including myself, had read them, as well as the book *The Best and the Brightest* by David Halberstam and Susan Wright. Viet Nam veterans who had gone on a personal quest to understand our war, had become fully aware of how we had been lied to. We were looking for a way to stop the war, and a number of us joined the Vietnam Veterans Against the War (VVAW). Yes, we were a small percentage of Nam veterans, but, because we had fought in Nam and had friends who didn't return from that war, we were a strong voice in opposition to the war. I don't remember seeing any WWII or Korean veterans participating in any of the antiwar protests. The American Legion and VFW were more about long meetings and even longer drinking bouts and swapping war stories at the organizations' canteens and bars, while members of the VVAW, like myself, were in the streets fighting to stop the killing and further destruction of an unjust war. We were not just trying to save American lives but also the lives of Vietnamese, Cambodians and Laotians.

In the spring of 1976, I really didn't know what to expect from these older men wearing their post hats proudly on their heads as they waited to testify in the committee room. I decided that I, too, would wear my WWI era Smokey the Bear campaign hat in the committee room. Their hats identified them as members of different clans; my hat showed my membership in the antiwar, hippie clan.

In a short while, the veterans bill was called up for discussion by the committee. The legislator sponsoring the bill took a seat at the table and spoke in support of his bill for what seemed like a pretty short time. In conclusion, he stated, there were several representatives of veterans' organizations and other veterans present who would like to speak on behalf of the bill. He turned and motion for all of us to join him at the table.

The men from the VFW and American Legion got up and took seats at the table to the right of the legislator. The president of the LSU Veterans' Association sat to the left of the legislator and I sat to the left of him. I had decided to sit at the end of the table in order to go last in the speaking order. Listening to the others' statements would help me craft what I would say to the committee. I didn't realize at that time that by going last, I would be responsible for tying up any loose ends that weren't covered by the others. As it turned out, I found myself being the one who had to drive home the point of why Viet Nam veterans deserved the same benefits of free tuition at state colleges and universities as the Louisiana National Guard.

What I didn't realize at the time was that both the VFW and the American Legion had members who were in the Louisiana National Guard. Their lukewarm statements of support for the bill made that fact abundantly clear. They stated their organizations supported the bill with the caveat that the bill did not endanger the Louisiana State Tuition Exemption Program (STEP) for the Louisiana National Guard.

On top of that, it turned out that the president of the LSU Veterans' Association had joined the Louisiana Guard in order to get free tuition at LSU. As I listened to their mealy mouthed statements, I started getting more and more pissed off. It was clear that the other individuals at the table with me weren't putting their hearts into fighting for this bill.

By the time my turn to speak came, I was in my "man the barricades" defiant attitude. I don't think the legislators realized what was about to hit them. At the time, I thought of the National Guard as part-time patriots, weekend warriors (little guessing that in the near future, there would be a vice president, Dan Quayle, and later a president, George W. Bush, who avoided service in Viet Nam by hiding out in the National Guard). My dander was up!

I knew I couldn't attack the National Guard directly, so, to counter my appearance, I started off by letting them think I was one of the "good ole boys" who must have gone astray due to the war. I told them that right after graduating from Istrouma High School in 1966, I answered my country's call and volunteered for the military.

Then I drove the point further home by explaining that I was a jock who had planned to run track at Istrouma High before pulling my plantar aponeurosis, a small muscle in the sole of my right foot. I stated that I was told by Istrouma Coach Lynn Amadee (in 1976 he was the LSU Offensive Coordinator) that I could probably get an athletic scholarship and didn't have to go into the military. I did what I am sure all of them thought was the right thing to do in 1966–67. I volunteered. Right after Boot Camp, I then volunteered for Viet Nam, served in a Navy IUWG 1 unit, and volunteered for a second tour in Viet Nam.

I could tell from the legislators' expressions that they weren't expecting to hear that. The five members in favor of the bill had smiles on their faces, while the faces of the eight members clearly showed that they were in a dilemma.

I explained that thousands of Louisianans had served in Viet Nam and that nearly 900 Louisianans had died in the war. I told them that my good friend was killed the second week in the country. When I volunteered for Viet Nam, I was willing to give my life for this great country of ours. Those of us Louisianans who survived the war came home only to be spat on by our fellow citizens for serving our country.

I could tell that some of the legislators were still holding out. So, I concluded with, "Wasn't there enough blood and sacrifice by your fellow Louisianans to earn us the same benefits that the State Legislatures gives to the National Guard? Haven't Louisiana Viet Nam veterans been spat on enough for answering our country's call to duty?" Then, with a firm look on my face, I sat back in my chair and looked each legislator in the eye. The coup de gras for the eight was when the audience broke out in applause.

The chairman banged on the table for quiet and thanked us. We returned to our seats in the audience. After a short discussion, one of the members called for a vote on the bill. The bill passed 12–1!

As we were leaving, the VFW and American Legion veterans shook my hand and thanked me for my statement to the committee. There was no doubt in my military mind that this was the first time they had said something positive to a long haired hippie, let alone shake a hippie's hand.

I felt great about what had just happened. I thought the bill was a shoo-in. The bill was next sent for a hearing in the Appropriations Committee. The author of the bill had told me he would contact me when he had a date for the hearing. I am not sure why he didn't, but a week or so later I found out that the bill had been defeated in the Appropriations Committee.

Later I was down at the State Capitol lobbying the legislature for more funding for LSU, or at least to not cut LSU's funding. If House Bill 154 passed, it would cut about one per cent from LSU's operating budget. The LSU administration was warning that could trigger a tuition increase, not only at Baton Rouge, but throughout the entire LSU university system.

I attended the committee hearings on House Bill 154 and was one of many individuals speaking in opposition to the bill. I stated how cuts to LSU's funding would inevitably lead to tuition increases at LSU, and that any fee increase would affect low income and poor students the most, possibly even preventing them from attending LSU. I argued that this would defeat one of LSU's main missions, that of providing the underprivileged students of Louisiana the opportunity to acquire a college education. I explained on a personal note, how I was one of those underprivileged individuals. I testified to how little money I received from the VA to attend LSU. This gave me the opportunity to bring up my two tours in Viet Nam. Any increase in the cost of attending LSU could shut the door to a higher education for individuals like myself. None of what the many speakers said against the bill prevailed. House Bill 154 won a favorable vote from the committee.

Later, one of the Baton Rouge representatives said to me, "Ted, you see that man over there? He's the LSU lobbyist." He added that man had told representatives that it was ok to vote for the bill in its present form. I was stunned!

When I later spoke with Chancellor Murrill about this, he stated it was likely that, if the cuts to LSU budget passed, the Board of Supervisors would authorize a $50–$60 tuition increase to make up for the cuts. With a sheepish look on his face, Murrill explained that this would be better for LSU financially in the future, since money raised from a tuition increase would be permanent and consistent revenue for LSU. In other words, it was better for budgeting and planning for the future to have funds that the university could count on instead of funding that was at the whim of the State Legislature every year. Well, I can see how, as chancellor, he could make those cold and calculating conclusions. I, on the other hand, was appalled by how easily Louisiana's poor children were being sacrificed. Huey Long was rolling over in his grave!

I felt that we would have to go more public to have any chance of eliminating the proposed rollback in funds. I started planning a newsletter to be mailed out to all 30,000 LSU students, present and incoming, who were home for the summer. If we informed all the students of what was happening, and if enough of them contacted their legislators, I believe we could put pressure on the legislature to reject the funding cut.

## SAVING THE STUDENT HEALTH SERVICE

The first attack by the administration on funding for the Student Health Service (SHS) started with an announcement by Vice Chancellor for Student Affairs Reddoch. He stated to the *Reveille* (July 1, 1976) that "he feels the administration's position is 'students who use the health services should pay for them.'" The plan was that, in the 1976 fall semester, students would have to pay $5 for each visit plus all costs for lab work or pharmaceuticals. Then beginning in 1977, the administration was going to start cutting funding for the Student Health Service by one-third per year. By 1979, university funding would be completely cutoff. All of this was being justified because of the university's financial situation.

The SHS officials warned that they would have to close the dental, eye and gynecology clinics. Staff physician, Dr. Barrelle N. Addis, pointed out that, if these services were stopped, students would have a hard time finding a local doctor due to a shortage of doctors near LSU. In the previous year, there had been 50,000 SHS visits by students.

I walked over to the infirmary to speak with SHS chief of staff, Dr. Robert Hyde. He explained that with a pay-as-you-go system, it would be very difficult to budget or plan, not knowing how much money would be coming into SHS in any given year. The administration's plan would eventually end health care services for students on LSU's campus. Since I had never had any kind of health insurance in my life, I appreciated the plight that students similarly situated would have to face with no SHS on campus.

The administration had already gotten the Board of Supervisors to cut funding for SHS by $183,000. As the Reveille reported, on July 11, 1976, the administration brought a resolution to the Board of Supervisors to change the status of the SHS into a self-supporting facility. Chancellor Murrill spoke in favor of the resolution. Murrill gave a very dire forecast of cuts in the legislative appropriations for the university for the coming year and stated that cuts would have to be made in many projects on campus. The SHS was just one of those projects. They had "tried to develop the kind of budget strategy that will do minimum damage to academics," Murrill told the Board. He agreed that this plan for the SHS was controversial, but so were other cuts that the university would have to propose.

Dr. Hyde, Dr. Addis and I had met just prior to the Board meeting to coordinate our efforts to derail the administration's plans. When Dr. Hyde spoke, he stated he felt that students would hesitate to come to the infirmary for a minor medical issue because of the $5 charge and would only come to the infirmary when the medical problem got worse. Further, he pointed out that, "there is no major university in the country without prepaid health care. It [pay-as-you-go] has never been done by any university," so why should LSU put its students at risk experimenting with it? I totally agreed with him.

I told Board members that students would be very upset when they returned to campus in the fall to find that the SHS had being turned into a pay-as-you-go infirmary while they were away on summer vacation. I stated that we had 30,000 newsletters being printed up to inform the student body about the administration's plans for the SHS. I asked the Board to delay the vote on the SHS funding pending the establishment of a committee to allow student input and more time to study the proposal.

Jerry McKernan said he agreed with me, stating, "I have talked with students on this issue and the students are very concerned." Then a motion to establish a committee to study the plan and to allow student input was moved and seconded. Murrill then asked that the committee report be ready by the July 23rd meeting of the full Board. Gordon Dore, who was appointed chairman of the task force, objected to Murrill's request saying, "I won't accept the chairmanship if we're going to be squeezed into that time schedule. If we're going to consider it, let's consider it correctly." Murrill's request died right there. Since I was the student member on the Board, the chairman agreed to put me on the task force. We now had time for the students to response to newsletter; we only had to get it mailed out to them!

At the Summer Executive Council of July 8, 1976, I had notified the Student Assembly of my plan for a newsletter to be mailed to all of LSU's registered students. It was to contain information relating to HB154 and the possibility of a tuition increase if the bill passed plus information pertaining to the LSU administration's plan to turn the

SHS from a prepaid healthcare service to a pay-as-you-go service. The newsletter would further provide information on how to contact legislators, the LSU Board of Supervisors, and Chancellor Murrill. I asked for help from the members of the Council in preparing and mailing the newsletter. To my great disappointment, none of the Council members, including both SGA vice presidents, helped in preparing the newsletter.

After the newsletter was printed, in order to get the cheaper bulk rate, the Post Office required us to organize the newsletters into bundles according to zip codes. Bundling 30,000 newsletters into zip codes was a mammoth task.

At the next Assembly meeting, I again pleaded for help in getting the newsletter mailed. With the exception of a couple of Assembly members, who only worked one day for a couple of hours, it was CPU members and my office staff who worked for days getting the newsletters prepared for mailing. At the end of each day, we would mail what we had gotten done, but, due to not having enough students to help us, we weren't able to get all the newsletters mailed on time to affect the legislative vote on HB154. Ned Wright and the conservative *Reveille* reporters he spoke with spread the lie that all 30,000 newsletters were mailed out after the bill had already passed. Only a few thousand newsletters were mailed out late. Even though the newsletter didn't have the impact on HB154 I had hoped for, it did have a great impact in relation to the SHS.

I was not sure how many calls or letters had been received by the chancellor, but, at the next Board meeting, Chancellor Murrill made it clear he was receiving a lot of feedback about the SHS from families of students. I am 100% confident that, without the newsletter, our victory would not have been possible.

At the Board meeting, Murrill offered me a deal. He rolled out on a table the blueprints for the renovations of the French House. Pointing to the ground floor, he stated he thought that would be a good location for the Book Rental once the renovations at the French House were completed. Murrill knew how invested I was in getting a nonprofit Book Rental at LSU. He explained to me that the administration was planning to propose a $55 fee increase to the Board. Tuition would rise from $165 per semester to $220 per semester. He stated that $40 of the $55 was a tuition increase and the remaining $15 would be allocated to SHS.

I realized that all this discussion by Murrill, about the ground floor of the French House being set aside for the Book Rental and that $15 out of the $55 fee increase would go to the SHS, was to get my support for the $55 fee increase. I didn't have a vote, but I did have the ear of a couple of the Board members who did have a vote. I believe what he was asking of me was not to bitch about the fee increase, either openly or to other Board members. What Murrill didn't know was that I already knew that the fee increases had the votes to pass. I therefore had no qualms about agreeing not to speak out against the fee increase when it was up for discussion. I did this in order to save the SHS and to get a location for the Book Rental.

I believe in the yin and yang, in that in every bad there is a good, and the good out of the student fee increase was that I was able to save the SHS from a pay-as-you-go death knell. Even the *Reveille* (July 22, 1976) had to write: "Schirmer managed to get $15 of the tuition increase allocated to support the infirmary, eliminating the threat of pay-as-you-go medical care for students."

In the fall, Dr. Hyde sent me a letter of thanks, which he provided a copy of to the *Reveille*. In the letter he expressed his appreciation for my coming to the aid of the SHS. In the letter, he stated "You gave us your help when we needed it and we certainly want you to know how thankful we are." The *Reveille* (August 10, 1976) reported, in an article titled "Schirmer gets thanks from Hyde, "when interviewed concerning the letter, Dr. Hyde told the reporter, "Ted backed us up on it and told the Board so….He was a lot of help….He did not like the fact that Reddoch tried to put it through in the summertime, when no students are around to fight it….Ted's viewpoints were necessary and helpful because he was the only one there to represent the students."

That summer the LSU rugby team went to Freeport, Bahamas, for a tournament. I had been a member of the team, and would be a member of the team after SGA, but then I was very busy as SGA president, so I hesitated about going. But it was only for a weekend, so I decided to go along. We stayed at a country club and the team we played was the club's team. I discovered, from pictures showing the building of the country club and casino, that it had been built in 1959–60. Knowing a great deal about Cuba, I put two and two together. After Castro kicked the mob out of Cuba, they went to Freeport, Bahamas. We were staying at the mob's country club!

Hell, it did not bother me. I have met a number of Wise Guys in the past. I lived next door to Dominick DiBella in McHenry, Illinois. He was a capo, one of the "Three Dons" in the Chicago Outfit. His showgirl wife once told me, when she heard I was from Louisiana, not to mess with the mob in New Orleans, 'cause there were bodies all over those swamps. I would find out much later, after I took DNA tests, that I was 28% Sicilian.

At the going away party for the LSU rugby team, the head man came up to me, put his arm around my shoulders, and said, "You should come work for us. We can fill your pockets full of gold." I had to remind him that all week I had been speaking to the Bahamian staff at the club on how they should rebel against their second class citizenship in their own country. He then glared at me saying, "Then we can fill your mouth full of gold!" I hit the door.

In 1976, ZZ Top World Wide Texas Tour scheduled a concert at the old Tulane Stadium in New Orleans. On the bill with ZZ Top was J. Geils Band and Lynyrd Skynyrd. Since ZZ Top was one of my favorite bands, as soon as I heard about the concert, I bought two tickets for Susanna and me. Tickets were $12.50 each. We sat on the field by one of the sound towers. I would find out decades later that, while we were inside the stadium, my future wife, Shelley, was outside trying to get into the concert.

What happened at that concert really shouldn't have come as a surprise to anyone who knew the New Orleans Police Department (NOPD). Of course, there were a lot of drugs being sold and used at the concert. J. Geils Band opened the concert. When they were finished, the audience was told that, due to plane problems, Lynyrd Skynyrd wouldn't make it. The following year Lynyrd Skynyrd would be in a plane crash, killing a number of the band members, including Ronnie Van Zant, the lead singer. Even though I had seen them perform at the Ozark Music Festival in 1974, I was disappointed that the band wasn't going to be able to make it. I didn't have much time to be down about that, however, because a police riot erupted.

It seemed that a New Orleans undercover narcotics officer had been discovered by the crowd, and his wellbeing was in serious jeopardy. Into the stadium, through a concourse leading to the field, came a phalanx of NOPD officers with their truncheons held high. They started beating and hitting everyone too slow or too stoned to move. They were beating the people in front of them and to the side as they worked their way to their narcotics officer. It was a dangerous assignment for a narcotics officer to go into a setting like the stadium in order to bust people for using illegal drugs, but that was New Orleans.

Susanna and I had been sitting within feet of where the narcotics officer was stranded and surrounded by some very angry individuals. I didn't know how far into the field this club wielding police phalanx was going to go, so I grabbed Susanna by the arm and told her to climb the tower. We both climbed to about 10 feet off the ground. I felt that was just enough to make it hard for the cops to hit us. Once the cops got to where their compadre was, they commenced to hit and beat everyone in the surrounding area, men and women alike. A number of those individuals were just trying to hold onto the spot on the field they had come hours early to the concert to get. A couple of the cops had worked their way right under us. They started beating the people who, just seconds ago, we had been talking to. I was glad I had the sense to make the quick judgement call I did.

Then I started yelling down at the cops beating those people below us. I, along with thousands of others, started cursing at them and yelling at them to stop. That was when the people in the upper seats of the stadium started throwing bottles. When I saw the bottles flying through the air toward the cops, I couldn't help but yell, with a smile, "In coming!"

As the bottles rained down on the cops, someone on the stage started telling everyone to calm down. At the same time, they were urging the police to leave the stadium. I don't really think the cops needed to be asked. It must have dawned on them that they were heavily outnumbered and in a precarious situation. Bottles were landing all around them and hitting several of them.

The officers gathered up the narcotics officer who appeared to have been roughed up and turned toward the concourse where they had entered moments earlier. By then hundreds of people had descended from the stadium seats and converged on top of the concourse where the police were headed. When the police phalanx got to the concourse, I saw bottles, cans, and even an ice chest raining down on the cops as they were trying to back their way out of the stadium. They were lucky that they all had their helmets on at the time, but even that didn't help the cop hit by the ice chest. When it hit the officer, cans, bottles and ice flew everywhere. That had to have really hurt.

Susanna and I climbed down from the tower. We thought about leaving as a number of people were doing, but I figured the worst was over. Even the NOPD would not attempt to come into the concert again after what had happened to them. We decided to stay to hear ZZ Top. We were glad we did! It turned out to be one of the better performances by ZZ Top or any band we had seen before. The band put on one hell of a show.

## THE REGISTRATION BLUES FESTIVAL

I was not looking forward to registration for the 1976 fall semester. By then I had been through eight registrations at LSU, counting summer registrations. I knew from experience what hell it could be to get all the classes you needed for the upcoming semester.

Registration for incoming freshmen, and those who needed to pick up a class or two, was organized chaos. Every semester there would be horror stories from students who couldn't get the class they needed because it was full, canceled, or the time had been changed. This chaos didn't just stop after the three days of formal registration but would stretch into the following week. Classes would be canceled because not enough students had signed up for them. This mostly happens to upper classmen on the second or third day of registration. Often one would have to run around at the last minute, trying to pick up another class in his major to keep him/her a full-time student.

Well, as the student body president, I felt the students needed a break. My experience with rock festivals over the years convinced me that music was a great vehicle for changing peoples' moods. Hell, if it could work with Viet Nam War veterans, then surely it could get students out of their funk due to the hassle of registration at LSU. What better way to change a sour mood into a party mood than through music? I came up with the idea of a Registration Blues Festival. Of course, to assist in this mood changing endeavor, alcohol would be served at the festival. So work on a Registration Blues Festival, to be held on the weekend at the end of registration for the 1976 fall semester, began a couple weeks into the summer semester.

My overall idea was to, not only provide a stress reliever from the hectic and frustrating registration process, but also to raise money for SGA. I was hoping, during my time as SGA president, that I could get SGA on the path of independence from the LSU administration by generating money for SGA from programs, like the Book Rental and concerts, like the Registration Blues Festival. If SGA could achieve that goal in the future, then student government wouldn't need to worry about the administration giving away their money to other organizations as a tool to divide students or stop the SGA from funding an event that the administration might be trying to stop. It was just common sense that any organization, which depended on money from another organization, would always be subservient to that organization.

When we started discussing where to hold the concert, we soon set our eyes on the Agricultural Center, aka, the Cow Palace. LSU began in 1853 as the Louisiana State Seminary of Learning and Military Academy (the Ole War Skule), but in 1870 changed to the Louisiana State Agricultural and Mechanical College. What I find ironic is that so many Louisianans hate the federal government while not realizing that so many of Louisiana's structures were built completely or in part using funds from the federal government. One such structure was the AgCenter or Cow Palace. It was built as a depression era WPA project under President Franklin Roosevelt, a person whom a lot of today's Louisianans dislike greatly.

We felt the AgCenter might just be the venue for the festival since, up to 1972, when Pete's Palace (the Pete Maravich Assembly Center) opened, the Cow Palace hosted not just rodeos but LSU basketball games and graduations.

We walked over to the AgCenter to see if it would be a good fit for what we had in mind. But for the fact that it was a bit large, it was perfect. We surveyed where the stage could go, and also the beer stands, food stands and stands for any other items we might sell during the concert. We just had to secure it for the weekend after registration in the fall. That's where my executive assistant, Naaman Eicher, was indispensable.

In as much as SGA was a recognized department of LSU, we had the right to rent the AgCenter if no other event was planned for that day. Even though this was true, I knew I would probably run into some resistance acting as the front person for this event. Therefore, I had Naaman negotiate with the administration for the Cow Palace for events scheduled for the coming fall and spring semesters. Looking back, I believe using Naaman to acquire the building for our concert was the key to our success.

We then had to figure out how to build a stage as cheaply as possible. I knew that SGA could purchase wood and other supplies through the university, but I was worried how much it would cost to pull this off. I walked over to the LSU maintenance and warehouse department in the hope we might be able to use some of their wood and tools to build the stage. I met the man who ran the warehouse, out front. I told him what I was looking for as we walked over to where the wood was stored. He pointed out what he had on hand, but then asked, "What about the wooden stage that was used for graduation at the AgCenter?" Graduations had been moved over to the Assembly Center in 1971, and the stage hadn't been used for anything else since. The AgCenter stage was in storage in the warehouse. The warehouse man asked if I wanted to see it. Sure!

The stage was in pieces, but, the warehouse man said, they were easy to assemble, though it would take a few men since the parts were heavy. I asked, what did I have to do to use the stage? He replied, as SGA president I only had to sign for it. Right on! He even stated he would have the parts delivered to the AgCenter when we needed it. After the event, he would pick up the stage parts and store them. All we would have to do was assemble and then disassemble the stage into the same manageable parts we got it in. And best of all, because SGA was a department of LSU, it was free. For the first time since coming up with the idea, I felt we were going to be able to pull this thing off.

I was on cloud nine as I walked back to the office. I couldn't wait to tell Marion and Naaman about all of this. I could envision future Registration Blues Festivals becoming an SGA tradition each semester, entertaining students while generating money so SGA could break away from the financial control of the LSU administration. By the end of the summer semester, we had ten campus organizations signed on to the festival. Those organizations would help in setting up the band's equipment, collecting tickets at the entrances, and operating the concessions stands, which would sell beer, sodas and hot dogs. All the student organizations would get a share of the profits from the concert. Then, as Naaman had told the *Reveille* (July 29, 1976), after all the debts were paid "the remainder of the profits will go toward the Second Registration Blues Festival" in the spring.

The festival was set for Thursday, August 26, 1976, after the three days of class registration at the Assembly Center was over. The festival was to start at 1 P.M. and run until 11 P.M. All the bands agreed to play for free, with SGA only having to pay for the expenses of the New Orleans bands getting to the festival. We charged $1 for students and $2 for all others. Children under six years old would be free. Some thought this wasn't necessary since they didn't think anyone would bring their young children to the concert, but I thought differently. Sure enough, a few dozen parents brought their kids for the afternoon hours.

We had to hire five Campus Police officers that Reddoch insisted we have on site for security. Well, we had to have them at the festival, but I told them they had to stay outside of the event. They were assigned the job of directing traffic and parking at the festival. We agreed that they were to come inside only if there was a disturbance. I knew there was going to be marijuana smoked inside by some students, like me, and I didn't want to put the Campus Police in a position where they might feel they had to arrest someone. One of the officers complained about not being allowed into the event, but I informed them that they were off duty from their university job and were working for SGA now.

To make sure that there would be no need to call them inside, I got the Rugby Club to handle security inside the Cow Palace. I explained to the ruggers that they had to make sure no fights broke out during the concert, giving the Campus Police outside an excuse to enter the event. There were only a few drunks who got rowdy, but the ruggers were on them in a flash, preventing any physical confrontations and ushering them out of the concert. I told them not to hand them over to the Campus Police, just escort them out of the festival.

Due to bad weather, attendance wasn't as high as we had hoped for, but we still generated around $2,600. In my executive address to the first Assembly meeting that fall, I announced that I had deposited the $2,600 generated from the Registration Blues Festival in a separate bank account off campus. Even though I had placed the account under my exclusive control, I explained that I wouldn't care "if all the Assembly members had their names on the account" since it was SGA funds.

In a *Reveille* (September 2, 1976) account of the meeting, I was quoted as saying that I wanted "to try to get us some damn money not under the administration's control." If I had deposited it in the SGA account with the university, they would have invested the money, and SGA would not get any of it." The point was that "I just want to get some money for us."

I told the Assembly that the money would be treated like any other SGA funds in that it would take action by the Assembly to spend it. In addition, all copies of any transactions with the bank on this account will be sent to the legislative vice president and financial vice president. I was sending a copy of all transactions to Ned Wright even though he still wasn't preforming his duties, including giving an executive report of SGA's finances as required by the SGA constitution.

The next day the editor of the *Reveille* (September 3, 1976), Marti Quinn, attacked my actions in an editorial titled, "For Students?" In it she stated that my placing the money in an off-campus bank account "raises a question of ethics, if not legality."

My actions weren't unethical for I did not lie or deceive the Assembly by placing the money in an off-campus bank. I informed the Assembly about what I had done at the first meeting that semester. And I didn't privately profit from my actions, either. Furthermore, my actions weren't illegal, as shown when she added that only some Assembly members that night "mildly protested" what I had done. She explained that "no action was taken" against my placing SGA funds off campus.

Conservatives! The way I saw it, this new editor of the *Reveille* was just another conservative student using her position to attack any and all changes that he/she personally disagreed with, like opening an off-campus bank account for SGA. She ended with "Schirmer's election slogan was Schirmer for Students, but his actions make that suspect." Really?!

Of course, I knew that this action of mine was going to cause a fire storm with the administration, especially with Vice Chancellor for Student Affairs "Buffalo Jim" Reddoch and some of the more conservative students at LSU. Nevertheless, as President Harry Truman said, "If you can't stand the heat, get out of the kitchen!" I was not about to get out of the kitchen.

After returning to school after Labor Day, I found a letter from Reddoch waiting for me. In the letter, he ordered me to remove the money I had deposited in American Bank and "return" it to the university. As the *Reveille* (September 8, 1976) reported in an article titled "Schirmer instructed to return cash," Reddoch cited, in the letter, a Louisiana Attorney General's opinion, "which states that SGA funds can be used for fund raising projects 'in conformity with university regulations regarding such projects.'" Reddoch wrote in his letter, "that the money could not be used in conformity to university regulations if the money is in a separate account." I knew what Reddoch was really saying: that the university couldn't control the monies raised by SGA if those funds were kept in a separate off campus account. That was exactly what I was attempting to achieve by placing the money in the American Bank.

When the *Reveille* asked what I had to say about what Reddoch had written, I replied, "I don't give a damn about the university's self-made rules….[T]he administration has always oppressed SGA, especially in financial matters….They can put me in jail or whatever they want….I think this is a good issue….SGA should try to stand on its own." Students weren't the administrators' children. I knew damn well I wasn't!

I told the reporter that I would bring the matter to the Student Assembly that night and "if they decided to support [me], [I] would 'fight this thing all I can." But if the vote was to comply with Reddoch's order, I would follow their instructions. "It's all up to the Assembly."

That night at the Assembly, it seemed as if the Assembly was going to cave in to Reddoch's order to close the account and "return' all the money to the university account. But as the *Reveille* (September 9, 1976) reported, after over an hour of argument between CPU Assembly members and Ned Wright's cohorts, Assemblymember Debbie Prevost rose to offer an amendment to the bill on the floor at the time. Debbie proposed SGA use those funds to pay the outstanding bills due from the festival, including reimbursing SGA's university account for the $1,600 dollars that SGA had appropriated to fund the festival. That would leave around $900 dollars in the SGA's American Bank account. The Assembly passed the amended bill almost unanimously with only one dissenting vote. Even though I understood that this was a compromise for both parties, I still didn't like it. I wanted to settle the issue once and for all and give future SGAs more control over their monies no matter what the university might or might not want.

Reddoch wasn't going to give up that easily. When I went over to American Bank to transfer the $1,600 to the university account, the bank clerk asked me to wait because the bank manager wanted to talk to me. I had met the manager when I first opened the account. As he approached me, I was preparing myself for bad news. Instead, he stuck out his hand to shake mine while saying, "Who the hell is this Reddoch guy?"

It kind of took me back. I asked, "Why?" He said this guy came to the bank demanding that he transfer the money in the SGA account to some university account. The manager told Reddoch he didn't know him from Adam, but the only person authorized to take money out of this account was me. He said that Reddoch appeared very upset as he turned and left the bank. I told him Reddoch was vice chancellor for student affairs, and he was pissed because I had put SGA money earned from a festival in the American Bank. The manager said not to worry, no one but me could do anything with the money.

I was to find out that, even though Reddoch didn't again bring up the subject of SGA money in the American Bank, he was not done with the issue. Toward the end of the fall semester, we were planning for the next Registration Blues Festival for the spring 1977 semester. When Marion Campbell attempted to get the required paperwork for the Cow Palace, he was told I would have to see Reddoch about the reservation. I went to see him in his office. Reddoch said that the AgCenter was not available the week of registration because the parking lot was going to be asphalted during that time. I was a little suspicious thinking that maybe the university had set it up that way to prevent us from having our second festival.

I still was determined to have the Second Annual Registration Blues Festival, as we had decided to call it. I figured we would just have to find another location that the stage we had modified last fall would fit into. We needed the exact measurements of the stage, so I went over to the warehouse to get them. When I learned what Reddoch had ordered, I was shocked at the extent he would go to in order to stop what I was trying to do. The headman at the warehouse told me he had received orders to burn the stage. I couldn't believe it! What excuse did the administration give for burning a perfectly good stage, a stage SGA had spent time and money making suitable for bands? The warehouse man said that they told him they needed the space to store other items. He said he was sorry and walked away.

It was too late to introduce a bill at the Assembly to fund building another stage; it probably wouldn't have passed anyway. We had no choice but to cancel our plans for the second festival.

That spring, at the start of registration, I made it a point to check on the Cow Palace's parking lot. There were some wooden barricades right in front of the entrances to the building, so I thought Reddoch was telling the truth about repaving. Then, after registration ended, I went back to the parking lot. There was no sign of the barricades or of any asphalting of the AgCenter's parking lot taking place.

# Fall Semester, 1976
## RACIAL DISCRIMINATION AT LSU

An article on the front page of the *Reveille* (March 11, 1976) reported on the LSU Forum's debate of the question, "Resolved, that we prefer racial segregation in the public schools of this country to the present system." The article stated that:

> Mark Noel, a Journalism major from Donaldsonville, led those favoring the resolution, saying that the real idea behind integration is the merging of cultures. "Whites are more intelligent than Blacks...and white education suffers under the present system. Whites cannot get a good education while being held back by Blacks," Noel asserted.

Even though the resolution was defeated, it does provide a window into where LSU was at that time, especially in relation to racial injustice.

A *Reveille* (October 5, 1976) article, titled "Group cites discrimination in pep pix," stated that Harambee and other Black organizations on campus were filing a grievance of racial discrimination in the selection of cheerleaders and varsity coaches. The Black students argued that the format for the selection of cheerleaders was racist and complained that there were no Black students on the 1976–77 football cheerleading squad. This lengthy article also raised the issue of how the basketball cheerleaders and coaches were selected. The Black student leaders ended their written grievances with the statement, "We know that LSU's racist policies must be abandoned, and we demand and expect it."

Early in my childhood, I became aware of systemic racism in our country, especially in the Deep South. The first time I was exposed to racism up close, and in a very personal manner, was at the early age of nine. In 1956, my grandma (who had raised me the first six years of my life and told me she was my mother) kidnapped my Black cousin, Phyllis, from a hospital in Rockford, Illinois and fled with her to our house in Kentucky.

My Aunt Barbara, my grandma's youngest child, had had an affair with a Black man. Barbara was 15 at the time, and the Black man was married. When Aunt Barbara got pregnant, she married an Irishman named Red Stringer who didn't know that Barb was pregnant. But, when Barbara gave birth to Phyllis, the baby was obviously of mixed race. When Red saw Phyllis, I am told, it took two orderlies and a doctor to pull him off Barbara. Barbara agreed to allow a middle-class Black family in Rockford to adopt Phyllis. My grandmother, on the other hand, declared that nobody was adopting her blood. She went to the hospital one day to visit and, when no one was looking, she left with baby Phyllis.

She next showed up with this little Black baby girl at the door of the one room shack on Hogg Ridge Road near Williamstown, Kentucky, where my family was living. I hadn't seen Grandma since Mom and my stepdad Bill took me away from her in 1953. Now she was standing at the door with my cousin Phyllis in her arms. Seeing her again was the greatest joy I had ever felt. Grandma pushed past Bill and placed Phyllis in my arms before she got into a very heated argument with my racist stepdad. As I gazed down into my baby cousin's face, I immediately bonded with Phyllis.

Years later, when I was trying to understand why I wasn't a racist, though I had grown up in an extremely racist society, I realized that the reason was this simple expression of love by my grandma toward my cousin Phyllis that I innately recognized as the same love Grandma had given me for my first six years. That is why I am not, nor have ever been, a racist. Later, at Free Speech Alley at LSU and at the Southern University Law Center, I stated that I strongly supported interracial relationships. I believed, based on my own personal experience, that it's hard to be a racist when your kin are members of another race.

To my mother's credit, she defended her mother and Phyllis. In today's terminology, she got in my stepdad's face and told him Phyllis could stay with us. Mom was never scared of a person just because that person was a man. However, the Ku Klux Klan (KKK) was very powerful in Kentucky at that time, and word spread quickly, not only among our neighbors but also throughout the little community nearby, that a little Black baby had turned up at our house. We were forced to do one of our quick pack and move jobs. We could not keep Phyllis with us, so Grandma had to go back to Rockford with her, but she did not give Phyllis up. Her friend and lawyer came to her aid and fought for her right to have full custody of Phyllis. She raised her granddaughter up to the time Phyllis died, at 14-years of age, of cancer.

At that age I didn't understand that what had happened with Bill and with the KKK was racism. I would first make that connection a year later when my mother, my brother Terry, and I were on a Greyhound bus from Rockford, Illinois, to Miami, Florida. That trip to Miami was the first time I had traveled on an interstate bus. When the bus crossed the so-called Mason-Dixon Line, there was a large area on the side of the road where buses could pull over. Our bus driver stopped the bus and, facing everybody, stated, "All Negroes to the back of the bus."

There were a few Blacks on the bus sitting a couple rows from the front. I remember them calmly getting up, taking their bags from the overhead rack, and, with their heads down and not making eye contact with any of the whites on the bus, walking slowly to the back of the bus. I did not understand what was happening and asked my mother, why did those people have to sit in the back of the bus? She said, "We are entering a different part of the country." I could tell from how she stated this in a low and sad tone that she felt as bad for what was happening to those individuals as I did. It was quite shocking to me, especially after bonding with Phyllis just the year before.

In 1965, I enrolled at Istrouma High School six weeks after school had already started and again witnessed institutional racism firsthand. At the time of my enrollment, there was only one Black student attending Istrouma: Mozetta Plummer. Since we both were seniors, we were in a couple of classes together. As I remember, she was one of the best students in our class, if not the best. In my opinion, she should have graduated at the top of our class but for the fact that she was Black. I have sad memories of what happened to her all during the school day, how terribly she was treated by other students, even at times in front of the white teachers who did nothing to stop the white students from harassing her.

Then when my friend Larry Foster got me a job at Barq's Root Beer loading the delivery trucks in 1966, I saw how racism was used to exploit hardworking, honest Black men. There was an older Black man named Huey who had been working at Barq's for about 15 years. Larry and I were told not to tell Huey that we were being paid $1.25 an hour.

I soon found out Huey was very proud that he was being paid $0.75 an hour. Huey could not read and could only write his name, but he was one of the hardest working men I have ever known in my life: an easy going, good man trying to support a family on $0.75 an hour. After all those years he was only being paid half of what a couple of white high school kids were being paid.

As I learned when I went to Viet Nam, racism traveled with the United States military. Most of the military personnel I observed treated the Vietnamese terribly. And I am not talking about just the enemy but also the civilian population. I found that the Vietnamese people were despised by many of our troops simply because they had a different skin color and a culture and lifestyle that was different from life in the States. I myself, having grown up in extreme poverty and forced to adapt to our constantly moving to new surroundings, didn't see the Vietnamese culture and lifestyle in a negative way but found it extremely interesting. Even some Blacks, despite the racist names they experienced in the United States, spoke badly about the Vietnamese, referring to them in the same racist terms that the white soldiers used: slope, zipper head, gook. Due to my observing this racist behavior in Viet Nam, I started saying that, "Hitler's super race is alive and well in the United States."

When I was released from the military in April of 1970, I found a place in our society that didn't embrace racism or tolerate any form of racism from others: the counterculture or the so-called long haired hippies. I attended a number of rock festivals before1976. At every one of these festivals there were numerous mixed couples and also groups and individuals educating people attending the festival about racial segregation, disfranchisement of Blacks in the South, and racial discrimination in jobs, education and housing. My exposure to those new ways of thinking helped me come out strongly against the Viet Nam war, for women's rights and environmentalism, and cemented my feelings of complete contempt for anything racist. In those days, one could tell if a person felt the same way as you did by the clothes he wore and the length of his hair.

In the academic year of 1970 and 1971, there were no Black football players on LSU's team. When I traveled to the Notre Dame game to watch LSU's all white football team play the Irish, I don't remember any big uproar about LSU not having any Blacks on their team. The following year that would change when I traveled to Wisconsin to watch the Tigers play the Badgers of Wisconsin.

When I got on the Wisconsin campus, I picked up the campus newspaper, The *Daily Cardinal* (September 24, 1971). The author of one of the articles, titled "LSU still fighting the Civil War—but not winning," wrote that "LSU is a racist school and the LSU Athletic Department is also racist." One of the articles stated: "Down there in LSU territory, where Abe Lincoln is as big a villain as Lester Maddox is a hero, they think they're pretty good at winning football games with a bunch of crewcut, all American white boys from down South."

The result of these articles, and the fact that the University of Wisconsin was one of the most liberal universities at the time, led to the LSU players, from the moment they stepped off the team bus on their way to the locker room, being greeted with a hail of taunting and insulting names and also thrown cans of beer and bottles of wine. It didn't get any better when the team ran through the players' gate onto the football field. Matter of fact, since the students were above them as they threw ice, cups, bottles and cans down on them, the LSU players had to wear their helmets each time they ran onto or off the field. Even though I fully realized how racist the LSU Athletic Department was, I still didn't like the way the players were treated.

LSU continued to resist and drag its heels in integrating its athletic teams. On September 30, 1967, the University of Kentucky became the first Southeastern Conference (SEC) team to play a Black athlete in a sporting event in the SEC. His name was Nathaniel "Nate" Northington, and he played in a football game against the Ole Miss Rebels. When LSU finally integrated its football team on September 16, 1972, it was second to last of all the SEC schools to integrate. It beat the Ole Miss Rebel's football team by two weeks. Ole Miss integrated its football team on September 30, 1972, exactly five years to the day after University of Kentucky integrated theirs.

Discriminatory actions on campus were supported by the LSU administration, specifically by Vice Chancellor for Student Affairs James Reddoch. This was pointed out at PSA's summer meeting on July 21, 1971, by Dr. Herb Rothschild, assistant professor of English and president of the Baton Rouge chapter of the American Civil Liberties Union. A Reveille (July 22, 1971) article, titled "Frisking Black youths discussed by alliance," quoted Dr. Rothschild when he "pointed out that about seven or eight Black students have been stopped and…two were detained by Campus Police." The *Reveille* reported that one of PSA's members stated: "One of the Blacks detained was a lecturer at Free University....When the lecturer questioned Chief of Campus Police Charles R. Anderson about the irregularity, Anderson said it was Vice Chancellor for Student Affairs James W. Reddoch's policy."

Reddoch was born and raised in Mississippi and attended Mississippi State University for his undergraduate and master's degrees. Mississippi had some of the harshest Jim Crow laws in the South. Even after the 1954 Supreme Court ruled in *Brown v Board of Education* that state laws establishing racial segregation in public schools were unconstitutional, in 1956 Mississippi passed laws requiring all state schools to remain racially separate and all state executive officers to prevent implementation of school integration by all lawful means. Public swimming pools and parks were to remain segregated, and the governor was authorized to close parks or swimming pools to prevent desegregation.

Reddoch's first job as an LSU administrator was as the personal assistant to LSU's President Troy Middleton. In 1962, Reddoch was named Dean for Student Affairs. When Dr. Martin Luther King Jr. was assassinated in 1968, students at LSU, both Black and white, wanted to lower the flag on the Parade Grounds to half-mast. An even larger group of white students didn't want the flag lowered. Dean Reddoch stood at the base of the flagpole preventing anyone from attempting to lower it. He justified taking this action by the fact that LSU had been started as a military academy and still had a military department, so the flag could not be lower without an order from the military. The President ordered flags to be lower to half-mast that same day. (James Reddoch, interview by Mary Hebert, audio recording, 1992, 4700.0174. Louisiana and Lower Mississippi Valley Collections, LSU Libraries, Baton Rouge, Louisiana.).

Reddoch's first boss at LSU, President Troy Middleton, had been born just 24 years after the Civil War ended in 1889. He grew up on a 400 acre plantation in Copiah County, Mississippi, and attended and graduated in 1909 from the Mississippi Agricultural and Mechanical College (Mississippi A&M), which later became Mississippi State University. Both of his grandfathers had served in the Confederate States Army, and Middleton followed them into military service. Joining the Army as a private in 1910, he served in both WWI and WWII, rising to the rank of Lieutenant General. After Troy Middleton was appointed LSU's president in 1951, he was addressed by faculty and staff as "General."

Over the period from the late 1940s to 1953, two legal cases were brought against LSU by the NAACP. Thurgood Marshall and Alexander Pierre Tureaud, a New Orleans native and Howard University Law School graduate, represented the NAACP. Those cases were discussed at length in an article titled "Opening the Doors: The struggle to desegregate LSU Law School" by Dr. Sharlene Sinegal Decuir.

On October 10, 1946, Tureaud filed a lawsuit on behalf of Charles Hatfield III, a senior at Xavier University in New Orleans, based on a rejection letter from the Dean of the LSU Law Center, Paul Hebert. In the letter, Dean Hebert, after whom the law school is presently named, stated that the "LSU Law School does not admit colored students." He further stated that Southern University was established by the state as "the principle state supported College for Negroes" and "authorized by statute to establish a law school for Negroes." In short, Dean Hebert was stating that LSU's law school was a racist law school, no Blacks need apply, and Mr. Hatfield would have to apply to Southern University if he wanted to attend a Louisiana state law school. The trouble was there was no law school at Southern University in the fall of 1946. This fact, coupled with Dean Hebert's letter, became the basis for the NAACP's lawsuit.

In response to the NAACP's lawsuit, the Louisiana State Board of Education pushed for the creation of a law school at Southern University. In 1947, the state legislature authorized this. The new law school was loaned four part-time law professors from the LSU Law Center and had a class of eight students. Even though Hatfield wasn't one of those eight students, his lawsuit resulted in the birth of the Southern University Law Center in a racist attempt to keep Blacks out of the LSU Law Center.

This was a positive thing for me personally since, in 1980, the Southern University Law Center admitted me while the LSU Paul M. Hebert Law Center rejected my application. That was a blessing in disguise considering how poorly educated I was at the time.

In 1950, the LSU Law Center still hadn't accepted a Black student, but that summer 12 Black students applied. Again, the LSU Board of Supervisors turned their applications down, stating that Louisiana had created a law school at Southern University for Blacks.

The NAACP saw this as a chance to finally integrate the LSU Law Center based on the fact that it and the Southern University Law Center were not equal, violating the United States Supreme Court's *Plessy v Ferguson* "separate but equal" ruling of 1896. Marshall and Tureaud chose, as the plaintiff for their second lawsuit, Roy Wilson, a veteran of the Army and a Louisiana native who met all of the qualifications for admission to LSU's law school.

After a lengthy argument before a three judge panel, the court agreed that the Southern University Law Center did not provide plaintiff with a legal education equal to that available at the LSU Law Center. The court ordered the defendant, the LSU Law Center, to admit Mr. Wilson, making him the first Black student enrolled at LSU. Of course, the LSU Board of Supervisors appealed the case to the United States Supreme Court, but the Court affirmed the ruling of the lower court. Those setbacks didn't stop Dean Hebert and the racist on the Board of Supervisors, from starting a so-called character investigation of Wilson, which led to his resignation from the LSU Law Center on January 17, 1951.

Shortly after Dean Hebert opened the character attack on Mr. Wilson, the president of LSU, Dr. Harold W. Stoke, resigned, and on December 28, 1950, at a special meeting of the LSU Board of Supervisors, Troy Middleton, the General, was hired as LSU president by the Board of Supervisors.

When the Board hired Troy Middleton, I guess they felt they needed a bona fide Southern man who would fight to keep LSU as white as possible. President Middleton proved he met the Board's requirements in a letter he wrote to the University of Texas chancellor in 1961. Asher Price, a reporter with the *Austin American Statesman* and the author of *Earl Campbell: Yards After Contact*, discovered Middleton's letter and reported on it in an *Advocate* (July 5, 2019) guest column titled "LSU icon Troy Middleton wanted to keep Black students off football team, journalist finds." Here is an excerpt:

> In October 1961, as the University of Texas found itself facing lawsuits—as well as student and faculty pressure—to integrate its dormitories, the university's chancellor wrote administrators at a number of other universities across the South to ask them how they had handled issues of desegregation.
>
> Middleton, then president of LSU, was among those to write back.
>
> "Though we did not like it, we accepted Negroes as students," Middleton wrote UT Chancellor Harry Ransom on Oct. 27 of that year.
>
> "At no time," the letter continues, "has a Negro occupied a room with a white student. We keep them in a given area and do not permit indiscriminate occupancy."
>
> The letter goes on: "Our Negro students have made no attempt to attend social functions, participate in athletic contests, go in the swimming pool, etc. If they did, we would,

for example, discontinue the operation of the swimming pool."

Middleton's letter concludes this way: "Since we have not had a Negro request that he be permitted to participate in athletics, we, of course, have not had to make a decision. If one should apply between now and February 1, 1962, (date for my retirement), I think I could find a good excuse why he would not participate. To be specific—LSU does not favor whites and Negroes participating together on athletic teams.

The letter is, of course, stomach turning and deeply disturbing, both rhetorically and practically speaking. It also reveals the machinery of segregation on university campuses in this post-Brown period. Like so many football programs in the South, LSU's didn't play an African American on the varsity squad till the early 1970s.

In 1973, the Department of Justice notified Louisiana twice that LSU was violating the Civil Rights Act. Governor Edwin Edwards' administration failed to respond to either notice.

In 1974, the same year I returned to LSU, the Department of Justice filed a lawsuit against LSU and the LSU Board of Supervisors. Also in 1974, the LSU Board of Supervisors appointed Paul Murrill chancellor.

What was it about Paul Murrill that led the Board of Supervisors to appoint him—at 39 years old the youngest LSU chancellor—after being in the administration for only four to five years? There were many individuals in the country with a much longer resume for the job and other administrators who had been at LSU longer. Granted that Paul Murrill was an intelligent and competent university administrator. He brought about many needed structural, administrative, and educational changes to LSU. He was also very effective at self-promotion, shown not only by his rocketed rise in the LSU administration ranks but even earlier when he attended Ole Miss. But it's possible a deciding factor was that the LSU Board of Supervisors was in the midst of their fight with the Office for Civil Rights (OCR) over integration.

The Board of Supervisors, a politically appointed body, would not have fought integration as hard as its history shows it did without popular support not only from the citizens of Louisiana but, more importantly, from the alumni of LSU. The civil rights lawsuit would continue through Murrill's tenure as chancellor, being settled finally in the winter of 1980. Murrill resigned in January of 1981.

Why did both Chancellor Paul Whitfield Murrill and Vice Chancellor James Reddoch work in tandem to maintain white privilege at LSU in 1976? They may have had different approaches relating to students, but I think their working relationship was grounded in the fact that they both had been raised and educated in Mississippi at the height of Jim Crow. Since members of both of their families had fought for the Confederacy to preserve slavery in Mississippi, it defies imagination to believe that Murrill and Reddoch didn't also have a reverence for the Confederacy.

I will be the first to admit that I was completely naïve when dealing with Paul Murrill. At the time I presumed that Murrill was an honorable man just doing his job as he understood it. I thought that pressure from the Board of Supervisors and alumni were determining his actions. I didn't agree with giving in to pressure. I have always believed that, despite what personal heat one might get for taking a controversial stand on an issue, if that stand was the correct stand, morally and ethically, then resisting pressure went with the responsibilities of being a leader. Still, I feel now that there had to have been more to it than just pressures from others for Murrill to condone racial injustice at LSU.

With the assistance of the internet plus what law school had taught me about researching issues, coupled with 30 years of practicing law honing those research skills, I went looking for the real Paul Whitfield Murrill. Due to this research, I acquired what I believe is a much more accurate impression of this man than I had when I was trying to prevent a racial injustice in 1976 at LSU. I learned a great deal about Paul Whitfield Murrill, the Southern Mississippian man.

Shortly after he was born in St. Louis, Missouri, to Horace and Grace Whitfield Murrill, the family moved to a farm outside of Pocahontas, Mississippi that his mother had inherited. His mother's family, the Whitfields, had the necessary pedigree for a respected Southern family: A long list of members who had served as soldiers and minsters in the Army of the Confederacy during the Civil War.

That kind of family heritage would have carried a lot of weight with Mississippians of the 1940s, '50s, '60s and '70s. The problem with pride in this family heritage is that it also carried with it the baggage of hatred, persecution, and subjugation of Blacks in Mississippi through institutionalized racism.

After Paul Murrill's family moved to Hinds County, he received his early education in a one room school house in Pocahontas, Mississippi. He finished his public school education in Clinton, Mississippi, graduating from high school in 1952. The fall after graduation, he enrolled at Ole Miss in Oxford, Mississippi, having won a Naval ROTC scholarship that, as he said, "*paid your way for four years—everything, totally—with a three-year active duty obligation. It was during the Korean War, and the draft was in effect, so I had to do something.*" (Article in "Control-2014 Process Automation Hall of Fame")

He referred to himself as just a "country boy" growing up in Hinds County, Mississippi and his decision to go to Ole Miss as a way to "get off the farm." He stated that his time at Ole Miss would always be "etched in his mind." "It was the best time of my life," he told the reporter. "I met many people who had a powerful impact on my life." Let's examine what kind of campus environment a student would have experienced at Ole Miss in 1952 that would have such a lasting "powerful impact" on that person's life.

As a new freshman on campus, and not knowing anyone, a student would most likely seek out like-minded Ole Miss students. Paul Murrill, considering his Confederate relatives, decided to pledge to the Alpha Tau Omega fraternity at Ole Miss. He would have been required to learn the unique history of Alpha Tau Omega fraternity: the chapter's founders, values, ideals, governance structure and bylaws. Alpha Tau

Omega's founder, Otis Allan Glazebrook, had been both a Confederate war veteran and a devout Christian, as many of the Confederate officers were, believing that God was on their side before and during the Civil War. Glazebrook and two other students founded the fraternity at the Virginia Military Institute (VMI) in Lexington, Virginia on September 11, 1865, just five months after General Robert E. Lee surrendered the Army of Northern Virginia to the Union Army under Lieutenant General Ulysses S. Grant on April 9, 1865. Over twenty VMI alumni had been officers in the Confederate Army, the most famous being Thomas Jonathan "Stonewall" Jackson.

In the 1954 Ole Miss yearbook, a picture of Murrill appears as a member of Alpha Tau Omega. There is a picture of the study area in their fraternity house showing a large Confederate battle flag on the wall. Paul Murrill would remain an Alpha Tau Omega fraternity member though out his time at Ole Miss and beyond. (University of Mississippi "The Ole Miss" (1954) page 244–245)

Today when you look up Ole Miss's yearbooks from that time, there is this statement:

> **Disclaimer**–Some of the images and language that appear in the University of Mississippi yearbooks depict prejudices that are not condoned by the University of Mississippi. The yearbooks are being presented as historical documents to aid in the understanding of both American history and the history of the University of Mississippi. The University Creed speaks to our current deeply held values, and the availability of past yearbooks should not be taken as an endorsement of previous attitudes or behavior.

University of Mississippi "The Ole Miss" (1954)

In Paul Murrill's freshman year, the front cover of the 1953 yearbook, *The Ole Miss* was the Confederate battle flag. (University of Mississippi "The Ole Miss" (1953). A photo showed ROTC cadets marching at parade, with the color bearers carrying both the United States flag and the Confederate battle flag. They seem to have forgotten that one had defeated the other in the Civil War. The Ole Miss band always played "Dixie" at games. (University of Mississippi "The Ole Miss" (1953) page 180)

In that same year the Supreme Court ruled, in *Brown v. Board of Education,* that "separate educational facilities are inherently unequal," effectively ending racial segregation in public schools. Surely this event in Murrill's second year at Ole Miss, had to have been a topic of discussion.

Defending racism became the issue of the day for white people living in Mississippi. They believed that if a Black person wasn't staying in "his place," then white men, either by themselves or as a member of an organization like the Ku Klux Klan, had the responsibility to punish the offending Black adult or child. There was no more egregious example of this than what happened to Emmett Till.

In 1955, two white Mississippian men kidnapped, brutally tortured, and lynched Emmett Till, a 14-year-old Black boy. He had been falsely accused of using vulgar language to a white woman in Money, Mississippi. Sixty years later, at the age of 82, that same woman would confess that she had lied about the whole thing.

That horrific event happened only 75 miles from Ole Miss, where Paul Murrill was attending college. One would think that this would cause a sea change in the young Murrill. How does a young man attending college just miles from where the torture and killing of a 14-year-old Black boy not see the horror in such a thing? Did attending a college that glorified the Confederacy and all that it stood for insulate him from hearing any voices speaking out against this heinous crime?

That environment had to have had an impact on LSU's top administrators, such as LSU President Middleton, who was born and raised in Mississippi; Chancellor Paul Murrill, who grew up in Hinds County and attended Ole Miss; and Vice Chancellor James Reddoch, who attended Mississippi State. Even Margaret Jameson, Dean of Women then later Dean of Students, was born and raised during the Jim Crow period in South Carolina. With the exception of Troy Middleton, who had retired before I started LSU in 1970, these were the administrators I found myself having to struggle with at LSU.

## THE HOMECOMING CONTROVERSY

Looking back at what happened during Homecoming in 1976, I see how difficult the work of a historian is when he tries to reconstruct an event 50 years after it occurred. This is especially so when many of the key actors in those events are either dead or, if still alive, have a poor memory of the events, or still have a vested interest in not being candid or truthful about those events.

In 2019, I returned to LSU to try to discover through research the motivations and roles of certain administrators and a handful of student leaders involved in events that took place during 1976. However, I found that the files of the administrators involved in the LSU 1976 Homecoming and the files relating to the attempt to recall me as student body president were either missing or undiscoverable. One of the key players, Chancellor Paul Murrill regretfully had sealed for over 70 years his many hours of oral interviews about his time at LSU that are kept in the T. Harry Williams Oral History Library. I also found that the records of my Code of Conduct hearing had been destroyed. Luckily, I had kept the heavily redacted copy of the hearing minutes that I had demanded from Dean Jameson before I left LSU.

Copies of the *Reveille* from 1970 to 1979 were available on microfiche, so I had them sent to a library in California near where I lived. I spent three months going through every issue. Then I flew back to LSU a half dozen times to listen and read the oral histories I could locate of administrators, such as Dean Jameson, Dean French, and Vice Chancellor for Student Affairs Reddoch, who were involved with the issues I fought for at LSU.

This is where my training in my last job before retiring as a criminal defense trial attorney in the Los Angeles Public Defender's Office came in handy. I developed skill in determining the facts of a case through investigation and/or legal discovery tools. Even using these approaches, in some cases there are still gaps in the facts. Therefore, in order to prevail on behalf of the client, a criminal defense attorney must formulate an argument by filling in those missing gaps so that a jury or judge can see the picture he believes explains the facts of his client's position in the clearest and most forceful way. What follows is my best effort at reconstructing those events which I considered then, and still do today, to be my most important fight at LSU, the fight against racism.

The 1976, LSU Homecoming was set for the October 9th football game against Vanderbilt University. According to the SGA constitution, the SGA president appoints the Homecoming Committee chairman. Mike Williams came into to my office on the first day of my administration asking to be appointed to that position.

I had not thought much about LSU's Homecoming when I ran for SGA president, and I had only a vague understanding about events that concluded with the crowning of the Homecoming Queen on the football field's 50-yard line in Tiger Stadium during half time. In the past it had been largely celebrated by the Greeks and their alumni. I knew Mike had previously worked on Homecoming, so, if he wanted to chair the 1976 Homecoming Committee, it seemed (at the time) a good idea. But to make the event as inclusive as possible I appointed Alphe Williams who was Black, as cochairman with Mike.

I attended one, and only, Homecoming Committee meeting prior to the Homecoming Queen election. I was busy during the summer of 1976 with lobbying the State Legislature, meeting with the Board to save the SHS, getting out the No Sweat Study Guide and the newsletter warning students about the fee increase and threat to the LSU Infirmary, and working on the Registration Blues Festival along with attending classes. I was even busier when the fall semester began. I felt that my attention and energies were needed on more important issues than Homecoming. Therefore, when I attended the first meeting that summer, as a member of the committee as the minutes from that first meeting reflected, I explained that I wouldn't be able to attend many meetings due to the many pressing issues on campus, but I expressed my desire for the committee to organize a more inclusive Homecoming than the ones in the past.

One of the issues that the SGA Homecoming Committee was concerned about was who would escort the Homecoming court. The tradition had been that the SGA president escorted the Homecoming Queen at half time of the Homecoming game, and the SGA legislative vice president escorted the runner-up. In the past, the SGA legislative vice president had been a male, but in 1976 the SGA's legislative vice president was a female: Dana Robert. The Homecoming Committee decided that a woman escorting the runner-up, another woman, was somehow improper. Michael Williams, the student I appointed as cochairman of the Homecoming Committee, stated in the *Reveille* (September 23, 1976) that the SGA legislative vice president escorting the runner-up wasn't a tradition, "'It's just been done that way in the past,' he said." Then he added that, "It would not have sat well with a lot of the alumni." Dana told the *Reveille* reporter, "that she [didn't] think her escorting the runner-up would shock the alumni."

Dana was told by the Committee that she would have to wear a dress, to which Dana responded, "If I'm not on the court, why should I be required to wear a dress?" She responded, "It's part of my job and duty to be a Homecoming escort, and I think I should be allowed to do it." and the only reason that she might not was " because I'm female.... It's obviously sexual discrimination."

I had already read *The Women's Room* by Marilyn French and *My Mother Myself: The Daughter's Search for Identity* by Nancy Friday, and I was blessed with having liberated women in my life since leaving the military. I told the *Reveille* that I "was '100 percent in favor' of Robert escorting the runner up." In an effort to express how ridiculous I thought it all was, I jokingly said that maybe Dana should wear my suit in order to escort the runner-up and I would wear a dress when escorting the Homecoming Queen.

In truth, the idea of a long haired student activist like me escorting the LSU Homecoming Queen in front of all of these Greeks and alumni fascinated me. However, the Homecoming Committee proposed changing that tradition, too, by having the chancellor and other administrators escort the Queen and her court. I explained to the committee that the Homecoming Queen finalists would be picked by our football team and voted on by the student body, not the administrators, and as SGA president I intended to follow tradition and escort the Queen. The committee dropped that idea. However, they would not agree to allow SGA Legislative Vice President Dana Robert to escort the runner up. She declined to fight it, so that decision stood.

No one had any expectation that the 1976 Homecoming would be any different from those of past years. But on September 29, 1976, the football team voted for Cynthia Payton to be the first Black finalist for Homecoming Queen in the history of LSU.

The names of the female students who had been selected by the football players to be finalists were spelled out in an article buried toward the back of the *Reveille*. I don't recall ever seeing the article but, even if I had, I would have found no mention of the fact that Cynthia was Black.

I was later told that the white players had voted for Cynthia out of respect for LSU's senior tailback Terry Robiskie, a Black football player, who, leading up to the Homecoming game, was first in all rushing categories, except for average per carry. He would finish first in all the same rushing categories at the end of the football season.

Cynthia Payton had been sponsored by one of the two Black sororities at LSU, Zeta Phi Beta. It had been founded at Howard University in Washington, D.C. on January 16, 1920, and an LSU chapter had been organized just the year before on May 2, 1975. The other nine finalists had been sponsored by other sororities, fraternities and student organizations.

A *Reveille* article (October 5, 1976) stated that the Homecoming Queen election would be held in the downstairs lobby of the Student Union from Tuesday, October 5, 1976, to Thursday, October 7, 1976, from 8 A.M. to 2 P.M. The top five finalists would compose the Queen's court, and the woman who received the most votes would be Queen. Thursday evening there would be a pep rally on the football practice field that included the football team. There the five finalists would be announced to the crowd, but the one who was elected Queen would not be announced until the halftime activities at Saturday night's football game. The only mention in the article about how the election was to be run was that students would vote for three of the finalists.

I arrived at the Student Union at LSU at approximately 9:30 A.M. on the morning of Tuesday, October 5th, the first day of voting for Homecoming Queen. I decided to vote then since I would probably not have the time to vote later that day due to the many issues I was dealing with at the time.

At the voting station on the first floor of the Student Union, I was handed a ballot by a member of the Army Scotch Guard who, along with Angel Flight (today known as Silver Wings), volunteered every year to work at the voting station for the Homecoming Queen election.

I already knew who I was voting for Homecoming Queen: Cynthia Payton. On the ballot was printed the notice: "vote for three." Nowhere did I see any sign stating that a voter had to vote for three or his vote would be thrown out.

After I voted, I went back upstairs to get breakfast at the Student Union cafeteria. I found myself daydreaming about how I was going to carry out my duties as SGA president at halftime at the game.

I knew that traditionally SGA presidents wore a suit for the occasion. I had been asked by friends of mine who were faculty members, History Professor Bob Becker and Anthropology Professor Miles Richardson, if I was going to wear a suit, if so, what kind of a suit? Or was I going to wear the same clothes I had worn for the Bicentennial Celebration last spring at LSU? (That was my Viet Nam jungle fatigue jacket with my WWI campaign hat and my Navy bell bottom dungarees that were being held together with numerous patches of various hippie designs.) I felt that this outfit would be over the top. Homecoming may not mean that much to me, but it sure did to the university and the alumni. A number of my friends and supporters urged me to wear my usual attire while some others offered to rent a tuxedo for me to wear. I was trying to visualize escorting Cynthia in front of 68,000 LSU alumni and students. What I didn't fully appreciate was the lengths that individuals in the administration would go to in their determination to keep that from happening.

While this was going through my head, a group of Black students, one whom I knew was an officer of the Black student organization Harambee, rushed up to my table and started yelling. They had just tried to vote for Cynthia Payton in the Homecoming election downstairs and were told that they had to vote for three candidates. There was a sign stating that if a student didn't vote for three candidates, his vote would be thrown out.

I told him I had just voted for Homecoming Queen and, even though the ballot stated "vote for three," I hadn't noticed any sign stating my ballot wouldn't count if I didn't. (I didn't brother to telling him that, due to my military training, when I read at the top of the ballot "vote for three," I didn't think, I just searched for two other candidates to vote for other than Cynthia Payton.)

It became clear that I wasn't the only student who didn't know about this mandatory rule the Homecoming Committee had established, a mandatory rule that would not only prevent Ms. Payton from being elected Homecoming Queen but would most likely prevent her from even being in the Queen's Court, making sure that the alumni would not see a Black participating in the halftime ceremonies at Homecoming. That kind of discrimination was exactly what I had tried to prevent when I appointed Alphe Williams as cochairman of the Homecoming Committee. There was no way I was going to allow it to happen on my watch as SGA president!

I left my breakfast and, with the Harambee officer, walked down to the first floor where the Homecoming election was being held. As we walked, I informed him that if what he was saying was true, I would quickly bring it to an end. I told him that I knew, from personal experience, that a voter's ballot cannot be thrown out simply because he had not voted the whole ballot. The Supreme Court had ruled on that issue. Since the Homecoming election was being run under the SGA, as president, I had a duty to stop that unconstitutional and racist requirement.

As the newly elected SGA president and newly appointed member of LSU's Board of Supervisors, I had to take an oath, "that I will support the constitution and laws of the United States and the constitution and laws of Louisiana and that I will faithfully and impartially discharge and perform all the duties incumbent on me." I had taken an earlier oath, in 1966, when I volunteer for military service to not only support the Constitution of the United States but to defend it. I took these oaths very seriously. I wasn't going to shirk my responsibilities.

We approached the table where the women's student organization, the Army Scotch Guard, were running the election. Sure enough, there, taped to the wall behind the voting table, in large bolded letters was a sign stating that students had to vote for three candidates or their ballot wouldn't count. That sign had to have been put up after I voted because there was no way I could have missed it.

I told the two Scotch Guard members that they would have to take the sign down. That the law was settled years ago when the Supreme Court decided that a voter didn't have to vote the whole ballot for his ballot to count. The students were confused as to what to do. They told me they didn't think they had the authority to take the sign down because Mike Williams had told them to put it up after Black students had complained about the mandatory rule. I appreciated their dilemma. I told them, no problem. As SGA president, I did have the authority to address an unconstitutional and discriminatory voting requirement of an SGA committee.

As SGA president I had appointed the chairman of the Homecoming Committee and Homecoming was funded by the SGA using state funds. In addition, as I had learned earlier when starting both PSA and the Book Rental, that students wishing to use the university's facilities could only do so as a student organization recognized by the university or be operating under a recognized student organization. Therefore, since the Homecoming Committee was not a recognized student organization, only a committee, the only way it could use university facilities, as they were doing, was by operating under a recognized student organization, and that organization was the Student Government Association.

I walked around the table and took the sign down. I informed the Army Scotch Guard students that I would go find Mike Williams to explain why I took this action. The Black students thanked me for taking swift actions in stopping this racial injustice and left for class. I went back up to the Union hoping my breakfast was still at my table. It wasn't.

After I had finished eating the second meal I brought that morning, I made it a point to find Mike Williams. I told Mike about the Supreme Court decision and explained why I felt I was obligated to intervene in the Homecoming elections. Mike stated he understood, and I walked back to my office. I didn't give the issue a second thought. Now all I had to do was figure out what I was going to wear for Homecoming.

Without notifying me, who as SGA president was an ex officio member of the Homecoming Committee, it met that evening to discuss the action I had taken. The Homecoming Committee voted to ignore my order and restore the mandatory three vote rule.

## WHO'S IN CHARGE OF HOMECOMING?

The next morning, Wednesday, October 6th, when I arrived at school, I ate my breakfast in the Tiger Lair, then went to my SGA office to work. Around ten that morning, as I was preparing to go to my first class for the day, some of the same Black students who had approached me the day before were standing outside my office.

They were really pissed off. They angrily told me that "they" were back to running a racist election. What! I couldn't believe my ears. What the fuck! One of the students told me this was bullshit, "I was being forced to vote for two girls I don't want to be Queen." He stated he was voting two to one against his preference.

We all went downstairs to the voting table. Sure as shit, there was a big ass sign stating that students had to vote for three or their ballots wouldn't be counted. I informed the Angel Flight women students manning the table that they had to take the sign down. They told me they had been instructed to call Assistant Dean Randy Gurie if I attempted to intervene again. I told them to call him and tell him to meet me in my office. I knew enough that, if there were to be a confrontation, it was better to have it on your choice of ground.

Gurie most have been waiting in the Union for the call he knew would come because I had just gotten to my office when he showed up. He informed me that SGA had no authorization to involve itself in the Homecoming Queen election and, since this was not an election for a public office, it didn't fall under federal and state rules governing election procedures.

I told him that, even if that were true, the Homecoming Committee is an SGA committee, and any committee funded with SGA funds was responsible to the SGA, therefore it was under the SGA's Election Board. In addition, the fact that the SGA president appoints the chairman, or, as in this case, cochairman, of the committee, makes it responsible to the SGA, and makes the SGA president an ex officio member of that committee. Since Gurie's job title was assistant to the dean of men, I said I was surprised that Dean French was taking that position. Gurie then told me that the ruling was coming from Vice Chancellor Reddoch.

After hearing that, I promptly called Reddoch's office. I was put through immediately, which in itself was highly unusually. Most times I would be put on hold for a while before Reddoch answered. In my view, it just confirmed what I had suspected that Randy Gurie was doing Reddoch's dirty work. Reddoch once again did his typical ploy, what I learned to call the administration shuffle, of sending a student off on a wild goose chase. He told me that, to his knowledge, it was the Alumni Federation that was in charge of the Homecoming activities, including the Homecoming Queen elections.

I hung up and immediately called Mr. J. Stan Landry, Director of the Alumni Federation. I told him what was happening and what Reddoch had said. Mr. Landry informed me that the Homecoming Committee wasn't the Alumni Federation's responsibility. The Alumni Federation only served in an advisory capacity and provided space for meetings. He went on to state that a few years ago, Homecoming had been dying out, and the only way the Alumni Federation could breathe life back into it was by getting SGA involved. Regardless of what Reddoch said, Mr. Landry believed that the Homecoming Committee was under SGA authority. He further added, but for SGA getting involved in Homecoming, he thought Homecoming would have died out years ago. I thanked him and told him I was going to call Reddoch back to inform him of what he had just told me.

I am not sure why Mr. Landry was so open with me. Maybe he didn't like Reddoch pushing this problem into his lap, or he didn't fully realize what was happening. At the time I had no reason to doubt what he told me was true. The Homecoming Committee operated under the authority of the SGA.

I had an appointment with Reddoch that afternoon, at 2:30 P.M. A group of concerned students went with me to discuss the situation. We all were in an uplifted mood. After what Mr. Landry had told me, we were confident that reason would prevail, and that the students would be allowed to cast a single vote for the finalist of their choice without fear that their vote wouldn't be counted.

When we got to Reddoch's office, I could tell that he wasn't expecting a group of students. As we all filed in, he stated that he would only see me in his office. I said that my fellow students, especially the Black students with us, had as much right to be in this meeting, if not more, as I did. I continued without waiting for a response, telling him that I had talked with the president of the Alumni Federation, Mr. Landry. Usually, the only expression I saw on Reddoch's face when dealing with him was one of smug superiority. But I noticed the slightest look of surprise. He must have expected that, since the university was in the middle of Homecoming Week, I wouldn't be able to locate and speak with Mr. Landry so quickly. Realizing that for once Reddoch appeared to be back on his heels, I quickly told him that it was Mr. Landry's position that the Homecoming Committee and the Homecoming Queen elections were under SGA's authority. After hearing that, Reddoch stated he didn't care what Mr. Landry had said, the SGA didn't have the responsibility or authority to oversee the Homecoming Committee.

Over mutterings by some of the other students in the room that "this is bullshit," I confronted Reddoch with the fact that essentially he was saying that the Homecoming Committee was not responsible to anyone for an election that was discriminatory and possibly against the law: "It appears you are saying that we have essentially a committee on the loose, responsible to no one!"

The mood in the room was rapidly rising to a boiling point. We all came to the realization that Reddoch was just fucking with us. He told us that he would compile a list of questions for the Homecoming Committee that day and wait for their answers the next morning.

Even though I had hoped that Reddoch would accept the Alumni Federation's position relating to the Homecoming Committee, I had brought with me a letter addressed to Vice Chancellor Reddoch, with a carbon copy I sent to Chancellor Murrill. It stated that, if the administration's position was that the Homecoming Committee wasn't under the authority of the Student Government, thus preventing SGA from correcting a discriminatory Homecoming Queen election, the SGA would be left with only the following options: 1) dismiss the Homecoming Committee's cochairmen, and/or 2) withdraw support and funds from the Homecoming Committee. The SGA wanted no association with an election that was discriminating against the only Black student finalist. As we got up to leave, I handed Reddoch my letter.

I went back to my office to work on preparations for that night's SGA Assembly meeting. The SGA president is responsible for giving a report to the Assembly at the beginning of all Assembly meetings. Most of my predecessors had not made this duty a top priority. I always felt it was important to keep the Assembly up to date on what projects and other matters the executive branch was handling that week. In my opinion, none was more important that night than stopping the racist Homecoming Queen election.

I was also hoping to get notified by the Homecoming Committee when their next meeting was going to be held so I could attend it. I still hadn't heard from the Homecoming Committee when we left the SGA office for the Assembly meeting in the Old Law School building.

When we got to the Assembly meeting, we had hoped to suspend the rules in order to present a resolution expressing SGA's condemnation of the racist Homecoming Queen election. But due to the objections of the fraternity and sorority members on the Assembly, our motion to suspend the rules was defeated.

I felt it was important to receive an expression of support from the Assembly, so we wrote a petition condemning the mandatory rule of voting for three finalists since it severely hampered the chances of the Black candidate winning the Homecoming Queen election, and also deploring the exclusion of SGA Legislative Vice President Dana Robert from the half-time ceremonies because she was a female. The petition further stated that if no corrections were made to stop those discriminatory practices by the Homecoming Committee, SGA would be forced to take action. A majority of the Assembly members signed the petition. The Greek Assembly members and a few others, who were opposed to anything our administration did, refused to sign.

I hurried home because Susanna needed the car for work. That night, Mike Williams called me to inform me that the Homecoming Committee was meeting to discuss the rules for the Homecoming Queen elections. I told Mike I wouldn't be able to make the meeting because I didn't have any transportation. At that time, I was living off of River Road, on Elbow Bayou, a good distance from the LSU's campus. Since I had complained about not being notified about the last meeting, I had figured I would get a late call about the next committee meeting, so I had made plans for an SGA delegation to go. It was led by Gary Simon, an Assembly member, and included Kenneth Barnes.

The next day the *Reveille* (Thursday, October 7, 1976) reported on the Homecoming Committee meeting the previous night. The SGA delegation was present along with the president of Harambee, Anthony Weaver, and other members of Harambee.

Harambee President Weaver pointed out that making him vote for three finalists instead of just the one finalist he wanted to see as Homecoming Queen infringed on his right to vote. The majority of students voting in the Homecoming Queen elections, he was quoted as saying, "didn't even know the girls in the race." He asked why the rule on Tuesday, the first morning of the Homecoming Queen election, which allowed students to vote for one, two or three candidates, was changed back on Wednesday to mandating that students vote for three candidates. This was when Alphe Williams, the Black student I had appointed to the Homecoming Committee in hopes of assuring a more diverse Homecoming, spoke up for the first time during this fight. He stated that he "changed the rule back because it gives more girls the opportunity to be elected, since they have a three-in-ten chance, rather than one-in-ten." I had never known a Black, especially in the Deep South, who was that "color blind." At the time, I couldn't figure out for the life of me why Alphe was giving cover to the committee. A few years later, when I was working in the Southside of Chicago as an AFDC case manager, I learned the name Blacks give another Black, who they believe has sold out to the white establishment: "Oreo," Black on the outside, white on the inside. Since learning that, whenever I think of Alphe, I think of that saying.

Then the Committee took up the rule that mandated students had to vote for three candidates or have their ballot thrown away. The *Reveille* reported that Mike Williams said, "In my interpretation, Ted Schirmer, SGA president, came to me today around noon and said.... the Supreme Court ruled that you can't invalidate any ballot because it doesn't show votes for a certain number of people....So, from about noon to 2 P.M. we had a sign up saying you could vote for one, two or three girls."

The article then quoted Williams saying "he "talked to some administrators" about the ruling. He then explained that the conclusion of those administrators was that the committee received funds from the university, therefore, Homecoming was a university event, not an SGA event. Williams added, "The election doesn't fall under SGA rules. The

Homecoming Committee as a whole can decide the voting procedure." Therefore, he stated, "All of the ballots cast today will count whether you voted for one, two or three girls. For Wednesday and Thursday, the maximum and the minimum number for voting will be three."

Afterwards, I found out that Reddoch had given Mike Williams and the Homecoming Committee the green light to blow off what SGA thought about how they were running the Homecoming Queen elections. Earlier in the day before that evening meeting of the Homecoming Committee, he had sent Mike Williams a letter stating that it was "his opinion that the Homecoming committee was a university committee and, therefore, not subject to the rules of the SGA election board." Reddoch further stated in the letter that, "My investigation also leads me to the conclusion that this committee is the only duly constituted committee charged with the authority and responsibility for staging the Homecoming Queen election." Thus, Reddoch gave the committee permission to continue the discriminatory election before the committee meeting even met that evening. It was clear that Reddoch wanted the committee to reject any change in their rules governing the election and didn't care that the discriminatory mandatory three vote rule would prevent a fair election for Cynthia Payton, the Black finalist.

After all, LSU had a very long history of fighting to remain segregated. A Black Homecoming Queen would offend alumni, politicians and citizens of Louisiana and probably also a good number of administrators, faculty and staff and the LSU Greek fraternity and sorority members also. And of course, Dean Reddoch had Randy Gurie sitting on the Homecoming Committee driving this message home.

Later, I researched all the files on past Homecoming Committees, and I couldn't find any minutes of the 1976 Homecoming Committee. I read the oral history of all the key administrators in this fight, other than those of Chancellor Murrill who had put a 70-year restriction on releasing his oral history. None of the other administrators mentioned the 1976 Homecoming Queen elections at all. I believe the 1976 Homecoming Committee members were ashamed of the role they played. Therefore, the minutes that had been taken at their meetings simply disappeared: That was another big reason I felt it was important for me to write this story.

The decision made by the Homecoming Committee infuriated the SGA delegation and the Harambee members in attendance. SGA Representative Gary Simon stated that he would move at next Wednesday's Assembly meeting to stop all funding for the Homecoming Committee based on the "unfairness of the election." The Harambee members threatened more immediate action. They told the committee that they were going to organize a picket line inside the Union tomorrow morning to protest the discriminatory committee rule.

## APPEALS TO THE CHANCELLOR

The next morning, Thursday, October 7th, I hadn't been in my office long when a group of students, the SGA delegations and the Harambee members who had been at the Homecoming Committee meeting the previous night, came in. They were very upset. They informed me that the Homecoming Committee last night voted to keep the mandatory voting requirement. I had convinced myself that, if not common sense, at least basic decency would lead the committee to do the right thing. I just couldn't understand why my fellow students could not see how wrong it was to insist on keeping a requirement that, if not outright discriminatory, was unfair to the only Black finalists, Cynthia Payton.

The SGA delegation had given Mike Williams and the Homecoming Committee the petition that had been signed by a majority of the SGA Assembly members objecting to the way the election was being run. In addition, I had put Vice Chancellor Reddoch on notice that SGA wasn't going to allow a racist Homecoming Queen election operating with SGA funds to go forward. Even with all that, I still felt it was important to get the input of more student leaders on how SGA should deal with this problem. I called an emergency meeting of all the SGA cabinet members who could be located on such short notice.

We were unable to contact all of them since a number were either not on campus or in class—after all, they were college students. But a number of cabinet members came to the SGA office that morning. Dana Robert, legislative vice president, was one of those members, along with my Executive Assistant, Molly Moss, and other department heads and SGA staff.

The meeting started with a summary of what had been happening during Homecoming week. The first question was whether SGA had the authority to intervene in the Homecoming Queen election. Everyone present felt that it did. Next, Dana Robert turned the discussion to whether any corrective action could be taken by the SGA Executive branch without the Assembly's approval. The next scheduled meeting of the Assembly wasn't until the Wednesday of the following week, and it was agreed that there wasn't enough time for me to call an extraordinary session before the Homecoming game on Saturday. If any corrective action was to be taken, it had to be taken immediately.

But what should SGA do? No one was in favor of stopping Homecoming from happening. The next question was, did cochairmen Mike Williams and Alphe Williams deserve to be fired? The cabinet discussed the fact that, under their leadership, the Homecoming Committee had not only blatantly established discriminatory voting requirements but, after I had taken corrective steps, it had reinstated the discriminatory mandatory requirement of voting for three finalists. It was decided by everyone in the meeting that, because of these actions, Mike Williams and Alphe Williams should be dismissed as chairpersons of the Homecoming Committee. It was agreed that, since the SGA president had the authority to appoint the chairman of the Homecoming Committee, I, as SGA president, had the authority to fire them.

Then the question became: if I fired Mike Williams and Alphe Williams, what then? Was there enough time to salvage the Homecoming Queen election? It was decided that there was enough time to setup a new election before the Homecoming game that Saturday night. It could run Thursday afternoon, all day Friday and Saturday up to 4 P.M., leaving plenty of time to count the ballots before half-time at the football game.

After all the debating was finished, the cabinet took a vote on whether to dismiss Mike Williams and Alphe Williams as cochairman of the Homecoming Committee. The vote was unanimous for their dismissal. Dana Robert had left for class before the vote was taken.

My staff prepared Executive Order #21. In it all the SGA officers and staff present were named, reasons for taking action were presented, and the results of the vote to dismiss Mike Williams and Alphe Williams as cochairman of the Homecoming Committee stated. In addition, the order named the students whom I appointed as the new cochairperson. Three students volunteered to take on those responsibilities and duties: Gary Simon, Sarah Soileau and Mike Richman.

I gave the new cochairpersons the use of my office. I told them that I didn't care how they decided to run the Homecoming Queen election. My only instruction to them was that the election was to be run in a way that was fair to all of the finalists and did not discriminate against any of them.

After about 30 minutes or so, they came out of my office to inform us of what they had decided: The election being run downstairs was to be stopped. Then they were going to print up new ballots at the SGA office with all of the finalist names on it. The instructions on the ballot would tell the student to vote for one of the finalists. The finalist receiving the most votes would be Homecoming Queen, and the next four finalists would be her court.

Mike Richman was chosen as the spokesperson for them. Mike told me that they felt they needed me, as SGA president, to go downstairs with them when they informed the Angel Flight students who were manning the voting poll at that time, that the election was being stopped. Since we were operating under severe time limits, we had to move quickly to set up the new election.

I agreed to accompany the new cochairpersons downstairs. John Crochet, an Assembly member and vice chairman of SGA's rules committee, joined the other cabinet members who didn't have to hurry off to class, and followed us downstairs. I also had a class to attend, but I didn't think twice about skipping it because I believed my duty to the student body overruled my personal education. John brought with him a copy of Executive Order #21 in the event it was needed to present to the Scotts Guard or Angel Flight students manning the table.

When we arrived at the polling table, there were some students with ballots in their hands trying to decide how to vote. I couldn't help asking them how they felt about the mandatory three vote requirement. Every one of them said that they had come to vote for who they wanted as Homecoming Queen but was having trouble picking the other two finalists required. That just reassured me that what SGA was during would be supported by the student body.

Mike Richman informed the Angel Flight students manning the table that this election was being stopped. The students at the table, with confused looks on their faces, glanced over at me for confirmation. I told them about decisions made at the meeting of the cabinet upstairs in the SGA office. SGA was going to start a new election that didn't force students to vote for two finalists that they didn't support and thus to discriminate against the only Black finalist on the ballot. One of the Angel Flight women told me that they had been dealing with complaints from a lot of students voting about the mandatory rule. She then added that, if we wanted, they would work the voting table once the new election started. I told them we would appreciate it.

As I was discussing this with them, the newly appointed cochairpersons were picking up the SGA supplies on the voting table, including the SGA's metal ballot box containing the ballots cast so far that day.

When we got back up to the SGA office, the SGA staff were already at work making the new ballots and posters. It wasn't until we opened the ballot box that we realized we had to do something with the ballots that had already been cast since we were going to need that SGA metal ballot box for our election. I decided to have the ballots dumped into an empty cardboard box and placed in a locked closet in my office. I was the only one with a key to this closet. I believe the reason none of us thought once about throwing the ballots out was because, no matter how flawed and discriminatory we all felt the election that we stopped was, those still were ballots that our fellow students had cast and therefore deserved a certain degree of respect.

I then attempted to contact Mike Williams and Alphe Williams. I discovered that they were in a meeting with the other members of the Homecoming Committee in the dean of men's office. A group of us, those not working on getting the new election up and running, headed over there. I accompanied the three newly appointed cochairman of the Homecoming Committee because I felt it was only proper that I personally inform both Williams that I had dismissed them since I had personally appointed them. In addition, it was important that they understood that it wasn't just me taking this action, but that all of the cabinet members present had supported the decision to dismiss them.

Furthermore, I wanted to speak to the other students on the Homecoming Committee to encourage them to remain on the committee. I believed it was important to avoid any further unnecessary disruption to the other Homecoming events that were planned.

We got to the dean of men's offices and just walked into the room. Seated around a conference table were the committee members, including Mike and Alphe Williams. To my surprise, Vice Chancellor Reddoch was also there. Everyone turned to look at us as we entered the room.

Assistant Dean Randy Gurie jumped out of his seat, yelling at us that we had to leave the meeting. The Homecoming Committee was in executive session, and only members could be present. I pointed at Reddoch who had a smug look on his face, and said that he wasn't a member of the committee. As Gurie was herding us out of the room, he said that Dean Reddoch was an invited guest of the committee. I told him that anything discussed in the meeting would be invalid because I had dismissed the two cochairmen. He just kept herding us out of the room, saying, "You will have to leave, you will have to leave."

I was thinking of going to see the chancellor, when John Crochet, the vice chairman of SGA's Rules Committee, informed everyone that Gurie couldn't keep me out of the meeting since, in accordance with the SGA constitution, I was an ex officio member of the Homecoming

Committee. The constitution stated that the SGA president serves as an ex officio member of all those student committees for which he appoints the chairman. I realized that I would need documentation establishing that, so I instructed John Crochet to run over to the SGA office and get a copy of the SGA Constitution. The rest of us waited in the hall for him to return.

I believe I understood why Dean Reddoch and Randy Gurie didn't want me in the meeting. They didn't want any opposition voices in the room. John got back with a copy of the SGA Constitution in record time. Glancing at the Constitution, it seemed that John was correct that as SGA president I was an ex officio member of the Homecoming Committee.

I told everyone else to wait in the hall and, armed with this information, I re-entered the room.

I noticed that Vice Chancellor Reddoch must have left the meeting by another door because he was no longer in the room. I immediately began waving the copy of the SGA constitution in my hand, as I stated in a loud voice that, as SGA president, I was an ex officio member of this committee and therefore allowed to attend this executive session. I looked over at Mike Williams and Alphe Williams and started to inform them again that they were no longer members of the committee when, again, Gurie jumped up again telling me that I had to leave and tried to usher me out the door. My blood was boiling at this total disrespect that Gurie was showing, not just to me but to the SGA as a whole, in attempting to keep me from speaking to the committee. I stood my ground this time, prepared to physically resist being removed from the meeting.

Randy Gurie, to his credit, didn't attempt to put his hands on me. He just kept loudly stating that I wasn't a member of the Homecoming Committee and had to leave the room. Even though I knew that I had every right to be present, I also knew that I had another recourse: to go to the authority above Reddoch and Gurie, Chancellor Murrill. At that time, I also believed that Chancellor Murrill was a fair man and, after showing him the SGA Constitution, that he would order my admission to the executive session. I let my eyes survey all of the committee members and said, "Fuck it, I'm taking this to the chancellor."

I hurried over to the chancellor's office with the other students and explained what was happening. I showed Murrill the SGA constitution to prove that I was allowed to attend an executive session of the committee. Murrill told me he would call Reddoch and ask him to see me, and, if I didn't receive satisfaction, to contact him again in twenty minutes. I got the impression that Chancellor Murrill and Reddoch had already talked.

When the other SGA members and I got to Reddoch's office, sure enough, he was expecting us. His door was open, and he was sitting behind his desk. Reddoch got up and signaled for all of us to follow him to the conference room where members of the Homecoming committee were still meeting. I again confronted Randy Gurie with the proof that the SGA president is an ex officio member of the Homecoming Committee. Gurie kept glancing over at Reddoch, who had taken a seat at the table, it appeared to me that he was looking for instructions but getting none from him. The committee members, including Mike Williams and Alphe Williams, sat there not saying a word.

Since Gurie hadn't stated any authority for my not being on the committee, I moved to have the minutes reflect that the SGA president, an ex officio member of the Homecoming Committee, was present to prevent future attempts by Reddoch to manipulate the committee. Mike Williams started discussing other matters involving the Homecoming rally that was to be held later that afternoon. I made a point of order that the topic on the table was the question of the SGA president being an ex officio member of the committee. I further restated that Mike Williams and Alphe Williams were no longer members of the committee, and I handed the two of them my executive order dismissing them. I pointed to the newly appointed cochairpersons sitting around the table stating, "These are the students I have appointed to replace them."

Well, that caused quite a row among the other members of the committee. As Reddoch and Gurie quietly sat in their chairs, the other members started yelling that I didn't have the authority to fire Mike Williams and Alphe Williams. I informed them that, after the committee reinstated the mandatory three vote requirement, I called an emergency meeting of my SGA cabinet to discuss the situation. The cabinet included SGA Legislative Vice President Dana Robert and the heads of Student Government departments, among others. All the Cabinet agreed that we were duty bound to act. I went on to explain that the cabinet's only purpose in taking this action was to ensure a fair Homecoming Queen election for all the finalists. The cabinet didn't want to interfere in any other Homecoming events and wanted to ask all the other members of the Homecoming committee to continue the fine work they were doing in order to make Homecoming a success.

My attempt to explain our actions fell on deaf ears. All the committee members, except Mike Williams, got up to leave, stating that the pep rally was to start at 4:45 P.M. and there was still a lot of work to be done setting it up. Reddoch also got up and returned to his office.

I continue to discuss the issue with Mike Williams. I explained that an easy way to solve this was by simply returning the voting process back to where a student didn't have to vote for three but could vote for one, two or three. Mike Williams refused to listen. He wanted the mandatory voting rule because that was the way other Homecoming Queen elections had been run. I pointed out that there was no proof that voting for three had been mandatory. Furthermore, the previous Homecoming Committees didn't have a Black finalist. Furthermore, the committee hadn't hesitated to change the previous actions of former Homecoming Committees when they denied Dana Robert, the SGA legislative vice president, the right to escort the runner-up for fear it would be upsetting to the alumni. I told Mike that it sure appeared that the driving force behind the mandatory three voting requirements was to prevent Cynthia Payton from getting elected. We were getting nowhere, so I told Mike what the chancellor had said about coming back to see him if I wasn't satisfied. He was welcome to come along with us. We all headed over to the chancellor's office.

When we got to the chancellor's office, it appeared once again that he had already spoken to Reddoch for he was waiting for us. I introduced Gary Simon, Sarah Soileau and Mike Richman to the chancellor as the newly appointed cochairpersons of the Homecoming Committee. With a nod to Mike Williams, the chancellor led us into his office. I thought it strange that Mike Williams didn't introduce himself to the chancellor, or, for that matter, that the chancellor didn't inquire Mike's name. It was then that I started to think that the chancellor may have been more involved in this matter than I had previously thought.

After we all were seated, I explained that all this hassle could be laid to rest just by endorsing SGA's new election being run without the mandatory rule of voting for three finalists for queen. The chancellor turned to Mike Williams and asked what he thought of dropping the mandatory requirement and just starting a new election. As reported in the *Reveille* (October 8, 1976), Mike Williams "rejected" having a new election. Instead, he started complaining that I didn't have the "power to confiscate the ballot box."

I explained to the chancellor that my cabinet had met and voted to stop the election, which obviously included returning SGA equipment such as the ballot box. I had the ballots that we found in the ballot box locked in my closet.

The chancellor said that it seemed the problem was Homecoming was too loosely organized, and that he was going to make sure that would be corrected in the future. At that point, I was seriously starting to question if the chancellor really was interested in correcting a discriminatory Homecoming election. I told him that SGA was going ahead with the new election without the discriminatory mandatory voting requirement. The student body deserved a Homecoming Queen elected in a fair and unbiased election, and that I hoped that would settle this controversy.

Except for Mike Williams, the rest of us got up to leave for class. He was looking straight ahead and hadn't moved. At the time I didn't give any weight to the fact that Williams was being left alone with the chancellor as I hurried to class. Unfortunately, my belief that the chancellor would do what was right ran smack-dab into the real world. I should have blown off class and stayed. As it was, I had to run flat out to get to my class on time.

After my class let out, I headed straight to the SGA office to check on how the new election was progressing. I found out that everyone was still organizing it. Packed into the office were a number of Black student members of Harambee who were all too familiar with the struggle for racial equality. They, along with several student government officers and SGA office staff members, were all working hard, side by side, to get the new non-discriminatory election up and running. As I looked around the room, I could see students, whom I had never seen in the SGA office before, working on getting the ballots, flyers and posters ready.

I found out that the new cochairpersons had made another important change in how the election was going to be held. Instead of having the voting location on the bottom floor of the Union, where few students went, they decided to move the voting table out onto the sidewalk, under the oak tree, across from the Union. This was the traditional location for student organizations to set up tables, because a large flow of students, leaving the Union and dormitories and heading to their classes on the other side of campus, passed that site.

I believed that the reason the Homecoming Committee had chosen that Union location was to discourage students, other than fraternity and sorority members, from voting in the election. Fraternities and sororities could easily inform their members where to go to vote.

I told the workers the new polling site was a great idea. The more students that voted, the fairer and more democratic the election. I also believed that after the student body heard about what was happening, they would turn out in large numbers to reject LSU's discriminatory past. I think that is exactly what the administration and others feared would happen.

I was surprised to see Ned Wright, financial vice president, in the SGA office. I hadn't seen Wright in the office since I had to remove his signature from SGA checks for questionable spending of SGA funds. I was told by staff workers that they had overheard Ned Wright on the telephone with someone discussing a recall petition against me, and that the petition was going to be circulated at today's pep rally.

In a story in the *Reveille* (October 9, 1976) the next day, Wright stated that he was in the SGA office Thursday afternoon when he received a call from Kip Knight, financial vice president of the Student Union, asking him how they could get rid of me. Wright went on to state that he next got a call from Jack Clegg, president of the Interfraternity Council about starting a recall petition to get rid of me. It appeared that Wright and the Greeks were going to try to seize on my fight to stop a racist Homecoming Queen election as an opportunity to remove me from office.

I decided I should go to the pep rally, but before I exposed myself to the welcome I knew I would receive, I wanted to make sure that, as SGA president, I could speak at the rally. I asked John Crochet if the pep rally was an SGA event. He told me indeed it was because they were using SGA equipment and funds for the pep rally. Therefore, he assured me, as SGA president, I had the right to address the students present and relate what was happening in the election of the Homecoming Queen. The Pollyanna in me still thought that if I could explain at the rally why the election had to be stopped, the students present, even though the vast majority of them were Greeks, would understand, and I could put a damper on any recall petition.

I instructed the students working on the posters and other items needed for the election tomorrow morning to keep working while I went to the pep rally. Some said they thought that was a bad idea since there would be predominantly fraternity and sorority student members, not to mention the LSU football team, in attendance. I just shrugged off the idea that I could be attacked by Greeks and white football players. I explained that it was important for all LSU students, especially the Greeks, with their long history of racism, to realize that the days of blatant racial discrimination on LSU's campus was coming to an end. I felt it was important to show solidarity with the Black football players on the team. I told them that I wasn't afraid of what might happen at the pep rally because I believed in standing up for what was right.

Hearing the concerns of some of the students, the Harambee members present decided to accompany me in order to cover my back. Pictures the next day in the *Reveille* (October 8, 1976) showed a number of these Harambee members present with me at the pep rally in a heated argument with Randy Gurie.

I asked if anyone needed a ride over to the pep rally. I realized that since it had already started there would be very few, if any, parking spots. Because I had a Board of Supervisor's sticker on my van, I knew I wouldn't have any problems parking, even if the only parking space open was Coach Charles McClendon's.

When we arrived, I noticed that a car, which I assumed to be Coach McClendon's, was in his parking space. After my personal experience with McClendon as the *Gumbo* sports reporter last year, I was more than a little disappointed that I was unable to park in his space. I had to settle for second best: I parked my van in one of the assistant football coaches' parking spaces.

The football practice field had very tall fencing all around it to prevent anyone, like scouts from other college football teams, from observing the team practicing. We saw that the gates had been left open for students attending the pep rally.

The pep rally was still going on as we entered. We must have been a sight to see because more and more of the students in front of the stage started turning their heads to look at us as we approached. A low buzz could be heard starting among the crowd, which appeared to be a few hundred students strong. The vast majority of students attending the pep rally were fraternity and sorority members plus the predominantly white football team, which was presently on the stage.

It was common knowledge that the majority of the Greek organizations despised me. At that moment I started looking for Ned Wright, but saw Randy Gurie. He walked quickly up to us. I brushed past him saying, "I am not here to talk to you." I proceeded to walk around the crowd to the front of the stage, all the while looking for Ned Wright. I didn't see him, but I did see a lot of worried looks as the Greeks stared at us.

The stage had been erected on the side of the football field. Standing on the stage with Coach McClendon and the football team were Mike Williams, Alphe Williams and a few other students on the Homecoming Committee. It appeared that the rally was wrapping up because the football team and Coach McClendon were preparing to leave the stage.

I couldn't help but notice that almost all the crowd of hundreds of fraternity and sorority students in front of the stage were white. On the stage with the football team was the Homecoming Committee, notable among them was Alphe Williams, the cochairman I had appointed to the Homecoming Committee in the hope of making Homecoming more diversified. That obviously hadn't worked!

I continued to scan the crowd for Ned Wright, but he was nowhere to be seen. I then heard Mike Williams up on the stage say he was going to read a statement from Chancellor Murrill relating to the Homecoming Queen elections. He said that Chancellor Murrill had stated, in part, that "because of the unfortunate breakdown in the interrelationships among various campus groups and in the election procedures, no one of the ten finalists can be fairly named queen. I have, therefore, regretfully decided that LSU will not have a Homecoming Queen this year. Instead, all finalists will be honored as the Homecoming court." Furthermore, "because of the controversy with the escorts, there would be none this year."

I was dumbstruck. I wasn't expecting this from the chancellor. He had given me no idea that he was going to take such a drastic step as declaring there would be no Homecoming Queen. First of all, I believed what Mr. J. Stan Landry, Director of the Alumni Federation, had told me: that the Homecoming Queen election was under SGA authority. Therefore, I felt that the chancellor couldn't stop us from crowning a Homecoming Queen if we didn't let him. Secondly, I feared that Murrill, like the other administrators I had dealt with, was attempting to prevent LSU students from electing their first Black Homecoming

Queen. This thought made me both sad and disappointed in the chancellor and, at the same time, very angry.

When Williams had finished reading the chancellor's statement, I started hearing abusive, harsh, obscene language coming from the Greeks directed toward the chancellor and me. The vast majority of it was directed at me.

I had forgotten all about Ned Wright and any recall petition. I just wanted to address the crowd from the stage to tell them that the chancellor had no right to stop the student body from electing and crowning a Homecoming Queen. Most of the finalists present had a look of despair on their faces. I decided, before going up on the stage, I would go over to them to comfort them by telling them not to worry, there would be a Homecoming Queen that year. After I had finished speaking with the finalists, I turned to go up on the stage.

But Mike Williams stepped in my way, telling me I didn't have any right to either go up on the stage or use the sound system to speak to the students. I stressed that he had no authority to stop me. I was really getting pissed off. As I was just about to push past Williams, Gurie stepped into the fray.

I had had it up to here with Randy Gurie. The assistant dean again came up with the same old shit, that I wasn't a member of the Homecoming Committee and therefore had no right to speak from the stage. I reiterated that I had the right to address the students from a stage that was paid for by SGA and using SGA's sound system—kind of like what Ronald Reagan said during a debate in the 1980 primary when editor Jon Breen, the debate moderator, told the sound man to turn off Reagan's microphone while he was attempting to speak. Reagan shouted, "I am paying for this microphone, Mr. Breen." It brought the house down. Of course, I am no Reagan.

I found myself face to face with Randy Gurie, Alphe Williams, and Mike Williams, arguing that it was the SGA's president right to use SGA equipment regardless if I was, or was not, a member of the Homecoming Committee. I hadn't noticed that Coach McClendon and the foot-ball team were leaving the rally until I heard an angry voice right behind me say, "Fuckin' asshole!"

I spun around, not knowing what to expect, only to see the number 77 on A. J. Duhe's football jersey. Duhe had been an outstanding defensive lineman for LSU. I had watched him flatten many of the opposing football teams' running backs. I presumed that he must have been the individual that called me an asshole. Maybe it was because he was in full pads, but I thought, "Damn, he's big." I wanted no part of him, and I was glad to see him board the bus with the other football players.

A lot of the students were also leaving the rally, so I decided to end this conversation with Gurie and the Williams. I turned back to the three of them, saying, "Fuck it. I'm tired of wasting my time with you three, I'm going to go talk to the chancellor." With that, the Harambee members and I headed to our vehicles to drive over to the chancellor's office.

When we got there, we were told that he had left for Welsh, Louisiana, to speak at a meeting of the LSU Alumni Welsh Association. I asked Murrill's secretary if she had a contact number. She said no, which I found hard to believe. I figured she was instructed not to give it out. After hearing that, we headed back to the SGA office.

I wasn't just going to roll over and allow the chancellor's statement to stand. I decided to try contacting him in Welch that night. I felt I had to move fast since the news that there wasn't going to be a Homecoming Queen that year was already on the local news stations.

That was before the internet, so we only had directory information to use. We called a couple of phone numbers, but no one picked up. It was getting late. If I didn't find him soon, I knew Welsh, like other small towns, probably rolled up its sidewalks early. I tried a couple of other numbers, but still didn't have any success in finding the chancellor.

When it was 9:30 P.M. I suddenly thought, "Hell, I'll call the police in Welsh; they should know where the LSU chancellor is." I called the Welsh police station direct, told the officer who answered that I was the president at LSU—failing to mention of the student body—and asked could he help me locate my chancellor. He said, "Yes, sir, I know where he is staying. If you could hold, I will go get him." I said, "I will hold for him, Thank you."

It wasn't long until I heard Murrill's voice on the other end of the phone, saying in a very sarcastic tone, "Evening, Mr. President." His sarcastic tone rolled off me like water off a duck since I was still mad about what I felt was a betrayal by him.

I started in on him. I didn't care what he thought he could do to stop the student body from having a Homecoming Queen. The SGA was going to go ahead with our Homecoming Queen election and crown a queen at Saturday night's football game. I then described the antics that Randy Gurie and Mike Williams had pulled at the pep rally. I felt the fault for all of this trouble lay at the feet of the administration for encouraging and supporting the stubborn insistence of Mike and Alphe Williams on continuing with a discriminatory Homecoming Queen election. When we all were in his office earlier, the chancellor could have taken a stand against Mike Williams' refusal to agree to a non-discriminatory election. I told him the actions of the administration, though Reddoch and Gurie, emboldened Mike Williams to dig in his heels.

Looking around the room at the other students in the office, I realized that my tone of voice must have become the loud fighting tone that would come over me when I was arguing with people like David Duke at Free Speech Alley. Seeing my comrades' concerned looks, I paused and took a deep breath to try to calm down a little, giving the chancellor the opportunity to say, "Now Ted, don't do anything foolish!" That was the worst thing he could have told me. I declared that I was going to fix this situation one way or another, with or without his help. I refused to be a part of any discrimination against Cynthia Payton, and I would resist any attempt by him to stop the student body from electing and crowning a Homecoming Queen at the Saturday night football game.

Paul Murrill had been chancellor less than four years at that time, but our relationship went back to my days as president of PSA in the spring of 1971. The fight at that time was about a different kind of discrimination: the College of Education denying male students who had hair a certain length and any facial hair at all, from enrolling in Education classes. Chancellor Murrill had been vice chancellor at that time. He learned then of my commitment to a cause I believed in and how hard I would fight for student rights at LSU.

At some point, the chancellor interrupted me asking me not to do anything rash, telling me that we could discuss the issue when he got back to the campus the next day.

I knew that his statement canceling Homecoming Queen that year had been on all of the local evening television news in Baton Rouge, but the late night 10 P.M. news hadn't started yet. I told him I would only wait if he immediately called the media stations and retracted his previous statement. After a short silence, he agreed to do that as soon as we hung up. I told him that SGA was still going ahead with the new Homecoming Queen election, which was non-negotiable, but I wouldn't take any further actions, nor make any statement to the press until we had a chance to talk. He agreed, telling me he would see me the next morning when he got back on campus.

The other students in the room had heard my side of the conversation but not the chancellor's. As I went over what Murrill had agreed to, their faces lit up. One of them shouted, "The Tiger Lair's TV should still be on." In a mad dash, we all took off to the Tiger Lair, taking the steps down to the second floor two at a time. When we got there, we had a few minutes to wait but, sure enough, Murrill had called the station and the news reporter stated that LSU's chancellor had retracted his statement that there wasn't going to be a Homecoming Queen that year at LSU. The reporter went on to say that the chancellor said that he would be meeting with the student body president and others to work out a solution so that there would be a Homecoming Queen.

Hearing that, we all started yelling and slapping each other on the backs. We decided to continue our celebrating at my friend Phil Brady's bar, Magoo's that was right off campus on Chime Street. None of us thought the war was won by far, but we did feel we had won that battle.

An important lesson for organizing and public defenders to learn: celebrate all the little victories because they may be the only ones.

## THE BETRAYAL

I arrived at the SGA office at 7 A.M. on Friday, October 8th, where I met with a handful of the other students who had been with me the previous night at Magoo's. We all had bloodshot eyes and hadn't gotten very much sleep the past few days, but we were all raring to go with the new non-discriminatory Homecoming Queen election. In my opinion, there is no greater feeling than being part of a group of people fighting against an injustice, be it marching to end the war in Viet Nam, civil rights, women's rights, anti-nukes, or whatever. Even though the system and the odds are against you, one really doesn't lose in such a fight even when the goal you are fighting for isn't fully achieved. The saying of Ralph Waldo Emerson is so true: Life is a journey, not a destination." Sure, we always thought in the long run we would win, but just standing up for what is right and just is a personal win in and of itself.

We carried the table, chairs, ballots, ballot box, and signs, and set up under the great oak tree on the corner across from the Union. We all were a little apprehensive about how the students would response to our new Homecoming Queen election.

We were up and running just as the students started passing us on their way to their 7:30 A.M. classes. We had two students standing out in front of the table calling for students to come vote in SGA's Homecoming Queen election.

I decided to get breakfast, as I usually did, at the Union before speaking with Chancellor Murrill later that morning. I still didn't know how I was going to approach this meeting with him. How firm should I be in demanding that whoever won our election was to be crowned Homecoming Queen at half time at the game Saturday night? And if he refused, what then? Should I threaten to go to the press about how LSU was preventing a Homecoming Queen to be crowned at the game for fear that the elected queen would be Black?

No sooner had I sat down with my scrambled eggs and grits than seven of the Homecoming Queen finalists appeared at my table. When I looked up, I was literally surrounded by "queens." I noticed immediately that Cynthia was not among them. I also noticed that every last one of them looked anguished, as if her lifelong dream had been completely destroyed.

Three of the "queens" sat down in the three empty chairs at my table while the others stood beside them. They must have chosen a spokesperson among themselves, because the finalist who sat across from me immediately said, "Ted, we all want one of us to be queen of Homecoming. For some of us, this has been a dream since, as little girls, our fathers took us to our first LSU football game." The tortured tone in her voice expressed the torment I could tell all of them were feeling at the chancellor's statement that there wasn't going to be a Homecoming Queen that year.

I told them, "There will be a Homecoming Queen this year, I promise you. SGA isn't alone in wanting one; the Alumni Federation also wants a Homecoming Queen." I told them that I was meeting with the chancellor that morning to work things out.

As I was explaining this to the "queens," a perfect way to approach the chancellor occurred to me. He had made it clear a number of times his concern at how all of this turmoil was affecting the finalist. Well, I had a plan to show him just how deeply his statement about no Homecoming Queen was affecting at least these seven finalists.

"I want y'all to come with me right now, before the planned meeting, to express to the chancellor the anguish you all are going through at the thought there might be no Homecoming Queen this year," I told them.

I could see that several of them were not comfortable with the idea of talking to the chancellor. I told them that Murrill had never met any of them personally, so it was easier to make the kind of decision he had made when there wasn't a human face attached to that decision. I felt that, if they would tell the chancellor the same thing they had just told me, it very well might get him to agree to having a Homecoming Queen.

The spokesperson looked around at her fellow finalists and said, "I think Ted is right. If we want to have a chance of achieving our dream of becoming LSU's Homecoming Queen, we must do everything possible." She looked back at me, saying, "I will go with you, Ted. I may not become Homecoming Queen, but I want one of us to be crowned queen Saturday night." They all slowly started nodding their heads affirmatively, even though some of them clearly weren't enthusiastic.

Still not having taken a bite of my breakfast, I got up from the table and said, "Let's go." I knew from the looks of some of those sorority girls that, if I didn't act soon, they would most likely back out. It was not only the idea of confronting the chancellor that troubled them, but doing it with me, the hated long haired, anti-Greek Ted Schirmer. I could see the wheels turning in their pretty little heads, hoping none of their sorority sisters saw them walking across campus with me.

As we were leaving, I started wondering how the voting was going at the Homecoming Queen voting table. None of us knew exactly how the student body would respond to our new election.

When I got to the sidewalk at the bottom of the Union's steps, I saw a large crowd of students standing around the voting table. There must have been 25 to 30 students who were voting or trying to vote. It was a few minutes before 8 A.M. on Friday morning, an hour that usually found few students on campus. Seeing this many students voting proved to me that there were students who supported what we were trying to accomplish.

I could tell that the "queens" were also impressed with the number of students trying to vote. Their demeanor changed from that point on, even those finalists who had doubts about going with us to see Murrill.

We were about to leave for the chancellor's office when I noticed a table being set up a couple of feet from our election table. Some students were preparing to collect students' signatures on a recall petition to have me removed as student body president. Much to the chagrin of the "queens," I stopped to talk with those students. I wanted to explain why I felt it was necessary to stop the other Homecoming Queen election.

I have never feared talking with others who disagreed with what I either said or stood up for, but those students manning the recall petition table made it clear that they weren't interested in discussing anything with me. I just couldn't understand why individuals who have a different point of view on a subject wouldn't want to discuss those differences with the other side, if for no other reason than to test that point of view. How else does one expand one's knowledge of an issue without discussions with others who hold different beliefs?

I told them that I thought that trying to recall me was a right of theirs, and I supported that right, but I felt that, if the recall petition was based on the actions I had to take relating to the Homecoming Queen elections, I believed it was misguided. One of the female students angrily stated that it was because I was anti-Greek. I explained to them I was against any forms of elitism, especially on a state college campus, like LSU, that is funded by Louisiana tax dollars. But again, I expressed my support for them to take this action since that is what a democracy was all about—freedom of speech and the right to petition their government about grievances—and the SGA was their government.

But as I looked at their faces, I knew I was wasting my breath. I turned and motioned to the "queens," and we once again headed to the chancellor's office. When we got there, Murrill's secretary, Mrs. Jean Van Volkenbery, was a little taken aback at seeing me coming into the office with a half dozen of the "queens" in tow. I told her we would like to talk to the chancellor. She said he is in a meeting, and it may be a long one. I told Mrs. Hubbard that we would come back later. Outside I explained to the "queens" that I would tell the chancellor all of you would like to talk to him and they should check back with me later that afternoon. I walked back to the polling table to help out with the voting.

As I approached the corner where the voting table was located, I couldn't even see it. There were students four to five deep standing around it. There were also students by the recall table, but I took comfort that there were not nearly as many.

When I made my way to the voting table, one of the students manning it gave me a big smile and said that it had been like that all morning. I saw a number of Blacks and long hairs waiting to vote. For the first time, I let myself start to believe that students were standing up against racism on campus. Sure, stopping a racist Homecoming Queen election and possibly electing a Black Homecoming Queen at a southern college with a history of racism wasn't going to stop all racism at LSU, but it would demonstrate that things were changing on campus.

I helped out with the voting until it was getting close to the time for the scheduled meeting with the chancellor. When I got to Murrill's office, the door was open and he got up from his desk to greet me. As he shut the door behind me, he motioned for me to sit down. Instead of returning to his seat behind his desk, he took the chair beside me.

The chancellor stated that Mr. Landry, Director of the Alumni Federation, was going to be a little late for our meeting. He handed me a letter that he had written referencing the long distance telephone conversation we had the previous night. He asked me to see if it accurately reflects our conversation. As I started to read it, he said he wanted to do everything he could to make sure that Homecoming was a success, including, if possible, the election of a Homecoming Queen. As I read the letter, I thought this letter sure didn't seem to reflect that sentiment.

In the letter, the chancellor reiterated his "keen disappointment in having to declare invalid the campus election conducted for the Homecoming Queen." He further stated that the election was carried out by the appropriately designated Homecoming Committee which was "composed of representatives of the Student Government Association [designated by me] and representatives of the LSU Alumni Federation and representatives of the administrative staff of the campus."

I pointed out that, if the committee members representing the alumni and the administration had any capacity other than a consultative to the students on the committee, there would have been a vote at the first meeting on who would chair the committee, instead of the SGA president appointing him.

Next, the chancellor justified his action declaring that there would be no Homecoming Queen this year by writing that there were "many irregularities and missing ballot boxes associated with this election." He further stated, as he had in our conversation the night before, that he felt there wasn't time to hold another election. This was the same weak ass excuse that Mike Williams was promoting. It seemed, at least on this point, that the two of them were on the same page. Obviously, I shouldn't have left Mike Williams alone with the chancellor yesterday when I went to class.

I pointed out that all other elections on campus, including the SGA elections, were held in one day. We had today, and if, since it was Friday, not a lot of students voted in our election, we could even run the election all day Saturday. But I had just left the polling station and students were voting in large numbers. I was confident that the majority of students wanted to elect a Homecoming Queen but wanted a fair election. I told him what the "queens" had said to me earlier this morning. I had brought them over to see him, but he was in a meeting.

He went on to write that "I will not be promissory with respect to any recognition" but he would not "attempt to prevent you from designating someone as your own selection for Homecoming Queen." I found this statement quite insulting since it appeared directed at me. Fighting to control my anger, I told him it wasn't going to be "my" selection of a Homecoming Queen but the vote of the student body in a fair election, purged of any discriminatory rules that would prevent the election of Cynthia Payton. Furthermore, Assembly members had signed a petition supporting my actions, calling the previous election both racist and sexist. Immediately I could tell he was getting uncomfortable with where this conversation was heading. He had learned that I will go to the barricades, or as in *The Godfather* "go to the mattresses," on behalf of the students. I had been doing that on campus since 1971.

Chancellor Murrill knew that, as a member of the Board, I had been briefed on the ongoing Justice Department's desegregation lawsuit against LSU. He also knew that I could appeal to other Board members, like Camille Gravel, Jerry McKernan and Gordon Dore, with whom I had a good working relationship. Since the chancellor worked for the Board of Supervisors, I could go over his head. I was just about to go there when Chancellor Murrill's secretary buzzed that Mr. Landry was there.

We both got up to greet Mr. Landry as he walked into the office. After Landry was seated, Chancellor Murrill brought him up to speed on what he and I had been discussing. When Murrill got to what I had said about Mr. Landry's telling me that the Homecoming Committee was under the SGA and that the alumni representatives were on the committee purely in an advisory capacity, I held my breath as I watched Mr. Landry's face. But he started nodding his head as he said, "That's correct." As quietly as possible I exhaled.

This was a very pleasant change from having to deal with an LSU administrator like Vice Chancellor Reddoch or Dean Jameson. I had learned that I couldn't trust either one of them. It was a relief to discover that a man, though I had met him only two days ago, was a trustworthy and honest person. He could have easily denied telling me that, since it would be my word against his, but he didn't. I looked over at the chancellor to see his response. As usual, Paul Murrill held his composure as he asked Mr. Landry what the Alumni Federation's position was relating to SGA's Homecoming Queen election.

It became apparent that Mr. Landry had been thinking about this very issue for he didn't hesitate as he stated that the Alumni Federation would sanction our Homecoming Queen election only if the election was conducted fairly and if more votes were cast in our election than in the first election.

I was ecstatic. I felt like jumping out of my seat and giving Mr. Landry a big hug. I noticed that the chancellor's usual composure had changed. I could tell that he wasn't expecting that answer from Mr. Landry.

With as much restraint as I could muster, I said that SGA agreed to those conditions. I realized if I didn't get out of the chancellor's office immediately, I would explode. As I got to my feet I said, "If there isn't anything else, I need to get back to my office to check on how the Homecoming Queen election is going." I thanked the chancellor for his professionalism in this matter. I turned to look at Mr. Landry, stuck out my hand and thanked him with a big grin on my face. I was afraid at any second the chancellor was going to say he wasn't in agreement. I started toward the door, dreading hearing the chancellor's voice. It seemed as if I would never get to the door, but neither man said anything to me as I exited the office.

I had to fight the urge to break out in a run as soon as I closed the door behind me. I managed to get out of the office before taking off like a bat out of hell for the polling station. Again, as I neared the corner, I could see an even larger group of students trying to vote in the election. I could tell that there was a very good chance that the number of students voting in the SGA election was going to far surpass the number that had voted in the election I had stopped.

When I got up to the polling table, I announced in a loud voice, so that the students manning the recall table next to us could hear, "I was just told by the Alumni Director that if our election is fairly run, which our election is, and if more students vote in our election than voted in the election I had to stop, then the Alumni Federation would accept our election results." A cheer went up from the students manning the table and even a number of the students waiting to vote.

The students at the table told me the turnout was phenomenal. They had already had to Xerox more ballots three different times. That meant that over 1,000 students had already voted, and it was only noon. They told me that many of the students had told them that they had seen the news about what was happening and, even though they didn't have any class on a Friday, they decided to come on campus to vote in the election. They told me that numerous other students were remarking how excited they felt that SGA was finally doing something by standing up against racism on campus and that this kind of action against racism at LSU was long overdue.

I headed to the Union to get some lunch. While there I let myself enjoy the moment. We had fought the good fight and damn if it didn't seem as though we had won. As everyone who has been involved in movements knows, you don't always win but that should never stop you from trying to correct, or change a wrong. A number of my friends, who were way more politically savvy than I was at that time, tried to persuade me to disengage from this fight. I told them I just couldn't do that. There were too many times in my past when I had remained silent and did nothing when I saw people being hurt by others' prejudices. Since Viet Nam, I was evolving into a better person. The war, along with marijuana and mushrooms, had opened my mind and, for better or for worse, I was becoming a completely different person than I was just a few years earlier. Some of the students, who had been fighting with me on this issue and others in the past, were the same age as I was when I went to Viet Nam. They, too, were looking for answers on why things were the way they were at LSU and in our country. It is easier for the younger generation to shake off the shackles of the prejudices and behaviors of the previous generation. They have no guilt, subconscious or otherwise, of placating, or worse participating, in the egregious events of that time. Maybe it was the civil rights movement, the antiwar movement, or just the music that opened their minds to the wrongs around them which, for whatever reasons, their parents hadn't challenged when they were growing up. Our generation was standing up and fighting for civil rights, stopping the war, or protecting the environment. I realize that fighting against a discriminatory Homecoming Queen election wasn't in the same category as the above mentioned movements, but racism in any form is wrong regardless of where one finds it. Thank God, unlike me, these students didn't need a war to wake their asses up.

As I sat down with my tray of food, the same half dozen "queens" appeared at my table. I thought, "Damn, are these women stalking me?" They told me that they had seen the crowd of students voting at the polling station and were anxious to know what was happening. Was there going to be a queen crowned at the game? I told them about my meeting with the chancellor and Mr. Landry of the Alumni Federation that morning. So, yes, there would be a Homecoming Queen.

I expected the "queens" to at least smile after hearing this news, if not outright cheer, but none did. Instead, a few of them got even graver looks on their faces. They didn't say another word to me but turned and left. I sat there for a while wondering what the hell that was all about?

Soon though, the excitement of our apparent victory swept back over me, and I didn't think of this question again until later that night. I had to eat quickly and get to the office for I had other issues I had to deal with now that the Homecoming Queen election issue was solved, or at least I thought it had been. Little did I suspect that Chancellor Murrill still had an ace up his sleeve that he hadn't yet played. It was a move I might have unintentionally encouraged when I took the half dozen "queens" over to see him that morning.

Around 4 o'clock, I decided to go down to the voting poll to help close it down for the day. I was curious if the large number of students voting had continued during the afternoon. I was not disappointed. I was told that the number of students voting that day had surpassed 1,500 students a couple of hours ago and was still climbing. There was still a large number of students gathered around the table trying to vote, so I decided to keep the poll open as long as anyone was attempting to vote.

I had only been there about 30 minutes when one of SGA's office staff came up to the table. He told me that the chancellor had called the office looking for me and asked if I would call him back. As I headed back to the office, I couldn't help but worry about what Murrill wanted to talk to me about. It would surely be about the election of the Homecoming Queen but what?

When I entered the SGA office, I could tell that everyone else must be wondering the same thing. I smiled at them and shrugged my shoulders as I went into my office to call the chancellor. I didn't close the door because I felt we were all in this together, and the other students had a right to hear our conversation. I took a deep breath as I picked up the phone and dialed Murrill's number.

The chancellor's secretary answered the phone, and I told her I was returning the Chancellor Murrill's call. She said he was expecting my call and transferred me. As always, the chancellor greeted me with a pleasant and friendly voice. He said that he had arranged for the ten Homecoming Queen finalists to meet with him in his office at five o'clock and wanted to know if I could come by at that time. I told him I would be there. I hadn't noticed that he didn't say anything about my attending his meeting with the finalists.

When I got to the chancellor's office, all ten finalists were already present. I was about to talk with them, but the chancellor's secretary must have been told to notify him as soon as I got there for Chancellor Murrill opened his door and motioned for us to come into his office.

At least that is what I thought, but, when I started toward the door, he held up his hand and said, "I want to talk to the girls alone." He followed the last finalist into his office and closed the door behind him. I was left standing there wondering what the hell. I didn't even have time to ask him why I was being excluded from his meeting with the finalists. I was worried.

I don't know how long they were in there; it seemed forever, but it probably was around 20 to 25 minutes. When the door opened, the "queens" walked out of his office and past me without saying a word. None of them even made eye contact with me. As a matter of fact, Cynthia was looking at the floor as she walked by me. I started to ask them what had happened, but the chancellor, who was standing in the doorway of his office, called for me to come in.

I walked past him into his office. As he closed the door, he motioned in the direction of the two chairs in front of his desk saying, "Have a seat." I walked over to one of the chairs and sat down, expecting him to take the other chair. Instead, he chose to sit behind his desk, clearly sending me the message: he was in charge, and I was subordinate to him. I was still attempting to get a handle on what was happening. I wasn't at all prepared for what came.

I was slowly learning that an individual can be two totally different people when he is occupying a position of power, like a chancellor for a university. He can be friendly and personable when interacting with a student, but, when it came to getting what he wants in his professional

299

role, he can be quite Machiavellian. In addition, I would learn that some people can readily switch back and forth between those two different personalities. I didn't have this awareness at the time. I was too trusting, and it hindered my effectiveness as a student leader. I had little experience dealing with this type of individual.

Chancellor Murrill didn't lean across his desk glaring at me as Reddoch or Jameson would have. Instead, he sat upright in his chair as he began to talk. He stated how distressed he was about what was happening to the ten finalists. That was why he had arranged to meet with them this afternoon. He had invited me to his office so that I could be the first to hear their decision. This was how smooth, some would say professional, Murrill was when he was about to lay down the law to a subordinate.

I had realized, when I hurriedly left his office after the meeting with Mr. Landry, that the chancellor had heard what he had wanted to hear. Still, I wasn't prepared for how far he was willing to go to stop the election of a Black as Homecoming Queen.

Looking at me sternly, but not glaring, he told me about his conversation with the "queens." He felt that they should have the final say on which election results he should sanction. He wanted me to think he had abdicated his authority to make the final decision of how to deal with the conflicting Homecoming Queen elections by allowing the "queens" themselves to make that decision.

Give me a break! I always felt at times I was slow on the uptake, but not that time. It quickly became clear to me that he had figured out a way around what Mr. Landry had told us earlier that morning. He must have come to the same realization that I and others on campus had. That, due to the very large student turnout all day voting in the SGA election, there was a high probability that there would be a Black Homecoming Queen crowned in Tiger Stadium at halftime on Saturday night.

If I had been chancellor, I would have been proud that I had been the head of LSU's Baton Rouge campus when another racial barrier had

300

been torn down, this time not because of a court order but by the students themselves. Then again, I guess the Board of Supervisors knew Paul Murrill way better than I did.

I didn't have to hear what he was about to say next to know the conclusion of our talk. Considering that the vast majority of the finalists were sorority members, I believed that they would choose the first election, where the students voting were predominantly members of fraternities and sororities, rather than the SGA election, especially after they had seen the number of, what appeared to be non-Greek students and most likely my supporters voting in our election. So I wasn't surprised when Murrill said that the finalists had picked the first election.

It became very clear to me then why he had me stay outside when he spoke with the "queens" privately. He didn't want me to bring up how discriminatory the first election was to Cynthia.

The chancellor didn't mention whether the finalists voted by a showing of hands or simply by voice vote. He stated that, based on the finalists' choice, he was only sanctioning the first election. Also, instead of the next four highest vote getters being the queen's court, all of the remaining nine finalists would make up the queen's court. Then he said something I hadn't anticipated him saying: "No students will be escorting the queen and her court. Only the Homecoming Queen would be escorted, and the chairman of the Alumni Federation has agreed to escort her." I thought to myself, well, that solved my question of what I was going to wear to escort the queen at halftime.

When he had finished, he just looked at me with that look of a parent telling his teenager he couldn't go out that night. He didn't ask me what I thought about his decision. It was clear that it wasn't up for discussion. Like it or not, it was clear that his decision was final. He had successfully stopped any possibility that members of the Board of Supervisor and LSU administrators would witness a long haired hippie SGA president escorting a Black Homecoming Queen at half-time of Saturday's football game in front of tens of thousands of conservative, and very possibly racist, alumni. Considering the Board's continuing fight with the federal government over integrating the university, if

Murrill had allowed that to happen, the Board might actually think that they had made a mistake when they made him chancellor.

I think the administration also had an agenda beyond maintaining the racial status quo. If the second election were sanctioned, so would be the actions I was forced to take to stop the first election. If they let me get away with this challenge to their authority, I think the administration feared it would encourage me to take even more similar actions in the future. What else might I do? Also, would other student leaders in the future be emboldened to attempt similar actions against the university's policies and procedures?

The chancellor had put me in checkmate by getting the "queens" to back the first election. Putting the whole weight of the final decision on the shoulders of the 'queens" relieved him from the responsibility of overruling the Alumni Federation.

I got up from my chair, shaking my head in the negative as I commented, "If that is what the finalists want, then I will have to accept that, but, as chancellor, you are sanctioning a racist election on LSU's campus. This is 1976, not the Jim Crow days of the past." Without waiting for any comment he might want to make, I turned and walked out of his office.

Like I said, I was pretty naïve then, but as my future clients in the Southside of Chicago would say, "My mother may have raised a fool, but she didn't raise no dummy." I definitely was foolish to have trusted Chancellor Murrill, but I had no choice except to capitulate to the fact that the Homecoming Queen was going to be elected by a racist election. There wasn't enough time for any more maneuvering on my part to try to prevent that from happening.

The more I thought about that as I walked to my office, the angrier I got, to the point I had to stop walking in order to calm down. I didn't want to get to the SGA office in a rage. I had to keep my composure in order to tell the others the bad news. My anger was only compounded with the pain I felt for the other students who had put so much work and time into pulling off this election. I realized that all of their hard work and the sacrifices they had made had been in vain.

When I got to the office, I was still struggling with my anger over what the chancellor had done. I found the same half dozen students, who had been working at the election table, putting away the items from the table. They still had that sense of excitement surrounding them they had when I was at the table with them earlier. I am sure the feeling of accomplishment they had for pulling off this election just added to the excitement they felt at seeing all those students coming out to vote in our election. I hesitated for a moment. I knew I was stalling, but, damn, I sure hated to be the one to throw cold water on their accomplishments. Damn Murrill!

I was brought back to earth when one of the students saw me standing in the hallway outside the doorway. "Ted's back!" he said. Everyone stopped what they were doing and turned to look at me. I once again cursed the chancellor in my head as I stepped farther into the office.

"I know of no other way to say this," I said, "but the chancellor found a way to void all of our work and is going to sanction the racist election's winner as Homecoming Queen." I hope no one else ever has to see what I saw at that moment. The expression on each face went from that of a victorious individual conquering an evil to a person who had just suffered a terrible defeat instead.

I still believe that Paul Murrill was a good man as defined by the norms of our culture: that, if a person has to do certain things required of him in his job that harm others, that doesn't make that person a bad person. In our culture, it is not only expected of him, but if he loses his job for refusing, he is thought a fool. A person can be a good and decent person outside of his workplace, but not at work if good behavior conflicts with his job responsibilities. I realized that blocking a Black from becoming LSU's Homecoming Queen was a part of the chancellor's job responsibilities, and, if he was able to find a reason to block a hippie student body president from escorting the Homecoming Queen at half time, well, that was just lagniappe.

After I was done talking to the workers, there was a very long moment of silence broken by one of the students saying, "I am going to go get drunk at Magoo's. Anyone coming with me?" I told her that I needed some time to work through what had just happened. The rest of the other students grabbed their personal belongings and headed out the door. Within a minute I found myself alone in the office. I closed and locked the front door and retreated into my office. I had just sat down when I heard a knock on the outside door. I thought someone must have forgotten something in the office. When I opened the door, to my surprise, there stood Bob Sappenfield.

Bob had been serving as one of the student members of University Court for a while and this semester was the Chief Justice. He looked a little nervous standing there in front of me. He told me that the chancellor had sent him to retrieve the ballots from the first Homecoming Queen elections.

Of course, I still had those ballots locked in my office closet. I could have used them as leverage with the chancellor, but I feared that could lead to a worst result. Chancellor Murrill had canceled the crowning of a Homecoming Queen once already. I believed that if I took any steps to block the return of those ballots, it would allow him again to cancel the crowning of a queen, but this time firmly placing all the blame squarely on me. Furthermore, any such action would bury any discussion of how the first election was racist.

It wasn't an easy thing for me, but I told Bob that I had locked them in my closet for safe keeping, and I waved for him to follow me. I unlocked the closet door, pulled out the cardboard box with the ballots in it and tried to hand it to him. Bob quickly held up his hands and asked if I minded putting them in the SGA's metal ballot box. He had brought a lock with him to secure the ballot box. I said no problem. I walked back to the outer office where I saw that the SGA metal ballot box was sitting, locked, on one of the desks.

Using my key, I unlocked the box and dumped the ballots from the second election into an empty cardboard box I found on the floor. So many students had voted in our election that the cardboard box was almost overflowing with ballots. I then dumped the ballots from the first election into the metal ballot box. Bob Sappenfield walked forward and, all official like, locked the lid with the lock he had brought with him. Then, without another word to me, he turned and left the office. Well, that's that, I thought, at least the chancellor had sense enough not to send Mike Williams to get the ballots. I wasn't sure how I would have handled that situation.

I found some tape and, pushing down the ballots from the SGA election, taped down the lid of the cardboard box. I carried the box back into my office and locked it in my closet. I had to chuckle to myself about the irony of it all. Here I was locking up our ballots after running a fair and non-discriminatory Homecoming election while turning over the ballots cast in the racist election in order for those votes to determine which finalists was to be crown LSU's Homecoming Queen.

Hey, if life has taught me one thing, it was that you had better be able to laugh at the absurdities people and life throw at you. No matter how bad things get, when those bad times subsided, you had better be able to laugh, if for nothing more than to relieve the tension in you. I did it in my childhood, in Nam, and I found myself doing it again. If there was one thing that kept me from becoming bitter over some of the conditions in my life, it was my sense of humor.

I locked the outer door again, went into my office, turned off the lights, sat behind my desk, and I said, not to myself this time, but out loud, "Fuck 'em!"

I found my Rolling Stones album, *Let It Bleed,* that had played during better times. I placed the tape in my 8-track player, pulled out the joint I had put in my pocket earlier that morning to celebrate what I thought was going to be a totally different outcome today. I selected my favorite song, cranked up the volume, and took a long drag on the joint, letting the music and lyrics of "You Can't Always Get What You Want" take me to a better place while saying one last time, in a louder voice, "Fuck 'em'!"

### HOMECOMING DAY

On Homecoming Day, Saturday morning, October 9th, I went as usual to eat breakfast at LSU at the Union. I stopped at the 7/11 store to get a newspaper before heading to the campus to read about the night's game. As I picked up the Saturday morning *Advocate* and headed to the checkout counter, I was struck like a lightning bolt by a picture in the bottom corner of the front page. There was Mike Williams, holding up the ballot box I had given Bob Sappenfield the night before. The caption over the picture was: "Homecoming Queen stolen ballots recovered."

I couldn't stop myself from saying loudly, "Goddamn those sons-of-bitches!" As I looked up, I saw the eyes of everyone standing in line in front of me were staring at me. I was so mad; I couldn't read anymore. Fuming, I just paid for the paper and left.

The sports page articles about the game must have already been written before the *Advocate* received that picture because there was no mention about the Homecoming Queen election in the articles I read while eating breakfast at the Union.

I was still coming to grips with why Murrill, Reddoch, Gurie, Mike Williams and the others had fought so hard to stop our election. Then, looking around the Union cafeteria, I came to the realization that I did not see any Blacks in the cafeteria. I saw only middle age, and older, white people, dressed in their purple and gold, sitting around tables eating their breakfast and socializing. It was one of those moments in one's life that a light bulb comes on in your head, and you realize something that had been right in front of you all of the time. It was like placing the final pieces of a thousand piece puzzle into place. Sure, I knew LSU was a racist school when I first started attending the school in 1970 but, not having the eyes of a Black person, the scene I was looking at in the cafeteria on this day had never come into focus before.

Maybe it was because I had always been so hyped to see an LSU football game that I hadn't noticed the whiteness of the fan base before. Even though I was aware of this country's original sin, slavery, and the pain and suffering it has inflicted on the Black citizens of this country, one really does not fully see racism in plain sight in our country when growing up white, even a poor white trash kid like myself. As was my habit ever since Viet Nam, I attempted to analyze this new awareness:

that, even though I was awaking to the blatant racism all around me, being white, I had never really seen it as clearly as I saw it that day.

I had never developed a hatred or mistrust of Black people. As the forever new poor kid in school, even though I was white, I had always been an outcast and never shared in the culture of white supremacy, though, with the exception of my senior year at Istrouma High, I had attended segregated public school in Kentucky, Florida, and Louisiana. That was true in the '60s, even though, in 1954, the United States Supreme Court in *Brown v. Board of Education of Topeka* had ruled that state laws establishing racially segregated public schools were unconstitutional. The southern states fought desegregation for decades. Certainly, the LSU Board and the top administrators, who all came from Mississippi, did.

After I finished breakfast, I would usually walk around the campus while listening to my transistor radio about the upcoming game, getting more and more psyched up for the game that night. I loved checking out all the fans and their amazing tailgating setups around campus. But that Homecoming Saturday, no matter how much I usually enjoyed meeting and talking with my fellow Tiger fans, my epiphany stopped me. Even if they didn't know what had been happening on campus this Homecoming, in part, it was the LSU alumni who had caused the administration to keep the first Black Homecoming Queen from being elected.

Even so, I wanted to see if there were many Black families and fans tailgating around campus. It took me about 30 to 40 minutes to walk from the Union, pass the Indian Mounds, down to the football stadium and the parking areas surrounding it. I should have known that I would not find any Blacks tailgating since it has only been recently that Blacks had graduated from LSU. I am sure Black alumni had not had the same enjoyable time at LSU that the white students, especially the Greeks, had.

I wasn't in the upbeat mood I normally was on game day, so I decided to just drive home, finish reading the paper, and catch some of the other college football games on television. Susanna and I had been invited to several pregame parties, but we just relaxed at home until it was time to go to the stadium.

I wore my usual clothing, my LSU sweatshirt and my well patched blue jeans. While I was waiting for Susanna to get ready, my mind drifted to thoughts of what kind of reception I was going to receive from the other Board members.

My worries vanished upon seeing Susanna emerge from our bedroom. She had out done herself. She was dressed in her finest hippie attire: a tie-dyed skirt with a beautiful flowery blouse. She wore an assortment of her beads, the silver turquoise bracelet I had bought her, and she had rings on every one of her fingers. Over her shoulders she had the stunning 1920s shawl she had brought at a secondhand store in Chicago. Her beautiful waist-long hair fell over her shoulders and down her back. Her peace sign earrings gleamed through her hair. I could tell by the toes of the shoes sticking out from under her long skirt that she was wearing her ankle high paisley pattern boots.

I got up from my chair, walked over to Suzanna, took her by her shoulders and said, "You're beautiful!" As I kissed her, I could smell her sandalwood perfume. I loved the smell of that perfume. I would burn sandalwood incense when I meditated. The scent would have the effect of instantly relaxing me, as it did then.

We walked out to my van, started it up and headed off for whatever awaited us at Tiger Stadium. Susanna lit up a joint as we drove down River Road. I smiled at her, knowing that she was getting us properly prepared for whatever was to come.

I was a little surprised that we didn't run into our first "stand still" traffic until we turned onto Alex Box Drive. That wasn't bad for a Homecoming game. Maybe some people didn't come because of the weak opponent we were playing. But it turned out the complete opposite was true. Fans had arrived on campus earlier to watch the Homecoming parade. I had been so wrapped up in the Homecoming Queen elections that I had forgotten all the other events that normally occur during Homecoming weekend.

As I approached the Board's parking area, I noticed that nearly all of the Board members vehicles were already in the lot.

I parked, and Susanna and I walked toward the elevator that would take us up to the level where the Board of Supervisors box was located. I was thankful that Susanna and I wouldn't have to pass through the students' entrances to the stadium. There was no doubt in my mind that some pretty nasty things would have been yelled at us, if not thrown at us, by drunken fraternity members waiting to get inside Tiger Stadium.

The two seats I was assigned were in the first row of the Board's box seats. I was told that all new members were always given the front row seats because the more senior members preferred the back seats due to the possibility of cold weather in November. Even though there was a saying "It never rains in Tiger Stadium on a Saturday night," trust me, it does rain at Tiger Stadium on a Saturday night, often really hard and accompanied by strong winds.

I was never comfortable "glad-handing" people. The exceptions were Jerry McKernan, Camille Gravel and Gordon Dore. Whenever they were present, I made a point of greeting them and their wives. I realized now that I should have made more effort to socialize with the other Board members to garner their support on the student issues, like the Book Rental program, that I brought before them. I did not know that, not only was that how it was done, but it was expected by the others if I wanted their support. Again, I showed my naivety in believing that just explaining an issue and the positive things it would achieve would win the day. In hindsight, if I had played the game like it had been played forever, more student issues might have been resolved. Then again, maybe no amount of "glad-handing" by me would have compensated for the way I looked and my frank way of talking about things.

Entering the Board's box, Susanna and I headed for our seats. I saw Gordon Dore was seated with his wife. As Susanna and I moved past him, he said to me, "Ted, I heard that they wouldn't let you escort the queen because you wanted to wear a dress."

The *Reveille* (September 30, 1976) had quoted me joking that maybe I should wear a dress and Dana Robert wear a suit to Homecoming, then maybe she could escort the Homecoming Queen runner-up. But I didn't think what had happened was a laughing matter. Though I was stoned, a part of me was still steaming about that damn picture in the *Advocate* that morning and its caption. I didn't find Gordon's statement humorous. I shot him a look expressing my displeasure with his comment. He quickly added, "Just joking, Ted." I turned around and took my seat beside Susanna as she whispered, not so quietly, "Asshole!"

As the second quarter was coming to an end, Susanna asked for something to eat. I was a vegetarian so there wasn't any food for me to eat, but Susanna did eat meat. Since we were in the Board of Supervisors' box seats, plus this being Louisiana, there were some mighty good eats available, though there were only non-alcoholic drinks since alcohol wasn't officially allowed in Tiger Stadium. As I hurried back with Susanna's food, I was wondering how they were going to handle the whole crowning of the Homecoming Queen.

In prior years, the names of the five finalists receiving the most votes were announced at the Thursday's afternoon pep rally, but the name of the queen would not be announced until the half-time ceremony on Saturday night in Tiger Stadium. At that time, the SGA president would escort the queen and the other SGA executive officers and the *Gumbo* editor would escort her court. The Homecoming Committee would provide each escort with a beautiful arrangement of a dozen red roses in a field of dark green ferns held together with a dark pink ribbon to give to each of the winning five finalists. The finalists would file out onto the football field with the one who received the least votes in front and the finalist who had won the last in line. They would walk under the drawn swords of LSU's ROTC Cadets. The president of the LSU Alumni Federation would crown the queen.

As the half-time ceremonies began, I watched as the ten finalists came out onto the field in single file, with no escorts, and proceeded to sit on chairs located on the sideline of the football field. Their names were called out in alphabetical order. Hearing her name, each got up and walked up to the Alumni Federation president who presented her with the traditional arrangement of red roses. After receiving the flowers, they formed a line and waited for all of the finalists to receive their flowers. There was no walking under drawn swords by the ROTC Honor Guard as in the past. After all the finalists had received their flowers, the name of the newly elected Homecoming Queen for 1976 was announced: Monica James. I definitely wasn't surprised that Cynthia didn't win.

In December of 1976, Chancellor Murrill created a committee to establish written rules governing the running of future Homecomings at LSU. He recruited and appointed six individuals to serve on the committee. Several were from the 1976 committee: Assistant Dean Randy Gurie and present and former student members of fraternities and sororities. None of them were Black.

I believe Chancellor Murrill was surprised when he received the committee's "suggestions and recommendations for [his] consideration in establishing general Homecoming policies" that they recommended the same "vote for one" ballot for Homecoming Queen as our election had proposed. I believe that the committee members, being fully aware of what had gone down in our Homecoming Queen election, wanted to establish rules that would not expose any future minority finalists to what Cynthia Payton had gone through. The only difference between the committee's recommendations and ours was, instead of the four runner ups being the queen's court, as we had proposed, the committee recommended that all of the finalists be allowed to go onto the football field at half-time as the queen's court.

But Chancellor Murrill made some changes. The committee had recommended that both full-time and part-time students be allowed to participate in selecting a Homecoming Queen. The chancellor changed it to only full-time students. A number of minority students went part-time, either due to the cost of attending LSU, working, or having children to care for, etc. This change would prevent them from voting for a minority finalist for queen.

Even more damaging to future minority finalists, Murrill changed the committee's recommendation that a student vote for only one finalist. He also changed the committee's recommendations that all ten finalists be allowed on the field. By reducing the number to five, he justified changing the number of votes a student might cast for Homecoming Queen from one to one, two, three, or four but no more than five finalists. This was even worse than the mandatory vote for three. If I had known of the committee's recommendations and that the chancellor changed essentially all of them, I would have spoken out against them at the Alley and in other media, but I did not learn of that until I researched the matter in 2019.

After the Homecoming weekend, Marion Campbell and I decided to count the ballots from our SGA Homecoming election, which I had kept in my office, to see how many students voted and who had won. On that one Friday, 1,848 students voted—a larger number than the 1,400 students who voted in the fall SGA Assembly election. The winner of our homecoming election was Cynthia Payton with 354 votes. The top four runners-up included Judy Fousch with 301 votes, Monica James with 266 votes, Lynn Herring with 222 votes, and Sloane Davis with 163. (See the 1977 Gumbo, Student Life, page 36)

That result, a Black being elected as LSU's 1976 Homecoming Queen, was exactly what the administration and others had been worried about. But that never happened while the man born and raised in Mississippi, Paul Murrill, was chancellor at LSU.

As far as I know, the Homecoming Committee never released the number of votes cast for each finalist as was customary. In my judgment, they probably knew there was a damn good chance that more students voted in our SGA election than in the Homecoming Committee's election. By not giving the number of votes for each finalist, the Homecoming Committee could continue their whitewash of how their mandatory voting requirement discriminated against the first Black finalist for Homecoming Queen.

LSU finally elected a Black Homecoming Queen, Renee Bouttee Myer, in 1991. LSU was the second to the last university in the south to do so, second only to Ole Miss. Myer was crowned in the middle of the football field during half-time in Tiger Stadium.

The *Reveille* (April 2, 2012 and October 25, 2013) reported, "As Renee Boutte Myer accepted her Homecoming crown, she smiled and waved to a silent audience who stared back at her with dropped jaws." The article went on to state that "with the exceptions of her close friends, family and sorority sisters" she was met with silence at the Homecoming ceremony. Myer said that when she walked back up to the student section in the stadium, she was met with glaring eyes of disbelief. I can only shudder to think what kind of reception Cynthia Payton would have received if she had been crowned Homecoming Queen in 1976.

## A PETITION TO RECALL ME AS SGA PRESIDENT

The Monday after Homecoming, I went through my usual routine. I bought a *Morning Advocate* at the Union, then headed to the cafeteria. As I moved through the line of students to get my usual breakfast of scrambled eggs, grits, and coffee, I couldn't help but notice that it appeared that some of the students were looking at me more than was typical. Judging by the smirks on their faces and their attire, they appeared to be Greeks. It wasn't unusual for that segment of the student population to throw me dirty looks, but these were different. They were the smug looks I would see at different times in my life when people believed they had me right where they wanted me. I wrote it off as just a continuation of the reaction by this particular group of students to what had happened during Homecoming week. After paying for my food, I sat at an empty table to eat and read my paper. I hadn't even taken a bite before Marion Campbell plopped down in the chair across from me.

Marion was one of my closest friends. He and his twin sister came to LSU together from New Orleans. Their family was from Lebanon. Marion had organized and worked on many SGA concerts, including the Bicentennial Concert on the Parade Ground, the Registration Blues

Concert, and numerous free concerts at the Greek Theatre. He was one of the hardest workers in the CPU, and I valued his advice and opinions greatly.

Before I could even greet him, Marion asked if I had seen the recall petition that the Greeks were circulating around campus. I responded, "Damn, I had forgotten all about that!" He told me that he had heard from a girlfriend of his, who was in a sorority, that the petition had been circulating through the fraternities and sororities all weekend. He said he had also heard that a number of other student organizations were going to endorse my recall. I was always impressed how Marion seem to know about everything that was happening on campus.

I said it didn't surprise me. I learned from my years in the military and as a student activist, if you are going to rock the boat, expect others in that boat to attempt to throw you out of the boat. I would add that the sharks weren't just in the water, they were in the boat.

I told Marion to go get some breakfast. After we ate, we went up to the SGA office to make plans on how to address the recall. John Crochet and Molly Moss were already in the office, and we were soon joined by Mike Moore, Mike Richman, and Susan Innes. We discussed what we were going to do about fighting the recall petition.

John had already prepared a brief on steps required to recall an elected officer as specified in the SGA's constitution. A recall petition would have to get 15% of the 24,000 full-time students presently attending LSU, a total of 3,600 signatures. After verification of the signatures by the Registrar's Office and submission of the petition to the Election Board, a recall election would be held within two weeks. A majority of those voting would be required to remove the incumbent, me.

After a brief discussion, I felt that it would take the rest of this week to get the necessary signatures. John pointed out that, if and when they got the necessary number of signatures, LSU's Registrar would still have to check all of the names against the enrollment records to verify the signatures. That would take quite a while. It was decided that we had time to organize for the recall if the Greeks got the 3,600 signatures needed to give to the Registrar's Office.

I knew we had all missed a hell of a lot of classes the previous week and needed to focus on our school work. I told them to return to their studies, and the meeting broke up.

The others were all carrying 12 or more hours of classes and, unlike me, their classes weren't cupcake classes. The only class demanding of my time, if I wanted to pass it, was Greek and Roman Mythology. Professor Clark, who usually taught it, had a reputation for going easy on football players and other jocks. But, because of the high enrollment in that class by student athletes and students like me, the university had added on another section and hired a new professor from Illinois to teach it. Unlike the jocks who, on the first day of class, seeing that it wasn't being taught by Professor Clark, all got up and left, I foolishly didn't. More than once that semester, I wished I had taken Professor Clark up on his offer to give me a class card to his course instead of sticking with the new professor.

The following morning, as I was heading to class, I picked up a *Reveille* (October 12, 1976) to read after class. In it were two articles about Homecoming. There was no mention that for the first time in LSU's history there had been a Black Homecoming Queen finalist nor any mention of the issue that triggered the fight. At the bottom of the page there was only a passing reference to the "cries of sexual and racist discrimination" with no explanation about the demand for a fair and non-discriminatory election for Homecoming Queen.

During that whole episode, journalism majors had either intentionally or unintentionally avoided or distorted the real reasons for what happened during Homecoming even though I had expressed them at every opportunity I had. Likewise, news articles in the *Morning Advocate* and the *State Times* rarely explained the reasons behind my actions. Instead, it was: the SGA president steals Homecoming ballots, stolen ballots recovered, etc.

Doug Manship, Sr., owned those newspapers, and at times it seemed as if he were sending a message to the LSU journalism majors: if you want to work for me this had better be your position on racism at LSU. After following a few of these journalism majors in their professional careers as journalists in the state and especially in Baton Rouge, I came to realize they constantly turned a blind eye to the ugly and hurtful history of racism at LSU and the lasting harm it caused to Blacks attending the university.

Another article in the *Reveille* (October 12, 1976) was titled "RHA resolution passes favoring Schirmer recall." Seeing that the executive committee of the Resident Hall Association (RHA) supported my recall didn't surprise me considering my successful fight to return the SGA money that Reddoch had taken away from the SGA and given to the RHA and the Association of Women Students (AWS) during my predecessor's administration. What I was pleasantly surprised to see was that the vote wasn't unanimous; it was 8-3. Even before becoming a public defender, I knew the importance of enjoying this little victory. In the following days, AWS would also endorse my recall.

The next morning, when I picked up the *Reveille* (October 13, 1976), I was taken aback to read a front-page headline boldly declaring that the number of recall petition signatures was nearing that required for a recall election. I thought, what the hell? I only had to get to the second paragraph to realize that the headline was misleading. It appeared that 1,100 signatures were still needed. This was just another example of what I had learned about the truthfulness of newspaper headlines.

I spoke to the reporter about the fact that her story was on point and fair, but the headline over the story was inaccurate and very misleading. She explained to me that she did not write the headline, that the *Reveille* had an editor responsible for that. She further explained that they were taught that many readers only read the headline of an article and maybe the first paragraph of a story. Therefore, one of the more powerful and influential position on a paper was the managing editor. The managing editor on the *Reveille* that fall was a very conservative student with whom I had had more than one heated discussion. I suspected he would love to see me removed from office.

In the article, Jack Clegg, the president of the Interfraternity Council and the one responsible for counting the signatures, stated that on Friday some students ripped up about 400 signatures, but they were able to tape the petition back together. The article also reported what I had told that same reporter the previous week: "I'll either get a vote of confidence or get the hell out of this job." The reporter wrote that, if I were recalled, Dana Robert, the legislative vice president, would be sworn in as SGA president.

On the editorial page was a political cartoon showing me being dragged behind a chariot driven by a bearded, uniformed ancient Greek looking soldier with the word in caps "GREEKS" and "RECALL PETITION" written on the front of the chariot. I thought, that pretty much summed up what was happening.

## THE SGA ASSEMBLY CENSURES ME

That night at the Assembly meeting, I was again taken by surprise by what was waiting for me. After all, I had gotten the backing of a majority of the Assembly members for my action involving the Homecoming Queen election. I failed to see that the Assembly members supporting my recall were playing political chess while I was playing school yard checkers.

As I walked into the meeting, my political adversaries were introducing a resolution to publicly censure me. As the *Reveille* (October 14, 1976) reported, it stated that I should be censured for "inaptitude in the office of the president, for his failure to complete the duties of this office and for his lack of responsibility with regard to not appointing department heads while presenting a budget allocating them money." The resolution argued that I had failed to make four appointments to university committees. In addition, the authors of the resolution told the Assembly that I had violated SGA bylaws. Those bylaws, they said, required the SGA president to appoint all chairmen of executive departments before midterms.

I had made it a point, right after taking office, to read the SGA constitution and bylaws in order to get a clear understanding of my duties and responsibilities as student body president. I was completely unaware of any such bylaw requiring me to make all appointments of committee chairmen by midterm. I walked over to John Crochet and asked, "Is there such a requirement in our bylaws?" John always carried a black binder containing the SGA constitution, bylaws, and other relevant documents for just such an eventuality. He started flipping through the pages of the SGA's bylaws. Finally, he looked up with a pissed off look on his face, while shaking his head negatively, and said, "There is no such bylaw!"

Just as I thought. I attempted to get the attention of the SGA legislative vice president, Dana Robert, who chaired Assembly meetings though she was not a member of the Assembly. She would not even look my way. I technically couldn't speak at the Assembly without a member of the Assembly being recognized by Dana and then yielding the floor to me. At that point, she was only recognizing Assembly members speaking in support of the resolution. Dana knew the SGA constitution and bylaws as well as anyone in SGA, and I suspect that she damn well must have known there was no such requirement that the president appoint committee chairmen by a certain time.

It was plain to me that the law students on the Assembly had a big part in writing this bogus resolution. That just further reinforced my opinion that the law school's student association should be independent from SGA. Law students were just using SGA as a place to cut their political teeth. I had several meetings with the Student Bar Association (SBA) president on this topic, and he was in complete agreement. I would speak of my support for this separation several times to the Board of Supervisors. The Board would eventually, the following year, separate the law school's student association from the SGA.

After John finally got recognized by Dana, he yielded the floor to me, and I was finally allowed to defend myself from these false allegations. I explained that in fact I had already made three of the four appointments alluded to by the authors of the resolution. I told them that there was only one committee, the Academic Committee, that I haven't been able to locate a qualified student to chair it. The Academic Committee was an important committee. I was not going to appoint just any student as chair. I pointed out that maybe the difficulty of finding qualified students who were willing to sacrifice their study time to chair an SGA committee, was why there was no time limit in the bylaws for those appointments.

Still being somewhat of a rookie at this political chess game, I didn't realize that the real motive behind my censure was to get negative news coverage about me before the recall election. As the *Reveille* (October 14, 1976) reported, in an article titled "Assembly Oks budget, censures Ted" this whole bogus resolution was simply an attempt to sow doubts about whether I had been performing my duties as SGA president. It was an effort to encourage more students to sign the recall petition and, later, to vote to recall me as student body president.

I was determined to file an appeal of the resolution with the University Court, not realizing that was exactly what they wanted me to do, because an appeal would just guarantee even more coverage in the *Reveille* of this bogus censure.

What's that line, "Fools rush in where angels fear to tread"? I was no angel, but I was both inexperienced at politics and was too rash in my actions at times to avoid making matters worse. ADHD you think?

On that same Thursday, the *Reveille* (October 14, 1976) section "On the Spot" asked the question, "Are you in favor of removing Ted Schirmer from office?" Of the 12 students whose responses were published, six were against the recall for various reasons, four students were for the recall and the other two students were Dana Robert and me. I thought it was kind of weird that the six students against the recall were all male students and the four students in support of the recall were female students. The six students against recalling me gave reasons that ranged from the serious (that I was the first president to stand up to the administration and was the most sincere president in four years) to the light hearted (my actions gave them something to read in the *Reveille*). The reasons that the four female students gave for recalling me as president were that I was anti-Greek and that I had stolen the Homecoming Queen ballot box. My answer to the *Reveille* was that, if the recall was based on logic and wrongdoing, I would support removing me from office, but it wasn't based on either. Dana said no comment when asked the question. But in my opinion, based on her past and future actions, along with statements she later made to the press, her answer to that question sure should have been in the affirmative.

The *Reveille* (October 20, 1976) reported on the front page that the University Court ruled it had jurisdiction over my appeal. At the same time, it was reported that the bylaw I was accused of having violated didn't exist. I felt that should have settled my appeal of the censure against me. Instead, Chief Justice Bob Sappenfield set a time the following Monday to formally hear arguments on my appeal.

Later that afternoon, I attended a meeting regarding the planning of the six concerts for which the Assembly had authorized funding, though only after cutting the number of concerts in the SGA budget from 12 to 6 over my strong objections. I argued there were many benefits for the SGA in providing concerts for students. First, and in some ways the most importantly: students actually experienced an event funded by the money allocated to SGA in their tuition fees. Second, concerts provided students living on campus a break from their studies without having to leave campus. And last but not least, the bands who played at the concerts were local bands playing for free. SGA's money was only for utilities and other costs set by Vice Chancellor Reddoch.

The meeting had just started when I received a call from Dana Robert informing me that Jack Clegg, president of the Interfraternity Council, and Naaman Eicher had informed her that they had 3,751 full-time students' signatures, the fifteen percent needed for the recall election to be called. They were requesting an immediate Election Board meeting. Robert said that she had already talked to the other three members of the Election Board. They were calling for a meeting for that Wednesday afternoon. Robert decided to do this herself even though I was the chairman of the Election Board with the responsibility for calling for meetings after consulting with the other members.

Even if the recall petition had the necessary number of signatures, they would still have to be verified by the LSU's Registrar's Office. How could a date for a recall election be set when the recall petition's signatures weren't even verified yet?

I was again thrown off balance by the political maneuvers of my adversaries. I had thought that Dana would remain neutral. After all, she had been present at the October 7th SGA cabinet meeting regarding the discriminatory Homecoming Queen election and had agreed with the rest of us that action needed to be taken. I had thought that would prohibit her from joining the recall movement. In my view, it only prevented her from taking a public leadership role in recalling me as SGA president. Her actions and statements in the *Reveille* suggested she was possibly involved in my recall behind the scenes. I should have realized that not only was she a member of a sorority backing my recall, but she would also become SGA president if I were recalled. I knew Robert was extremely interested in politics after college. Being able to say she had been the LSU student body president would help her in that effort. But I didn't have time to spend on speculating who might and might not be involved in my recall. It would drive a person crazy trying to guess what another person was doing or not doing.

Late Wednesday night shortly after arriving home, I received a call from a *Reveille* reporter informing me that, indeed the other four members of the Election Board had met that night, and Dana Robert chaired the meeting. They voted unanimously to set a recall election on October 29th, the Friday before the Saturday Ole Miss game.

Clegg and his supporters were obviously banking on a number of my supporters leaving campus early on that Friday in order to get into their costumes for the number of Halloween parties to be held around campus. Susanna and I also enjoyed attending Halloween costume parties. I could hide my identity from others while enjoying the party. My supporters also didn't give a damn about the LSU v. Ole Miss football game, so a number of them might not even attend school Friday in order to drive home for Halloween parties and parades, while my opponents would not go far because of the game and tailgate parties on campus that weekend.

In addition, unlike other SGA elections, the Election Board had set no limit on the amount of money either side could spend. Considering we were up against the richest students on campus, the Greeks, that was just another example of the four Board members giving a huge advantage to my adversaries. All of this was before even one of the petition signatures had been verified by the Registrar's Office.

I told the reporter that I was going to appeal that bullshit Election Board decision to the University Court.

## MY APPEALS TO THE UNIVERSITY COURT

On October 25th, the Monday before the scheduled Friday recall election, the University Court met to hear my appeal on my censure of the Assembly. I was out of town on Board of Supervisors matters; therefore, I was unable to attend the hearing, but I was not worried. I believed that the censure was based on my violating a nonexistent bylaw, and that I wasn't needed at the hearing because John Crochet, a future lawyer who was well versed on the facts and SGA laws and regulations, would represent me.

In addition to my appeal of the Assembly censure resolution, I had filed a second appeal with the Court, asking them to rule on the Election Board's decision to set the recall election for that coming Friday. The Court decided to hear that appeal the following night. Even though Chief Justice Bob Sappenfield was friends with Robert, setting our appeal the next night was very fair since the Court had received our appeal only that morning.

With regard to the Assembly censure resolution, the Court agreed with our argument that there was no such SGA bylaw requirement. However, Sappenfield ruled "that the court was not concerned with the validity of the contents of the resolution in making its decision." They were concerned only with whether or not the rules of procedure had been followed. John had claimed my right to due process under the U.S. Constitution had been violated.

At the hearing Dana Robert and Dan Parker, the current and previous SGA legislative vice presidents, argued that "the censure was merely an instrument for the Assembly to publicly show its dissatisfaction over the president's efficiency." Based on the rules of procedure, the Court found that the Assembly had the right to pass the resolution by suspending the rules and allowing the resolution to proceed to the floor for a vote.

As reported in the *Reveille* (October 26, 1976) article "Court rules in favor of power to censure," Robert told the reporter covering the hearing that the censure had the desired effect because, "Schirmer was 'busy in his office trying to find students to appoint as the heads of the committee[s].'" She used the plural "heads" even though I had only one position to fill at the time of the censure.

After finding out the results of Monday's University Court hearing, there was no way in hell I was going to miss Tuesday night's hearing on the Election Board ruling. Under the leadership of Robert, it had set the date of the recall election for Friday, the 29th. I realized I was in for a battle royal if I was going to overturn their decision and get a new election date. I had to get a representative who would be willing to "go to the mattresses" beside me in this fight. I had a student friend who fit this need perfectly: Vic Bell. And he did not disappoint!

Tuesday morning, we heard from supporters working in the Office of the Registrar that Vice Chancellor Reddoch had sent three of his staff to that office Monday morning to assist in verifying the recall petitions signatures. They had been told to keep working until all the signatures had been verified. The informant said that Reddoch's staff had to work well into the evening.

That just confirmed my opinion that there were certain individuals working behind the scenes in an effort to make sure that the recall election was held on the Friday before the Ole Miss game. Sure enough, that same day, I received a call from Dana telling me that she had received a letter from Harold M. Parker, associate director of Records and Registration, stating that his office had verified the necessary signatures for the recall election to go forward.

Later that morning, I was informed that the other four members of the Election Board were setting a Board meeting for 12:30 P.M. that day to accept the petition as valid, therefore sanctioning Friday's election. It was clear that nothing I said would slow down their efforts to see me recalled.

Understanding that fact, I decided to attend the meeting. I was still the chairman of the Election Board. At the meeting, I told them that I was going to recuse myself since the recall was about me, and I argued that Dana Robert and Mark Schroeder should do the same since Robert would become SGA president if I were recalled and Schroeder was one of the first to sign the recall petition.

Schroeder admitted he had signed the recall petition but claimed he could still perform his duties on the Election Board. On the other hand, as the *Reveille* (October 27, 1976) reported in an article, titled "Validation of petition names clears way for recall election." Robert, in my opinion, put on a show of indignation, stating that she "resent being asked to recuse myself. That is an insult to my sense of fairness." She went on to make it clear that, "under no circumstances will [she] recuse [herself]." She must have realized (as I did) that, regardless of my being chairman of the Election Board, she, along with the other three members, controlled all aspects of the running of the recall election.

When the other two members joined Robert and Schroeder in voting down my motion, I decided I wasn't going to participate in my own railroading. I therefore informed them that I was still going to recuse myself in order to do my part in protecting the credibility of the Election Board. I got up and left the meeting.

Vic Bell and I attended the University Court hearings that night. The fireworks started immediately after Vic argued that there was a conspiracy between Greek leaders and certain SGA officers, helped by the administration, to throw me out of office because I took action against a racist Homecoming Queen election. He pointed out that the leaders of the recall went to Robert with the petition pushing for a recall election as soon as possible. He then raised the issue of Vice Chancellor Reddoch's complicity in speeding up the verification of the signatures in order to finish before October 29th, the date set by the Election Board for the election. Then, for good measure, Vic went after not only the four Election Board members but the Greek leadership and other SGA officers, alluding that they had indeed invited Reddoch's involvement in recalling the SGA president. Vic despised Reddoch more than me and, for him, the worst insult student leaders could have thrown at them was that they were working with Reddoch on anything. The other side blew up over that comment and the fight was on.

I quickly realized that I couldn't have picked a better advocate for me at this crucial hearing than Vic Bell. As in Alice Cooper's song, he was sending a clear and very loud message, "No more Mr. Nice Guy." The other side had made it clear that they sure as hell weren't going to play nice. For them, this was just how the political game was played: the Machiavellian way.

At the University Court hearing, the shouting from both sides rose to such a level that, for a moment, I thought a physical fight would break out. After insults and accusations thrown by both sides rose to a fever-ish pitch, Chief Justice Bob Sappenfield started banging his gravel so continuously that it made all of us stop and look over at him. He then began chastising all of us for our behavior before he officially repri-manded all of us.

I not only thought that the reprimand was fair, but it showed again how Sappenfield was bending over backward to make sure that his Court did not show favoritism to either side. It was the first time since the Election Board started the railroad job on me that I thought that their train just might get derailed, thanks in large part to Vic Adam's strong advocacy.

After over three and a half hours of argument and deliberation, the Court first addressed our accusation that Reddoch conspired with the student leaders of the recall movement by ruling that the Court didn't have jurisdiction over the actions of LSU's administrators. We didn't think that the Court had that kind of authority, but we felt that it was important for them to hear about the administration's heavy handed-ness in the recall.

A *Reveille* (October 28, 1976) article, titled "Schirmer-Robert schism grows, SGA image suffers," reported that Sappenfield then ruled that the Court didn't have the authority to require members of the Election Board to recuse themselves but "upon a showing of bias or impropriety on the part of the board, the University Court may order a new election." I had hoped that the Court would put pressure on Robert and Schroeder to recuse themselves but still I felt good that it was publicly warning Robert and the other three students on the Election Board to be careful in the future relating to the recall election.

Then Sappenfield moved to the main issue in our appeal, stopping Friday's election. The Court, in a unanimous decision, ruled that Friday's recall election should be reset to a future date no later than 14 days from receipt of the petition in accordance with the SGA constitution. Even though the court found that the certification of the petition's signatures occurred at 2:30 P.M. last Tuesday, placing the proposed Friday election within those fourteen days, it ruled that "fundamental fairness" alone required the court to order a seven day minimum time limit before the recall election could be held.

In addition, the Court reasoned that this seven day window would "insure that adequate opportunity be given for the fullest possible debate and discussion of the issues raised in a recall petition."

I was ecstatic. I believed that, given enough time to educate the non-Greek part of the student body, we had a chance to beat the Greeks again. We truly couldn't have asked for a better result. The one negative point in the court's ruling was upholding the Board's decision to allow unlimited spending by both sides. The court argued that a recall election was different from an SGA election for office where there were spending limits. Other than that, we were close to achieving a total victory.

Meanwhile, we figured that, since the recall election was happening, let's put some important pending issues to a student vote. John Crochet got busy writing three resolutions of our own that were introduced and passed at the Assembly meeting Wednesday night. A *Daily Reveille*

(October 28, 1976) article reported on these in an article titled "Addition of three referenda to recall ballot requested."

One referendum was aimed at blocking Reddoch's move to put Dean of Women Margaret Jameson, a small minded authoritarian person whom Reddoch had personally recruited from Mississippi, into the newly established position of Dean of Students. I calculated there were an overwhelming majority of students who despised Jameson as much as me and never wanted to see her become Dean of Students. This included the Greeks, especially the frat boys. They were technically under Dean of Men Arden O. French, who had been dean of men since 1941. But due to Dean French becoming less and less hands on over the last few years as he approached his retirement, Jameson, with the support of Reddoch, was stepping into that void. Therefore, the fraternities were starting to experience Jameson's authoritarian rule that the sororities had been experiencing ever since Jameson set foot onto LSU's campus. Our resolution relating to her included the wording, "Do you wish Dean of Women Mary Margaret Jameson to fill the position of Dean of Students…when it becomes open?" and "that the results of the referendum be forwarded to Chancellor Paul W. Murrill."

The second resolution concerned my long time desire to get law students out of the SGA. It turned out that the law school student leaders wanted the same thing: to amend the SGA constitution to allow the Student Bar Association to depart from SGA.

The third referendum had to do with our ongoing struggle with certain members of the Assembly who were trying to stop the SGA "Free Press" paper we had started. They were blocking funding in the hope that I would be recalled, and then they could kill the idea of an independent SGA newspaper whose purpose was "to provide students and student organizations a forum to express their opinions and announce their meetings." I felt that the *Reveille* was under way too much control by the Journalism College faculty. If the referendum passed it would force the funding of the paper, which had already been approved by the Assembly when there were more Campus Political Union members on the Assembly.

Thursday morning, a day after the University Court's ruling stopping their Friday's recall election, Dana Robert and Ricky DeJean, the law school representative on the Election Board, approached me to ask if I would please consider chairing the Election Board meeting. They said that they wanted to hear my thoughts and ideas about a date for the recall election that would be fair to me. The Election Board had to also address adding to the ballot the three referenda that the Assembly had passed Wednesday night. They told me that they had called a meeting of the Election Board for later that day.

I agreed, thinking that they wanted to follow the Court's example of "fundamental fairness," that they really would take into consideration a date that was fair to both parties, which would still be within the 14-day window mandated by the SGA constitution. I walked right into their trap.

Before the Election Board meeting that afternoon, I spoke with Marion Campbell and others working on the recall campaign about when our campaign literature would be ready. I was told that there was still a lot of work to be done getting the material ready. If we could finish the artwork for the stickers and write the arguments against the recall that would go on our pamphlets, then the campaign material would be ready on Monday at the earliest, but more likely on Tuesday, November 2nd. Everyone agreed that Friday, November 5th would give us time enough to prepare our campaign material and leave us either four or possibly five days to pass it out to the students.

Once the Election Board meeting began, I introduced a motion to set Friday, November 5th, as the date for the recall election. I explained that date would give the Board five full days to publicize the election and would also give me time to prepare and hand out my campaign material.

Immediately, one of the Board members made a counter motion to reset the election for Tuesday, November 2nd. This was the earliest possible date established by the University Court. Another Board member argued that an election on Friday would be bad since many students would be going home after class on Friday. I wondered why the Board had previously argued that Friday, October 29th, was an ideal date for the election but now thought Friday, November 5th was a bad date. Most likely the problem was that LSU was playing Bear Byrant's Alabama team on November 6th and a shit load of Greeks would be leaving Friday for the game. Then Dana moved to hold the election on Thursday, November 4th, to show that they were being fair by compromising. I pointed out that November 4th wasn't enough time for me to print my campaign material and organize my campaign. This argument fell on deaf ears.

My viewpoint was that the four members of the Election Board had no interest in affording me even the minimum "fundamental fairness" but were only interested in closing the door to any possible appeal I could make. After that, I permanently recused myself and stepped down from the Election Board. I wrote a letter to the *Reveille* and spoke at the Alley, before the recall election, publicly informing the student body that I was permanently stepping off the Election Board for the remainder of my time as SGA president, be that just days or the five months left on my term.

## CODE OF CONDUCT COMPLAINT AND HEARING

The next day, as I was attending one of our recall strategy meetings in the SGA, I received a written notice from Dean Margaret Jameson that a complaint had been filed against me for violating the Code of Conduct governing students' behavior at LSU. I knew that a guilty verdict could result in expulsion.

There were four charges in the complaint. Count one: "Knowingly making in public a false oral statement with the intent to deceive and/or mislead or knowingly publishing and or distributing a false written or printed statement with the intent to deceive and/or mislead." Count two: "Theft, larceny, shoplifting, embezzlement, or the temporary taking of the property of another." Count three: "Intentional disruption of, obstruction of, or interfering with teaching, research, or other university academic activities or other university sponsored and university cosponsored activities, programs, and events conducted on campus." And Count four: "Vandalism, malicious destruction, damage, or misuse of public or private property, including library materials."

In addition, Dean Jameson's letter stated that a hearing date had already be set for October 28th, just days before the scheduled recall election on November 4th. Immediately my military training told me that my adversaries, both students and administrators, were trying to make me fight a two-front war in the hope of defeating me, if not in one, then surely in the other. I was determined not to take my eye off of the more serious threat, the recall election. After all, I was up against a united Greek front, plus the leaders in AWS and RHA. Therefore, I was going to apply all my time and energy to defeating the recall.

I took Jameson's letter to my friend and SGA ombudsman Bernard (Beno) Duhon. Beno had not been involved in the Homecoming events, but fortunately he was aware of what had gone down, so I didn't have to bring him up to speed on those facts.

I told him that I didn't know what false statement I allegedly had made but I did recall mentioning at the Alley what Mike Richman had told me: that Randy Gurie and officers of the Interfraternity Council had run off the recall petition on the dean of men's mimeograph machine. I thought that maybe that was what the complaint was referring to. I told Beno I would talk with Mike Richmond about testifying on that point.

Monday morning, I had to attend a function in New Orleans, but I hurried back to campus to meet with Beno. He started the meeting by saying he wanted to get the bad news out first. It was Mike Williams who had filed the complaint against me. That didn't surprise me even though I didn't know what alleged lie I was supposed to have said about him. Then Beno hit me with the really bad news: Vice Chancellor Reddoch would be picking the committee members to hear my case. Hearing that, I couldn't help but break out in a laugh while saying, "Oh yeah, who's going to be on the committee, Jameson and Gurie?" We knew that Reddoch was going to stack the committee with individuals who felt I should have been thrown out of LSU a long time ago.

Beno told me that, the day before the hearing, we would be given the names of the committee members and a list of all material observers (since witnesses were not sworn in or questioned by attorneys, the university labeled them "material observers"). That was also the cutoff date for submitting the names of our "material observers" and documents. The university would then be allowed to identify any "material observer" needed to rebut any information presented by us.

Beno felt that I should just focus all my efforts on the recall election and leave the hearing to him. It was due to start at 1:30 P.M. on October 28th in David Boyd Hall. My worry, ever since learning that Vice Chancellor Reddoch was the one picking the hearing committee, was that it was just going to be a railroad job.

As I walked into the room and saw who was on the committee, that fear was quickly confirmed. Sitting at the front of the table was the chairman Reddoch had appointed; Dr. George L. Robertson, Head of the Animal Science Department at LSU, later an inductee into the Hall of Honor in LSU's Cadets of the Ole War Skule. I had had a brief run-in with him when I was securing the AgCenter for the Registration Blues Concert earlier that year. He didn't seem to like me much or the idea of having a concert at the AgCenter, but, as SGA president, I had the authority to reserve the Cow Palace for our concert. The other four faculty members I didn't recognize.

I looked over at the three student members of the committee. The way they were dressed plus their expressions when I walked into the room made me believe that they were Greeks. Someone had said that the student members were appointed by the previous SGA administration. I think that was just a bullshit line from Reddoch in order to cover up the fact that he stacked the committee against me. Seeing the makeup of the committee, Beno was more nervous than I was.

I took my designated seat at the conference table, looked around with a smile on my face at all the committee members and gave them all a hearty hello. Hell, my SERE training alone taught me the mentality of "never let them see you sweat."

Over the next three and a half hours, what happened was a clear example of a kangaroo court, i.e., one with a total disregard of due process and any kind of fairness. There was no *voir dire* of the committee members. Even though my recall election was all the campus was talking about, we were not allowed to question the committee members about any bias toward me. One would think the principle of fundamental fairness would at least have allowed us that line of questioning. In addition, no questions as to the credibility or possible bias of any of the student "material observers," who had been asked to give statements at the hearing, would be allowed.

Ironically, I had been working on the committee writing the new Bill of Student Rights since the previous fall. It had passed overwhelmingly in the spring elections of 1976 but was under review by Reddoch. Some of the changes our committee had proposed included a student having the right to challenge members sitting on the conduct review committee that was hearing his case, the right to have evidence in the case produced for them before the hearing, and, if convicted, the student's right to remain in school until any appeals in their case were decided. At that time, I had none of these rights, but today the LSU's Code of Conduct Hearing Rules does guarantee them to students (see *Code of Conduct Hearing Rules:* 6.3 Rights and Responsibilities of a Charged Student or RSO During a UHP).

Realizing there was no way in hell was I going to get a fair hearing, I leaned back in my chair and, staring at the chairman, gave him my best smile, expressing that I fully understood what he was doing. This wasn't my first rodeo when individuals in positions of power attempted to strike out at me for something I had said or done. I just wished I had found a railroad engineer hat to wear to this kangaroo hearing. Speaking at Free Speech Alley later I would say that same thing.

I felt bad for Beno for having to go through with this sham of a hearing. I knew he had worked hard preparing for it, not just as the SGA ombudsman but also as my friend. As I watched Beno arranging his papers in front of him, I could tell he hadn't come to the same conclusion I had about the foregone conclusion of this farce of a hearing.

I later asked Dean Jameson for a copy of the minutes of the hearing, but she only gave me a summary. On May 24, 1978, Dean Jameson sent a letter asking me to acknowledge receipt of "a written summary of the committee hearing from October 28, 1976, and also a copy of the letter written by Dr. James W. Reddoch to Chancellor Murrill on November 23, 1977." When I looked into getting the full record, including all the minutes of the hearing, I was told they had been destroyed. Any testimony quoted below is from the summary of the Code of Conduct hearing.

Next, the charges against me were read out loud and I was asked how I would plead. I stood and, in a loud and clear voice, said, "I plead not guilty to all of the charges."

The student "material observers" were asked to step outside and wait until they were called in to give their statements to the committee. The students filed out of the room, then the discussion started. I don't say testimony, for no one was sworn in. Each student was called back in and asked to tell the committee what he or she knew about what happened during the Homecoming Queen election.

The first "material observer" was one of the Army Scotch Guard students who had manned the voting table on October 5th. She stated that I had threatened to remove the ballot box if they didn't change the voting procedure from the mandatory three votes to a maximum of three votes, thereby allowing a voter to cast one, two, or three votes. She added that this was in violation of the established procedure as set forth by the Homecoming Committee. I leaned over and whispered to Beno that I never threaten to take the ballot box at that time or, for that matter, at any time.

She told the committee that on October 7th, between the hours of 12 noon and 1 P.M., I again approached the voting table and removed the ballot box, ballots, and ID punches and took these items to the SGA president's office.

Actually, the other students with me, members of SGA's new Homecoming Committee, picked up the ballot box and other SGA supplies, which were needed to run SGA's new Homecoming Queen election. At the time I didn't give that act any notice. My only thought had been to get a new election setup and running as soon as possible.

The student then blew my mind when she ended her statement by saying to the committee that I had said Randy Gurie and Mike Williams were plotting the downfall of Homecoming for political reasons. I couldn't suppress saying out loud, "What!" before Beno nudged me to be quiet.

If there was any doubt that she had been coached on what to say at the hearing, that last statement cleared that up. It wasn't until four days later, on October 13th at Free Speech Alley, that I said that Mike Williams and Randy Gurie had done what they did in order to help the recall movement against me. After I made that statement at the Alley, neither Williams nor Gurie ever said to me that it wasn't true. Beno pointed that out later in his hasty summation.

Then Mike Williams addressed the committee, stating that I had appointed him and Alphe Williams as cochairmen of the Homecoming Committee, and that I was an ex officio member of that committee. Williams then began to read from a memorandum from Reddoch, dated October 13, 1976, written six days after we had had to stop the Homecoming election.

In it Reddoch concluded, that the source of authority for Homecoming on the LSU campus was the university administration, as represented by the chancellor (something that Reddoch or the chancellor never said to me). The memo went on to state that the responsibility for coordinating all aspects of Homecoming rests with the Office of Alumni Affairs and the president of the Alumni Federation. They gave the authority to establish the procedures for and the implementation of these procedures to select the Homecoming Queen to the Homecoming Committee.

Reddoch had completely taken SGA out of any role in Homecoming despite the fact that the Homecoming Committee functioned under SGA, SGA provided all of the supplies and funded the committee, and the SGA president appointed the chairman of the committee.

Beno and I immediately recognized Reddoch's handy work as a "phantom history" of the origins of the Homecoming Committee and who had authority over it. We had never seen this document before, and Beno objected to the October 13th memorandum being presented to the committee. He argued that the memo was what Article 1, Section 10, Clause 1 of the United States Constitution prohibited as *ex post facto* law. Here Williams, through Reddoch's memo, was attempting to show that the Homecoming Committee was solely under the administration and Alumni Federation, and SGA had no say in Homecoming. Therefore, I, as SGA president, had no authority to intervene in the Homecoming Queen election. During the five days of the Homecoming election no one ever expressed this position. Even Reddoch himself stated that Homecoming was under the authority of the Alumni Federation, while Mr. Landry said it was under SGA.

In addition, Beno argued that we had the right to confront witnesses and to question Reddoch on the reasons for his conclusions and the source of his information, especially since the October 13th memo was being introduced to establish an element of the charge: that I intentionally interrupted a university function.

Beno pointed out that he wasn't questioning the credibility of the person giving the information, (for questioning the creditability by anyone, especially someone as powerful as Reddoch, was not permitted) but the reliability of the source of the information.

What a fuckin tightrope to have to walk just to try to get to the foundation and sources of Reddoch's conclusion. There was little doubt in my mind that, if we could question Reddoch, we could prove that he took it upon himself to prepare this memo after the fact, thus leading to the conclusion that the memo was written to assist in convicting me at this hearing. As he had told me several times, he wrote the rules that govern students on LSU's campus. And he took pride in the power to produce documents to support a position anytime he wanted to.

Chairman Robertson said that, if the committee decided that they would like to call Reddoch to discuss his memorandum, they would call him for this purpose only. It was clear that, even if the committee sent for Reddoch, only the committee members would be allowed to ask Reddoch questions. We would be prevented from questioning him about anything.

To my surprise, one of the committee's faculty members, whom I didn't recognize, moved to summon Reddoch, and another faculty member, whom I also didn't recognize, seconded his motion. The look on Robertson's face was priceless. He had no choice but to ask everyone to leave the room while the motion to summon Reddoch was discussed and voted on. We all got up and left the room.

After about 10 to 15 minutes, we were called back into the room. After we were seated, Robertson stated that the committee did not wish to call Reddoch for further information. His presence in the hearing was not necessary.

Williams said that the information in the October 13$^{th}$ memo was relevant and important to his case and asked that the memo be accepted into evidence by the committee. Chairman Robertson let the committee examine the memorandum from Reddoch.

Then Williams called several of the Angel Flight students who were manning the voting table on October 7$^{th}$. They stated that I and other SGA people came to the voting table and took the ballot boxes, ID punches, and ballots saying that the voting procedures were unconstitutional. They said I informed them that I had appointed another Homecoming Committee, and the new committee had decided to hold a new election for Homecoming Queen.

Chairman Robertson asked the first Angel Flight student if she saw who took the ballot boxes. She only stated, "SGA people." (Code of Conduct minutes). Then he asked her "if she saw Mr. Schirmer take the boxes." (Code of Conduct minutes) She answered that "She did not see who took them." (Code of Conduct minutes) I believed Robertson asked that hoping to prove the charge of "theft, larceny, shoplifting, embezzlement, or the temporary taking of the property of another."

Williams next called Bob Sappenfield, Chief Justice of University Court. I realized that Williams was calling him to establish that indeed

I had the ballots in my office, but I am confident that he wasn't expecting what Sappenfield testified.

As the minutes of the hearing show, Sappenfield stated to the committee, "that in order to ensure that *whatever election results* [emphasis added] were used were properly determined, he thought it best that whatever ballots were cast in the first election should be in the hands of a neutral third party." He further stated "that on the agreement of the original Homecoming Committee and Mr. Schirmer, he took custody of the ballots that had been cast on Tuesday and Wednesday." I thought Sappenfield's testimony clearly established that there had been an agreement that whichever election had more students voting in it would be the election that the Alumni Federation and administration would recognize.

At this time, it was announced that Chancellor Murrill was outside the hearing room and requesting to give his statement to the committee since he had a later afternoon meeting to attend. Robertson objected to any appearance by Murrill, saying, "The committee should consider the question as to whether they can hear the testimony from the chancellor knowing that he will have an appellate function later on." I thought to myself, he has already blocked the appearance of Reddoch, now he was attempting to block Murrill's appearance.

Beno told Dr. Robertson that we agreed to waive any rights of appeal on any points which might be due to the irregularity of the chancellor's appearance as a witness.

Murrill entered and stated that, during Homecoming week, Reddoch told him of some of the events that were going on, and that he was aware of the fact that the Homecoming Committee had said that students should vote for three candidates and that, sometime during the course of the election, ballots had been accepted for one or two.

He never mentioned that it was mandatory that students vote for three finalists or have their ballot disqualified. In addition, he never told the committee that all I wanted was for that mandatory rule to be dropped, giving the students the option to vote for one to three finalists.

Murrill went on to state, "that on Thursday afternoon he received a telephone call from Reddoch in which he indicated that the ballot boxes had been picked up." Again, he avoided explaining the reason it had come to that point, and that it was Reddoch's and Gurie's involvement that brought about the need to stop the election. He mentioned that he learned that the new Homecoming Committee SGA had established was going to undertake a new election for Homecoming Queen. He had some doubts that anyone could have a clear title in such an election and prepared a statement which he released to the press canceling the crowning of a Homecoming Queen that year.

He never told me or anyone one in SGA that he was going to take this action. I only heard about it at the pep rally when Williams read the statement. Why wasn't I told of this action by the chancellor or given a copy of the letter?

The chancellor then stated that, while speaking to the Alumni Federation at Welch, he had received a telephone call from me in which we discussed a new election. He told me that he would not be promissory about the way in which such an election would be viewed, but that he would not interfere with the SGA conducting such an election. He stressed that he had stated three times that he would not be promissory about the way in which such an election would be viewed.

Again, I shuddered at hearing what he said. He failed to mention that he said (and wrote in his letter he gave me the next day) that it would be up to the Alumni Federation to decide whether our election would be recognized. A couple of things were becoming painfully clear. One, Murrill was leaving out key parts of our conversation about my reasons for the actions I took. Secondly, without Mr. Landry confirming that he had told me the Alumni Federation would accept whichever election had the more students voting in it, it could come down to my word against the chancellor's. Murrill never mentioned anything about this agreement with the Alumni Federation at any time during his statement to the committee.

The chancellor went on to describe his meeting with the finalists. He stated that when he spoke with me afterward, he told me that he knew that I had worked hard on this matter, and I said that it wasn't a problem for we now had a Homecoming Queen. Even though that was not 100% accurate, it was the most positive thing he had said in his whole statement to the committee.

The committee then took a recess. It was almost 3 P.M., and we still hadn't been allowed to present our case. As I headed out the door, I had to pass Williams and the others to get to the exit. I just smiled at them as I walked past. Show no fear or hurt even if your insides are in turmoil.

When the committee finally came back into the room, Robertson called the hearing in session and told Williams to continue. Williams called a student to come forward. That student stated that he had attended a Free Speech Alley where he heard me say that Randy Gurie and Mike Williams took the actions that they did to prevent the crowning of a Homecoming Queen for political reasons. The student failed to mention that the Free Speech Alley he attended was the Wednesday after Homecoming.

After this student finished his statement, I was expecting Williams to make a statement to the committee that he never wanted to prevent the crowning of a Homecoming Queen in order to hurt me politically. Instead, to our surprise, he called Dana Robert, SGA legislative vice president.

That surprised us, and Beno and I both listened intently to Robert's statement, hoping it wasn't going to be a revisionist history of what had happened. She said that she had been present on the Thursday morning before Homecoming when the cabinet members who could be located came to the SGA office for an emergency meeting. The staff was able to contact only half of the cabinet's members. Robert went on to explain that I had called the Cabinet meeting because I had concerns about how the Homecoming Queen election was being run (without explaining what those concerns were). Eventually, she said, the members of the cabinet discussed stopping the election and appointing new chairmen to organize a new Homecoming Queen election. Then she stated that she "contended that Mr. Schirmer did not have this authority to fire the two cochairmen of the Homecoming Committee."

This was different than what I remembered her saying at the time, which was that she didn't think we could take corrective action without taking it before the Assembly. It was my opinion that we didn't have time to call the Assembly into special session, and that we already had a petition signed by a majority of Assembly members supporting stopping a racist election.

At the next break in the hearing, Beno told me how taken aback he was at the distain Robert and the other witnesses showed toward me. I realized that the only exposure Beno had had to Robert was during my fight to get him appointed SGA ombudsman back in the spring. Since then, he and his staff, consisting of the two other law students, had been fighting in a whole different arena than I had been. Beno would point out, in his appeal to Chancellor Murrill, the "overwhelming prejudice" shown against me at the hearing.

Then Williams circulated copies of the SGA constitution and pointed out Article VII, Section 4. I didn't know the constitution by heart and thought to myself, did he find something in it to support the proposition that I didn't have the authority to fire Mike and Alphe Williams? As I waited for a copy to be handed to Beno, I thought there was no way that John Crochet would have missed that.

As I read the page over Beno's shoulder, a smile spread across my face. Article VII, Section 4 of SGA's constitution stated, "Employees and department heads of the student government association may be dismissed by the president and shall be filled in accordance with the constitution and bylaws." Really, this was their best shot? There was no language that the president could only dismiss those individuals and not the chairmen he had appointed.

Williams had been allowed in excess of two hours to prosecute his case, which also included a 15-minute break called by Robertson. It was well after 4 P.M. when Beno began presenting his case. This was when the chairman first started hassling Beno to hurry up with his presentation, saying that the faculty members had responsibilities to tend to and that the hearing was ending at 5 P.M.

340

Beno was forced to choose which part of the case he would have to skip in order to make Robertson's deadline. At the start of our defense, Beno again objected to using Reddoch's October 13th memo since it was admitted to establish an element of the case against me relating to the charge of intentional disruption of a university event. Beno again requested that Vice Chancellor Reddoch be sent for to answer questions about his memo. Beno's request had been denied earlier, but this time more committee members agreed to call Reddoch, and Robertson left the room to contact his office. Upon his return, Robertson said that Reddoch had left the campus and was unavailable. Beno moved that Reddoch's memo of October 13th not be used as evidence because the defense could not cross examine Reddoch. That was denied by Robertson without any further discussion with the committee. As Beno pointed out in his appeal, once again, I was denied the right to confront a witness against me. This was especially damaging to my case since this was the only evidence presented that SGA had no authority in Homecoming at all and that, therefore, I had no authority over the Homecoming Committee or any say in how the election was run.

At this point, Beno felt it was very important for the committee to hear my side of what happened and why I took the steps I did. First Beno asked me to tell the committee why I felt that Gurie and Williams were taking their actions based on political reasons.

I explained to the committee that my intent, and continuous effort, had been to bring about a non-discriminatory Homecoming Queen election. My one and only objection was that the requirement to vote for three finalists for Homecoming Queen was unfair and discriminatory to Ms. Payton, the first Black Homecoming Queen finalists. I found myself confronted by Mike Williams and Randy Gurie, telling me that the SGA, and I as president, had no authority over the Homecoming Committee. When Vice Chancellor Reddoch told me that the Alumni Federation was the organization with authority over the Homecoming Committee, I spoke with Mr. Landry, Director of the Alumni Federation. He assured me Reddoch was wrong, that SGA had that authority. After that, I didn't accept what Randy Gurie and Mike Williams were saying. I did what I felt was necessary to fulfill my responsibilities as student body president and put a stop to a discriminatory election.

I stated that on Friday, October 8th, I was informed by Mike Richmond that Dean French's secretary had told him recall petitions were being run off in the dean of men's office by Assistance to the Dean of Men Randy Gurie and leaders of the recall movement. Then he and Mike Williams would not let me address the students at the pep rally, at which the recall petition was circulated. When I reflected on those actions by Gurie and Williams at the pep rally, it appeared to me they had been done to support the removal of me as SGA president. Based on these events, I made the statement at Free Speech Alley on Wednesday, October 13th, that I thought Gurie and Williams had been trying to hurt me politically. At no time since had either of them told me otherwise.

I ended my statement explaining that my devotion to the vows of the SGA Presidency, to uphold the Louisiana and United States Constitutions, required me to step in and stop a discriminatory, and, I believed, unconstitutional Homecoming Queen election.

Beno presented the committee with a sign used by the Homecoming Committee promoting the Pep Rally stating that it was sponsored by SGA. In addition, he presented the committee with the petition that had been signed by thirty SGA members of the Assembly requesting a new Homecoming Queen election the Wednesday before the cabinet voted to stop the election and appoint new chairmen. Answering a question from Mike Williams on whether this was an Assembly resolution, I stated it was meant to be, but Robert adjourned the Assembly before it could be introduced and voted on. After that, the resolution was converted into this petition with the same language as in the resolution.

Beno then called Molly Moss and John Crochet, two members of my cabinet, to state what had happened at the cabinet meeting. Molly Moss stated the cabinet felt that they couldn't turn a blind eye to blatant discrimination that was being endorsed by the present chairmen of the Homecoming Committee; therefore, they voted to fire Mike Williams and Alphe Williams to allow Ted to appoint new chairmen. Those students would have the authority to decide the next steps to take to correct the election. John Crochet, in turn, agreed with Molly's statement, adding he helped prepared the Executive Order firing Mike and Alfie Williams, presenting the signed order to them.

At the predetermined time of 5 P.M., Beno had only presented a small portion of our defense to making a false statement when, as pointed out in Beno's appeal, "I was forced to terminate the hearing… when the chairman stated, 'I don't want to hear from anyone else unless somebody's just got to speak.' ….It should be pointed out that no such interruptions were made of the case presented by Mike Williams, nor was anyone even informed of the supposed deadline until well after 4 P.M." Quoting from a copy of the Appeal that Beno wrote immediately after the hearing while having access to a full transcript of the hearing: "An example of the chairman's repeated attempts to rush the presentation of Ted's case can be related as follows, we were told again to wrap it up…make a summary statement…we are faced with a shortage of time…say what you need to say as quickly as possible…people need to be out of here to teach a class….This stricture on time seriously prejudiced the case of Ted Schirmer."

Before Beno was done with his case, in what sounded mighty close to a military order, Robertson told Williams and Beno to make their closing statements. Beno had not been able to present anywhere close to his entire case at that time.

Williams reiterated the charges and the evidence which had been presented. Beno started off his summation by saying that it was alleged I lied when I publicly stated that Randy Gurie and Mike Williams were plotting to bring Homecoming down for political reasons, and when I claimed to have held a cabinet meeting to take action on the Homecoming problem. Beno stated that there was no evidence presented that the statements were false, nor that I had been aware that those statements were false before making them at the Alley.

Beno went on to tell the committee that only one of the witnesses stated she saw me take the ballot boxes and other supplies while the

343

other witnesses only saw "SGA people'" or didn't see who picked up the ballot box.

He added that the decision to stop the election was made by the SGA Cabinet executive committee operating under the auspices of the SGA constitution and bylaws. That there was no theft in the first place because the ballot boxes, the hole punches, etc. belonged to the SGA. He argued that one can't steal nor vandalize one's own property.

Beno then discussed the sign advertising that the Pep Rally was sponsored by the SGA, establishing that the Homecoming Committee and the election were under SGA. Therefore, my actions, as SGA president, were to assure that the university would have a Homecoming Queen elected in a fair and non-discriminatory election. He pointed out that the chancellor did not question my motives, and that there was no proof that I had any evil intent in either my actions or my speech.

It was then a little after 5 o'clock, the witching hour, and Robertson was once again signaling for Beno to wrap it up. Beno ended his summation, and Robertson asked everyone to step outside while the committee went into executive session to discuss the case and to vote by secret ballot on each charge. I thought it was a little strange that, with time being so limited, they would decide on the case immediately.

It was less than an hour when we were told that the committee had reached a verdict.

On the charges of "intentional disruption of, obstruction of, or interfering with teaching research, or other university academic activities or other university sponsored and university cosponsored activities, programs, and events conducted on campus," I was found guilty by a vote of 6 to 2.

On the charge of "knowingly making in public a false oral statement with the intent to deceive and/or mislead or knowingly publishing and/or distributing a false written or printed statement with the intent to deceive and/or mislead," the committee found me guilty by another vote of 6 to 2.

On the remaining two charges of "theft" and "vandalism," I was unanimously found not guilty.

I figured that the two votes for acquittal came from the same two faculty members who were trying to give me a fair hearing. That was confirmed when I looked over at them as the decision was read. They both had their heads slightly bent down, eyes looking at the table. Most of the rest of the committee, particularly the three students, had what could only be described as a smirking look of satisfaction.

Robertson moved that the committee place me on probation to the Committee on Student Conduct until I graduated. Another faculty member seconded the motion. The vote was five for the motion and three against. Damn, I figured that the two who voted for my acquittal were two of the three votes, but who was the third? And just as interesting, did that third member want lesser or worst punishment?

I could not fathom how the committee, in less than an hour, had, not only discussed, debated and voted on my guilt or innocence on four charges, but also debated and voted on the recommendations of my punishment. It wasn't just a railroad job, it was a 'bullet train.'

Beno appeared crushed. I knew it was not just that he had lost the case, but more because we were good friends and he probably felt he let me down. I put my arm around his shoulders, trying to comfort him, as I told him not to worry. He had done the best he could under the circumstances. We would appeal the verdict to the chancellor and then see where that went. I again reminded him that they were in a pickle if they tried to expel me since I was the student representative on the Board of Supervisors. None of that seemed to help and I would soon find out why.

I didn't know what to do next and, since Beno was having such a hard time dealing with the verdict, I asked Robertson before he left. He told me that Dean Jameson was in Dean French's old office, and she was expecting us. Then he walked out of the room.

How the hell did Jameson already know what had happened? The only thing I could think of was that Robertson called her with the verdict before calling us back into the room. At least I hope that was how she found out so soon because the other explanation was that she already knew I was going to be convicted of something at the hearing. I was pretty damn sure that, if I had been found not guilty on all charges, I wouldn't have to be seeing her, and she damn sure wouldn't be in her office since it was close to 6 P.M. Beno was still just staring at his hands, so I put my hand on Beno's arm while saying, "Let's go see Jameson."

When we got to the dean's office, we were told to take a seat in the waiting room, and that Jameson would be with us in a moment. After we sat down, Beno told me that the committee's recommendations of probation until graduation was just that, a recommendation. Dean Jameson didn't have to accept it. She could change it, as she had many times before, for better or for worse. As this sunk in, I knew damn well, as Beno obviously knew, that if Jameson could change the committee's recommendation, she could expel me from school.

Then I started to worry! If expelled from LSU, I not only wouldn't be SGA president but also, not being a student, I could no longer be the student representative on the Board of Supervisors. They could kill two birds with one conviction. Shit!

As I have done my whole life when shit hits the fan, I found myself just shaking my head while smiling and saying to myself the modified Laurel and Hardy line, "Well, this is another fine mess you have gotten yourself into."

I believe Jameson left us sitting there for a while to give me time to dwell on my fate before calling us into her office. As we walked in, I could see her sitting behind the desk with that same contemptuous smile on her chubby, made up face that I and other student leaders had seen way too many times. Then, with what could only be described as glee, she told us to take a seat, waving her hand toward the two chairs, not across from her desk but against the wall, several feet away from where she was sitting. I think she was worried a little about what I would do after she told me her decision. I could tell she was savoring this moment, like a spider savors its upcoming meal of a fly caught in its web before eating it.

Beno still hadn't been able to compose himself while I was fighting to control my anger at this contemptuous display toward me. As long as I can remember, my self-respect was all I had to get me through times like this, and rarely did I not strike out at people who displayed such a level of contempt toward me. I asked her in a firm voice, "What now?"

As she leaned forward on her desk, looking straight at me, she said in that sickeningly sweet southern voice of hers that she used to coverup the evil that lay just below the surface, "Mr. Schirmer, you are going to be expelled."

I could see Beno kind of jerk like a person feeling a whip hit his back. I put my hand on his arm and looked Jameson in the eyes as I said, with the most bravado I could muster, "Is that all?" I could tell she wasn't expecting that response from me, rather more of what Beno was going through.

I got Beno to his feet and headed toward the door, but turned back toward her, as I had done in 1971 during the protest over the rights of women students. I think she thought I was going to give her another Hitler line, but I simply said, "Of course, I am going to appeal this decision of the committee." And I turned and left her sitting there. I had come a long way since 1971. As emperor Marcus Aurelius, who was one of the so-called Five Good Emperors, said, "The best revenge is not to be like your enemy." Still, it was difficult for me to leave her sitting there thinking she had struck a fatal blow against me.

Beno and I said very little as we walked through the campus back to the SGA office. When we arrived, I again attempted to comfort him. I knew, with the fight over the recall election just heating up, that I would not have much time to work on any appeal of the case with him. I told Beno that and added that I was confident that he would convince the chancellor to overturn the committee's verdict and order a new hearing. Beno had composed himself enough to tell me he would have the notice of appeal ready for my signature tomorrow morning. With that, he left for home.

Since there was a chance that I wouldn't be SGA president much longer, I did what I did the night I won the office, I decided to smoke a joint and contemplate what had just transpired.

I closed and locked the SGA office door and went into my inner office. Closing the door behind me, I pulled out the bath towel I kept in

347

my desk for just such an occasion and stuffed the towel into the crack under the door. I walked back to my desk while pulling a joint out of my pocket. I always thought about these types of things better when I was stoned. It always opened my mind to all the various angles while also mellowing me out. As I took hit after hit, (marijuana wasn't as potent then as it is now that it is legal in California) I replayed in my head the hearing and what Jameson had said. Then, after running all the different scenarios of what might lie ahead, I told myself, as I had many times before, "Fuck it!" and left the office to go home to tell Susanna what had happened.

The next morning, true to his word, Beno came to my office before heading to class at law school with the Notice of Appeal. The notice authorized Beno to represent me in any appeal proceedings. The only note I added under my signature was, "Could action on this appeal be scheduled after the upcoming Recall Election of November 4th." (See Notice of Appeal). Chancellor Murrill agreed to extend the time to submit my appeal to November 9th, five days after the recall election on November 4th.

I knew how busy I was going to be the next few days fighting the recall. Yes, even though there was a possibility that I might be thrown out of LSU, I wasn't going gently. At the time, I didn't realize that the chancellor probably wanted to wait until after the recall elections also, believing like so many others that I would lose and be removed from office, therefore giving him an out.

## THE RECALL ELECTION

It didn't take long to see the effect of no spending limits in the recall election. The Greeks flooded the campus with flyers and posters calling for my recall. In addition, they bought a half page ad in the *Reveille* saying that I had illegally spent $2,000 and making other false allegations. Their flyers, in very large print, typically ended with, "And of course there was Homecoming." Everyday leading up to the election, it became more and more obvious that we were not only being outspent but outspent by a lot!

The Wednesday before the recall election, I spoke as usual at the Alley. I pointed out that the election was set for a Thursday because the recall leaders were worried about a large turnout. They knew that a large turnout would be to my advantage. I also stated that the ad in the *Reveille* supporting my recall as president was a pack of lies and even slanderous. No students' names appeared on the ad; it only stated that it was paid for by "The Committee to Recall Schirmer."

I told everyone who was interested in getting some of our leaflets, which detailed all that we had accomplished and stated reason to oppose my recall, that they should walk across the street since it was against university regulations to hand out political material in front of the Union.

After the Alley, I spoke at student meetings in the Union and around campus, explaining the many accomplishments of my administration. Therefore, I wasn't present at that evening's Assembly meeting when Dave Tuttle, a Sigma Nu member and an Assembly member, one of the four members of the Election Board and a backer of the recall, alleged that I had illegally spent $21.20 to print flyers for the Rugby Club's tournament that had been held on the LSU Parade Ground. When I was contacted about the allegation by reporter Ken Kleinpeter for a *Reveille* (November 4, 1976) article titled "Tuttle charges Schirmer in fund misuse," I told him that the SGA president had an executive contingency fund, so he didn't have to run to the Assembly to get approval for small amounts money, such as that which I had authorized for the Rugby Club. It was clear that the editors of the *Reveille* knew that there was no basis for what Tuttle was doing other than a desire to get a negative story in the *Reveille* on election day. To the credit of the editors, the story was buried deep in the middle of Thursday's paper. But there were a number of negative political cartoons, editorials, and letters to the editor printed every day leading up to the recall.

The day of the election, Marion Campbell had built a 10-foot sign to put at our table, located at the corner of the Parade Grounds across from the Union and under the big oak tree that sometimes was referred to as the Liberty Tree, mostly by history and political science majors. On the sign in letters over a foot high, were the words, "ANYONE OF THESE 10 REASONS IS REASON ENOUGH TO VOTE NO ON RECALL."

Attached to each side of the sign were the 10 leaflets we had been handing out to students. They listed the accomplishments of my administration in the past six months: saving the students thousands of dollars a year by removing the president's private phone line in the SGA office and reducing the overall cost of the phones by eliminating five single lines and installing a six-line phone system; getting SGA's secretaries paid through the Federal Work Study program; starting the first SGA Newsletter to alert students to the move by the Board to increase their tuition. A leaflet told the students how, as a member of the Board of Supervisors, I was able to save the campus infirmary by stopping the administration from making it a "pay-as-you-go" healthcare facility. I had made SGA funds independent of the administration by depositing the profits from the Registration Blues Festival in the American Bank. Then there was the Book Rental program, whose goals were to make textbooks more affordable for students, raise money toward SGA's financial independence, and provide paying jobs for students. I had gotten Murrill to give the Book Rental program the use of the bottom floor of the French House.

We had a leaflet explaining the "professional budget" our administration presented and passed through the Assembly, allocating specific funds, with oversight to all SGA committees and departments for the first time in LSU's history, and saving SGA thousands of dollars every year.

There was a leaflet explaining how my negotiations with Mayor / President Woody Dumas of Baton Rouge Parish resulted in getting free shuttle buses to make voter registration easier. In addition, negotiations with the Baton Rouge Bus Company had led to a policy whereby a student only had to show his LSU ID to ride free on any bus in Baton Rouge. This benefit was paid for by money from the student tuition fee.

Then there was, of course, a leaflet telling of all the free concerts in the Greek Theater and Memorial Oak Grove, which my administration put on for the students, among them the Bicentennial concert on the Parade Grounds. SGA also provided free strawberries and ice cream during Free Speech Alley, which we got donated by the Ponchatoula Strawberry Festival and LSU's own ice cream making department.

There was a leaflet about the *Free Press*, SGA's first newspaper, and another about our legislative lobbying effort during the summer. We also kept the Foster Commons, for the first time, open until 2 A.M. each night during finals and offered half priced coffee and other drinks. SGA paid the other half of the cost.

I vetoed putting out a leaflet proclaiming how I was honored by the Student Assembly last year, when they voted me "as the student who best exemplifies the characteristics of sincerity, dedication and good will in the work of student government at LSU," to show that I could and did work with Assembly members who were truly interested in helping the student body and not their own future political ambitions. I protested that that flyer would embarrass the shit out of me. That didn't stop some of my campaign staff from using it as a counter to people claiming I couldn't work with the Assembly.

On November 4th, the day of the recall election, the *Reveille* pages were filled with pros and cons on the recall, including lengthy opinion articles, letters to the editors and full-page stories by *Reveille* reporters interviewing me and the leaders of the recall movement.

All day, the Greeks were in a festive mood on the Parade Grounds where the voting was taking place. It appeared they were extremely confident that the outcome was preordained. They were going to win the recall election and remove me as SGA president. I, myself, was very relaxed, sitting at our table under the big oak tree on the corner. Win or lose, I was just glad this part of my struggle was in its final hours. As I told reporters, when asked how I felt about the recall, that either way I would come out a winner. In short, as silly as it sounds, I felt I was in a win/win situation. I would get either a vote of confidence by a majority of the student body and keep my job, or, if I lost, I would be liberated from the hassle of being president. I had gotten damn tired of having a target on my back for simply standing up for what I believed to be right and just causes.

Of course, I still had my appeal of the Code of Conduct conviction hanging over my head. But I hoped that having been appointed the student member of the Board of Supervisors by Governor Edwards protected me from being thrown out of LSU. As I have said many times, including in our campaign material, even if I were recalled, I would still be a member of the Board of Supervisors. I was to find out later that, all during this time, Vice Chancellor Reddoch had LSU's attorneys researching the issue: If I were recalled as student body president of the LSU Baton Rouge campus, what did they have to do to remove me from the Board of Supervisors? I believe that Reddoch knew I was going to be convicted before the Code of Conduct hearing even got started. Beno had been working on the appeal since that bullshit conviction to meet the extended due date of November 9th set by the chancellor.

As I watched the recall voting, I could see Greeks with clipboards standing outside the voting area, checking off the names of the Greek students who passed them on their way to vote. I thought, that is one way to make sure their people voted: make it mandatory. Along with the recall question, the Election Board members had put two of the three referenda on the ballot for a vote by the student body.

One of the two was whether or not students wanted Dean of Women Margaret Jameson to be appointed dean of students, and the other was whether to allow the law school to separate from SGA and the *Gumbo* fees paid by law students to go to the *Law School Yearbook* instead.

The four members of the Election Board left off the third referendum relating to Assembly members blocking funding for the SGA's newspaper *Free Press*, in spite of the fact that the funding had already been approved by the Assembly. It was a blatant attempt to kill the project we had worked hard to get up and running. I guess my opponents thought that question might dilute their argument that I was a "do nothing president."

While my adversaries might have thought that both the Jameson and law school questions would bring more of their supporters out to vote, I thought those two questions would just as much help bring out our people. I only lost the law school by 29 votes in the runoff election for SGA president, and the vast majority of the student body despised Jameson and were unlikely to pass up a chance to show their contempt for her.

Because of the large turn out and how relaxed I was, everyone working at our table was in a very good mood. The 1977 *Gumbo* yearbook published a number of photos of us taken at that time.

Our mood improved even more after we got some other students to hold down our table while we left to smoke a joint. With my Board of Supervisors parking sticker, I had purposely parked my van nearby for just such an occasion.

After piling into the van and locking the doors, one of our party lit up a joint while I put the Stones' *Let it Bleed* album in my 8-track player. Considering what we were attempting to do, beat the Greeks again, and with so many believing it was already a foregone conclusion that we were going to lose, I skipped to the song "You Can't Always Get Want You Want" and cranked up the volume. We all started to sing along. I remember the smiles that broke out on the faces of some students walking by my van when, after sliding open the side door, a pillar of marijuana smoke followed us out of the van. Hey, everyone had worked so hard, we needed to chill out at times and enjoy what was happening around us. Life is hard enough not to lighten up (or light up) at times.

All morning and afternoon, students flooded the Parade Grounds to vote. Two pictures on the front page of *Reveille* (November 5, 1976) showed students voting in the election with the caption, "LARGE TURNOUT—Voting was heavy in Thursday's election to recall SGA President Ted Schirmer. Students stood in lines most of the day."

The Election Board intentionally didn't have enough polling places (only one), ballot boxes, or workers, which caused the voting lines to stretch a hundred feet or more at times. To my mind, that was to discourage non-Greeks from voting by making it hard to participate in the election, a ploy that conservatives apply even more today. That was just another example that conservatives sharpen their political teeth in colleges politics and, more times than not, to the detriment of the student body.

Even with the long lines, I didn't see one student leave before casting his or her vote. Our workers, who were allowed by the Election Board to observe the voting, said that there was really only one significant issue that arose. That involved students who wanted to vote but had forgotten or lost their student IDs. Our people and the recall people met with election officials and agreed that those students who knew their student ID number (at LSU at that time the student's ID number was their social security number—this was before identity thief had become a major problem in the United States) and who could show a valid driver license would be allowed to fill out a ballot, and then have their votes placed in a sealed envelope for later verification by the Registrar's Office that they were indeed full-time students.

By the time the poll closed at 4 P.M. and the ballot boxes were taken into the Union to be counted, a large crowd of students supporting both sides had gathered in front of the Union to learn the results of the recall election. The relaxed mood of the day was replaced by a mounting tension among the students on our side who had worked on the recall campaign and, for a number of them, the Homecoming election also.

The Greeks, on the other hand, were still in an upbeat, festive mood. I thought at the time, they were pretty damn cocky. I had to remind myself that most Greeks, especially the leadership, have an innate feeling of superiority. The accepted theory was that the Greeks were all unified behind recalling me, and, when Greeks were united in SGA elections, they would, of course, prevail.

The difference between the two groups was striking. Whereas our people sat on the steps speaking in low tones among themselves, the Greeks were strutting around with broad smiles and a swagger, offering an occasional slap on the back for, I guess, mission accomplished. I really so disliked watching those arrogant Greeks that I found myself, for the first time during this whole campaign, hoping that we would win just to wipe those smiles from their faces.

The number of students voting that day turned out to be the largest fall election turnout in LSU history, with 4,252 students voting compared to around the 1,400 students who usually voted in a fall SGA election. Due to the unexpectedly large turnout, it would take a while for all the votes to be counted.

We, along with the other side, had observers in the room as the ballots were dumped on the table and counted. I had my friend, and close adviser, John Crochet, observing the count, writing down the tally as each ballot was read out loud by Dana Wicks, a Union Governing Board member appointed by the Election Board to count the votes. John told me that he sat on one side of Wicks with a notepad, and Naaman Eicher sat on the other side of him. First, Dana Wicks would unfold the ballot, then read the votes on each issue on the ballot out loud as another student, assigned by the Election Board, wrote the vote down, as would John and Naaman. I was sure glad that I had John in the room to cover our backs.

Finally, I heard someone in our group say, "Here they come!" I looked over at the doors of the Union and saw a large group of students coming out. It was obvious that the group consisted of the students from the counting room and a large number of other students who must have been waiting for them inside the Union. I saw John Crochet among them. As I watched, they approached the top of the steps of the Union.

All the students in our group, who had been sitting on the steps, stood up and moved closer to Wicks. The other students milling around the steps also gathered closer to hear what Wicks was about to announce.

As I would later do watching a jury coming back into court with a verdict, I scanned the faces of the group to try to get an impression of what was about to be announced. I saw a number of the students had the look of a person going to a loved one's funeral. I knew immediately that we had won the election when I glanced over at John. He had a mile-wide smile stretching from ear to ear!

John later told me that Wicks had instructed everyone to stay together as they walked out of the Union and wait for him to make the announcement of the election results. This was smart on his part, for it let all of the waiting students know that both sides were in agreement as to the total as it stood at that moment.

Before Wicks began to read the results of the election, I turned, with an equally broad smile on my face, to look at the students standing around me who had fought with me through so many battles. Some had seen John's beaming smile and deduced the same thing: we had beaten them! I saw that they were shaking hands and hugging each other, and I joined in with them. None of us waited for the official ballot count to start celebrating what we already knew: we had won!

As the Greeks went silent, Wicks, in order to be heard over our celebrating, announced loudly, "The results of the election are…" I saw John give me a look that seemed to say, "Wait till you hear this!" In true dramatic fashion, Wicks first read the results of the referendum on whether the student body wanted Margaret Jameson to be appointed dean of students. The vote was 2,598 nays to 1,127 yeas. It was an overwhelming denouncement by the student body of her as dean of women and as a person. Then Wicks moved on to the question of allowing the law school to separate from SGA. That vote was 2,561 in favor and 1,007 against. We had pushed for both results. By the total of votes cast in these two issues, I knew that the large crowd of students voting that day was a record breaker.

At this point, the Greeks seemed to be on the verge of rushing Wicks and ripping the tally sheets out of his hands. We didn't really care about what the margin of victory was, just that we had won. Those students who had stood with me, at great sacrifice to their studies and social life, to defeat this recall were still celebrating. That was about to change when we heard Wicks read out the votes on the recall question.

I could not help but notice that Wicks' tone of voice seemed to change to a more sober one as he read out the results. The first words out of his mouth, words that he hadn't used when announcing the other two results, were, "The unofficial count in the issue of Ted Schirmer's recall as president of SGA…2,119 votes for the recall and 2,133 votes against the recall. And there are still 80 outstanding votes that need to be verified by the Registrar's Office." None of us had to be math majors to quickly realize that the margin of victory was tiny. We won by a mere 14 votes out of 4,252 cast. It got more worrisome when Wicks said that there were 80 ballots still uncounted.

Anyone who has never won an election by a scant number of votes won't understand how, after hearing how close the vote was, we started laughing, cheering and clapping even louder. A number of us were shaking our heads in disbelief, realizing how close we had come to losing the election. In LSU football terms, it was another Kentucky Bluegrass Miracle.

I looked over at the Greeks. It was sinking in what had happened. Their strutting and laughter had stopped and was replaced by expressions of shock, disbelief, and anger.

Wicks announced that the 80 ballots were being sent to the Registrar's Office to be verified that they had been cast by full-time students before being counted. He then added that those 80 votes consisted of 53 votes by students who knew their student ID number and showed a valid driver license before voting and 27 votes by students who had their student IDs but whose names didn't appear on the printout provided by the administration of the names of full-time students as of the date of the election.

Our people who had been poll watchers told me not to worry, that the vast majority of students being allowed to vote without their student ID were our supporters. I asked them, how they could be so sure. They said, by the way those students dressed and talked while voting. Then, with a smile, they added, "Coupled with the fact that most of them reeked of marijuana." I said with a laugh, "No wonder they forgot their student IDs! I am just glad they were able to find the Parade Ground to vote."

A vision of all my fellow long haired freaks at LSU coming out to vote in this election caused a warm feeling of camaraderie to sweep over me. It was similar to my feelings of camaraderie for my Nam buddies who stood by my side through thick and thin.

No matter what the final count, I felt good that we had fought the good fight. In my opinion, as a people's activist who over the years lost many fights, fighting the good fight is just as noble as winning the fight. To be knocked down, when standing up and fighting for the people, doesn't dilute the fact that you were at least in the ring. As Theodore Roosevelt put it in his speech known as "The Man in the Arena":

> It is not the critic who counts; not the man who points out how the strong man stumbles, or where the doer of deeds could have done them better. The credit belongs to the man who is actually in the arena, whose face is marred by dust and sweat and blood; who strives valiantly; who errs, who comes short again and again, because there is no effort without error and shortcoming; but who does actually strive to do the deeds; who knows great enthusiasms, the great devotions; who spends himself in a worthy cause; who at the best knows in the end the triumph of high achievement, and who at the worst, if he fails, at least fails while daring greatly, so that his place shall never be with those cold and timid souls who neither know victory nor defeat.

> —Theodore Roosevelt
> Speech at the Sorbonne, Paris, April 23, 1910

The next morning, we would read that the Election Board had met directly after the vote counting was completed to certify the election, I guess thinking that would be the finish of me as SGA president. They were in for a big disappointment since the election results showed that I had won the election by 14 votes. They voted to recount the votes cast in the recall election tomorrow.

358

I suppose what they then did next would have been more shocking but for the blatant basis I believed the four of them had already exhibited in their past actions. The Election Board voted to disqualify all of the 53 votes cast by students who didn't have a student ID with them but had been allowed to vote after giving their name and student ID number and showing a valid driver's license to the poll worker as had been agreed to by all parties. By reasonable assumption, this action by the Election Board was just another heavy-handed approach by the four remaining members on the Board to tilt the election against me.

The weak ass rationale given by the Election Board members was that, since the election rules clearly stated that a student ID would be required to vote, those votes should not be counted. When the agreement had been reached by all sides to allow those students to vote and then have the Registrar's Office verify them as full-time students, the election had just started, so the Election Board had no way of knowing that rule would apply to such a large number of students, and that a majority of them might be my supporters. Undoubtedly that was the real reason for them reneging on the agreement.

After reading about the Board's decision the next morning, I instructed John Crochet to begin working on our appeal in the event that the outcome of the election was shifted by the verification and counting of the remaining 27 votes by students who had their student IDs but were not on the list provided by the administration of full-time students.

As reported by the *Reveille* (November 5, 1976) in an article titled "Schirmer still in office, but…" a reporter asked, did I think that, after those 27 votes were counted, would I still win the election? I replied that I was confident I was going to win. Out of the 27 votes, 21 of them would have to be for the recall for me to lose. I added, however, that I wasn't so confident that my campaign staff weren't, as we spoke, preparing our appeal in the eventuality that we fell behind.

In a report by Marti Quinn, the editor of the *Reveille* (November 5, 1976), titled "Both sides pledge to seek unity after recall outcome" I am quoted as saying that, "I thought we were going to win by a bigger margin than we did. We had a good effort...[I]n two days, we organized and brought out the vote better than they did in two weeks." I further said, "I only spoke in four sorority houses, but if I could have spoken at all the houses, I think the vote would have been more lopsided. The girls I spoke to didn't really know the issues and were very receptive."

All the fraternities and most of the sororities had refused to allow me to speak at their houses on campus during the recall. I told the four sororities, which allowed me to speak, that "The whole issue was created through the emotional mess of Homecoming. It's like we had all our dirty linen aired, and people didn't like that." I went on to explain why I had to stop the original racist Homecoming Queen election. Most of the women at the sorority houses I spoke at had never heard that part of the events and thought that I was doing it because I was anti-Greek. I told the *Reveille* that I was very proud of the student body since, "A fall election where we had over 4,000 students vote is fantastic."

Jack Clegg stated in that same article that, "he wanted to publicly thank the Election Board 'for doing a super job. It was a very emotional issue and the Board kept it straight.'" He specifically thanked, "Mark Schrodeder, Dana Wicks, and Dave Tuttle [for doing] a fine job." He further stated that, "Ted knows a lot about the campus and the students; it's just the way he does things that bothers me. He doesn't represent all the students, but it appears he represents a good many of them." I had to smile when I read that and wondered, was this the next Greek running for SGA president?

Then to my utter surprise, the next day, in what appeared to be an attempt to overcome our lead and head off our appeal, which could have caused the whole election to be disqualified and a new one called by the University Court, the Election Board reversed its decision of the evening before and agreed to open and count the 53 disqualified votes. I am confident that at some time they did the math and realized that the 27 votes were most likely not enough to put them over the top.

That was exactly what happened. When those 27 ballots returned from the Registrar's Office, only 19 of the voters were found to be full-time students whose votes could be added to the count. Of those 19 votes, 9 were in support of the recall, 10 were opposed.

But those 53 votes didn't help the Greeks win the election either. Of the 53 votes, 24 supported the recall, while 29 votes were against it. You have got to hand it to the members of the Election Board, they tried everything they could to swing the election their way.

Regarding Robert's role in these shenanigans, I could not help but think, that, while there might not be a proverbial smoking gun, the number of spent shell casings scattering around from the bullets fired at me by Dana Robert during the Greeks' attempt to recall me sure were mounting up. And those were just the bullets fired at me by her that I knew about. Damn, despite her claims of neutrality, all the circumstantial evidence sure seems to me to point to her working with the recall movement behind the scenes. Maybe I'll never know that for sure, but to quote poet James Whitcomb Riley, "When I see a bird that walks like a duck and swims like a duck and quacks like a duck, I call that bird a duck."

After all of the tricks by the Election Board, the recall finally failed, not by 14 votes, but by 20 votes. If winning by 20 votes looks like barely winning, one has to realize that, in the '70s, it was very rare for a non-Greek candidate to defeat a Greek candidate for student body president. Plus, in the recall election the Greeks were united. There was no competition among the different Greek houses as there might have been in a normal election. Those factors led nearly everyone to believe I didn't have a snowball's chance in hell of surviving the recall election.

That Monday, November 8th, I wasn't waiting for the final count to get back to work. I met with my department heads in order to crank back up the many projects we had been working on before Homecoming and the recall. My newly appointed director of Academic Affairs, Kevin Frindik, put a notice in the *Reveille* (November 9, 1976), titled, "SGA looking for aid," that said students were needed for the SGA academic appeals and the teacher course evaluation programs, the F grade abolition committee, and the teacher removal petitions committee. Also, with the fall semester nearing an end, the Book Rental program needed volunteers for program organizer, poster planner, sales personnel, and helpers to stack, move and store books at the end of the semester and, at the start of the spring semester, to collect and rent books.

All of this we got underway even though my appeal from the Code of Conduct hearing had just been submitted to Chancellor Murrill that Tuesday.

## APPEAL OF CODE OF CONDUCT DECISION

Beno and I knew that I had been railroaded in the Code of Conduct hearing, but believed it had all just been an attempt by the recall leaders to assist their recall movement. We hoped that Murrill would overturn that biased decision and allow us a new hearing. Beno submitted our appeal on November 9th.

In his appeal he raised the same issues he raised during the hearing. The first was that I was not allowed an opportunity for reasonable cross examination of the witnesses appearing against me. Specifically, the committee had denied us the opportunity to question Vice Chancellor Reddoch about his October 13th memo and the sources he relied on when he wrote it. Yet Reddoch's October 13th memo was used to "establish an element of the case against" me in that it stated "the SGA and [I] as president possessed no authority over the Homecoming Committee." I felt that just reading the minutes of the hearing would prove that point.

The second error we appealed was the charge of "knowingly making, in public, a false oral statement with the intent to deceive and/or mislead." Beno argued that anything I said at the Alley was protected speech under the First Amendment to the United States Constitution. I wasn't too sure about that argument.

Third, Beno stated that there were apparent inconsistencies in the verdict of the hearing committee, in that I was found innocent of the charge of "theft or temporary taking of the property of another" but found guilty of disruption or interfering with the election, a university function.

Finally, Beno's last point was about the restraints, interruptions, and manner in which his presentation of my case was cut off by the chairman of the committee. Dr. Robertson's demand, that Beno hurry up because the hearing had to end at 5 P.M., prevented us from presenting our defenses to the charge of interrupting a university sponsored activity, i.e. the Homecoming Queen election.

Beno's requested remedy was to have a new hearing with a different committee on the two charges of which I was found guilty.

On November 22nd, just before leaving for McHenry, Illinois, to spend Thanksgiving with my brother and Susanna's mother, I received the chancellor's ruling on the appeal. Murrill wrote, "I asked Dr. James W. Reddoch, vice chancellor for student affairs, to make a detailed review of this appeal." Shit, I thought, I'm fucked!

Sure enough, the very next line read:

> Based on the facts put forward in your behalf by Mr.
> Duhon, on the analysis prepared by Dr. Reddoch, and on
> the minutes of the meeting of the Student Conduct Com-
> mittee itself, I do not find any basis on which to grant your
> appeal. As a result, I am not changing the findings of the
> Committee with respect to paragraph A-3-i and paragraph
> A-3-e in which the committee found you guilty as charged.
> In the Code of Student Conduct...a student on such proba-
> tion is prohibited from holding an office or standing com-
> mittee chairmanship in any student organization... [but he
> was]...granting specific exemption will not use the findings
> of the committee or the recommended sanction of the
> committee as a vehicle or basis to remove you from your
> office...unless there are new or additional charges brought
> against you before a new Code of Student Conduct Hearing
> Committee or unless there is further conduct by you which,
> in my judgement, would merit my taking further action in
> this case.

Murrill made it very clear that I had the Sword of Damocles hanging over my head. He sent copies of his decision to LSU President Martin Woodin; Vice Chancellor James Reddoch; Dean of Men Arden O. French and Mr. William Brown, chairman, LSU Board of Supervisors. It was clear to me that Murrill had been discussing these matters with them. He also sent a copy to Dr. George L. Robertson, chairman, Code of Student Conduct Committee for this case. This was all done apparently without violating the Buckley Amendment protecting students' privacy.

Murrill went on to write in his appeal decision:

> While in this probation status, you will be prohibited from assuming any new offices or new standing committee chairmanships in any student organizations and, *also, you will be prohibited from being a candidate for re-election [emphasis added]* or reappointment to such offices or chairmanships.

It must have scared the shit out of the administration that, since I had won the recall election, I might decide to run for SGA president again, and that I could win. There was no way in hell that I would run for re-election. I was not that much of a masochist.

In the last sentence of his decision, Murrill stated, "I will not consider any appeals for a change in this status for one calendar year."

Attached to the decision was a copy of Reddoch's five-page opinion to Murrill. In it, Reddoch summarized his October 13th memo:

> In this memorandum, the vice chancellor [meaning himself] outlined conclusions drawn concerning authority for staging Homecoming. These conclusions were based upon the Regulations of the Board of Supervisors, which outline the duties, powers, and authority of the chancellor on each campus, conversations with other administrators, including the Director of Alumni Affairs, and a review of the SGA constitution.

I could have written a chapter on the many pertinent questions I had about each of these areas but it was clear that, by giving my appeal to Reddoch, Murrill meant the review to be a white wash of the kangaroo court's decision.

Reddoch concluded by writing that I:

> was afforded a Code of Student Conduct hearing that met all generally accepted criteria established to assure substantive and procedural due process in university disciplinary hearings. I, therefore, recommend that his appeal be denied.

I believed that many of the "powers that be" wanted me removed from both the SGA presidency and the Board of Supervisors, if not outright expelled from LSU, but something was stopping them. What I overlooked at the time was the fact that LSU was in court fighting a Department of Justice civil rights lawsuit charging LSU with racial discrimination. If the Department of Justice and the court had become aware that the LSU administration had condoned a racist Homecoming Queen election, it could have caused them some real headaches. It is now clear to me that it was the pending civil rights lawsuit against LSU and the Board of Supervisors that prevented them from striking out at me as forcefully as they wanted to. Taylor and Porter, the law firm representing LSU, must have warned them what could happen if the discriminatory Homecoming Queen election came out in court.

A number of friends and adversaries thought that Murrill was doing me a kindness by not allowing Jameson and Reddoch to throw me out of school when he modified the repercussions of my being placed on probation by allowing me to serve out the remainder of my term as SGA president. But I am sure that, if they had removed me, the storyline in all of the news outlets would have been, "Hippie SGA president recalled and kicked off of Board of Supervisors due to Homecoming controversy."

I would have surely been sought out for interviews by the media, not only in Baton Rouge but throughout the state, possibly even by the national press. That would have been one hell of a story. The press would start digging into the reason all of this started, i.e., the discriminatory Homecoming Queen election and the role that LSU's administration had played in blocking the possible election of LSU's first Black Homecoming Queen. Suspending judgment and putting me on probation was a clever solution to their dilemma of what to do with me.

Each time I read Murrill's letter, the more disappointed I got with him. This disappointment soon turned to anger. I later realized that Chancellor Murrill had made a wise decision to send his decision to me as I was leaving for McHenry, Illinois, for the Thanksgiving break. I would not be back until November 29th.

As it turned out, that gave me time to realize no real harm had been done to me by Murrill's decision. Still being president, I could push for projects that were unfinished. What I was yet to realize was that, while Murrill's decision may not have harmed me personally; it sure did harm the student body's hopes for a Book Rental and a new Bill of Student Rights, both of which they had voted for overwhelmingly when I was elected.

## BOOK RENTAL AND THE BOARD OF SUPERVISORS

Soon after, I won the November 4th recall election, but while still waiting for Chancellor Murrill's decision on my appeal of the Code of Conduct hearing verdict, a front-page article appeared in the *Reveille* (November 18, 1976) titled "Schirmer slapped by conduct board." In it, Ken Kleinpeter wrote that I had been found guilty by a Code of Conduct hearing on charges relating to the Homecoming controversy. He had been told by his source, who was close to the matter, that the committee had put me on probation to the Code of Conduct Committee, and that I would not be able to hold office if Murrill rejected my appeal of that decision. The article also mentioned I could be facing suspension or expulsion from LSU. When questioned, Murrill had no comment, citing the Bill of Student Rights and the Buckley Amendment, the federal law that covered students' right to confidentiality of their records.

The article further raised the question that I was sure was on the mind of many people: if I were forced out of office, how would that affect my position on the Board of Supervisors? Murrill stressed that issue was solely in the hands of the Board of Supervisors. But the reporter pointed out that sources told him that Vice Chancellor Reddoch had instructed LSU's attorneys to research the issue of removing me from the Board of Supervisors. When the reporter contacted Reddoch by phone, he at first had no comment but then stated that it was "not unusual" for LSU's attorneys to research university issues governed by Louisiana state law. I guessed he added that to try to make me sweat. I have to admit, it did get my attention.

The proposed Book Rental program was coming up for Board approval. Had my fighting with the administration damaged the chances of getting the votes it needed? I had faith that my fellow Board members Camille Gravel, Jerry McKernan and Gordon Dore would understand why I did what I had done and would still support it.

They were the only Board members who had accepted my invitation to appear at Free Speech Alley. I had told them that students needed to see the individuals who ran LSU. Camille told me afterwards that he thoroughly enjoyed the experiences of answering students' questions at the Alley, but, he added with a grin, he would never forget it. I thought the students went pretty easy on him. After all, this is the South where children were still raised to say "yes, sir" or "yes, ma'am" to all adults.

I attended the meeting of the Financial Committee of the Board of Supervisors on Saturday, November 20th. Camille had placed the Book Rental on the committee's agenda. A number of students opposed to the Book Rental appeared at the committee hearing to give their input on it. They included Bob Sappenfield, chief justice of the University Court, Dana Wicks, president of the Student Governing Board, and William Crews III, representing the Young Americans for Freedom (YAF). Their comments ranged from "it's not workable" to "it's a good idea but it would not be able to cover junior and senior students for years, yet they would still be required to pay the $1 fee."

When I was given the floor, I walked the committee through the rising high cost of textbooks and the groundswell of support from students as shown by their voting for the $1 fee referendum and donating their textbooks to the Book Rental instead of selling them back to the LSU Bookstore for pennies on the dollar. I explained how Professor Hilary Zaunbrecher of the Accounting Department, had found that both the plan and the budget for the program were sound and workable. I then addressed the fact that, even though juniors and seniors would be paying the $1 fee, but graduating before receiving any benefit from the Book Rental, I was sure that they would see their dollar as both a statement against the high cost of textbooks at LSU and an expression of their willingness to help present and future LSU students.

Ultimately, as reported in the Reveille (November 23, 1976) article "Supervisors' panel passes book rental," the Financial Committee voted 6-3 in favor of the Book Rental. I felt good that, despite the November 18th article about my being found guilty by the Code of Conduct Committee, what had happened at that kangaroo court hadn't stopped the Finance Committee from approving the Book Rental program. As far as I knew, any matter receiving a positive vote by any committee of the Board of Supervisors was usually approved by the whole Board.

I allowed myself to start feeling optimistic about the Book Rental passing at the next full Board meeting on December 4th. I began discussing with student leaders in the SGA and other student organizations plans for operation of the Book Rental the following spring semester. That included looking into hiring a manager and staff to run the Book Rental along with part-time student workers to assist them. I realized that there was going to be a lot of work to get the Book Rental up and running by the spring semester, but I wasn't worried because everyone, who had been working so hard to make it a reality, was really psyched since it appeared it would finally be approved. My optimism lasted until a *Morning Advocate* article shook it right out of me.

After Murrill ruled on my appeal on November 22nd, the *Morning Advocate* finally took notice of what had been happening on campus. The paper published an article, on November 25th, about Murrill's decision not to remove me from office. In addition, Ken Kleinpeter subsequently wrote a *Reveille* (December 1, 1976) article titled "Ted keeping post, despite probation." It was published just three days before the next Board meeting in New Orleans. I began to worry again about the fate of the Book Rental.

I figured that there was a damn good chance that all of the Board members would be present at the December 4th Board of Supervisors meeting in New Orleans. If there was one matter that they all took a keen interest in, it was LSU football. I had learned that, due to three plus years of dismal football seasons, the contract of Charlie McClendon (Coach Mac) was going to be discussed in Executive Session at the Board meeting.

When I first started at LSU in 1970, our football team had been a national contender. In the 1970 AP poll of the top 25 football teams in the country, LSU was ranked seventh and, more importantly, our win/loss record in the SEC was 5–0. In 1974, LSU had fallen completely out of the AP poll and had a 2–4 SEC record. It was not better the next two years.

I fully appreciated the interest in Coach Mac's future at LSU. I would not be able to vote on his contract renewal, but I looked forward to asking him questions and making comments at the Board meeting.

On December 4th, I left the house early in the hope of missing New Orleans' Monday morning traffic, but, as I got to the outskirts of New Orleans on the I-10, I ran into it anyway and found myself running late. It didn't help that I hadn't been on UNO's campus before and didn't know exactly where the building hosting the meeting was located. That was way before Google maps.

As I slowly drove in New Orleans traffic, I worried about how the Board members would vote on the Book Rental. How much would the *Advocate* and *Reveille* articles affect their votes? Would I still be fighting against those Board members who didn't want me on the Board with them? Even though I was trying to get my head around what might be waiting for me at the Board meeting, I was still excited by the prospect that the Book Rental could finally have the votes it needed to pass.

I finally found the UNO campus and made it to the building where the meeting was being held. I was hoping that I could have a few words with Camille, Gordon, and Jerry before the meeting started, but, due to the number of coffees I had drunk, I had to urgently go to the head (restroom) and missed out on talking with them. I did get a chance to ask Camille how the vote looked on the Book Rental, and he told me we had the necessary votes to pass it. "Great!" I said, and went to take my seat next to Ruth Miller.

As I sat down next to Ruth, I flashed on the memory at the last Board meeting. Ruth and Clarence Romero had said that they felt not enough students had voted in favor of the Book Rental referendum to make that vote an adequate representation of the total student body's support for an additional tuition fee of $1 to fund the program. I pointed out that I was elected in that same election, and, under that logic, I should not be on the Board representing the student body as SGA president at the Baton Rouge campus. I never heard that reasoning again. I figured I wouldn't hear it at this meeting either.

When the Board meeting was called to order, there were 16 members present, 15 with a vote and me, which meant we needed eight votes to pass the Book Rental. The meeting was also attended by the largest number of individuals I had ever seen at a Board meeting. I knew it wasn't because of the Book Rental; rather, the debate on the fate of Coach McClendon had drawn them.

Kitty Strain, the Board secretary, read the history of the Book Rental proposal, which included the vote on the resolution in the spring SGA election when students approved the $1 per term student tuition fee increase for one academic year with 2,432 voting for it and 1,181 against.

The proposal that was in front of the Board included the two additional sections which Camille and I had agreed to include in order to address the concerns of some of the other Board members. These two changes were:

BE IT FURTHER RESOLVED that this Book Rental Service is viewed as an experiment to be conducted during the fiscal year 1977—78 with a full accounting and analysis of its operation to be made in an administrative report to the Board of Supervisors in August of 1978. This administrative report should also include recommendations as to whether the Service is justified and, if so, under what conditions.

BE IT FURTHER RESOLVED that the Board of Supervisors specifically limits its liability in the operation of the Book Rental to the amount of the fee collected from this special assessment and all income, including the value of gifts, generated from the operation of the Book Rental, and the university administrator responsible for the general administration of the Book Rental Restricted Fund is directed to take all actions necessary to keep financial commitments within the bounds of available funds.

When Kitty finished reading the proposal, the floor was open for any statements by Board members. I had learned from my time in the SGA Assembly that, once you have the votes you needed to pass an issue, keep any further comments brief. I quickly went over an abbreviated version of my argument for why a nonprofit Book Rental was needed at the Baton Rouge campus. Then I pointed out that, according to Professor Zaunbrecher's detailed proposed budget, the Book Rental was a feasible proposal.

The other Board members, who have been supporting the Book Rental from the beginning, gave statements of their support, and the members who had voted against the Book Rental previously gave their reasons for not supporting the Book Rental proposal at that time.

What caught my attention and worried me was that some of the nine members who had expressed their support to Camille had remained silent. I tried not to read too much into their silence, but it turned out not to bode well for the upcoming vote.

The vote was called and I saw Vice Chairman Oliver Stockwell switch sides. He was followed by the Shreveport car dealer and gambling buddy of Edwards, William Hanna, Jr., who joined Charles Cusimano and Murphy Foster in voting "no." I didn't panic for we only needed eight votes to pass. Finally, we had five votes and there were five more members to vote. Four out of those remaining five members had voted for the Book Rental at previous meetings of the Board. I felt the Board was going to finally pass the Book Rental. I looked over at Camille and Jerry, and the looks on their faces didn't seem to match my optimism. I was soon going to find out why.

William Peck Jr. voted for the Book Rental, giving us six "yes" votes for the Book Rental. Then Dr. James Peltier followed with a "no" vote. I was starting to sweat as Clarence Romero voted "no," as he had before. His vote was followed by a "yes" vote by John Sherrouse, Jr. It was tied again with only Carlos Spaht left to vote. When he voted "no" it felt as if someone had punched me in the gut.

Without waiting to be recognized, I immediately went into a strong diatribe. I asked, what kind of message was the Board sending to the student body at the Baton Rouge campus, the future voters of this state and country, by not respecting their vote on an issue to improve their experience at LSU. I told them it was outrageous. Students deserve not to be treated like children. I pointed out that if 18 or 19-year-old students, like myself, were old enough to go to war for our country, they were old enough to vote to assess themselves a fee of $1 in an effort to solve a serious financial problem affecting many students at LSU. As I spoke, I scanned the faces of the members who had not supported the Book Rental. I guess that my anger was obvious, not only in my words and tone of voice, but in my face, for none of them would look at me.

I stopped when I saw that Camille had anger written all over his face, too. He stated that he had been told by some of the Board members that, if changes were made, they would vote for the proposal. In his long career at the State Capitol, no one had ever not honored the commitment to vote for a bill if changes were made to that bill. He wanted a discussion of how the redrafted resolution had been rewritten to please members who had just voted "no."

Mr. Fitzmorris' motion for a discussion of the redrafted resolution was seconded by Mr. Brown. But this motion would only allow a discussion of how the redrafted portion of the resolution was made, it would not allow another vote on the Book Rental. There was no way that the four members who had reneged on their agreement with Camille and me wanted this discussion to go any further, and the motion failed by one vote.

Ruth Miller, sitting beside me, leaned over and said she hoped I wasn't mad. I looked at her and told her: "I don't get mad, I get even." She looked startled as she said, "Governor McKeithen told her the same thing."

I was still steaming, when I felt a hand on my shoulder. Looking up, I saw UNO's student government president. He asked if he could speak with me outside. Realizing that I needed to calm down before the Board moved on to discuss what to do about Coach McClendon's contract, I got up and followed him out a back exit to the meeting room.

I tried to find out what he wanted to see me about as he led me down a hallway and around a corner. He told me he would like to talk with me in his office. I didn't know where UNO's SGA offices were located, but I knew I didn't want to miss the Board's discussion about Coach McClendon. I told him I couldn't go to his office, I needed to get back to the Board meeting before they called Coach McClendon.

He began asking my advice about starting a Book Rental at UNO. I told him I would call him next week, and we could discuss it. As I turned to leave, he again took my arm and asked if our Bill of Student Rights had passed. Since he had been my only ally at the Student Presidents Committee, I was trying my best to be patient with him, so I told him the trouble I was having getting the bill that the students had voted for out of the committee of administrators and faculty who were reviewing it.

He started to ask me something else, when I held up my hand, telling him I had to get back to the meeting, and that I would call him next week. When I opened the door to the meeting room, I found it was empty. "Damn it!" I muttered. I was definitely disappointed.

It wasn't until years later that, while researching for this story, I came to realize that Board members and/or administrators must have convinced the UNO student body president to lure me out of the meeting before the Board dealt with the issue of whether or not to fire McClendon. For Board members, the hiring and firing of an LSU football coach was a sacred act that they didn't want any damn student present to observe. Maybe, like making sausage, the hiring and firing of an LSU football coach is better not seen.

I had a long drive back to Baton Rouge. To say I was crushed about the vote on the Book Rental would be a huge understatement. It helped that after finals, Susanna and I went back to McHenry, Illinois, to spend the holidays with my friends and family. That was great for distracting me from what had happened.

After I returned to campus in January of 1977, I had lost any belief that I could accomplish anything through the Board and thought that my remaining months as SGA president would be more beneficial spent working to get the Bill of Student Rights out of the University Review Committee. Therefore, I didn't attend the next meeting of the Board on February 11, 1977.

It was fortunate that I didn't attend since the Board agreed to a mortgage guarantee for a loan of over $500,000 to rebuild the Sigma Chi fraternity house that had been destroyed by fire in 1974. Keep in mind we are talking about $500,000 dollars in 1977, which would be roughly $2.2 million in today's dollars. This generous act by the Board failed to consider the racism exhibited by all fraternities on campus in denying minorities membership, not to mention the violation of university rules prohibiting hazing. Hazing at Sigma Chi would eventually lead to the death of a pledge in 2015, and the banning of the fraternity from LSU's campus.

My term as SGA president ended with the March 25th spring elections, but I still had two more Board meetings remaining in my one year appointment. Even though the next meeting on April 2, 1977, was being held at Shreveport at 9:10 A.M. on a Saturday morning, I was determined to attend since the Student Health Service fee was on the agenda. I had been fighting to save the infirmary at the Baton Rouge campus since becoming SGA president, and I wasn't going to stop fighting for it just because I no longer was SGA president.

At the meeting, I spoke about how important it was to have an infirmary on campus for all students, but especially the students living on campus. Unlike the vote on the Book Rental, the Student Health Service fee passed unanimously. As I drove back home, I couldn't help but think the Board had just approved a $15 Student Health Service fee indefinitely that wasn't voted on by the student body, but would not approve a $1 Book Rental fee for one academic year that had been approved by a student vote. I guess I couldn't completely forget what some of the Board members had done.

There was only one more Board meeting before the new SGA president became the student member on the Board. The meeting was set for May 9th, during dead week and final exams. I was in trouble in a few of my classes due to how much time I had spent with SGA and the Board, so I wasn't planning to attend the meeting even though it was being held in Baton Rouge.

Then, a few days before the meeting, Professor Paul Grosser called me at home and asked me to come see him at his office. Paul was a Political Science professor who had worked with Cesar Chavez in the National Farm Workers Association (NFWA) and later in the United Farm Workers (UFW) before coming to LSU. He had helped me out last semester by allowing me to take a reading class with him. That class and another taught by a professor friend of mine, allowed me to put in as much time as I did as SGA president, and still pass that semester.

Paul's favorite saying to me about all the time I spent fighting the administration and Greeks was: just let the finks run the place. But when I got to his office, he told me that the finks wanted to fire him for not publishing.

He took me into a conference room to show me a manuscript he had written about the Holocaust. He had it neatly laid out in stacks of paper, one for each chapter. He told me he was preparing to ship it to the publisher. The head of the department knew that he was wrapping up his book, but still informed him that he was being terminated. I wondered to myself if it was because he had helped me. Paul asked for my help in keeping his job. Paul may not have published like the other political science professors in the department, but he was by far the best lecturer in the whole department.

All departments at LSU knew it was important to have a professor, who was an excellent lecturer, teach that department's freshmen and sophomore courses if they hoped to recruit student majors for their departments. That is why Paul taught the freshmen and sophomores courses in political science. The students who took Paul's classes loved them.

I told Paul I would speak with Camille Gravel about bringing this matter up in front of the Board. In addition to contacting Camille, I decided to also contact Jerry McKernan and Gordon Dore to line up support for overturning Paul's termination notice. I was in luck, for I got through to all of them on the first try. All three agreed to support a motion that the Board should investigate this matter. I felt that was the best I could do. I called Paul to tell him about my progress and say that, even though I had exams, I would make it a point to attend the Board meeting.

On the morning of May 9th, the final exam in my anthropology class on Ancient Civilizations of South America, taught by Dr. Robert West, was scheduled. I was fascinated with the Olmecs, Mayans, Inca and Aztecs, so I had signed up for Dr. West's course, assuming that he was an anthropology professor. I would find out later that he was a renowned geography professor, an outstanding authority on Latin American, and even a former cultural geographer for the Smithsonian Institution. But he didn't have the sense of humor that I found so attractive in anthropology professors. He was the typical dry and intellectual professor that LSU sought out in order to boost their standing among other universities in the country and the world.

That morning I went to Professor West's office to tell him that I would need to make up his final exam, but he had already left. I then hurried to the classroom where the exam was to be held. There I found him and told him I couldn't take the test because there was a Board of Supervisors meeting starting in about five minutes that I needed to attend. Without looking up, he said, "There are no make-up tests in my class." I explained that I was a member of the Board of Supervisors, and I needed to attend the meeting that morning. He then looked up at me with a slightly puzzled look on his face, saying, "I don't allow make-up exams in my classes." Dr. West was very old, probably in his late 70s or early 80s. I could tell he was having problems with understanding what I was telling him, and I began getting worried that I would miss Camille's motion to discuss Paul's termination. I told Dr. West in a stern tone, "You don't understand: you technically work for me since I am a member of the Board of Supervisors." That really confused him. As he turned away from me, he said, "I could only allow you to make up my test later with a note from the chancellor." Hearing that, I spun around and took off as fast as I could for the Board meeting that was underway.

The Board meeting room was all the way on the other side of the campus in Boyd Hall. I was out of breath when I got there. Kitty Stain was not at her desk. Another Board secretary was in the outer office, but I rushed past her and entered the Board Room. Chancellor Murrill and Vice Chancellor Reddoch were sitting in their usual seats up front. I noticed Camille looking at me, but I had eyes only for the chancellor. I excused myself and squeezed past President Woodin, telling him I needed to speak with the chancellor. I leaned over and told Murrill that I needed a note from him to make up a test that I had to miss so I could attend this meeting. With a smile, the chancellor turned to Reddoch saying, "I have to write a note for a Board member so he can attend this meeting!" As Reddoch looked up at me, that too familiar cynical smile of his spread across his face. I had to fight hard not to make one of my smart comeback lines. I needed that note from the chancellor.

Murrill took his sweet time as he wrote on the note pad in front of him, "Please excuse Ted Schirmer and allow him to make up today's test so that he can attend a Board of Supervisors meeting." He signed the note, and, with the smile still on his face, handed it to me. I spun around quickly, bumping into President Woodin. I muttered, "Excuse me," as I took off for the Geography and Anthropology Building.

I took the steps two at a time up to the third floor where the classroom was located. I was really breathing heavily as I opened the door. My classmates were already taking the final exam with Dr. West sitting at his desk. He looked up at me as I asked, "Is this what you require?" and handed him the chancellor's note.

Dr. West looked amazed as he read the note. I asked him if I could go now. Without looking at me, he said first he had to find a date for me to take the make-up test. I asked if I could come to his office later to get the date for the test. He didn't even respond. He opened his calendar and gave me a date and time, but I had to tell him I had a final in another class at that time. He then said that the only other date I could take the make-up final exam was the following Wednesday at lunch time. Without waiting for my responses, I saw him write it down on his calendar. By that time, my anxiety level over missing the Board meeting had risen to such a point that I just didn't care, and I took off for the meeting.

As I entered the Board Room, the meeting was just adjourning. I was really panicky. I wanted desperately to help Professor Grosser. I went up to Camille and asked what had happened. It turned out that six Board members, not counting me, were absent, so they had adjourned early. Camille knew what was on my mind and quickly added that he got Professor Grosser's matter on the agenda for the Board's next meeting. I was so relieved that for a moment I didn't realize that I wouldn't be on the Board for that meeting. As it turned out, press coverage by the *Reveille* and many speakers at the Alley, including me, stood up for Professor Grosser.

I thought, considering how I had failed to get the Book Rental passed by the Board, that this was a sad but appropriate ending to my time on LSU's Board of Supervisors.

# Spring Semester, 1977
## REVISION COMMITTEE REVIEWS
## THE BILL OF STUDENT RIGHTS

Meetings of the University Revision Committee on the Bill of Student Rights had been going on and on since the committee was formed in the summer of 1976. Bernard (Beno) Duhon, my ombudsman, had warned me that very little progress was being made. When the Revision Committee met, the chairman, political science Professor Cecil Crabb, was meticulously going over every sentence of every paragraph of every article of every page of our Bill of Student Rights. Beno told me that it appeared that the administration, i.e., Reddoch, was stalling until a new SGA administration was in office. After being told this by Beno, I had no doubt it was so. The administration knew that I was an anomaly: a student activist and a non-Greek SGA president. They were counting on a return to the norm.

That train of thought made me fear that the faculty was going to do the administration's bidding and change the bill by taking out the important parts, such as protecting the students against the unwarranted entering and searching of their dorm rooms or the teacher evaluation requirement, to mention just a couple—the same rights that other college students had throughout the country, except in the South.

I felt that the committee chairman, Professor Crabb, and Reddoch were working hand-in-hand. When the *Reveille* (January 19, 1977), in an article titled "Reddoch creating own little empire," asked Professor Crabb if Reddoch were the one holding up the release of the bill, he said that Reddoch didn't even have to set up the University Revision Committee in the first place. Reddoch could have just made any decisions about the bill himself. The committee showed how much Reddoch wanted to assist the student body in preparing a new Bill of Student Rights. What a load of crap. I thought about going to see Reddoch to ask what was holding up the committee's report, but I had a sudden flash back to the bullshit game he had played with me during the Homecoming Queen election fight. There was no way I was going to fall for his crap again.

On February 18, 1977, I received a letter from Vice Chancellor Reddoch informing me of changes that were being made to the Bill of Student Rights by the review committee. Major sections of the student approved Bill of Student Rights were being either taken out altogether or changed in such a way that the meaning of the section was totally altered.

In my February 24th response to Reddoch, I informed him that I had spoken with an officer of the National Student Association (NSA) in Washington, D.C. He had told me how many of the major universities' Boards of Regents had sanctioned Bills of Student Rights that had been written and voted on by the student body without major changes in the document. In addition, I informed Reddoch that the NSA officer sent me a list of student governments that were totally independent of their university's administration in all areas.

In Reddoch's reply to me, he wrote that I should read the Report of the Attorney General's Special Commission of Inquiry on the Southern University Tragedy of November 16, 1972. The incident took place after weeks of demonstrations by Southern students protesting inadequate services. When students marched on Southern University President Leon Netterville's office, 300 police officers arrived to break up the demonstrations. During the subsequent confrontation, a still-unidentified officer fired a shotgun at students in violation of orders. When the smoke cleared, two 20-year-old students —Leonard Brown and Denver Smith—were dead. Reddoch wrote, "Students should have a meaningful input into university life. But students cannot be given the final voice. This must rest with the university authorities."

My response to Reddoch was that that was the type of authoritarian ideology that led to tragedies such as that at Southern University. I told him that if he did not realize, as I did, that the fault lay, not with the Southern students, but with the administrators and the sheriffs who cold-bloodily shot the students, then that was another example of his blatant misunderstanding of the student body of 1977. I went on to state, "As I personally know in dealing with you at Homecoming, you would rather…force the issue upon the students. This kind of action, as it has been proven in the past, leads to tragic results." I concluded my letter with, "What you consider meaningful and what the students consider meaningful are obviously different, as shown by your past actions."

## MY LAST THREE MONTHS AS PRESIDENT

As the spring SGA elections of 1977 approached, I returned to the Election Board to perform my duties as chairman and start setting the rules and dates for the upcoming SGA spring elections. Soon, though, I ran into the same election road blocks I had experienced in my recall election.

I raised the idea of allowing a party's candidates to have their party affiliation listed on the ballot beside their names. I made the point that a new political party had been organized. The students who started that party included Dana Robert's ex-boyfriend Naamen Eicher, Jamie Prevost, Joe Wills and, even though he wasn't running for any office, Ned Wright. They had followed CPU's lead and formed a political organization of their own and called it Action Alliance. Their overall theme was to oppose CPU's candidates and my administration's programs. Since a number of the students running under the Action Alliance banner, like Naamen Eicher, who had been a member of CPU from the beginning and also my executive assistant, and Joe Wills, who was a founding member and the former chairman of the CPU, I felt that seeing their names on the ballot would cause confusion among our supporters and the student body in general.

I also argued that the elections should be on dates as convenient as possible for the student body, i.e., on a Monday, Wednesday or Friday when more students were on campus, and should not be on or near mid-terms and finals to encourage more students to participate in the election. We adjourned the meeting without any action being taken due to the lack of a quorum.

From my standpoint, I had serious doubts about the willingness of the other Election Board members to be fair on these issues. The board had the same six members as during the recall meetings. Four members were needed for a quorum. Since there was no quorum, I set the next date for an Election Board meeting, and we all left.

Then, late on the night of March 3rd, I received a call from Robert saying that she and the other board members had called an emergency meeting at her home at 11:30 P.M. I told her I was studying for an exam the next morning, and I couldn't make the meeting. I asked for the meeting to be set the day after my exam. Robert stated that the deadline for establishing the election rules and dates was getting close. I interpreted that to mean, in other words, no.

As far as I'm concerned, the board had taken the same type of action during the recall election, calling a meeting that was impossible for me to attend in order to put into place rules and dates for that election which were way more advantageous to the recall effort.

At the next meeting, on March 8th, I complained that, just as before, they were attempting to tip the scale in the election, in this case in favor of candidates on the Action Alliance ticket and against the CPU candidates by setting dates that would make it more difficult for CPU's supporters to vote. I had only one vote, so I couldn't stop them, but I felt I had to protest.

Therefore, I once again decided to recuse myself from the Election Board until after the election. According to the SGA constitution, for the president to recuse himself from the Election Board, the announcement had to be in writing. I wrote that, "I do hereby recuse myself from participation in any meetings or decisions of the SGA Election Board until further notice, at which time I will resume my duties as chairman of the Election Board." This left Robert to chair the Election Board. There was an effort to make me resume my duties as chairman of the Election Board, but it failed.

In the March 25<sup>th</sup> SGA elections, Jay Dardenne, a Sigma Chi, was a leading candidate for SGA president after, as reported in a *Reveille* (March 18, 1977) article "Sewell gives support to Dardenne." It seemed to me Dardenne had pulled a classic maneuver by politicos running for office: getting people to sign up for the same office, then, at some point, dropping out of the race and endorsing you. Sewell told the *Reveille*, "I'm withdrawing because Jay is a very acceptable SGA presidential candidate. For once, students have a candidate who's acceptable for everyone....Yes, that is correct, you could say I withdrew to work in Jay's campaign." In addition to Sewell, the article pointed out that Dana Wicks also removed his name as a candidate.

Another politico maneuver Dardenne's campaign appeared to use was to attempt to disqualify his opposition. As the *Reveille* (March 18, 1977) reported, Bob Richey, who was Dardenne's most serious opposition in the election for SGA president, was informed that he was disqualified "for not being a full-time student for the past three semesters." Randy Gurie quoted the memo I had received on April 23, 1976, when I had dropped down to part-time after winning the SGA presidency: a full-time student is reclassified as a part-time student "if his remaining courses total less than 12 semester hours in a regular semester." Richey had to appeal the disqualifying decision, but his appeal took him away from working on his campaign until it was cleared up.

Even though CPU ran a full ballot for SGA president and both vice presidents, we lost all offices to the Greeks led by Jay Dardenne and his Sigma Chi fraternity brothers. Jay won in the primary election and did not have to face a runoff even though his vote total was much less than mine the prior year. The *Reveille* (March 25, 1977) reported, in an article titled "Dardenne makes difference as promised in campaign," that he had promised in his campaign he would make a difference and take on a "new look." The article stated that the difference he made was winning with 50.8 per cent of the vote in the primary and "that the conflict associated with his predecessor would be a thing of the past."

I was taking a class during the 1977 spring semester on the Geology of the Grand Canyon. The highpoint of the class was to be a 10-day trip through the southwest: a 3,000-mile tour that would include camping at the Grand Canyon, the White Sands National Monument, the Carlsbad Caverns, and other parks and interesting geological locations.

This class trip was scheduled to run over LSU's Spring Break, which corresponded with my last 11 days as SGA president. We were to return on Easter Sunday, April 17th, the day before Jay Dardenne and the other newly elected SGA officers were to be sworn in at the SGA inauguration banquet on April 18th.

About 40 geology students assembled on the morning of April 7th to load their gear on the bus. They piled all of the sleeping bags, duffle bags, pillows, etc. up in the back of the school bus. The tents, coolers and other bulky items went in the storages area on the top and in the bottom of the bus.

I arrived a little late due to getting stoned the night before with Susanna and other friends at a little going away party. On top of being stoned, I was really exhausted since Susanna and I had been up late the night before, as was our habit, when either one of us was going to be gone for a number of days. I was the last one on the bus, and everyone else had taken a seat. As I was throwing my seabag on the pile at the back of the bus, I decided to make a bed out of it and the other soft bags. I laid down and fell fast asleep. Slowly but surely, a few of the guys joined me on the pile. I didn't wake up until we got to our first campground in Texas.

I had borrowed a great sleeping bag and a tent from a friend, but I didn't use the tent since I enjoyed sleeping under the stars. Due to living in Las Vegas a number of years, I knew that the night sky was big out west. Of course, Texas's skies were the biggest 'cause, as everyone knows, everything is bigger in Texas.

At that first campground in Texas, I asked if anyone wanted to go with me to smoke a joint. I was told that the professor had specifically ordered the class not to bring any drugs or alcohol. I said, I must have missed that class. I missed many classes during my time as president—hell, even when I wasn't president.

Seeing those geological sites was a great way to learn geology. I think because of my age, military service, and being the SGA president, the grad students let me follow them around during the whole trip as they told me about the rock formations. I am a visual person after all, so for me, it was a wonderful introduction to geology. Learning it in a classroom can be as exciting as, I guess, a rock.

Even though we stopped at a number of national and state parks the first few days, everyone, including myself, was excited to get to Arizona and the Grand Canyon. Finally, we arrived in Arizona, but we discovered that we were stopping at one more site before the Grand Canyon, Sunset Crater Volcano National Monument, to learn about volcanic cones. We would be spending the night before heading to the canyon the next day. Most of us were bummed out about this. When we reached the geologic site, it was getting dark, so we were driven straight out to the cinder cones for a lecture before it got dark. My disappointment about not heading directly to the canyon quickly disappeared as we listened to the lecture and then walked around the base of a cinder cone, learning how the first plant life evolved from such cones.

The next day we arrived at dusk at the campgrounds at the Grand Canyon. The following morning, the class hiked down about a mile and a half to a plateau for our lecture on the canyon. On the way down, I asked the professor, Ray Ferrell, if I could skip the lecture since I had been to the canyon once before and wanted to hike down to the bottom. He said, no, I had to stay for the lecture. After he finished, I told him I was heading to the Colorado River at the bottom of the canyon. He said that the bus would be leaving just before dusk for the campgrounds, and he wasn't holding it up for me. I said, "No, sweat."

As I was preparing to leave, two of the younger guys said they wanted to come with me. I told them that it was going to be a very hard and exhausting hike. I felt I could make this "forced march" since I have been getting into shape to play rugby. They assured me that they could do it, too. Well, I couldn't stop them, so off we went.

The trip down was not very hard, and we cooled off by soaking our feet in the Colorado River. There I found some Vishnu schist at my feet

(Vishnu schist is around 1.75 million years old). Then we began the long, winding trip back up to the canyon rim. About halfway, both of my companions started having troubles. One even had severe leg cramps. I was forced to take on the role of a drill instructor, screaming at him when he collapsed, "Get to your feet and keep going because it's getting dark."

When we got to the Bright Angel parking lot it was dark and the parking lot was empty. Since one of the guys was suffering from severe leg cramps, I had to use the park's emergency phone to call the Park Ranger's station and ask them to pick us up and take us to our campsite.

On the drive home, I got my classmates singing: "Easter Parade" and "Leaving on a Jet Plane." We practiced for hours traveling through Texas. Some students played the comb (they were, after all, Louisiana kids), and we added the sounds of our fingers snapping. We got so good, I talked them into performing "Easter Parade" in a packed McDonalds on Easter morning. After we finished, we got a standing ovation from everyone.

We had no exams in that class, only a paper due at the end of the semester. With a little help from my friends, I managed to get a C.

## SWEARING IN THE NEW SGA ADMINISTRATION

The planning and organizing of the swearing-in banquet for the newly elected SGA executive officers was performed by Dana Robert and members of the Assembly. SGA rented the same room in the Union that was used when I was sworn into office: the Cotillion Ballroom, which seats 350. I thought, as before, that the ballroom was too large and too expensive for an SGA swearing-in ceremony. But since the newly elected SGA president, Jay Dardenne, was a prominent Greek, maybe a lot of people wanted to attend, so I stayed out of those decisions. My only input was to demand that all administrators wanting to attend would have to buy their own tickets to the banquet, the same as the students. Some of the administrators, like Dean of Men French, refused to pay to attend. I thought that was pretty funny considering he had a good salary while many students had to scrape by on just a few dollars a day. Well, due to that and other reasons, there were once again a number of empty tables.

Prior to going to the banquet, I was attending a rugby team practice game on the Parade Grounds. The practice game was set to finish before the banquet was to start. Just before it ended, John Crochet, came rushing out of the Union. John was one of our people who had decided to attend the banquet. He hurried over to tell me that there were even more empty tables in the Cotillion ballroom that night than there had been at my swearing-in banquet. "Well," I said with a smile on my face, "I know just how to fill those tables up."

Inviting LSU's rugby team to the banquet was the obvious solution. After all, I had done the same thing at my swearing-in banquet and, as SGA president—at least for the next few hours—I had the authority to fill those empty places that SGA had already purchased meals for.

As the rugby team gathered around to discuss how the practice had gone and when to set the next practice, I told all of the ruggers that I had heard there were a lot of empty tables at the SGA banquet I was heading to. Since SGA had already paid for the dinners, as my last act as SGA president, I was inviting them to a free meal, courtesy of their student government. Some of them pointed out that they didn't have time to go shower and change clothes. I told them I was going as I was because I was damn tired of dressing in suits; that wasn't me. If they were comfortable with it, come as they were to the banquet. Anyone who knows ruggers would not be surprised that it was of little concern to the vast majority of ruggers that they were still in their rugby practice clothes, dirty and sweaty. They were excited about getting a free meal and attending the banquet with me.

When we walked into the ballroom, the sound of rugby cleats on the floor got everyone's attention. The heads of the people, who were already sitting at the tables or at the speaker's dais in the front of the room, turned to watch us enter. I noticed that everyone there was wearing a suit or dress.

I saw several empty tables in the front near the empty seat on the dais, which had my name on the place marker. I guess the people in this crowd didn't want to be mistaken as my supporters. I pointed to the empty tables saying, "Some of y'all can sit there." As I headed to the dais, a dozen or so ruggers followed me and took their seats at the tables just a few feet away.

Already seated on the dais were Louisiana State Sen. Ken Osterberger, the newly elected Past President's Association president; Assistant Dean of Men Randy Gurie; Beno; Jay Dardenne; Dana Robert, and others. As I took my seat I looked out at the other people in the room, which, I was to find out a little later, included a number of former SGA presidents.

A large number of individuals seated in the audience were not at last year's banquet. I couldn't believe that all of those people came just because Jay Dardenne had won; more likely it was to see me go. The expressions on their faces ran from complete disgust and shocked disbelief to outright anger at what I looked like in my sweaty and dirty rugby practice clothes, and, I am guessing, that I had dared to bring the LSU rugby team with me. Even when I wasn't playing rugby, I always felt the ruggers had my back, and I felt that way about those who came to the banquet with me that evening.

I had made sure that there were vegetarian meals for those of us who were vegetarian. That number, unsurprisingly, was a grand total of one, me. Therefore, to some of the ruggers' disappointment, they were served a vegetarian meal. That didn't stop them from wolfing it down though.

While I was eating, I heard one of the ruggers sitting at the front table start to complain that they had run out of bread at their table. Well, the dais table had baskets full of dinner rolls. I picked up a basket and yelled down to the rugger, "We have plenty of rolls up here. Here you go." And I began tossing rolls down to him. As I did this, the other ruggers at that table and the one next to it started raising their hands, asking me to toss them a roll. To their credit, all of the ruggers I tossed rolls to didn't miss catching any.

I don't think I have to tell you how that went over with the well-to-do attendees, especially the individuals from the administration, like Reddoch, his wife, and Jameson, to mention a few. I actually heard a couple grasps, which were soon replaced by a low angry buzz. I had to smile to myself, seeing how careful they were to keep their expressions of disgust at our behavior to a very low decibel, as though they feared that, if they got any louder, the ruggers might attack them.

I had insisted Beno Duhon be the master of ceremonies. I sure in the hell didn't want one of those individuals in the SGA who had tried to recall me to introduce me at the banquet. Even though Beno had known me since the early PSA days, I could tell he wasn't too happy at my choice of attire, for he was wearing a suit like the others. He slightly shook his head in disapproval, but he had a slight smile on his lips as he got up and made some welcoming comments. Then Beno introduced me to the audience as the outgoing SGA president.

Due to a lot of factors, at that time in my life, when I was to speak at an event, I never wrote down, or even thought about, what I wanted to say to the audience. One could blame it on ADHD, or simply my mental block about writing anything down on paper. I just spoke what I was thinking at that time about the subject or subjects on the agenda. As usual, I didn't know what I was going to say until I heard it come out of my mouth.

This was a little different, though, since it could be said that I did practice what I was going to say at the banquet because, days earlier, I had delivered my farewell speech at the place I felt was the proper forum: at Free Speech Alley and to the students who regularly attended the Alley. What I said to the Greeks and administrators and their wives attending the banquet didn't deviate far from what I had told those students at the Alley.

Standing there at the podium, I realized I had a captive audience: the key LSU administrators who had prevented the election of the first Black Homecoming Queen and were the stumbling blocks to students taking more control of their own lives at LSU. They were there to see me leave office and a new SGA president more to their liking get sworn in. Well, they would find that I hadn't lost any of my frankness in speaking my mind just because of the setting.

The *Reveille* (April 19, 1977) reported my speech in an article titled "SGA leaders reflect on past, future." With a smile on my face and looking straight at Reddoch and Jameson, with a glance at Randy Gurie, I said, "People predicted this would be a controversial year, and I'm glad I didn't let them down." I went on to talk about my attempt to make SGA more independent of the administration by placing funds raised at the Registration Blues Festival in an off-campus account under the SGA name, where, I added as I turned my gaze to Reddoch, they still remain. I expressed my opinion that I felt, in the past, the SGA had been just a puppet of the administration and at times had served the administration more than the students. I added that I hoped that SGA would continue to increase the amount of money in the account in order to eventually break the dependence on student fees. My efforts to increase SGA independence were consistently being fought by a faction in the Assembly, so I warned them, "You can't expect to be 100 per cent successful in what you do when your own camp is divided."

Despite my struggles with the Assembly, I felt my administration's accomplishments had been significant: saving the infirmary, sending out the first summer newsletter to inform the whole student body of important events happening at LSU, and the Homecoming Queen election. Then, as I looked at Randy Gurie and Reddoch, I stated that, "The Homecoming dispute was my proudest accomplishment because it was the hardest to fight for."

I said that I felt that when the SGA was working smoothly with the administration, you could count on the students being sold down the river. But I added, that is only my opinion, as I smiled over at the new incoming executive officers: Jay Dardenne, John Price, and Mark Schroeder. The *Reveille* reported me saying:

> "I know they will have a different administration, as different as their dress is from mine here tonight," Schirmer said. He spoke in his rugby practice clothes and his usual and

recognizable Smokey the Bear hat. The new officers were in suits and ties. With that said, "I wish you luck but I don't think you'll need it. People will be bending over backwards to show that Schirmer's tactics weren't right. If you play your cards right, you'll have all the benefits just to prove a point."

Then Beno announced that Randy Gurie would be presenting the Art Ensminger Award for the Outstanding LSU Student of the Year. I felt that, since I was awarded the Art Ensminger Award the previous year, I should have been the one presenting it. Regardless, I was keenly interested in who was going to win the award. To my total surprise, it was given to Dana Robert. I heard myself say, "What the fuck?" Fortunately, not very loudly. I looked at Dana as she got up to receive the award, wondering what she was going to say, but she just took the plaque from Gurie's hand and returned to her seat without a word. Maybe, like me, she had hoped we would end our terms as SGA officers on a more positive note than we did.

So, Jay Dardenne was sworn in as the new SGA president. His first acts were to close SGA's off campus bank account, cancel the SGA Free Press, and kill the Book Rental. Also, Dardenne didn't fight the Athletic Department's proposal to move the student section of Tiger Stadium from near the 50-yard line to closer to the end zone and to sell tickets for football games to students at regular prices. That was in spite of an SGA Assembly resolution and petition protesting the change from the system where all full-time students paid an athletic fee for access to any LSU sporting event. Dardenne was quoted in the *Reveille* as saying, "The plan would make payment for football attendance voluntary instead of mandatory. Some students would find that very attractive." He went on to say that "LSU students get treated very well right now, and we would like to keep it that way." Spoken like the Greek he was, who benefited from their pledges reserving the best seats in Tiger Stadium for them. In addition, the plan would also block off special seating arrangements for law students. Jay was in his first year at law school. In the same article, Dardenne stated that he would have to miss the Board meeting on this issue because he would have to "devote his attention" to exams.

## Fall Semester, 1977

### A DEBATE WITH DARDENNE

At the end of the 1977 spring semester, I had used up my VA Educational Benefits and still had at least another year before I had enough hours to graduate from LSU. Instead of attending summer school, I needed to find a job and earn some money to cover the next academic year. I had discovered that I could not work and go to school and maintain a full class schedule at the same time. I found a job framing houses for two brothers from Walker. In addition, I started going to Alvin Roy's gym to get in shape to play rugby. Unfortunately, two months into the job, while playing rugby-softball, I was tripped by David Jensen and fell and broke my collar bone. With no insurance, I had to go to Earl K. Long Charity Hospital. That ended my construction job, and I spent the rest of the summer in McHenry, Illinois, with Susanna.

I didn't give much attention to what was happening back in Baton Rouge at LSU until I returned just before time to register for the 1977 fall semester. I soon found out that Dardenne had been bad mouthing me and my administration. We all worked too hard and sacrificed too much to let a "want to be" future politician use us as some kind of whipping boy.

I also wasn't going to stand by idly and do nothing as Dardenne took SGA back to the days of a "do nothing" SGA, a Mickey Mouse Club of the LSU administration. I inherited such an SGA when I took office and knew full well the effort it took to reform SGA into a true advocate and voice for the student body. One of my ideas was to challenge Dardenne to a debate at Free Speech Alley about his administration's unwilling-ness to stand-up and fight for what the students wanted.

As the *Reveille* (October 7, 1977) reported, I told the students at Free Speech Alley, "I'm not gonna be a platform for any little politicians to climb on." I pointed out that the projects the Dardenne administration was working on were projects we had started and didn't have time to bring to completion with the exception of the Tiger cage expansion, and really, it appeared that was just a Greek project to impress his fellow Greeks. I challenged Dardenne to come to the next Alley so we could "debate and compare our administrations." I told the crowd, "I'll be here Thursday. It should be interesting." I was coming armed with nu-merous *Reveille* articles that had statements from Dardenne bad-mouthing my administration.

On the following Monday, Dardenne was quick to tell the *Reveille* (October 11, 1977) that he wasn't going to debate me at Free Speech Alley, stating that "Ted Schirmer has had his chance." He went on to say, "The success or failures of his year in office are left for the students to determine in their own minds" and that "SGA is breaking free from its negative image."

Reading this, my friend Mike Moore, circulated a petition request-ing that Dardenne come to the Alley to debate me. Mike got a couple of hundred students to sign the petition and took it up to the SGA office and gave it in person to Dardenne. As Mike told the *Reveille* (October 21, 1977), "The Alley is, in a way, more valid than other forums because the speakers' arguments must be reinforced....If a speaker's argument is full of holes, someone will call him out on it at the Alley."

Shortly after receiving the petition, Dardenne told the *Reveille* (Oc-tober 25, 1977) he would come to the Alley in order to inform the stu-dents what his administration was doing but would not debate me. When I read this, I thought Dardenne didn't have a clue how the Alley worked if he thought he could just get on the Alley's "soap box" and only talk about what he wanted to talk about.

Even though Dardenne's administration had changed the day of the Alley from a Wednesday, when more students were on campus, to

Thursday, when fewer students were on the campus, the day of the showdown between Dardenne and me at the Alley drew the largest crowd of students that semester. An article in the *Reveille* (October 28, 1977), titled "Dardenne, Schirmer clash at Alley," reported: "Some 200 students crowded in front of the Union Thursday to listen to the awaited debate between SGA President Jay Dardenne and last year's SGA President Ted Schirmer."

Dardenne showed up well after the Alley had started. Maybe he was hoping that the crowd would have thinned out, with students going to class at the change of the hour. If he thought that, he really didn't know the type of students who attended the Alley. Those students believed, rightly so, that the Alley was the best place to find out what was happening on campus for the non-Greek student population. With the exception of when the religious preachers would get on the "soap box," students who spoke at the Alley raised issues that affected their lives on campus. In all the years I attended and spoke at the Alley, rarely do I remember a fraternity or sorority student speaking on issues affecting the campus. Of course, why would they? Their fellow fraternity alumni and sorority alumnae ran LSU's administration.

When I had the opportunity, I asked Dardenne about his statement to the *Reveille* shortly after becoming SGA president that "he would 'try to get programs working that the administration would accept.'" I stressed that the administration had its own priorities and agenda that many times didn't take into account issues of importance to the majority of the student body, like the high cost of textbooks and healthcare on campus. I stated that the administration has the attitude that the students should just pay their tuition and attend class and not cause trouble, like demanding more rights as students, like enrolling and attending colleges of their choice regardless of their personal decision to grow their hair long or have a beard and mustache, like establishing a path to less expensive textbooks even if it took money from LSU's bookstore, or like wanting available and inexpensive healthcare.

Dardenne's response was, "I see no student versus administration struggle." He stated that any of SGA's decisions had to be approved by the administration.

I said that the only project his administration appeared to be working on was the expansion of Mike the Tiger's cage. I argued that the issue shouldn't be about whether to expand Mike's cage. Instead, we should be debating "should LSU have a live mascot?" To the cheers of the crowd, it was pointed out that the traditional practice of pounding on Mike's cage at football games to get him to roar was cruel. Many other students agreed that the expansion of Mike's cage was the wrong priority for the SGA. Instead, Dardenne's administration should be focused on the needs of the students. But when the issue of revising the Bill of Student Rights came to a head, it became painfully clear that Dardenne and the SGA weren't going to fight for student body rights.

## MY PROBATION ENDS

On November 22, 1976, Chancellor Murrill upheld the ruling of the kangaroo Code of Conduct hearing that placed me on probation. Although Murrill did not remove me from my office as SGA president, one of the terms of that probation prohibited me from running for office. He ended his decision with the statement, "I will not consider any appeals for a change in this status for one calendar year."

I had been waiting a year for November 22, 1977, to arrive so I could confront Murrill on why he had upheld the hearing's decision to place me on probation for "life" as a student at LSU. That morning had finally arrived, and, as I drove to the campus to get an early breakfast, I was determined to do just that and demand to be taken off probation.

I knew that Murrill got to his office early, but that his secretary wouldn't open the office until 8 A.M. I planned to be sitting outside his office, waiting.

I was one of the first people to enter the Union that morning. I wanted to eat before confronting Murrill, since I learned a long time ago that, if you were going into a fight, it was better to have eaten first.

As I stood in line for the cafeteria to open, I kept going over in my mind the many different ways that my upcoming conversation with Murrill could go. My mind was so focused on my thoughts that the student behind me had to nudge me before I realized that the cafeteria had opened. I got my usual breakfast of scrambled eggs and grits (no meat, being a vegetarian) and coffee, sat down at a table by myself, and continued mentally running through the possible scenarios.

Murrill knew damn well that the charges I had been found guilty of in that Code of Conduct hearing were bullshit. It seemed clear to me that the only possible reason he had for rejecting my appeal was that he and others in the LSU administration, like Reddoch, feared that I would run for reelection.

I don't even remember eating and drinking my coffee before I was out the door of the Union, heading to the chancellor's office in Thomas Boyd Hall. When I got there, I tried the door, even though I knew that the office would not officially open for another twenty minutes. It was locked. I took a seat right beside the door. In a few minutes I saw the chancellor's secretary coming down the hall toward me. She looked at me with a slight smile and gave a shake of her head as she greeted me with, "Good morning, Mr. Schirmer." I stood up as I told her, "Good morning," and sat back down. I couldn't help but think that I wasn't the only one who knew the importance of this day to me. She entered the office, locking the door behind her. There were still ten minutes or so before the office would be opened.

At eight o'clock sharp, I heard the door unlocked from inside. I stood up and took a big breath to fortify myself for the anticipated upcoming fight to clear my name. As I opened the door and walked into the outer office, Murrill's secretary was sitting behind her desk. She looked right at me with an even broader smile on her face, and, before I could even say that I wanted to see Murrill, she said, "The chancellor is waiting to see you."

I interpreted that smile as a sarcastic acknowledgement that, not only did everyone anticipate that I would be there bright and early, but I wasn't going to get what I came for: an end to my probation. This thought triggered memories of the many times people in my life had expressed their contempt for me by sneering at me.

I saw that Murrill's office door was open and there was the chancellor, sitting behind his desk, looking in my directions. By then my growing anger hit the same level it had gone to when, as the poor new kid in school, I was about to get into a physical confrontation with my classmates.

As I stepped into Murrill's office, glaring at him, I angrily spit out the words, "I want off this bullshit probation right now!" A big smile spread across his face as, to my total surprise, he said, "Just write it out, and I will sign it."

To say I was taken aback would be an understatement, but I learned very early in my life not to let an adversary, and Murrill had become my adversary, see that he had knocked me off balance. I just said, "Good!" I spun around, walked out of his office and, nodding to his secretary, walked into the hall. As I closed the door behind me, I paused for a moment to allow my adrenaline to settle down.

I started walking back to the Union to get a coffee and think about what had just happened. It confirmed to me that Murrill knew I had been railroaded, that I had not been given a fair and open-minded hearing committee, rather one stacked against me by Reddoch.

Later, I requested my personnel file from Jameson before moving back to McHenry, Illinois. Among the material I received was a memo from Vice Chancellor Reddoch addressed to Chancellor Murrill, dated that same date of November 22, 1977. On the subject line was: Mr. Theodor A. Schirmer.

The very first sentence was, "Since our phone conversation this morning, I have reviewed Mr. Theodor A. Schirmer's file." Damn, Murrill must have called Reddoch right after I left his office. Reddoch summarized the facts: the Code of Conduct hearing had found me guilty of two counts and put me on probation until my graduation, and that I had filed an appeal of that decision to the chancellor. Then he added that, on appeal, Murrill had modified the sanction of probation to the extent that I was allowed to remain as SGA president and finish my term in office. Reddoch noted that, in Murrill's last sentence, the chancellor had stated that he would not "consider any appeals for a change in this status for one calendar year."

He then pointed out the obvious: "One calendar year is up today." Was Reddoch watching the calendar, too? He ended his memo to Murrill by writing one of his classic bullshit lines, "Consistent with the idea that university discipline should primarily be for the purpose of counseling and not punitive in nature, it would seem to me that no good purpose would be served by continuing this period of probation beyond one year."

When I read this last part, I couldn't help but laugh out loud. Try telling that to all those students who had been thrown out of school under the university's disciplinary policies, a fate that Jameson had told me after the hearing was waiting for me. That was straight up propaganda for future consumption by others.

Due to the imminent Thanksgiving holidays and that I had been told by Murrill he would sign whatever I prepared, I didn't bother writing anything at that time. I had tests to study for, and Susanna and I were going back to McHenry for the holidays.

While up in McHenry, I typed up what I felt was a simple statement of what I wanted: "I hereby petition you to rescind the order which placed me on probation November 22, 1976." I addressed it to the chancellor and signed it with my student number and address. Upon returning to Baton Rouge after Thanksgiving, I walked it over to the chancellor's office. I handed his secretary an envelope containing what I had written and asked her to give it to the chancellor.

A few days later, I received my petition back in the mail and written in the bottom corner was: "11/30/77 Approved." Murrill had signed it and sent copies to me and, of course, to Vice Chancellor Reddoch. And that was that, I thought, the final chapter to the Homecoming saga.

# Spring Semester, 1978

## FIGHTING THE REVISED BILL OF STUDENT RIGHTS

In order to graduate at the 1978 commencement, I had to take and pass, not only 17 hours of classes that spring, but 17 hours of actual class subjects: no sports classes like swimming, golf, racquetball, or bowling. I had hoped that I could for once just be a student, but due to Dardenne's failure to fight for the Bill of Student Rights, I had to throw myself once again into campus politics. When I had my Code of Conduct hearing, I had been screwed by not having the rights we had included in our new Student Bill of Rights, and I did not want others in the future to suffer similarly.

I didn't give a second thought to whether or not taking time away from my studies would increase my risk of not graduating that semester. Of course, it could have been my ADHD kicking in. It just was part of who I had started becoming since I had decided to fight against the grooming standards in the College of Education back in 1971, even though the grooming standards didn't affect me.

As a *Reveille* (1978) article pointed out, "for almost three years, Reddoch's committee to revise and update the Bill of Student Rights has been stalled." When the revised Bill of Student Rights finally came out of Reddoch's University Revision Committee a few weeks later, it became clear that the bill had been completely rewritten to strengthen the positions of the administration and faculty. It was a real slap in the face of all those students who had worked on the original bill. Four important sections had been deleted from the Bill of Student Rights, which had been approved by the student body in the 1976 SGA spring election.

1) The first casualty was the constitutional protection from unannounced searches of dorm rooms by the resident assistant (RA), an upper-class student assigned to individual floors or communities of students living in LSU housing. We had received numerous complaints of

RA's entering students' rooms without authorization while the students were not present, or just entering their dorm rooms unannounced while the students were present.

2) The revised bill removed the right of students brought up before the Code of Conduct Committee to challenge the committee members appointed by Reddoch. I had personal experience in how a biased committee can prevent a fair and just hearing for the student.

3) All language we wrote addressing the long history of discrimination to the present day that occurred at fraternity and sorority houses was removed. Federal laws required all of the Greek organizations with houses on campus to have language in their constitutions and charters forbidding discrimination. But the administration continued to allow discrimination in the face of dozens of letters to the *Reveille* and numerous complaints filed with the administration by students of color who claimed they were being discriminated against when they attempted to join a fraternity or sorority.

4) Also, deleted was language we wrote establishing a teacher evaluation that included the right of a class to take their evaluations to the dean of that college in order to discuss concerns about their professors.

Thanks to the agreement I had gotten from Chancellor Murrill to allow the student body to vote on the final version of the bill that came out of the University Revision committee, the student body had the right to express their approval or disapproval of this weaken and pro-faculty and pro-administration bill. I realized that we had to organize the students to reject it and put pressure on SGA leaders to see that the original bill, which had been passed by the student body, was instituted. This led me and other members of CPU to organize the Committee of Rights and Education, CORE. I decided not to take a leadership role in CORE, rather just focus on educating and mobilizing the student body to vote in the upcoming SGA election set for the spring of 1978.

My good friend Mike Moore and I met for lunch in the Union one Thursday before we were to go to the Alley to speak on the bill. We both were terribly upset with the direction that Dardenne had taken the SGA. Both of us had sacrificed a great deal of our time and energy to make SGA more responsive to students' needs. We discussed what we could do to get the SGA back on course to being the champion of the students and not the floor mat for the administration.

The more we talked about it, the madder I got. I knew that the administration had feared that I was going to run for reelection last spring and had put me on probation to forbid it, but I was finally off probation. So I mentioned that, if I weren't graduating that semester, I had half a mind to run for SGA president again. However, I pointed out that I had had to drop to part-time right after I won the election in 1976, and, if I did that again, I would not be able to graduate. And even if I thought being SGA president again was worth postponing my graduation, the administration would use their rule that SGA officers had to be full-time students to block me from running.

It occurred to me that what I could do was point out to the students at the Alley the vast differences between Dardenne's administration and mine. I could say something to the point that Dardenne is nothing like us. Hell, I bet he doesn't even get high. With a smile on his face, Mike said, "What if you showed that by smoking a joint at the Alley?" Yeah, I liked it. I added, "What the hell, I could also declare I am going to run for SGA president again." That might put pressure on Dardenne and anyone planning to run for SGA president in the spring election to reject the revised Bill of Student Rights and insist on the one that had been passed by the student body.

I had learned in my Speech classes that a shocking action gets people's attention, so I told Mike to stand close by and hand me a joint when I was speaking at the Alley.

Mike and I both headed for the Alley, where he took a spot right in front of the speaker's "soap box." When it was my time to speak, I got up on the platform and started off by saying that Jay Dardenne not only was politically different from the non-Greek students on campus but also socially different. Then Mike handed me a joint and I asked the crowd, "Does anyone have a light?" The students went crazy, hooting and howling. Mike, with a big smile on his face, held his lighter up to me. I leaned down, lit the joint, and inhaled deeply. I stood back up and exhaled the marijuana smoke into the crowd. This act took the students up another notch or so.

I stated, "Jay Dardenne and his other flunkies produced the most chicken shit document in the currently proposed Bill of Student Rights the university has ever seen." After taking a second hit on the joint, I handed it down to Mike, who took a hit and passed the joint around the crowd. Of course, there was a front-page Reveille (March 2, 1978) article titled "Glutton for punishment? -Ted to run again" with a photo of me at the Alley smoking the joint.

The next day, I went to Blimpie's for lunch. Blimpie's was one of the few eateries in Baton Rouge where a vegetarian in the '70s could get a vegetarian sub sandwich. As I was placing my order, I heard a voice coming from the entrance saying, "Schirmer, I see you declared your candidacy yesterday." I turned to see a captain on the Baton Rouge Police Department, who had been in one of my law enforcement classes at LSU, coming through the door. With a big smile on my face, I said to him, "I bet that got a lot of peoples' attention." "Oh yeah," he said, "a lot of people!"

I signed up to run in the 1978 spring election for SGA president but didn't campaign, with the exception of saying to the Reveille, and later at the Alley, that I would gladly drop out of the race if the other candidates for SGA president would take my position on the Bill of Student Rights. I was surprised at the number of students who sought me out and volunteered to work on my campaign. I told them, "No thanks," but that some of us had started an organization to fight approving the revised Bill of Student Rights, and they could work with us on the Committee of Rights and Education (CORE). However, the administration quickly stated that I was disqualified from running for office. Since I was only trying to force the presidential candidates to take a stand on the proposed Bill of Student Rights and never actually intended to run, I did not fight that ruling.

In the spring 1978 SGA elections, the referendum on the revised bill was on the ballot. A Reveille (April 6, 1978) article reported the election results:

The vote that drew the most debate was not an election at all. The referendum on the proposed revision of the Bill of Student Rights was the cause of more debate, more advertising, and more organizing than even the presidential primary. Students, led by the Committee of Rights and Education (CORE), defeated the bill with 84% of the vote.

## GRADUATION-AT LAST!

As the 1978 spring semester neared its end, I realized I was passing all the classes I needed to graduate, and I began to think about commencement and my departure from LSU.

My only experience with something similar to a college commencement ceremony was in the spring of 1966, when I graduated from Istrouma High School, and, later that fall, when I graduated from Navy boot camp. Both of these ceremonies weren't my cup of tea, although I did kind of enjoy my company's boot camp's graduation ceremony due in large part to the military band.

A commencement ceremony was a rite of passage into the class of people that had a long history of looking down on the working class and poor. Intentionally or not, it drove a wedge between the blue-collar working class and the educated white collar management class. Some LSU students came from blue-collar working-class families, and some, like myself, even from the working poor and the poverty stricken. Being a part of the establishment, graduates would now be called on to protect the establishment by paying taxes and supporting law enforcement while not understanding, or wanting to understand, that law enforcement's main job was to sit on the lid of the garbage can where the poor were dumped by the capitalist socioeconomic class they were being invited into.

I had long ago come to the realization that, when I thought of my future, I had no desire to ever join the middle class or upper class. I simply wanted to work for the "people" in whatever capacity I could

403

after graduation. A door was opening for me to, hopefully, play a role in the fight for justice in our country.

Therefore, I saw the upcoming commencement ceremonies as a chance to express one's own feelings of joy and relief at the ending of four (or more) years of struggle, to celebrate the sacrifices and hard work so many of my fellow students had put in to get to this point of their lives. I was determined to express how I felt about finally graduating from LSU and to hell with the establishment if they didn't like it.

For graduating students to participate in commencement ceremonies, it was required that they order, pay for, and wear the caps and gowns used for the graduation ceremonies. If anyone attended one of these regimented and pompous ceremonies at a university at that time, one saw hundreds to thousands of students marching in formation like robots, all wearing robes and caps identical to their classmates. The requirement that all students look the same and march into the Assembly Center in single file was way too much like Navy boot camp for my taste. Well, I was damn sure that I was somehow going to put my own mark on my graduation.

I always was into throwing big parties both up north in McHenry, Illinois and here in Baton Rouge, so naturally a big event like my finally graduating from LSU (an event that I can easily say a number of LSU's administrators and some faculty had been looking forward to since the early '70s), deserved a big party. Mike Richman and his roommate Andy, who were also graduating with me, agreed to hold a joint graduation party at my place on River Road right after the ceremonies at the Assembly Center. I talked with my neighbors living on Elbow Bayou to warn them we anticipated a few hundred people would attend our party.

I wanted there to be live music, so I asked Greg Wright how much he would charge for him and his band, Light Years, to play at the party. Greg told me that the band would play for free. I explained that I could put together a couple hundred dollars, but he told me he was very grateful to me for booking his band so many times at LSU when it was newly formed. Playing at all our free SGA concerts and the Registration Blues

Festival at LSU helped establish the band in Baton Rouge. Due to that exposure, they had developed a large local following that helped them book gigs all over town and around the state.

My good friend, Marion Campbell, who had done so much of the work putting those concerts together, lived in the shot-gun house next to mine. Marion and I had to figure out where to build a stage, how to provide the electrical power the band would need, and all the other things it would take to pull this off.

I was once again amazed at the can-do attitude of Marion. He and other friends of ours gathered the wood to build a small stage under one of the big trees in our front yard. My neighbor in the front, Red, had a shed with 240-volt outlets for his power tools just 15 feet or so from the stage. I asked him if we could plug our extension cords into his outlets to power the band's equipment and offered to pay the electrical bill.

Red was one of the best neighbors I ever had. He once drove over fifty miles to tow my VW van back home after it broke down on Interstate 10 at one o'clock in the morning. He not only said we could hook our extension cords to his 240 outlets, he refused to accept any money. In addition, he pitched in with the building of the stage.

I invited Red and his family to come to the graduation party. I told him there was going to be lots of good Louisiana food and drink. He thanked me but graciously declined. I thought he might feel uncomfortable about coming to a party where he knew only me, so I did not push it. However, when Greg and his band members, who were mostly Black, and other Black friends of mine arrived, I saw Red and his family had joined us and were eating and drinking by the stage while talking to Greg. Maybe Red had thought there would be just a bunch of white people at the party.

I asked one of my artistic friends if he would draw up an invitation to the party. I still have a framed copy of that flyer, which showed LSU's bell tower with two large eyes and tears coming down its face. The bell tower's clock hands were drawn waving goodbye to three flying cartoon characters labeled Mike, Andy, and Ted, who were flying past the tower and calling out to everyone, "We will miss y'all." The flyer included a map to my house with a BYOB statement, and, since I was a vegetarian, a notice that guests would have to bring their own meat to cook at the party.

Susanna didn't attend the graduation ceremonies. She, along with a number of my friends, brought tables, chairs, ice chests filled with ice, drinks, and a ton of good Louisiana food to our house. A dozen large folding tables were set up around the yard, along with a volleyball court and two horseshoe pits. At the height of the party, there had to have been well over two hundred guests, including Mike's and Andy's parents (who didn't stay all that long after the smell of marijuana started drifting through the air).

As Mike, Andy and I were planning the party, we all agreed that the commencement ceremonies were more for the administration and faculty. We didn't like how the students were left out of any planning of the event. As I passed a joint around, I brought up an idea I had about performing a skit from a song in the cult movie classic *The Rocky Horror Picture Show*, which was, and still is, the longest -running movie based on a theatrical play in movie history. I had attended my first performance of *Rocky Horror* with them at the Varsity Theater right off campus on Highland Road. I thought that we three should all paint our faces and perform a pantomime of the "Time Warp" song from the movie outside the Assembly Center before graduation.

Mike and Andy both stated they were in. I tried to set a time for us to practice, but they said they just couldn't take any time away from preparing for finals. They assured me they had both seen the movie so many times that they knew the song and the performance by heart.

I too, was cramming for my finals. I knew I wouldn't graduate if I failed any of my classes, and I was determined not to let that happen. I wanted back my private life that I had lost when I became SGA president. Andy and Mike arranged to meet me at the Indian Mounds the day of graduation to put our makeup on our faces and to discuss how we were going to perform the "Time Warp."

As I was heading to our prearranged rendezvous site, I was thinking to myself, "I am about to graduate college!" Then it dawned on me that

I was graduating despite not being able to write. I didn't even know the alphabet. I tried to say it but couldn't get entirely through it. I shook my head, thinking, "The only reason I am graduating from LSU is that I am a freak with a high IQ and a damn good memory." I was still shaking my head in disbelief when I arrived at our meeting place.

Only Andy had shown up with his girlfriend Rebbie. Andy told me that Mike wasn't coming. I knew that his mother and brother had flown in from California, so I wasn't surprised that he was spending time with them. Then Andy confessed that neither of them wanted to perform the skit outside of the Assembly Center, nor did they want to paint their faces, fearing it would upset their families. I didn't have any family coming to the graduation ceremonies to worry about.

Remember, this was a time when graduation was a solemn event full of pomp and ceremony, and only a few graduating students would even dare to write messages on top of their mortarboards.

I was a little disappointed, but I could understand my friends' reasoning. For a graduating student to paint his entire face, let alone perform a skit from a movie like *The Rocky Horror Picture Show*, was highly unusual. Plus, we hadn't worked on any kind of routine to perform.

Well, I wasn't able to do the "Time Warp," but Andy's girlfriend was kind enough to paint my face. I had her paint one half of my face white and the other side black with a black line dividing them. Then she added the shape of two large tear drops of the opposing color on my face. I felt that the Yin and Yang expressed exactly the divided feelings I had about finally finishing this stage in my life.

Andy and his girlfriend left to meet his family and friends, who were attending commencement. Similar to the night I had won the SGA presidency, I pulled out a joint and, as I smoked it, I thought about how big of a milestone graduating from LSU was in my life. I was not only the first in my family to graduate high school, I was also about to achieve the next milestone in the history of families: graduating college. After finishing the joint, I carefully put the mortar board squarely on my head, making sure not to mess up the paint on my face, and headed to the Assembly Center.

As I walked past other graduates and their families and friends heading to the Assembly Center, I saw out of the corner of my eye many a look of shock and disgust. Those looks just increased as I approached the Assembly Center, leading me to stare only straight ahead. Yes, I had second thoughts about what I had gotten myself into this time. But like the many times before, when I did things without fully thinking it through, I just steeled myself for whatever was to come. I expected some curses and name calling. Thankfully, I didn't hear any of that. I realized that luckily, because I had short hair and my whole face was hidden under face paint, no one seemed to recognize me. I used to say I had the luck of the Irish, back when I thought I was Irish.

The time seemed to slow down as I waited with the other students to be called into the Assembly Center by college. It didn't help that University College was going to be called in last. When University College was finally called, we were ushered into lines alphabetically. This was the first time anyone realized that the dude with the painted face was me. The student behind me tapped me on the shoulder and asked if I were Ted Schirmer. I smiled and said, "Yes." When the word passed down the line, since these were my fellow University College mates, I only received smiles from the other students in line.

When Chancellor Murrill began speaking at commencement, he congratulated all of us. He went on to announce the names of students who were graduating at the top of the class and those with 4.0+ GPAs. Then he mentioned the names of other students who were graduating with academic honors.

I was only half listening to him pointing out the youngest and oldest graduating student, when I heard him say, "And former student body president, Ted Schirmer, is in the graduating class." I didn't know he was going to do that. Hearing him, I half expected him to add, "At last!" The student on my left started lightly pushing me to stand up. Still being stoned, I had no desire to stand up, but he kept pushing me to do so. I realized that he likely wanted to see how the audience would react to seeing me with my painted face. I shrugged and stood up, did a slight bow, almost losing my cap, and quickly sat back down. I heard no boo-ing or hissing.

After all the speakers were done, including the commencement speaker, we had to wait as the students in other colleges got into line to receive their degrees from the dean of their colleges. Finally, our college was next. As I was waiting in line, I watched the University College's dean, who had frequently expressed his dislike of me, handing the students ahead of me their diplomas, and shaking their hands, congratu-lating them.

When I got to the front of the line, the dean had turned back toward his long-time secretary, who handed him my diploma. Even though she was behind him, she saw my face before the dean did, and a very disap-proving motherly look came over her face as she shook her head incred-ulously. When the dean turned toward me and saw my painted face, his eyes immediately narrowed and his face started turning red with anger. He dropped his hand holding my diploma to his side and hissed, "I shouldn't even give you this!" I narrowed my own eyes and replied in a firm voice, "You haven't got the power not to!"

At that point he shoved my diploma at me with his left hand while keeping his right hand at his side, obviously not wanting to shake my hand in congratulation. I sure as hell didn't want to shake his hand ei-ther so, while sarcastically smiling at him, I defiantly yanked my di-ploma out of his hand and walked away.

Later, as I was heading back to my VW van, I took a slow look around. I realized that there was one thing I was going to miss more than anything else at LSU: Tiger Stadium. I might never be able to at-tend another Tiger football game there. Susanna had already told me that she was moving back to McHenry with or without me. She added, "NO DISCUSSION!"

At the time, I didn't realize that I would be back in Baton Rouge just two years later, due in large part to Susanna and me breaking up. I moved to Chicago after the breakup and worked first at the Illinois Pub-lic Action Council, a statewide citizens' action organization, then for over a year at the Illinois Department of Human Services as an AFDC case manager on the South Side of Chicago. Working in the ghetto, I came to realize that I wasn't really helping my people out of their plight, but, in a lot of ways, being a part of the system that was keeping them and their children in the ghetto. This led me to want to get the tools to do a proper job of helping the poor. That made me rethink going to law school.

At that time, I had what would turn out to be a very naïve understanding of what the practice of law really entailed. With that said, the desire to be more effective as a citizen activist led me in 1979 to take the City of New Orleans train back to Baton Rouge in order to apply for law school. I graduated with a J.D. from the Southern University Law Center in 1983.

I enjoyed my time at LSU, fighting for students' rights. There is no doubt in my mind that those experiences encouraged me later in life to fight against injustice and corruption in politics and for people's rights as a civil rights attorney and public defender.

# Epilogue
## THEODOR A. SCHIRMER FREE SPEECH ALLEY

About a year after graduating from LSU, while working as an AFDC case manager in the South Side of Chicago, I was told that there was a long distance call for me from Sabrina Rabe, a reporter for the *Reveille* at LSU. As I waited for the call to be transferred to my desk, for the life of me, I couldn't think what the hell a reporter from the *Reveille* wanted to talk to me about. In a thousand years I couldn't have guessed.

After confirming with her that I was "the" Ted Schirmer, former SGA president, the reporter told me she wanted to know my thoughts about the possibility of my name being taken off Free Speech Alley. All I could say was, "What?!" She than explained that the SGA had named Free Speech Alley after me in the summer of 1978. I said, "I'll bet a lot of people were up in arms over naming anything after me, even Free Speech Alley where I had spent so much time while I was at LSU."

Ms. Rabe didn't go over who had been complaining, but I was to learn that the biggest complaint came in the form of an Op-Ed in the *Reveille* (September 21, 1978) written by Edwin K. Hunter, the son-in-law of Board of Supervisors member, Mrs. Ruth Miller. Mrs. Miller had been my key nemesis stopping the Book Rental from becoming a reality at LSU in 1976.

In the Op-Ed, Mr. Hunter stated, among other things, that a Louisiana Revised Statute prohibited naming public facilities in honor of any living person. He maintained that Free Speech Alley was a public facility and, unless a death certificate established that I have been dead for at least two years, Free Speech Alley couldn't be named after me.

Another *Reveille* reporter, Lawrence Zeilinger wrote a *Reveille* (September 26, 1978) editorial titled, "The Alley must not fade away" in response:

411

Remember the front-page picture of Schirmer in the *Reveille* this past spring, the one that showed him toking on a joint at Free Speech Alley—all smoky eyed and smiling? That was a political act, one that would not necessarily have been tolerated elsewhere in American society, and in other countries not at all...It has been those traditionally neutral areas, like Hyde Park Corner in London, England, or Free Speech Alley in Baton Rouge, that have allowed men to express their deepest-felt, innermost beliefs, no matter how unpopular or non-conformist. It is this very type of ultimate freedom of speech that creates a marketplace for the exchange of ideas, a marketplace that true democracy is strong enough to endure and must promulgate it if it is to survive.

Several other students wrote Letters to the Editor in response that were published in the *Reveille* (September 28, 1978). In one, SGA president Bob Richey pointed out that Free Speech Alley didn't fall under La. R.S. 14:316. He then wrote that, when I spoke at the Alley, I was:

...never at a loss for words: grammar maybe, but never for words...We named the Alley after Ted because he kept it alive during those hard years when nobody cared about how the bad guys in the ivory towers treated us students...I can still see Ted on the soap box, toking on a joint (he never could roll worth a damn).

In reply to Ms. Rabe's question asking how I felt about my name being removed from Free Speech Alley, I told her that I was "honored that Free Speech Alley bears [my] name" but since I had no plans of dying anytime soon, I felt that "an institution should not have the name of a living person." When Bob Richey and his executive assistant Steve Triche heard this, my name was taken off of Free Speech Alley.

# About the Author

Theodor "Ted" Schirmer graduated from Louisiana State University (LSU) in 1978, worked as a case manager for the Illinois Department of Welfare in the South Side of Chicago, and then enrolled in the Southern University Law Center. After graduating in 1983, he opened a law practice in Baton Rouge that focused on civil rights and handicap discrimination. Due to a family health issue, Ted moved to California where he worked for New Directions, a long term drug and alcohol rehabilitation center for homeless veterans, helping his fellow veterans with their legal issues. In 2006, Ted joined the Los Angeles County Public Defender's Office where he worked until he retired.

After retirement, Ted decided to write his life story for his children and grandchild. When he began writing about his years at LSU, he discovered through research that events that took place during his time as Student Government Association (SGA) president were being swept under the rug. He could locate nothing in the administrative files or oral histories open to the public that covered what happened at the LSU Homecoming in 1976.

In the '70s, twenty years after Brown v. Board of Education of Topeka, 347 U.S. 483 (1954), LSU was still refusing to give up its racist past. While most students attending LSU were primarily focused on obtaining a better life through getting a college degree, some could not turn their backs on injustice. The students who fought at Ted's side were not the wealthy fraternity or sorority members. They were from middle or lower-middle class families and the working poor. It was Ted's goal in writing this book to honor their sacrifices and tell what it was like to fight the system—the LSU administrators, the Board of Supervisors, and the Greek organizations—in the deep South in the turbulent '70s.